GALLERY OF

Best

RESUMES

*A Collection of Quality Resumes
by Professional Resume Writers*

SECOND EDITION

DAVID F. NOBLE

Gallery of Best Resumes
A Collection of Quality Resumes by Professional Resume Writers
Second Edition

© 1994, 2001 by David F. Noble

Published by JIST Works, an imprint of JIST Publishing, Inc.
8902 Otis Avenue
Indianapolis, IN 46216-1033
Phone: 800-648-JIST   Fax: 800-JIST-FAX   E-mail: editorial@jist.com

Visit our Web site at http://www.jist.com for more information on JIST, free job search information and book chapters, and ordering information on our many products!

Other books by David F. Noble:

Gallery of Best Cover Letters
Gallery of Best Resumes for People Without a Four-Year Degree
Professional Resumes for Executives, Managers, and Other Administrators
Professional Resumes for Tax and Accounting Occupations
Professional Resumes for Accounting, Tax, Finance, and Law
Using WordPerfect in Your Job Search

Quantity discounts are available for JIST books. Please call our Sales Department at 1-800-648-5478 for a free catalog and more information.

Proofreaders: Rebecca York and Gayle Johnson
Interior Designer: Debbie Berman
Page Layout: Debbie Berman

Printed in the United States of America.

03 02 01 00   9 8 7 6 5 4 3 2 1

ISBN: 1-56370-809-4

Contents

This practical "idea book" of best resumes has three parts: Best Resume Writing Tips; a Gallery of 215 resumes written by 72 professional writers; and an Exhibit of 30 cover letters, together with tips for polishing cover letters. With this book, you not only have a treasury of quality resumes and cover letters but also learn how to view them as superior models for your own resumes and cover letters.

This book is for *any job searcher* who wants to know how the professionals write resumes. It's for *active job seekers* who want top-notch ideas for creating a first-rate resume in today's competitive job market. It's for *all job searchers* who must have an ahead-of-the-pack resume—from *high school students* looking for their first job to *retirees* wanting to stay active. This book is also for *career changers,* those *terminated* by downsizing, and the *overqualified* who must look in new directions and tailor their resumes in special ways. Because of the wealth of quality resume models in this book, it is for *anyone* who wants examples of top-quality resumes to create an outstanding resume.

This idea book can transform your thinking about resumes so that you have a better sense of what kind of resume is best for you and the interviews you schedule.

In this section, you learn experience-tested, resume-writing strategies, such as how to put the most important information about you as a worker near the top of your resume, how to highlight key information so that it is seen, and how to showcase your experience and skills.

A quality resume can make a great impression, but it can be ruined quickly by a poorly written cover letter. This section shows you how to eliminate common errors in cover letters. It amounts to a *crash writing course* that you won't find in any other resume book. After you read the following sections, you will be better able to write and polish any letters you create for your job search.

In this section, you learn how to evaluate 30 sample cover letters that accompanied resumes submitted for use in the Gallery. After you study this exhibit, you will have a better feel for designing your own cover letters to make them distinctive and effective.

Foreword

Y ou just have to ask whether the world needs yet another resume book. There are hundreds of them out there, and each year there is a new crop. So a legitimate question is, Why is this resume book worth while?

After looking at hundreds of resume books, I can tell you that most people who write them really don't know much about looking for work—and too few seem to know much about what makes a good resume. They often have backgrounds as personnel directors (who use resumes to screen people out, not in) or teachers (with little practical experience in actually looking for work). Nice people, I'm sure, but not all that well qualified.

Gallery of Best Resumes is different from most resume books for two reasons:

1. The resumes have all been created by people who write resumes for a living.

2. David Noble

I think that these two reasons make this a more useful and important book. Let me explain.

While most books are based on one person's opinion of what makes a good resume, *Gallery of Best Resumes* includes resumes written by dozens of professional resume writers. These people make their living helping others produce good resumes, and they sent us their best work. This approach allows for a wide range of writing styles, formats, and designs that just is not possible through any other approach.

But behind this extraordinary collection of resumes is the author, David Noble. Educated in the classics and a graduate of prestigious universities, he brings to this collection a discipline of thought and an understanding of good writing that is simply lacking in most resume books. When I asked him to explain to me how this book was developed, he used this analogy:

> If Plato had been asked, "What is a resume?" he would have asked the questioner what it was for, how it was used, and what it did. Plato would then have tried to imagine the ideal form that a resume should take to fulfill those functions. That, David explained, is deductive reasoning (an advanced form of intuition).

> Aristotle, a pupil of Plato, responding to the same question, would have asked, "Who makes resumes?" and asked a number of those persons to show him examples. Aristotle would then have sorted through those examples and arranged them into types. From this, he would have determined what a resume is. That, David explained, is inductive reasoning (a scientific method).

Aristotle's method is the one that David used to examine the question, What makes a resume a best resume?

There are, it seems, some things that make one resume stand out above others. Instead of just making assumptions, David Noble examined hundreds of professionally written resumes. After careful analysis, he presents his conclusions in this book—along with lots of outstanding resumes.

One good thing about this book is that you don't have to read Plato or Aristotle to find out how to write a good resume. It's all here. You can examine carefully on your own the resumes presented in the Gallery or spend some time learning from David the principles of resume writing and, more importantly, how to *use* a resume.

J. Michael Farr

(Mike Farr is the author of many career planning and job search books, including his own books on resumes, *The Quick Resume and Cover Letter Book* and *America's Top Resumes for America's Top Jobs*. Collectively, his books have sold more than one million copies.)

Acknowledgments

To all those who helped to make possible this second edition, I would like to acknowledge my appreciation. I am most indebted to all of the professional resume writers who sent me many examples of their work for inclusion in this book and other books. These writers took the time—often on short notice—to supply multiple copies, files on disks, and any other requested information.

I want to express my gratitude to Mike Farr for his Foreword to this book and to Michael Cunningham for overseeing this project. Debbie Berman makes desktop publishing look easy, and her design changes are always pleasing. Working with Becca York remains a pleasure. Gayle Johnson's sharp eye spotted some important inconsistencies.

Introduction

The *Gallery of Best Resumes,* Second Edition, is a new and an expanded collection of quality resumes from professional resume writers, each with individual views about resumes and resume writing. The second edition contains some resumes that were in the first edition, but most of the resumes in the second edition are new. Similarly, some of the writers of resumes in the first edition are included in the second edition, but some are not for various reasons (the writer has retired, become inactive as a resume writer, changed careers, or become unavailable for some other reason), and others are new, having become active contributors to my other resume books.

Unlike many resume books whose selections "look the same," this book, like the first edition, contains resumes that look different because they are representations of *real* resumes prepared by different professionals for actual job searchers throughout the country. (Certain information in the resumes has been fictionalized by the writers to protect, where necessary, each client's right to privacy.) Even when several resumes from the same writer appear in the book, most of these resumes are different because the writer has customized each resume according to the background information and career goals of the client for whom the resume was prepared.

Instead of assuming that "one resume style fits all," the writers featured here believe that a client's past experiences and next job target should determine the resume's type, design, and content. The use of *Best* in the book's title reflects this approach to resume making. The resumes are not "best" because they are ideal types for you to copy, but because resume writers have interacted with clients to fashion resumes that seemed best for each client's situation at the time.

This book features resumes from writers who share several important qualities: good listening skills, a sense of what details are appropriate for a particular resume, and flexibility in selecting and arranging the resume's sections. By "hearing between" a client's statements, the perceptive resume writer can detect what kind of job the client really wants. The writer then chooses the information that will best represent the client for the job being sought. Finally, the writer decides on the best arrangement of the information, from the most important to the least important, for that job. With the help of this book, you can create this kind of resume yourself.

Most of the writers of the resumes in this Gallery are members of either the Professional Association of Résumé Writers (PARW) or the National Résumé Writers Association (NRWA). Some of the writers belong to both organizations. Those who have CPRW certification, for Certified Professional Résumé Writer, received this designation from PARW after they studied specific course materials and demonstrated proficiency in an examination. Those who have NCRW certification, for National Certified Résumé Writer, received this designation from NRWA after a different course of study and a different examination. Some of the writers are currently not members of either organization but are either past members or professional writers in Indiana, Michigan, and Ohio who were invited by the author to submit works for possible selection for the *Gallery of Best Resumes for Two-Year Degree Graduates.* For contact information about PARW and NRWA, see their listings at the end of the Appendix (List of Contributors).

How This Book Is Organized

Like the first edition, the *Gallery of Best Resumes,* Second Edition, consists of three parts. Part 1, "Best Resume Tips," presents resume writing strategies, design and layout tips, and resume writing style tips for making resumes visually impressive. Many of these strategies and tips were suggested by the resume writers who contributed resumes to the first edition. From time to time, a reference is given to one or more Gallery resumes that illustrate the strategy or tip.

Part 2 is the Gallery itself, containing 215 resumes from 72 professional resume writers. The location of several of these writers has become unknown since the first edition of this Gallery. Included also are a few "before" resumes from clients so that you can see how the writers improved these resumes.

Resume writers commonly distinguish between chronological resumes and functional (or skills) resumes. A *chronological resume* is a photo—a snapshot history of what you did and when you did it. A *functional resume* is a painting—an interpretive sketch of what you can do for a future employer. A third kind of resume, known as a *combination resume,* is a mix of recalled history and self-assessment. Besides recollecting "the facts," a combination resume contains self-interpretation and is therefore more like dramatic history than news coverage. A chronological resume and a functional resume are not always that different; often, all that is needed for a functional resume to qualify as a combination resume is the inclusion of some dates, such as those for positions held. All three kinds of resumes are illustrated in the Gallery. Most of them are combination resumes.

The resumes in the Gallery are presented in the following occupational categories:

> Accounting/Finance
> Administrative Support
> Animal Care
> Career Change
> Communications
> Consultant
> Education/Training
> Graduating/Graduated Student
> Insurance/Real Estate
> Maintenance and Material Handling
> Management
> Medical and Health Care
> Professional Service
> Psychology and Social Work
> Sales/Marketing
> Technology/Engineering/Science

Within each category, the resumes are generally arranged from the simple to the complex. Most of the resumes are one page, but a number of them are two pages. A few are more than two pages.

The Gallery offers a wide range of resumes whose features you can use in creating and improving your own resumes. Notice the plural. An important premise of an active job search is that you will not have just one "perfect" resume for all potential employers, but different versions of your resume for different interviews. The Gallery is therefore not a showroom where you say, "I'll take that one," alter it with your information, and then duplicate your version 200 times. It is a valuable resource of design ideas, expressions, and organizational patterns that can help make your own resume a "best resume" for your next interview.

Creating multiple *versions* of a resume may seem difficult, but it is easy to do if you have (or have access to) a personal computer and a laser printer or some other kind of printer that can produce quality output. You will also need word processing, desktop publishing, or resume software. If you don't have a computer or a friend who does, most professional resume writers have the hardware and software, and they can make your resume look like those in the Gallery. See the List of Contributors in the Appendix for the names, addresses, phone numbers, and e-mail addresses of the professional writers whose works are featured in this book. A local fast-print shop can make your resume look good, but you will probably not get there the kind of advice and service the professional resume writer provides. Of course, if all you have is a typewriter, you can still produce versions of your resume, but you will have to retype the resume for each new version.

Part 3, "Best Cover Letter Tips," contains a discussion of some myths about cover letters, plus tips for polishing cover letters. Much of the advice offered here applies also to writing resumes. Included in this part is an exhibit of 30 cover letters.

The List of Contributors in the Appendix is arranged alphabetically by state and city. Although most of these resume writers work with local clients, some of the writers work with clients by phone from anywhere in the United States.

You can use the Occupation Index to look up resumes by the current or most recent job title. This index, however, should not replace careful examination of all of the resumes. Too many resumes for some other occupation may have features adaptable to your own occupation. Limiting your search to the Occupation Index may cause you to miss some valuable examples. You can use the Features Index to find resumes that contain representative resume sections that may be important to you and your resume needs.

Who This Book Is For

Anyone who wants ideas for creating or improving a resume can benefit from this book. It is especially useful for active job seekers—those who understand the difference between active and passive job searching. A *passive* job seeker waits until jobs are advertised and then mails copies of the same resume, along with a standard cover letter, to a number of Help Wanted ads. An *active* job seeker believes that a resume should be modified for a specific job target *after* having talked in person or by phone to a prospective interviewer *before* a job is announced. To schedule such an interview is to penetrate the "hidden job market." Active job seekers can find in the Gallery's focused resumes a wealth of strategies for targeting a resume for a particular interview. The section "How to Use the Gallery" at the beginning of Part 2 shows you how to do this.

Besides the active job seeker, any unemployed person who wants to create a more competitive resume or update an old one should find this book helpful. It shows the kinds of resumes that professional resume writers are writing, and it showcases resumes for job seekers with particular needs.

What This Book Can Do for You

Besides providing you with a treasury of quality resumes whose features you can use in your own resumes, this book can help transform your thinking about resumes. If you think that there is one "best" way to create a resume, this book will help you learn how to shape a resume that is best for you as you try to get an interview with a particular person for a specific job.

If you have been told that resumes should be only one page long, the examples of multiple-page resumes in the Gallery will help you see how to distribute information effectively across two or more pages. If you believe that the way to update a resume is to add your latest work experiences to your last resume, this book will show you how to rearrange your resume so that you can highlight the most important information about your experience and skills.

After you have studied "Best Resume Tips" in Part 1, examined the professionally written resumes in the Gallery in Part 2, and reviewed "Tips for Polishing Cover Letters" and the cover letters in Part 3, you should be able to create your own resumes and cover letters worthy of inclusion in any gallery of best resumes.

1
P·A·R·T

Best
Resume Tips

Best Resume Tips
at a Glance

Best Resume Tips

I n a passive job search, you rely on your resume to do most of the work for you. An eye-catching resume that stands out above all the others may be your best shot at getting noticed by a prospective employer. If your resume is only average and looks like most of the others in the pile, the chances are great that you won't be noticed and called for an interview. If you want to be singled out because of your resume, it should be somewhere between spectacular and award-winning.

In an active job search, however, your resume complements your efforts at being known to a prospective employer *before* that person receives it. For this reason, you can rely less on your resume for getting someone's attention. Nevertheless, your resume has an important role in an active job search that may include the following activities:

- Talking to relatives, friends, and other acquaintances to meet people who can hire you before a job is available

- Contacting employers directly, using the *Yellow Pages* to identify types of organizations that could use a person with your skills

- Creating phone scripts to speak with the person who is most likely to hire someone with your background and skills

- Walking into a business in person to talk directly to the one who is most likely to hire someone like you

- Using a schedule to keep track of your appointments and callbacks

- Working at least 25 hours a week to search for a job

When you are this active in searching for a job, the quality of your resume confirms the quality of your efforts to get to know the person who might hire you, as well as your worth to the company whose workforce you want to join. An eye-catching resume makes it easier for you to sell yourself directly to a prospective employer. If your resume is mediocre or conspicuously flawed, it will work against you and may undo all of your good efforts in searching for a job.

The following list offers ideas for making resumes visually impressive. Many of the ideas are for making resumes pleasing to the eye, but a number of the ideas are strategies to use in resumes for special cases. Other ideas are for eliminating common writing mistakes and stylistic weaknesses.

A number of the ideas have come from comments of the professional resume writers who submitted resumes for the first edition of the book (*Gallery of Best Resumes,* JIST Works, 1994). The name of the writer appears in brackets. Resumes that illustrate these ideas are referenced by resume number.

Some of these ideas can be used with any equipment, from a manual typewriter to a sophisticated computer with desktop publishing software. Other ideas make sense only if you have a computer system with word processing or desktop publishing. Even if you don't have a computer, take some time to read all of the ideas. Then, if you decide to use the services of a professional resume writer, you will be better informed about what the writer can do for you in producing your resume.

Best Resume Writing Strategies

1. **Although many resume books say that you should spell out the name of the state in your address at the top of the resume, consider using the postal abbreviation instead.** The reason is simple: it's an address. Anyone wanting to contact you by mail will probably refer to your name and address on the resume. If they appear there as they should on an envelope, the writer or typist can simply copy the information you supply. If you spell out the name of your state in full, the writer will have to "translate" the name of the state to its postal abbreviation.

   Not everyone knows all the postal abbreviations, and some abbreviations are easily confused. For example, those for Alabama (AL), Alaska (AK), American Samoa (AS), Arizona (AZ), and Arkansas (AR) are easy to mix up. You can prevent confusion and delay simply by using the correct postal abbreviation. As resumes become more "scannable," the use of postal abbreviations in addresses will become a requirement.

   If you decide to use postal abbreviations in addresses, make certain that you do not add a period after the abbreviations, even before ZIP codes. This applies also to postal abbreviations in the addresses of references, if provided.

   Do not, however, use the state postal abbreviation when you are indicating only the city and state (not the mailing address) of a school you attended or a business where you worked. In these cases, it makes sense to write out the name of the state in full.

2. **Adopt a sensible form for phone numbers and then use it consistently.** Do this in your resume and in all of the documents you use in your job search. Some forms for phone numbers make more sense than others. Compare the following forms:

123-4567	This form is best for a resume circulated locally, within a region where all the phone numbers have the same area code.
(222) 123-4567	This form is best for a resume circulated in areas with different area codes.
222-123-4567	This form suggests that the area code should be dialed in all cases. But that won't be necessary for prospective employers whose area code is 222. This form should be avoided.
222/123-4567	This form is illogical and should be avoided also. The slash can mean an alternate option, as in ON/OFF. In a phone number, this meaning of a slash makes little sense.
1 (222) 123-4567	This form is long, and the digit 1 isn't necessary. Almost everyone will know that 1 should be used before the area code to dial a long-distance number.

222.123.4567	This form, resembling Internet addresses, is becoming more evident.

Note: For resumes directed to prospective employers *outside* the United States, be sure to include the correct international prefixes in all phone numbers so that you and your references can be reached easily by phone.

3. **Make your Objective statement focused, interesting, and unique so that it grabs the reader's attention.** If your Objective statement fails to do this, the reader might discard the resume without reading further. An Objective statement can be your first opportunity to sell yourself. For examples of effective Objective statements, see Resumes 1, 11, 12, 13, 24, 31, and many others. Check out Objective in the Features Index for the numbers of those resumes that have an Objective statement.

4. **In the Experience section, state achievements or accomplishments, not just duties or responsibilities.** Duties and responsibilities for a given position are often already known by the reader. Achievements, however, can be interesting. The reader probably considers life too short to be bored by lists of duties and responsibilities in a stack of resumes. See, for example, Resumes 2, 10, 16, 22, 51 (bulleted items), 57 (bulleted items), and 84.

5. **If you feel you must indicate duties, call attention to special or unusual duties you performed.** For example, if you are an accountant, don't say that you prepared accounting reports and analyzed income statements and balance sheets. What else is new? That's like being a dentist and saying, "I filled cavities and made crowns." What did you do that distinguished you from other accountants? To be noticed, you need to stand above the crowd in ways that display your individuality and work style.

6. **Instead of just listing your achievements, present them as very brief stories, perhaps indicating what you did when something went wrong or needed fixing.** See, for example, Resume 93. [Young]

7. **When skills and abilities are varied, group them according to categories for easier comprehension.** See, for example, Resumes 17, 32, 40, and 62.

8. **To make your promotions stand out, list your work experiences chronologically, with the range of dates for each position.** See, for example, Resume 16. [Baskin]

9. **Summarize your qualifications and work experiences to avoid having to repeat yourself in the job descriptions.** See, for example, Resumes 22, 25, 45, and 49. [Lowry]

10. **Create a prominent Skills or Abilities section that draws together skills and abilities you have gained in previous work experience from different careers.** See, for example, Resumes 1, 4, 40, 41, and 55.

Best Resume Design and Layout Tips

11. **Use quality paper correctly.** If you use quality watermarked paper for your resume, be sure to use the right side of the paper. To know which side is the right side, hold a blank sheet of paper up to a light source. If you can see a watermark and read it, the right side of the paper is facing you. This is the surface for typing or printing. If the watermark is unreadable or if any

characters look backward, you are looking at the "underside" of a sheet of paper—the side that should be left blank if you use only one side of the sheet.

12. **Use adequate "white space."** A sheet of white paper with no words on it is impossible to read. Likewise, a sheet of white paper with words all over it is impossible to read. The goal is to have a comfortable mix of white space and words. If your resume has too many words and not enough white space, the resume looks cluttered and unfriendly. If it has too much white space and too few words, the resume looks skimpy and unimportant. Make certain that adequate white space exists between the main sections. For examples that display good use of white space, see Resumes 1, 4, 7, 8, 11, 12, 13, 14, and many others.

13. **Make the margins uniform in width and preferably no less than an inch.** Margins are part of the white space of a resume page. If the margins shrink below an inch, the page begins to have a "too much to read" look. An enemy of margins is the one-page rule. If you try to fit more than one page of information on a page, the first temptation is to shrink the margins to make room for the extra material. It is better to shrink the material by paring it down than to reduce the size of the left, right, top, and bottom margins. If you do your resume on a computer, lowering the point size of the type is one way to save the margins.

14. **Be consistent in your use of line spacing.** How you handle line spacing can tell the reader how good you are at details and how consistent you are in your use of them. If, near the beginning of your resume, you insert two line spaces (two hard returns in a word processing program) between two main sections, be sure to put two line spaces between main sections throughout the resume.

15. **Be consistent in your use of horizontal spacing.** If you usually put two character spaces after a period at the end of a sentence, make certain that you use two spaces consistently. The same is true for colons. If you put two spaces after colons, do so consistently.

    Note that an em dash—a dash the width of the letter *m*—does not require spaces before or after it. No space should go between the *P* and *O* of P.O. Box. Only one space is needed between the postal abbreviation of a state and the ZIP code. You should insert a space between the first and second initials of a person's name, as in I. M. Jobseeker (not I.M. Jobseeker). These conventions have become widely adopted in English and business communications. If, however, you use other conventions, be sure to be consistent. In resumes, as in grammar, consistency is more important than conformity.

16. **Make certain that characters, lines, and images contrast well with the paper.** The quality of "ink" depends on the device used to type or print your resume. If you use a typewriter or a dot-matrix printer with a cloth ribbon, check that the ribbon is fresh enough to make a dark impression. If you use a typewriter or a printer with a carbon tape, make certain that your paper has a texture that allows the characters to adhere permanently. (For a test, send yourself a copy of your resume and see how it makes the trip through the mail.) If you use an inkjet or laser printer, check that the characters are sharp and clean, without ink smudges or traces of extra toner.

    After much use, a cloth ribbon in a typewriter or a daisywheel printer may cause some characters (especially *a, e, o, g,* and *p*) to look darker than others. The reason probably is that ink has collected in the characters on the type bars or print wheel. To fix this problem, use a toothbrush and a safe solvent to clean the type.

17. **Use vertical alignment in stacked text.** Resumes usually contain tabbed or indented text. Make certain that this "stacked" material is aligned vertically. Misalignment can ruin the appearance of a well-written resume. Try to set tabs or indents that control this text throughout a resume instead of having a mix of tab stops in different sections. If you use a word processor, make certain that you understand the difference between tabbed text and indented text, as in the following examples:

Tabbed text: This text was tabbed over one tab stop before the writer started to write the sentence.

Indented text: This text was indented once before the writer started to write the sentence.

Note: In a number of word processing programs, the Indent command is useful for ensuring the correct vertical alignment of proportionally spaced, stacked text. After you issue the Indent command, lines of wrapped text are vertically aligned automatically until you terminate the command by pressing Enter.

18. **For the vertical alignment of dates, try left- or right-aligning the dates.** This technique is especially useful in chronological resumes and combination resumes. For examples of left-aligned dates, see Resumes 12, 20, 22, and 23. For right-aligned dates, look at Resumes 1, 4, 7, 8, 9, 11, 14, and 15.

19. **Use as many pages as you need for portraying yourself adequately to a specific interviewer about a particular job.** Try to limit your resume to one page, but set the upper limit at four pages. No rule about the number of pages makes sense in all cases. The determining factors are a person's qualifications and experiences, the requirements of the job, and the interests and pet peeves of the interviewer. If you know that an interviewer refuses to look at a resume longer than a page, that says it all. You need to deliver a one-page resume if you want to get past the first gate.

20. **Make each page a full page.** More important than the number of pages is whether each page you have is a full page. A partial page suggests deficiency even if the information on page 1 spills over onto page 2. There, it becomes evident that you don't have enough information to fill two pages. In that situation, try to compress all of your information onto the first page. If you have a resume that is almost two pages, make it two full pages.

21. **If you use a later Windows version of WordPerfect (6.1 or later), use the Make It Fit Expert to compress or expand your text into whole pages.** If you are a resume writer or write many letters, this feature is worth the cost of the program.

22. **When you have letters of recommendation, use quotations from them as testimonials in the first column of a two-column format or somewhere else in the resume.** Devoting a whole column to the positive opinions of "external authorities" helps to make a resume convincing as well as impressive. See, for example, Resume 189. [Culp Coury]

23. **Unless you enlist the services of a professional printer or skilled desktop publisher, resist the temptation to use full justification for text.** The price that you pay for a straight right margin is uneven word spacing. Words may appear too close together on some lines and too spread out on others. Although the resume might look like typeset text, you lose readability. See also Tip 4 in Part 3 of this book.

24. **If you can choose a typeface for your resume, use a serif font for greater readability.** Serif fonts have little lines extending from the top, bottom, and end of a character. These fonts tend to be easier to read than sans serif (without serif) fonts, especially in low-light conditions. Compare the following font examples:

Serif	**Sans Serif**
Century Schoolbook	Gill Sans
Courier	Futura
Times New Roman	Helvetica

   Words like *minimum* and *abilities* are more readable in a serif font.

25. **If possible, avoid using monospaced type like this Courier type.** Courier was a standard of business communications during the 1960s and 1970s. Because of its widespread use, it is now considered "common." It also takes up a lot of space, so you can't pack as much information on a page with Courier type as you can with a proportionally spaced type like Times Roman.

26. **Think twice before using all uppercase letters in parts of your resume.** A common misconception is that uppercase letters are easier to read than lowercase letters. Actually, the ascenders and descenders of lowercase letters make them more distinguishable from each other and therefore more recognizable than uppercase letters. For a test, look at a string of uppercase letters and throw them gradually out of focus by squinting. The uppercase letters become a blur sooner than lowercase letters.

27. **Think twice about underlining some words in your resume.** Underlining defeats the purpose of serifs at the bottom of characters by blending with the serifs. In trying to emphasize words, you lose some visual clarity. This is especially true if you use underlining with uppercase letters in centered or side headings.

28. **If you have access to many fonts through word processing or desktop publishing, beware of becoming "font happy" and turning your resume into a font circus.** Frequent font changes can distract the reader, AND SO CAN GAUDY DISPLAY TYPE.

29. **To make your resume stand out, consider using headings in unconventional type.** See, for example, Resumes 56 and 61. When you compare this idea with the preceding idea, you can see that one of the basic rules of resume making is, "Anything goes." What is usually fitting for resumes for most prospective jobs is not always the most appropriate resume strategy for every job opportunity. [Busby]

30. **Be aware of the value differences of black type.** Some typefaces are light; others are dark. Notice the following lines:

   A quick brown fox jumps over the lazy dog.

   A quick brown fox jumps over the lazy dog.

   Most typefaces fall somewhere in-between. With the variables of height, width, thickness, serifs, angles, curves, spacing, ink color, ink density, boldfacing, and typewriter double-striking, you can see that type offers an infinite range of values from light to dark. Try to make your resume more visually interesting by offering stronger contrasts between light type and dark type. See, for example, Resume 198.

31. **Use italic characters carefully.** Whenever possible, use italic characters instead of underlining when you need to call attention to a word or phrase. You might consider using italic for duties or achievements. Think twice about using italic throughout your resume, however. The reason is that italic characters are less readable than normal characters.

32. **Use boldfacing to make different job positions more evident.** See, for example, Resumes 4, 9, 10, 11, 13, 15, and many others.

33. **If you use word processing or desktop publishing and have a suitable printer, use special characters to enhance the look of your resume.** For example, use enhanced quotation marks ("and") instead of their typewriter equivalents (" "). Use an em dash (—) instead of two hyphens (--) for a dash. To separate dates, try using an en dash (a dash the width of the letter *n*) instead of a hyphen, as in 1993–1994.

34. **To call attention to an item in a list, use a bullet (•) or a box (❑) instead of a hyphen (-).** Browse through the Gallery and notice how bullets are used effectively as attention getters.

35. **For variety, try using bullets of a different style, such as diamond (♦) bullets, rather than the usual round or square bullets.** For diamond bullets, see Resumes 7, 13, 15, 18, 49, 63, 65, 66, and many others. For other kinds of "bullets," see Resumes 5, 11, 14, 22, 35, 41, 47, 49, 64, 71, 81, 83, 84, and many others.

36. **Make a bullet a little smaller than the lowercase letters that appear after it.** Disregard any ascenders or descenders on the letters. Compare the following bullet sizes:

    • Too small   ● Too large   • Better   • Just right

37. **When you use bullets, make certain that the bulleted items go beyond the superficial and contain information that employers really want to know.** Many short bulleted statements that say nothing special can affect the reader negatively. Brevity is not always the best strategy with bullets.

38. **When the amount of information justifies a longer resume, repeat a particular graphic, such as a filled square bullet (■) or a right-pointing arrow, to unify the entire resume.**

39. **Use a horizontal line to separate the name (or both the name and the address) from the rest of the resume.** If you browse through the Gallery, you can see many resumes that use horizontal lines this way. See, for example, Resumes 2, 3, 9, 14, 15, and 19.

40. **Use horizontal lines to separate the different sections of the resume.** See, for example, Resumes 31, 53, 72, 75, and 83. See also Resumes 35 and 171, whose lines are interrupted by the section headings.

41. **To call attention to a resume section or certain information, use horizontal lines to enclose it.** See, for example, Resumes 5, 10, 18, 23, 40, 42, 45, 47, 58, 59, 61, 63, 81, 87, 94, 95, 106, 119, 120, 122, 128, 138, 144, 155, 157, 180, 187, 191, and 215. This device is powerful for increasing the chances that whatever is between the lines will be seen.

42. **Change the thickness of part of a horizontal line to call attention to a section heading below the line.** See, for example, Resumes 72 and 105.

43. **Use a vertical line (or lines) to spice up your resume.** See, for example, Resumes 12, 56, 172, 173, 189, 201, 205, and 214. See also Resume 11, in which both a vertical line and a horizontal line are used.

44. **Use boxes, shaded boxes, or shadowed boxes to make a page visually more interesting.** See, for example, Resumes 12, 16, 97, 108, 123, 126, 170, and 188.

45. **Use a theme-related graphic to make a page more interesting.** See, for example, Resumes 104, 109, 145, 157, 163, and 207.

46. **If your computer system has the capability, use "white on black" to make a page more interesting.** See, for example, Resumes 33, 44, 66, and 93.

Best Resume Writing Style Tips

47. **Avoid using the archaic word *upon* in the References section.** The common statement "References available upon request" needs to be simplified, updated, or even deleted in resume writing. The word *upon* is one of the finest words of the 13th century, but it's a stuffy word at the beginning of the 21st century. Usually, *on* will do for *upon*. Other possibilities are "References available by request" and "References available." Because most readers of resumes know that applicants can usually provide several reference letters, this statement is probably unnecessary. A reader who is seriously interested in you will ask about reference letters.

48. **Check that words or phrases in lists are parallel.** For example, notice the bulleted items in the Volunteer section of Resume 1. All the verbs are in the past tense. Notice also the bulleted list in the Management Experience section of Resume 34. Here all the entries begin with verbs in the present tense.

49. **Use capital letters correctly.** Resumes usually contain many of the following:

    ■ Names of people, companies, organizations, government agencies, awards, and prizes

    ■ Titles of job positions and publications

    ■ References to academic fields (such as chemistry, English, and mathematics)

    ■ Geographic regions (such as the Midwest, the East, the state of California, and Oregon State)

    Because of such words, resumes are minefields for the misuse of uppercase letters. When you don't know whether a word should have an initial capital letter, don't guess. Consult a dictionary, a handbook on style, or some other authoritative source. Often a reference librarian can provide the information you need. If so, you are only a phone call away from an accurate answer.

50. **Check that capital letters and hyphens are used correctly in computer terms.** If you want to show in a Computer Experience section that you have used certain hardware and software, you may give the opposite impression if you don't use uppercase letters and hyphens correctly. Note the correct use of

capitals and hyphens in the following names of hardware, software, and computer companies:

LaserJet III	Hewlett-Packard	dBASE
PageMaker	MS-DOS	Microsoft
WordPerfect	PC DOS	Microsoft Word
NetWare	PostScript	AutoCAD

The reason that many computer product names have an internal uppercase letter is for the sake of a trademark. A word with unusual spelling or capitalization is trademarkable. When you use the correct forms of these words, you are honoring trademarks and registered trademarks.

51. **Use all uppercase letters for most acronyms.** An *acronym* is a pronounceable word usually formed from the initial letters of the words in a compound term, or sometimes from multiple letters in those words. Note the following examples:

BASIC	Beginner's All-purpose Symbolic Instruction Code
COBOL	COmmon Business-Oriented Language
DOS	Disk Operating System
FORTRAN	FORmula TRANslator

An acronym like *radar* (*ra*dio *d*etecting *a*nd *r*anging) has become so common that it is no longer all uppercase.

52. **Be aware that you may need to use a period with some abbreviations.** An *abbreviation* is a word shortened by removing the latter part of the word or by deleting some letters within the word. Here are some examples:

adj. for *adjective*	*amt.* for *amount*
adv. for *adverb*	*dept.* for *department*

Usually, you can't pronounce an abbreviation as a word. Sometimes, however, an abbreviation is a set of uppercase letters (without periods) that you can pronounce as letters. AFL-CIO (A-F-L, C-I-O), CBS, NFL, and YMCA are examples.

53. **Be sure to spell every word correctly.** A resume with just one misspelling is not impressive and may undermine all the hours you spent putting it together. Worse than that, one misspelling may be what the reader is looking for to screen you out, particularly if you are applying for a position that requires accuracy with words. The cost of that error can be immense if you figure the salary, benefits, and bonuses you *don't* get because of the error but would have gotten without it.

If you use word processing and have a spelling checker, you may be able to catch any misspellings. Be wary of spelling checkers, however. They can detect a misspelled word but cannot detect when you have inadvertently used a wrong word (*to* for *too,* for example). Be wary also of letting someone else check your resume. If the other person is not a good speller, you may not get any real help. The best authority is a good dictionary.

54. **For words that have a couple of correct spellings, use the preferred form.** This form is the one that appears first in a dictionary. For example, if you see the entry **trav·el·ing** *or* **trav·el·ling**, the first form (with one *l*) is the

preferred spelling. If you make it a practice to use the preferred spelling, you will build consistency in your resumes and cover letters.

55. **Avoid British spellings.** These slip into American usage through books published in Great Britain. Note the following words:

British Spelling	American Spelling
acknowledgement	acknowledgment
centre	center
judgement	judgment
towards	toward

56. **Avoid hyphenating words with such prefixes as *co-, micro-, mid-, mini-, multi-, non-, pre-, re-,* and *sub-*.** Many people think that words with these prefixes should have a hyphen after the prefix, but most of these words should not. The following words are spelled correctly:

coauthor	microcomputer	minicomputer
coworker	midpoint	multicultural
cowriter	midway	multilevel
nondisclosure	prearrange	reenter
nonfunctional	prequalify	subdirectory

Note: If you look in a dictionary for a word with a prefix and can't find the word, look for the *prefix* itself in the dictionary. You might find there a small-print listing of a number of words that have the prefix.

57. **Be aware that compounds (combinations of words) present special problems for hyphenation.** Writers' handbooks and books on style do not always agree on how compounds should be hyphenated. Many compounds are evolving from *open* compounds to *hyphenated* compounds to *closed* compounds. In different dictionaries, you can therefore find the words *copy-editor, copy editor,* and *copyeditor*. No wonder the issue is confusing! Most style books do agree, however, that when some compounds appear as an adjective before a noun, the compound should be hyphenated. When the same compound appears after a noun, hyphenation is unnecessary. Compare the following two sentences:

> I scheduled well-attended conferences.

> The conferences I scheduled were well attended.

For detailed information about hyphenation, see a recent edition of *The Chicago Manual of Style*. You should be able to find a copy at a local library.

58. **Be sure to hyphenate so-called *permanent* hyphenated compounds.**
Usually, you can find these by looking them up in a dictionary. You can spot them easily because they have a "long hyphen" (–) for visibility in the dictionary. Hyphenate these words (with a standard hyphen) wherever they appear, before or after a noun. Here are some examples:

all-important	self-employed
day-to-day	step-by-step
full-blown	time-consuming

59. **Use the correct form for certain verbs and nouns combined with prepositions.** You may need to consult a dictionary for correct spelling and hyphenation. Compare the following examples:

start up	(verb)
start-up	(noun)
start-up	(adj.)
startup	(noun, computer industry)
startup	(adj., computer industry)

60. **Avoid using shortcut words, such as abbreviations like *thru* or foreign words like *via*.** Spell out *through* and use *by* for *via*.

61. **Use the right words.** The issue here is correct usage, which often means the choice of the right word or phrase from a group of two or more possibilities. The following words and phrases are often used incorrectly:

alternate (adj.)	Refers to an option used every other time. OFF is the alternate option to ON in an ON/OFF switch.
alternative	Refers to an option that can be used at any time. If cake and pie are alternative desserts for dinner, you can have cake three days in a row if you like. The common mistake is to use *alternate* when the correct word is *alternative*.
center around	A common illogical expression. Draw a circle and then try to draw its center around it. You can't. Use *center in* or *center on* as logical alternatives to *center around*.

    For information about the correct *usage* of words, consult a usage dictionary or the usage section of a writer's handbook.

62. **Use numbers consistently.** Numbers are often used inconsistently with text. Should you present a number as a numeral or spell out the number as a word? One approach is to spell out numbers *one* through *nine* but present numbers 10 and above as numerals. Different approaches are taught in different schools, colleges, and universities. Use the approach you have learned, but be consistent.

63. **Use (or don't use) the serial comma consistently.** How should you punctuate a series of three or more items? If, for example, you say in your resume that you increased sales by 100 percent, opened two new territories, and trained four new salespersons, the comma before *and* is called the *serial comma*. It is commonly omitted in newspapers, magazine articles, advertisements, and business documents; but it is often used for precision in technical documents or for stylistic reasons in academic text, particularly in the Humanities.

64. **Use semicolons correctly.** Semicolons are useful because they help to distinguish visually the items in a series when the items themselves contain commas. Suppose that you have the following entry in your resume:

    Increased sales by 100 percent, opened two new territories, which were in the Midwest, trained four new salespersons, who were from Georgia, and increased sales by 250 percent.

The extra commas (before *which* and *who*) throw the main items of the series out of focus. By separating the main items with semicolons, you can bring them back into focus:

> Increased sales by 100 percent; opened two new territories, which were in the Midwest; trained four new salespersons, who were from Georgia; and increased sales by 250 percent.

Use this kind of high-rise punctuation even if just one item in the series has an internal comma.

65. **Avoid using colons after headings.** A colon indicates that something is to follow. A heading indicates that something is to follow. A colon after a heading is therefore redundant.

66. **Use dashes correctly.** One of the purposes of a dash (an em dash or two hyphens) is to introduce a comment or afterthought about preceding information. A colon *anticipates* something to follow, but a dash *looks back* to something already said. Two dashes are sometimes used before and after a parenthetical remark a related but nonessential remark—such as this—within a sentence. In this case, the dashes are like parentheses, but more formal.

2

P·A·R·T

The Gallery

The Gallery at a Glance

How to Use the Gallery

You can learn much from the Gallery just by browsing through it. To make the best use of this resource, however, read the following suggestions before you begin.

Examine the resumes on special paper at the beginning of the Gallery. These 16 examples show how quality paper can enhance the appearance of a resume. The papers range in color from whites to blues and include cream, tan, warm grays, and cool grays. Some of these papers are watermarked, and all are laser-compatible. Most have a weight of 24 lb. or more, which is widely used for resumes, and most contain recycled content. Some of the paper samples have subtle differences in texture that you can sense by rubbing your fingers over the surface and listening to the sound. Notice what colors are not included: orange, green, purple (the secondary colors), and darker values of any color.

Look at the resumes in the category containing your field, related fields, or your target occupation. Notice what kinds of resumes other people have used to find similar jobs. Always remember, though, that your resume should not be "canned." It should not look just like someone else's resume but should reflect your own background, unique experiences, and goals.

Use the Gallery primarily as an "idea book." Even if you don't find a resume for your specific occupation or job, be sure to look at all of the resumes for ideas you can borrow or adapt. You may be able to modify some of the sections or statements with information that applies to your own situation or job target.

Study the ways professional resume writers have formatted the names, addresses, and phone numbers of the subjects. In most instances, this information appears at the top of the first page of the resume. In one of the resumes, you will find this information in the middle of the first page. Look at type styles, size of type, and use of boldface. See whether the personal information is centered on lines, spread across a line, or located near the margin on one side of a page. Look for the use of horizontal lines to separate this information from the rest of the resume, to separate the address and phone number from the person's name, or to enclose information for higher visibility.

Look at each resume to see what section appears first after the personal information. Then compare those same sections across the Gallery. For example, look just at the resumes that have a Goal or an Objective statement as the first section. Compare the length, clarity, and use of words. Do these statements contain complete sentences, or one or more partial lines of thought? Are some statements better than others from your point of view? Do you see one or more Objective statements that come close to matching your own objective? After you have compared these statements, try expressing *in your own words* your goal or objective.

Repeat this "horizontal comparison" for each of the sections across the Gallery. Compare all of the Education sections, all of the Qualifications sections, and so on. As you make these comparisons, continue to note differences in length, the kinds of words and phrases used, and the effectiveness of the content. Jot down any ideas that might be true for you. Then put together similar sections for your own resume.

As you compare sections across the Gallery, pay special attention to the Profile, Summary, Areas of Expertise, Career Highlights, Qualifications, and Experience sections. (Most resumes won't have all of these sections.) Notice how skills and accomplishments are worked into these sections. Skills and accomplishments are *variables* that you can select to put a certain "spin" on your resume as you pitch it toward a particular interviewer or job. Your observations here should be especially valuable for your own resume versions.

After you have examined the resumes "horizontally" (section by section), compare them "vertically" (design by design). To do this, you need to determine which resumes have the same sections in the same order, and then compare just those resumes. For example, look for resumes that have personal information at the top, an Objective statement, an Experience section, an Education section, and finally a line about references. (Notice that the section heads may differ slightly. Instead of the word *Experience,* you might find *Work Experience* or *Employment.*) When you examine the resumes in this way, you are looking at their *structural design,* which means the order in which the various sections appear. The same order can appear in resumes of different fields or jobs, so it is important to explore the whole Gallery and not limit your investigation to resumes in your field or related fields.

Developing a sense of resume structure is extremely important because it enables you to emphasize the most important information about yourself. A resume is a little like a newspaper article—read quickly and usually discarded before the reader finishes. That is why the information in newspaper articles often dwindles in significance toward the end. For the same reason, the most important, attention-getting information about you should be at or near the top of your resume. What follows should appear in order of descending significance.

If you know that the reader will be more interested in your education than your work experience, put your Education section before your Experience section. If you know that the reader will be interested in your skills regardless of your education and work experience, put your Skills section at or near the beginning of your resume. In this way, you can help to ensure that anyone who reads only *part* of your resume will read the "best about you." Your hope is that this information will encourage the reader to read on to the end of the resume and, above all, take an interest in you.

Compare the resumes according to visual design features, such as the use of horizontal and vertical lines, borders, boxes, bullets, white space, graphics, and inverse type (light characters on a dark background). Notice which resumes have more visual impact at first glance and which ones make no initial impression. Do some of the resumes seem more inviting to read than others? Which ones are less appealing because they have too much information, or too little? Which ones seem to have the right balance of information and white space?

After comparing the visual design features, choose the design ideas that might improve your own resume. You will want to be selective here and not try to work every design possibility into your resume. As in writing, "less is more" in resume making, especially when you integrate design features with content.

Resumes on Special Paper

Resumes at a Glance

MELISSA M. MARCHESE

1255 West Shaw Avenue
Fresno, California 93711
(209) 222-7474

CAREER GOALS

Association with an organization that will benefit from my initiative, capabilities, and contributions, ultimately qualifying for advancement and increased decision-making responsibilities.

EDUCATION

CALIFORNIA STATE UNIVERSITY, FRESNO

Degree: Bachelor of Science (December 1993)
Major: Economics
Emphasis: Political Science and International Economics

FRESNO CITY COLLEGE

Degree: Associate of Arts (December 1991)
Honors: Participated in the college's Honors Program

SUMMARY OF SKILLS

- Extensive general office experience encompassing administrative, secretarial, computer data entry, light bookkeeping (A/P, A/R, payroll), and special projects.

- Proficient in IBM computer environment; familiar with WordPerfect, Quattro, Multimate, Q & A, One-Write Plus, Lotus 1-2-3, Org Plus, and DOS.

- Exceptional organizational/planning skills; simultaneously managed and monitored multiple tasks; developed new systems and forms to increase office efficiency.

- Excellent computer keyboard skills; typing speed of 85 wpm; composed correspondence and memoranda; word processed lengthy proposals/reports (60+ pages), legal documents, and architectural specifications.

- Maintain composure under pressure; able to work autonomously with little direct supervision.

PROFESSIONAL EXPERIENCE

Personally financed majority of education, holding part-time or full-time employment while maintaining above average GPA and completing degree in 4½ years:

Office Manager/Secretary -- James L. Manachek, Attorney at Law	8/90 to Pres.
Temp Office Worker/Secretary -- Denham Personnel	5/90 to 7/90
Temp Office Worker -- Snelling Temporaries	12/89 to 4/90
Legal Secretary -- John Duffy, Attorney at Law	5/89 to 1/90
Telex Typist -- Sumitomo Corporation	11/88 to 5/89

Combination. *Susan Britton Whitcomb, Fresno, California*

A resume that is easy to size up at a glance because of bold type for the individual's name and section headings, plus adequate white space (blank lines) between and within sections.

LINDA M. STRONG

1000 Crescent Drive
Tyler, Texas 75700

(903) 666-9999 (Home)
(903) 555-4444 (Pager)

HIGHLIGHTS OF QUALIFICATIONS

- 20+ years of experience with progressive responsibility in **Office Administration / Management**; strong **organizational**, **time management**, and **conflict resolution** abilities.
- Proficiency in **accounting** and **secretarial/clerical functions** (computer, A/R, A/P, payroll).
- Excellent **employee relations** and **team-building** abilities; interview, hire, train, supervise, motivate, and counsel 25 employees; develop team committed to optimal productivity.
- Ability to evaluate problems or unsatisfactory situations and make astute decisions to effect positive change. **Results-oriented.**
- Effective **oral** and **written communication** skills.
- Loyal, conscientious, and dependable. Flawless attendance.

EDUCATION / PROFESSIONAL DEVELOPMENT

TEXAS WOMAN'S UNIVERSITY – Denton, Texas
Bachelor of Science Degree

Stress Management   •   Employee Relations   •   Time Management

CAREER EXPERIENCE

MASON ENTERPRISES   Tyler, Texas
Office Manager / Executive Secretary   1970 – Present

- Began as **Administrative Assistant**; assumed additional responsibilities and promoted to **Office Manager/ Executive Secretary** in 1977 for cattle company and wholesale nursery operation shipping in excess of five million rose bushes to nationwide retailers annually.
- Interview, hire, train, schedule, supervise, motivate, counsel, and discipline/terminate staff.
- Manage A/R, A/P, payroll, taxes, correspondence, records management for both companies.
- Interface extensively with 50 sales representatives located all over the country; coordinate travel plans; book reservations and car rentals; schedule and organize meetings.
- Organize and coordinate two "Employee Appreciation" parties annually; prepare bonus checks for every employee; purchase fruit baskets for every employee and gifts for all children of employees at Christmas; deliver to those who cannot attend party.
- Organize and attend trade shows twice a year to promote roses.
- Negotiate with shippers to attain lowest shipping rates; ensure on-time delivery.

Significant Achievements

- Planned and implemented **"Employee Incentive Award"** program. Designed to promote safety in the workplace and good attendance. Awards presented to all employees with no injuries or lost time; **substantially reduced absenteeism and injuries**; personally received award every year after inception.
- Conducted **Time Management Studies** which **significantly improved quality of performance.**
- Completely reorganized filing system which **increased efficiency and accessibility.**

2

Combination. *Ann Klint, Tyler, Texas*

Thicker top and bottom page borders make this resume stand out. Boldfacing for embedded key words helps them to be seen. Center-alignment for Education offers relief.

Hardy Rock

2410 Armor Way
Camptonville, CA 95835
(916) 555-1212

Objective: Position as a full-time air personality

SUMMARY OF QUALIFICATIONS

- More than 9 years progressive air talent experience.
- Extensive experience in radio broadcasting
- Skilled in programming, production, and promotion
- Vast knowledge of artists and their music
- Philosophy: *"Have a passion for what you do.*
  You're only as good as your last break."

EDUCATION

A.S., Broadcasting, American College, San Francisco, CA, 1995

RELEVANT EXPERIENCE AND ACCOMPLISHMENTS

AIR WORK/PRODUCTION/PROGRAMMING:
- Performed as Air Personality in various dayparts including full-time Evenings.
- Filled in as Morning Drive Host and Newscaster.
- Assembled creative production including origination of Image Liner beds.
- Voiced and produced commercials and promos using multi-track machine.
- Served as programming assistant to David Andrews—KROK.
- Operated SELECTOR: Scheduled music while monitoring diverse flow of artists and styles.
- Printed music logs, and gave input on music selections.

INTERVIEWS:
- Researched, wrote and conducted on-air interviews with Graham Nash; Bonnie Raitt; Crash Test Dummies; John Hiatt and other artists.
- Reported at 1995 Oakland A's Spring Training, Phoenix, interviewed Tony La Russa, Mark McGwire, and other Major League players, coaches and administrators.

SPECIAL PROJECTS/PROMOTIONS:
- Contributed album reviews and artist interviews to *Print Tracks*, KRON Newsletter.
- Wrote, produced, and narrated the *"Top 80 Songs of the 80's."*
- Served as promotions assistant to Randy Swift—KUPD.
- Involved in strategic planning of on-air contests and station events.
- Made numerous personal appearances at concerts, clubs and other events.

TELEVISION/VIDEO:
- Served as guest announcer for PBS Station KWIE, Channel 8, San Francisco.
- Featured on KFOB, Channel 35, San Francisco.
- Appeared in video for, *"The Way It Is,"* by Geffen Recording artists, TESLA.

EMPLOYMENT HISTORY

Air Personality	KRON -FM, THE PRINT, San Francisco, CA	1991-Present
Air Personality	KUPD-FM, Oakland, CA	1990-1991
Air Personality	KROK-FM, San Francisco, CA	1989-1990
Air Personality	KRES-FM, 95 ROCK, San Francisco, CA	1987-1989

3

Combination. *Nancy Karvonen, Galt, California*

Horizontal lines after the contact information and before the Employment History display vertical symmetry. The impressive Employment History provides a strong ending.

MICHAEL SMITHERS

Plate Shop Production

5433 S.W. Lakeview Court, Lake Oswego, Oregon 97035   (503) 636-3055

**TECHNICAL
SKILLS**

Fully qualified journeyman with solid skills in plate shop production and press brake operations. Known for speed, accuracy and quality of work.

- Extensive experience in sheet metal production.
- Accustomed to working with various types of metal—aluminum, mild steel and hardened steel (16 gauge to 1/2").
- Able to read blueprints and schematics.
- Expertise in CNC programming.
- Capable of working with engineers and co-workers at all levels.

Able to operate, maintain and repair:

Pacific 500 ton press brake	Cincinnati 1000 ton press brake
Cincinnati 12' and 24' shears	Drill presses
Cincinnati 12' CNC control shear	Promecam 12' CNC press brake
Ironworkers	Wysong 16' shear
Hand grinders / hand tools	Roll press
Punches	Pacific 6" shear

EXPERIENCE

PEERLESS - Tualatin, Oregon   7/85-Present
Journeyman (Plate Shop)
Shear plates for various projects and manufacture custom parts from blueprints. Work with all types of metal, from thin aluminum to heavy steel plate. Utilize press brakes, shears and other types of shop equipment; perform routine maintenance and repair as needed.

ACKERMANN-SMITHERS TOOL & DIE GRINDING - Frankfurt, Germany   5/79-3/85
Partner / Maintenance Mechanic
After 20 months of on-the-job training, was accepted as partner in family-owned tool and die repair business. Helped build company into a respected, efficiently run business. Operated, maintained and repaired all equipment on the premises. Worked as sole operator after partner retired.

MERCEDES BENZ - Frankfurt, Germany   7/76-4/79
Mechanic
Responsible for routine maintenance on heavy trucks and buses.

UNITED STATES ARMY - Frankfurt, Germany   11/72-6/76
Mechanic
Repaired jeeps and various types of heavy construction equipment.

EDUCATION

General: Graduated from Frankfurt-American High School.

Technical: Completed comprehensive Mechanics Training School (U.S. Army); continuing education related to equipment operation and repair.

REFERENCES

Provided upon request.

4

Combination. *Pat Kendall, Aloha, Oregon*

Below the address, the content could be presented as a one-tall-row, three-column table without lines. The space between the headings and the text is the second column.

THOMAS RICHARD MANSON

3802 Winchell Way, #A306 – Kalamazoo, MI 49008 – (616) 555-5432

PROFILE

Assertive professional with practical experience in and solid understanding of a diverse range of business management applications, including profit and loss, market analysis, sales and marketing, team-building, and quality assurance. Demonstrated ability to select, train, and retain self-motivated, customer-oriented employees. High-caliber presentation, negotiation, and closing skills. IBM / Macintosh computer skills: Lotus, Excel, Windows, WordPerfect, Investors, etc. Expertise in:

- ❖ Staff Hiring / Training / Supervision
- ❖ Vendor Sourcing / Competitive Purchasing
- ❖ Debt to Equity Ratio Analysis
- ❖ Corporate Financing / Risk Management

- ❖ Customer Relationship Management
- ❖ New Market Penetration & Development
- ❖ Professional Sales Training
- ❖ Business Communications: Verbal / Written / Computer

Consistently successful in outselling market competition, increasing revenues, and capturing key accounts.

EDUCATION

Western Michigan University, Kalamazoo, Michigan

<u>Bachelor of Business Administration</u>, <u>Finance</u>, 1995
Special emphasis in Security Analysis
Self-financed **100%** of all educational and living expenses.

PROFESSIONAL EXPERIENCE

CO-MANAGER: Richardo's Fine Dining / Maxie's Tavern, Kalamazoo, Michigan, 1993–1996

- Hired, trained, motivated, scheduled, and supervised **20–25** employees; conducted regular performance evaluations; and administered disciplinary action as required.
- Ensured total customer satisfaction in all areas (front / back of house and waitstaff) of fine dining establishment.
- Coordinated party / group / banquet bookings, ensuring consistently high profit ratios were achieved.
- Performed debt to equity analyses on a weekly basis to identify areas requiring attention (maintained **33%** or less food costs and **17%** or less beverage costs).
- Assessed restaurant staffing needs and implemented successful strategy to hire a more professional waitstaff which reduced employee turnover and significantly increased customer service quality and consistency.
- Launched several new employee incentive programs designed to successfully increase customer service.

FOOD SERVICE REPRESENTATIVE: Dandyman Food Service, Kalamazoo, Michigan, 1992–1993

- Recruited from Van Dyke Food Service to serve as territory developer for distributor of **4,500** different food items.
- Began employment with no (0) accounts and built to **70+** accounts with $1 million in gross sales within a year.
- Facilitated profitable business relationship between Western Michigan University and Dandyman Food Service, forming "win-win" partnership with McDonald's to secure sponsorship at various sporting events.
- Added another rep's territory to own with no replacement rep being hired.

FOOD SERVICE REPRESENTATIVE: Van Dyke Food Service, Mattawan, Michigan, 1990–1992

- Initiated "cold call" sales visits to potential customers; presented new products to existing account base.
- Won sales contest for most new accounts opened among **30** sales reps.
- Monitored daily market prices of pork, beef, seafood, and produce to determine customer pricing.
- Introduced and test marketed numerous new food items to existing and potential customers.

Combination. *Mary Roberts (city withheld), Florida*

Each pair of horizontal lines makes conspicuous the heading between the lines. If you want to draw attention to certain information, enclose it within a pair of horizontal lines.

John Richardson   *Hospitality Executive Management*

15 Circle Way
Redwood City, California 94433
Telephone (514) 515-2333

Background includes practical experience and education, which have provided good working
knowledge of these key areas:

Restaurant & Club Operations	**Cost Controls Management**
Profit/Loss Responsibility	**Strategy Planning**
Business Development	**Fine-dining Ambiance**
Inventory & Purchasing	**Food & Service Quality**
Staff Motivation & Training	**Marketing & Advertising**
Menu Development	**Remodels & Expansions**

Deliver highly motivated and effective performance in all areas of hospitality operations management. Experienced with multiple-site operations. Provide strong leadership and staff motivation.
Excellent communications, presentation and promotions abilities. Exceptionally guest oriented.

Operations Director

HOLOGRAM RESTAURANT CORP.   Redwood, California August 1987 - Present
Report to the owner/CEO and to the senior vice president of this company that has 55 restaurants in nine states—with a $33-million sales budget for 13 of the properties. Joined Hologram as
an assistant manager of in San Anita and was promoted to general manager of flagship
restaurant in 1989, Named to current post in May 1993. Key areas of accomplishment and
responsibility include:

- Strengthened controls and accountability, reduced costs, and improved profits by 25%.
- Oversaw re-opening of a property that involved development of a new concept and name.
- Direct-reports include three division managers and 14 general managers; responsible for
  recruiting, hiring, training, performance evaluations and relocations.
- Manage promotional activities to achieve market recognition and increased sales; pro-active
  in menu planning & design, food testing and quality assurance.
- P/L responsibilities include budget forecasts, and cost controls.

At the Cala and Topline restaurants, which had dining room, banquet and lounge facilities,
played key roles in organizing catered events, promoting patio dining, and installing a national
reservation system.

Director of Food & Beverage

FAR INN WEST   Harvey, Louisiana 1986 - 87
Managed all restaurant, banquet and room service sales and personnel at this 200-room property
operated by Vista Host, Inc. Launched a promotional drive to attract business lunches, dinners
and catering that increased sales by 15 percent.

General Manager

GOOD TIMES ENTERPRISES   Boca Raton, Florida 1982 - 86
Successfully managed three restaurants in College Station and Houston, including planning and
managing the openings of the bar/restaurant operations for Sam's Cantina and Zephyr Annex for
this rapidly expanding restaurant chain.

BA Degree Program - Business Administration

FLORIDA A&M   Boca Chica

Extensive Food & Beverage Management seminars and workshops

6

Combination. *Ted Bache, location unknown*

Notice that whatever is bold is seen first. The smaller font size and line spacing are characteristics
of executive resumes, providing more text without sacrificing white space.

GEORGE A. WHITELEY

1111 East Tuolumne
Fresno, California 93700
(209) 111-1000

QUALIFICATIONS

Accomplished 17-year career encompassing strengths in:

♦ Administration/Management
♦ Resource Development/Fundraising
♦ Human Resources/Personnel

PROFESSIONAL EXPERIENCE

Administration/Management:

- Planned and managed business operations for non-profit organizations, including finance, budgeting, facilities management, staffing, programming, and public relations.
- Prepared comprehensive business operating plan with short-range and long-range goals.
- Negotiated contractual agreements pertaining to purchase of property, rental of facilities valued at $2 million, refinancing, and construction/remodel projects.
- Balanced budget after long history of deficits.
- Supervised seven department directors and support staff.

Human Resources/Personnel:

- Managed all facets of Human Resource Department including start-up of new department.
- Experienced in recruiting, interviewing, placement, and evaluation of personnel (program managers, departmental supervisors, construction/trades, educators, and support staff).
- Conducted orientation and wrote curricula for training.
- Researched, presented for CEO approval, and administered employee benefits program.
- Wrote policy and procedures manual.
- Developed personnel forms.

Resource Development/Fundraising:

- Directed resource development programs for multi-state region.
- Targeted untapped cities through direct mail, generating $25,000 in revenue.
- Achieved $10,000 through direct mail alone, using segmented list with genesis series of letters.
- Developed prospect lists and data files for new donor acquisition.
- Took over planning for annual banquet and generated $25,000 (prior year's event lost money).
- Assisted in developing a deferred giving and financial counseling program.

EDUCATION

Master of Arts Degree, Regent University
Bachelor of Science Degree, Biola University

EMPLOYMENT HISTORY

Director of Personnel/Resource Development: His Ministries, Inc., Fresno, CA	1991-Pres.
Senior Administrative Pastor: Intercity Ministries, Norfolk, VA	1988-1991
Senior Administrative Pastor: Fellowship Alliance, Norfolk, VA	1981-1988

Combination. *Susan Britton Whitcomb, Fresno, California*

Small caps, an enhancement of upper- and lowercase text, tie together visually the individual's name and the side headings. Diamond bullets point to key strengths.

Thomas J. Thurgood

444 E. Cincinnati
Fresno, CA 93722
(209) 222-2222

■■ **Career Focus: International Business** ■■

EDUCATION

CALIFORNIA STATE UNIVERSITY, FRESNO

B.S., Business Administration (12/92)
Emphasis: **International Business**

REPRESENTATIVE COURSEWORK

Intro to International Business   International Finance
Management of Multinational Enterprises   International Marketing
World Commerce and Development   International Management

RELATED EXPERIENCES

- **Pacific Rim Trip:** Visited Hong Kong, Bangkok, Thailand, Singapore, and Seoul, Korea in connection with CSUF coursework. Opportunity provided exposure to conducting business in the Pacific Rim.
- **International Business Internship:** Under direction of CSUF Department Chair, worked with entrepreneurs from Ireland in researching, identifying, and contacting companies offering potential for import/export business.
- **Import Experience:** Presently employed with Skorich International which specializes in importing watches from Hong Kong, Malaysia, and India; make buying recommendations and organize shows for sales in five western states.

COMPUTER

Extensive computer coursework (60+ hours) with knowledge of various desktop hardware and software applications, including Lotus 1-2-3, WordPerfect, and D-base III+ and IV.

EMPLOYMENT SUMMARY

Personally financed 100% of education through the following employment:

Import/Sales: Trade International	1992-Present
Assistant Manager/Driver: Best Courier Services	1989-1990
Shift Supervisor/Waiter: Holiday Inn	1988-1989
Banquet Supervisor: The Marriott	1986-1988

AFFILIATIONS

International Business Association
Central California International Trade Association
Toastmasters International

Available for Relocation • References Upon Request

8

Combination. *Susan Britton Whitcomb, Fresno, California*

The bold page border keeps the attention of the reader on the information within the border. Follow the bold down the page, and you'll see what the writer wants you to see.

JASON DEAN

(209) 222-2222 • 1255 West Shaw • Fresno, CA 93711

EXPERTISE: Sales Management ... Marketing ... Account Management

SUMMARY OF QUALIFICATIONS:

Over 14 years' successful experience in sales management and sales. Consistently made significant contributions to corporate goals for business growth and profits. Created, implemented, and managed productive marketing programs for tangibles and intangibles.

Customer-driven focus: Built strong business partnerships, maximized account retention, and improved customer loyalty. **Team-oriented:** Recruited, motivated, and managed productive sales and sales support teams.

PROFESSIONAL EXPERIENCE:

GENERAL SALES MANAGER -- Pacific Sales, Fresno, CA   4/92 - Present
                                                                   and 2/80 - 11/87

- Promoted from Sales Manager to General Sales Manager in less than one year.
- Directly accountable for sales management, marketing, promotions, and programming.
- Manage national accounts. Negotiate co-op advertising and sponsorship packages.
- Was recruited to **revitalize sales** -- accomplished this goal through restructuring sales force, conducting intensive sales training, and implementing successful incentive programs.
- Personally **generated significant new business.**

AGENT MARKETING COORDINATOR -- Western Sales, Fresno, CA   10/89 - 3/92

- Liaison between Western Sales and 30 retail outlets to coordinate indirect distribution channel for cable service.
- Motivated and trained sales force; created successful incentive programs.
- **One of 20 nationwide** to earn "Manager Achievement Award" (awarded for design of successful promotions and management of outside agencies in a highly regulated market).
- Selected to **"Circle of Excellence"** (awarded to one per market nationally for overall performance).
- Featured in national monthly newsletter for consistently exceeding monthly goals.
- Won numerous incentive awards (including trip to London) for quota achievement.

GENERAL SALES MANAGER -- Americom Leasing, Fresno, CA   11/87 - 2/89

- Managed and motivated sales team. Coordinated marketing strategies.
- Personally sold to and serviced regional accounts.
- Increased sales 500%; advanced from 15th to 3rd highest billing station in market among 30 stations.

EDUCATION:

DEGREE PROGRAM: A.S., Business Merchandising & Management, Sacramento City College

Sales and Sales Management Seminars:
- Jones & Associates: "Fundamentals of Consultant Sales," "Leading High Performance Sales Teams"
- IBM Training: "Selling Technology," "Selling Naturally," "Retail Sales Skills and Management"
- CareerTrack Seminars: "High Impact Communication Skills"

9

Combination. *Susan Britton Whitcomb, Fresno, California*

The partial, thick-thin lines (reading from the bottom line upward) call attention to both the contact information and the Expertise areas. Underlining highlights the job positions.

REBECCA CALDERWOOD

714 East 9th Street ▪ Astoria, New York ▪ 11222
Phone: (718) 434-7872 ▪ E-mail: RCalderwood@msn.com

HEALTHCARE ADMINISTRATOR / PROGRAM DIRECTOR

Experienced administrator with a proven ability to run successful programs. Proficient at setting, expecting, and achieving high standards of quality. Currently direct a facility regarded as a model program. Respected leader with excellent team-building, communication, and interpersonal skills.

EDUCATION

Master of Science in Health Administration, Hunter College, New York, NY, 1990
Bachelor of Arts in Psychology, Union College, Schenectady, NY, 1984

EMPLOYMENT

Heartland Agency, Woodside, NY
Director, 1990 to present
Administer program that serves adults with disabilities. Manage $5 million in funding. Oversee more than 50 management, clinical, and direct care staff members. Devise systems for admission, discharge, organization, and staffing. Monitor all facets of the 20,000 square foot plant and comply with OSHA standards. Ensure compliance with NYS OMRDD Part 690, 633, 635, and 624 policies.

Key Accomplishments:

- Fostered an environment of teamwork and cooperation that boosted staff morale.
- Initiated a recruitment campaign that increased consumer enrollment from 73 to 129.
- Undertook a classroom reorganization project that improved quality services and increased consumer independence.
- Developed a positive relationship with other departments so that all programs work toward common goals.
- Set-up and chair the interagency Human Rights and Informed Consent committees.
- Selected to direct a satellite program for geriatric consumers.

United Samaritans, Flushing, NY
Program Coordinator, 1985 to 1990
Managed department that received more than $2 million in funding. Hired, supervised, and evaluated professional and support staff. Supervised the work activities of 350 consumers in the Extended Rehabilitation Department. Acted as Director of Rehabilitation in her absence.

Key Accomplishments:

- Secured three new agency programs by responding to Request for Proposals.
- Prepared statistical reports and handled external audits for all programs.
- Devised consumer satisfaction survey that sparked improvements in programming.
- Promoted from Case Manager and maintained a large caseload as Coordinator.

COMPUTERS

Advanced user of WordPerfect, Microsoft Word, R&R Relational Report Writer, Lotus 1-2-3, SPSS, and Microsoft Publisher. Train colleagues on how to use a computer and provide technical guidance. Experience with installing network systems and computer hardware.

10

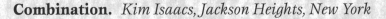

Combination. *Kim Isaacs, Jackson Heights, New York*

The Education section is placed near the top because of the importance of the degrees for health-care management. Square bullets highlight key accomplishments.

5555 North Glenn, #555
Gloucester, Nevada 55555
(209) 439-9581

NATALIE F. JENSEN, R.D.H.

OBJECTIVE: Continued career growth as a Registered Dental Hygienist within a progressive dental practice whose emphasis is on periodontal therapy and preventative dentistry.

SPECIALTY PROCEDURES:

★ Local Anesthesia   ★ Gingival Curettage
★ Nitrous Oxide   ★ Periodontal Therapy
★ Coronal Polish   ★ Orthodontics
★ Endodontics   ★ Periodontics
★ Pedodontics   ★ Radiology

LICENSURE: **California State Board of Dental Examiners** (License Number 55555)

EXPERIENCE: **Registered Dental Hygienist:** Perform a full range of RDH responsibilities, including FMS, BW, prophylaxis, scaling, root planing, local anesthesia, nitrous oxide, OHI, and periodontal charting. Excellent record with former and present employers:

Keenan Wynn, D.D.S., Gloucester, Nevada	7/94-Present
Angela Berrins, D.D.S., Gloucester, Nevada	2/93-6/94
Warren Minnis, D.D.S., Gloucester, Nevada	9/91-1/93

EDUCATION: GLOUCESTER CITY COLLEGE, Gloucester, Nevada

★ **Associate of Science Degree, Dental Hygiene** (1991)
★ **Advanced Training** in Periodontal Therapy (scaling and root planing)

AWARDS: **Clinical Award** -- Selected by instructors as top graduate with exceptional clinical skills. Award is given jointly by the Glouster Dental Society, the County Dental Society, the Waxahachie Dental Society, and the Gloucester Dental Foundation.

Special Honors -- Chosen by Dental Hygiene graduating students for demonstration of leadership and clinical skills.

AFFILIATIONS: American Dental Hygienists Association; Nevada Dental Hygienists Association; Gloucester Dental Hygienists Association (Vice President)

VOLUNTEER:

★ Provided public health information as Dental Hygiene Representative at City High School's Health Fair.

★ Informed students of Dental Hygiene career opportunities at Gloucester College's Career Day.

★ Presented lecture series on dental hygiene to elementary school children and senior citizens in connection with "All Smiles" and "Target Group" programs respectively.

★ Assisted in organizing the first annual National Dental Hygiene Week at Gloucester City College.

REFERENCES: Provided upon request.

Selected comments from performance evaluations: "it is critical to the health and prosperity of my practice that staff *care* about our patients -- Natalie is exemplary in her rapport with patients which stems from her belief in, and appreciation for, the uniqueness and worth of every individual, whether young or old."

11

Combination. *Susan Britton Whitcomb, Fresno, California*

The crossing lines are striking design elements. The format of the Experience section avoids duplication of similar job descriptions. The closing testimonial is a strong, convincing ending.

Frances L. Noval

7777 HISSY ROAD • BETHESDA, MD 88888 • (000) 000-0000

| CERTIFIED NURSING ASSISTANT |

OBJECTIVE

Position as a <u>medical office assistant</u> offering opportunity for continued professional growth in the health care field.

HIGHLIGHTS OF QUALIFICATIONS

- Six years experience in patient care.
- Patient care experience in home and institutional environments.
- Excellent care-giving skills.
- Experience working with physicians, nurses and other health care professionals.
- Team player. Works well with people on all levels.
- Well organized. Excellent time management skills.
- Reliable. Dependable.
- Career directed in health care.
- Certified PC specialist.

EXPERIENCE

2/96 to Present — **HOUSE CALL INC., BETHESDA, MD**
Home Health Aide
Provides direct patient care services in private residential and nursing care facilities. Maintains documentation on patient activities and provides daily reports for nursing staff. Implements varying care plans designed to support the highest quality of day-to-day life for all patients.

2/94 to 2/96 — **CHRISTIAN HEALTH CARE CENTER, BRADLEY, MD**
Certified Nursing Assistant
Assisted nursing staff in helping provide and meet day-to-day living needs of 15-20 alzheimers and psychiatric patients. Conducted daily patient rounds; took vital signs/blood pressure, etc.; helped plan and conduct patient activities; helped provide patient supplies; helped dress, feed, and bathe patients; helped transport patients and provided other support services for nursing staff.

12/90 to 7/94 — **FAIR ACRES MANOR, WILLIS, MD**
Certified Nursing Assistant
Worked mainly in the alzheimers unit planning and implementing patient care programs and activities. Responsible for planning successful fashion show, costume parties and holiday related events. Helped escort patients on off-site outings. Took patients for walks, organized games and provided other patient support services for nursing staff.

12/89 to 12/90 — **CHRISTIAN HEALTH CARE CENTER, BRADLEY, MD**
Certified Nursing Assistant

EDUCATION/TRAINING

1996 — **HOUSE CALL INC., BETHESDA, MD**
Completed orientation training.
1996 — **INTERNATIONAL CORRESPONDENCE SCHOOLS INC., MUNRO, PA**
Completed course requirements for certification as a PC Specialist.
1995 — **INTERNATIONAL CORRESPONDENCE SCHOOLS INC., MUNRO, PA**
Completed requirements for high school diploma.
1990 — **MD DEPARTMENT OF HEALTH AND MENTAL HYGIENE, BALTIMORE, MD**
Received license as a Certified Nursing Assistant.
1987 — **SHADYSIDE NURSING CENTER, LINCOLN, MD**
Received license as a Geriatrics Nursing Assistant.

Other: Completed numerous in-service workshops on nursing assistance at Fair Acres Manor. Holds current certification in CPR.

12

Combination. *Thomas E. Spann, Easton, Maryland*

Bold initial caps with small caps gives this classy resume extra punch. Smaller type for section headings and dates makes the individual's name and main information stand out.

MARIA CARDOZA

555 Courtney Boulevard   Home: (555) 555-5555
Boston, MA 55555   Work: (555) 555-5555

PROFESSIONAL GOALS

Immediate: Secure a Physical Therapy Aide position providing exposure to evaluation, treatment, and discharge planning for a variety of patient populations.

Long-Term: Pursue a Masters Degree in Physical Therapy and obtain designation as a Registered Physical Therapist.

PROFESSIONAL SUMMARY

Physical Therapy Aide	Foundation Medical Care, Boston, Massachusetts	(part-time)	2/96-Pres.
Physical Therapy Volunteer	Orthopedic Services, Cambridge, Massachusetts	(part-time)	12/95-Pres.
Physical Therapy Volunteer	St. Francis Hospital, Boston, Massachusetts		1/95-12/95
Physical Therapy Aide	Physical Performance Center, Boston, Massachusetts		10/93-1/95

PHYSICAL THERAPY EXPERIENCE

♦ Over three years' experience as Physical Therapy Aide and Physical Therapy Volunteer in a variety of environments including acute medical (orthopedic, neurological, cancer, cardiac, and burn units), cardiac rehabilitation, outpatient rehabilitation, outpatient orthopedic, sports medicine, and hydrotherapy settings.

♦ Under supervision of Registered Physical Therapist, assisted with treatment, monitoring, and documentation. Populations represented a variety of geriatric orthopedic, neurological impairment, and adolescent/adult sports injuries. Attended interdisciplinary team evaluation meetings, treatment sessions, and family conferences.

♦ Familiar with various physical therapy technologies and modality equipment. Under supervision, prepared patients for hot/cold packs, ultrasound, electrical stimulation, cervical or pelvic traction, and other modalities. Interpreted and implemented exercise lists to sustain recovery from a variety of impairments and disabilities.

♦ Assisted in other clinic areas as needed: regulated chemical balance for hydrotherapy, purchased clinical supplies, input patient data on computer (familiar with Microsoft Word, WordPerfect, and basic programming).

EDUCATION

BOSTON UNIVERSITY, Boston, Massachusetts

Bachelor of Arts Degree in Sociology (1996)
Completed a number of pre-med requisites.

UNIVERSITY ACTIVITIES

Teaching Assistant: Performed cadaver dissections for Human Anatomy Laboratory and instructed undergraduate students in class material.

Intramural Sports: Active participant in flag football, co-ed softball, tournament tennis, and soccer.

References Upon Request

13

Combination. *Susan Britton Whitcomb, Fresno, California*

The candidate had little paid experience, so the writer added volunteer experience to it under Physical Therapy Experience. "Long-term" suggests commitment to career growth.

DONALD D. DIXON, M.D.

1234 27th Ave. N.W.   Tel.: (909) 999-9876
Seattle, WA 98777   Fax: (909) 999-8765

QUALIFICATIONS

SUCCESSFUL OPHTHALMOLOGIST offering the benefit of both clinical expertise in vitreo-retinal surgical and general ophthalmology and strong business acumen to thrive in highly competitive managed care environments. Broad experience in quality management and utilization management for all clinical specialities.

EDUCATION AND LICENSURE

Fellowship	Vitreo-Retinal Surgery, UCLA Harbor Medical Center, Los Angeles, California	1991
Residency	Chief Resident, New York Medical College, New York, New York	1983-1986
M.D.	Honors Graduate, Univ. of New York School of Medicine, New York, New York	1982
B.S.	Massachusetts Institute of Technology (MIT), Boston, Massachusetts	1978
Medical Licenses	California, New York	
Board Certified	American Board of Ophthalmology	1990

PROFESSIONAL EXPERIENCE

Private Practice: Vitreo-Retinal Surgery and General Ophthalmology, Seattle, Washington   1986-Present

Experience includes critical start-up and management of high-volume ophthalmologic practice. Trained in cataract surgery, pars plana vitrectomy, trabeculectomy, RK, PRK, and refraction. Actively involved in quality improvement activities within the hospital setting and throughout the community. Supervise staff of four. *Accomplishments:*

- Built practice from start-up levels to servicing more than 3,000 patients per year.

- Developed successful satellite office in outlying rural community which has grown in excess of 200% in one year.

- Applied cross-cultural business development strategies to tap emerging Hispanic market (speak ophthalmologic and colloquial Spanish).

- Envisioned and brought to fruition Washington Eye Group, a medical group without walls which negotiates and services managed care contracts for ophthalmology services. (Founding Member, Treasurer)

AFFILIATIONS

Fellow, American Academy of Ophthalmology; Washington Association of Ophthalmology; Washington Medical Association; Lecturer, Medicus Medical Center Medical Residents, Grand Rounds and Community Groups

PUBLICATIONS, HONORS

"Paraneoplastic Syndrome Presenting as a Posterior Uveitis," *American Journal of Ophthalmology* (in progress).
"Ocular Apex Syndrome Resulting in Rapid Blindness," *American Journal of Ophthalmology* (in progress).
American Medical Association Physicians Recognition Award in Continuing Medical Education with Special Commendations for Self-Directed Learning (11/95-12/98)

OTHER SKILLS, ACTIVITIES

Volunteer Ophthalmologist (Holy Cross Clinic and Children's Hospital).
Computer proficient in IBM and Macintosh environments (spreadsheets, word processing, programming).
Multi-lingual (intermediate Spanish skills; basic knowledge of French, Italian, and German).

◆ ◆ ◆

14

Combination. *Susan Britton Whitcomb, Fresno, California*

This professional was seeking a position with another group. Rather than a curriculum vitae, the writer used this resume with Qualifications statements and bulleted accomplishments.

CHRISTOPHER D. ATHLETE
11092 Runaway Bay
Longview, Texas 75600
(903) 777-1155

HIGHLIGHTS OF QUALIFICATIONS

- ◆ **Efficient, enthusiastic Golf Professional** with proficiency in **individual / group golf instruction, tournament organization / management**, and **pro shop merchandising / administration**.
- ◆ Successfully completed **GPTP Level I**; pursuing Class A designation.
- ◆ Astute **financial / accounting manager**; experienced in governmental, not-for-profit, and public auditing, tax preparation, and **cash management**. Accurate with attention to detail.
- ◆ Exceptional **public relations**, **communication**, and **interpersonal** skills; quickly establish positive rapport with people of diverse ages, cultures, and personalities. **Customer satisfaction oriented**.
- ◆ Computer literate: Windows, Logical Solutions, WordPerfect, MS-Word, Excel, Lacert, Unilink, Fast Advantage, Lotus 1-2-3.
- ◆ Outgoing personality. Patient. Highly **career-** and **goal-oriented**.

EDUCATION

BAYLOR UNIVERSITY – Waco, Texas
Bachelor of Science Degree, Accounting (1996)
Graduated Cum Laude with GPA of 3.40; Dean's List; Recipient of academic and athletic scholarships

PROFESSIONAL EXPERIENCE

PROFESSIONAL GOLF CLUB   Longview, Texas
Assistant Golf Professional   January 1997 – Present
- ◆ Manage entire 18-hole private golf operation encompassing 480 members, pro shop, and staff of five in the absence of Head Golf Professional; activity approximately 70,000 rounds annually.
- ◆ Plan, organize, and execute tournaments and clinics; independently manage tournaments and clinics. Mark course and supervise range; provide assistance to members/guests; resolve member complaints/conflicts.
- ◆ Teach golf lessons to individuals and groups; establish excellent rapport with members and guests.
- ◆ Pro shop management includes customer service, administration of books, cash management, purchasing, merchandising, displays, inventory control, sales, and club repair.
- ◆ **Nominated for "Assistant of the Year"** for the East Texas Chapter of the PGA.

THOMAS & BROWN, L.L.C.   Waco, Texas
Accountant   June 1996 – November 1996
- ◆ Audited governmental and public entities. Prepared tax returns for corporations and individuals.

BAYLOR GOLF COURSE   Waco, Texas
Golf Shop Manager   Summer, 1995
- ◆ Managed golf shop; purchased and displayed merchandise; organized tournaments.

EAST TEXAS GOLF WORLD AND DRIVING RANGE   Longview, Texas
Sales Associate / Range Assistant   Summer, 1994
- ◆ Began as Range Assistant; promoted quickly to Sales Associate due to acquired knowledge and outstanding performance.

GOLF HONORS / ACADEMIC ACTIVITIES

Captain of University Golf Team ◆ 10 All-Tournament Teams ◆ Men's Sun Belt All-Conference Team
Athletic Advisory Committee ◆ Beta Alpha Psi Accounting Society ◆ Business Students Association

15

Combination. *Ann Klint, Tyler, Texas*

Observe the use of boldfacing in this attractive resume. As you look down the page, you notice first the bold words. They help you see the key information about this individual.

John L. Robertson

1411 Vine Street
Cincinnati, Ohio 45202
(513) 555-5555

SUMMARY

- Skilled press operator with a commitment to producing top-quality work through attention to detail, thorough planning, and sound knowledge of color printing operations.

- Expert in color matching, mixing, and production on the press.

- Strong communication skills and the ability to maintain positive professional relationships that lead to better planning and higher quality.

- Proven ability to analyze and adjust to varied equipment to achieve maximum output and quality.

PROFESSIONAL EXPERIENCE

QUEEN CITY PRINTING, INC., Cincinnati, Ohio   1982-Present

Commercial printer producing high-quality four-color business communications including brochures, catalogs, and magazines.

Web Pressman (1991-Present)

Maintain color and ink quality throughout the press run by diligent attention to detail and quality control. Monitor all production facets, including folding, compensation, registration, pagination, etc.

- Specialize in precise color mixing to achieve customer's desired output.
- Apply knowledge of individual presses to achieve maximum output and consistent quality.
- Thoroughly review specifications for upcoming job so that adequate planning and preparation can be made to ensure timely press operation.
- Troubleshoot print runs, monitoring for quality and conformance to specifications.
- Maintain open communication with MIC (Man in Charge, chief pressman) and Assistant Pressman to promote teamwork and ensure shared job knowledge.
- Coordinate computerized press operations to set appropriate color levels.

Accomplishments

- Analyzed operation of unique printing press and established appropriate settings that significantly reduced waste and increased production from 25,000 to 40,000 impressions per hour. Documented and explained findings to management.
- Recognized for ability to find errors and prevent them from contaminating the entire press run; contribute to company profitability by reducing waste in printing operations.
- Earned incentive compensation for hundreds of money-saving catches and ideas for efficient operations.
- Developed formal job description for Pressman position, at the request of management.

Assistant Pressman (1985-91)

Assisted in all phases of web press operation.

- Went beyond job parameters to initiate checking and pre-planning routine for upcoming jobs.

Packer (1982-85)

Performed printing-related tasks and learned the printing business.

- Promoted to Assistant Pressman based on initiative and demonstrated knowledge and ability.

16

Combination. *Louise M. Kursmark, Cincinnati, Ohio*

The writer added an Accomplishments section to the current job description so that readers could see the "extras" this individual might bring: increased production and profitability.

Special Paper Information

The papers are arranged from white to blue and from warm to cool colors, including warm grays and cool grays. Ivory is avoided because of overuse. Heavy textures are avoided because of their resistance to laser printing. Laser-printed characters on heavy textures tend to break up with frequent handling.

Besides comparing colors, compare subtle textures by rubbing your fingers rapidly over the surface and comparing sounds. Compare weights by using your thumb to press an edge of a sheet against the other fingers of your hand. Consider using 70-lb. paper for an executive's resume.

Not shown are 100% rag-content papers, which are ideal for resumes. Such papers feel more substantial and tend to be watermarked. Look for them in local stationery stores and office supply stores.

Resume 1
Brand: Crane's Crest
Parent company: Crane & Company, Inc.
Color: Flourescent White
Kind: Wove
Weight: 24
Contains 100% cotton, tree-free
Acid-free: Yes
Watermarked: Yes
InkJet compatible: NA
Laser compatible: Yes
Copier compatible: NA

Resume 2
Brand: Hammermill Laser Bond
Parent company: International Paper Company
Color: Radiant White
Kind: Writing, Imaging Finish
Weight: 24
Contains 25% cotton fiber
Acid-free: Yes
Watermarked: Yes
InkJet compatible: Yes
Laser compatible: Yes
Copier compatible: Yes

Resume 3
Brand: Mosaic
Parent company: Fraser Papers
Color: Stucco
Kind: Writing, Smooth
Weight: 24 lb.
Contains 30% postconsumer waste
Acid-free: Yes
Watermarked: NA
InkJet compatible: Yes
Laser compatible: Yes
Copier compatible: Yes

Resume 4
Brand: Proterra
Parent company: Georgia-Pacific Papers
Color: Marble
Kind: Writing, Smooth
Weight: 24 lb.
Contains 60% recycled fiber (30% of total fiber content is postconsumer waste)
Acid-free: Yes
Watermarked: NA
InkJet compatible: Yes
Laser compatible: Yes
Copier compatible: NA

Resume 5
Brand: Graphika!
Parent company: Crown Vantage
Color: Pueblo
Kind: Writing
Weight: 24 lb.
Contains minimum of 20% postconsumer fiber
Acid-free: Yes
Watermarked: NA
InkJet compatible: Yes
Laser compatible: Yes
Color copier compatible: Yes

Resume 6
Brand: Skytone
Parent company: Georgia-Pacific Papers
Color: Natural
Kind: Text
Weight: 24/60 lb.
Contains 50% recycled fiber including 30% postconsumer fiber
Acid-free: Yes
Watermarked: NA
InkJet compatible: NA
Laser compatible: Yes
Copier compatible: Yes

Resume 7

Brand: Nekoosa Solutions
Parent company: Georgia-Pacific Papers
Color: Spice
Kind: Text, Smooth
Weight: 60 (24)
Contains 50% recycled fiber; 20% of total
fiber from postconsumer waste
Acid-free: Yes
Watermarked: NA
InkJet compatible: Yes
Laser compatible: Yes
Copier compatible: Yes

Resume 8

Brand: Nekoosa Solutions
Parent company: Georgia-Pacific Papers
Color: Pepper
Kind: Text, Smooth
Weight: 70 (28)
Contains 50% recycled fiber; 20% of total
fiber from postconsumer waste
Acid-free: Yes
Watermarked: NA
InkJet compatible: Yes
Laser compatible: Yes
Copier compatible: Yes

Resume 9

Brand: Skytone
Parent company: Georgia-Pacific Papers
Color: Pewter
Kind: Text
Weight: 24/60 lb.
Contains 50% recycled fiber including 30%
postconsumer fiber
Acid-free: Yes
Watermarked: NA
InkJet compatible: NA
Laser compatible: Yes
Copier compatible: Yes

Resume 10

Brand: Graphika!
Parent company: Crown Vantage
Color: Gray Riblaid
Kind: Writing
Weight: 24 lb.
Contains minimum of 20% postconsumer fiber
Acid-free: Yes
Watermarked: NA
InkJet compatible: Yes
Laser compatible: Yes
Color copier compatible: Yes

Resume 11

Brand: Nekoosa Solutions
Parent company: Georgia-Pacific Papers
Color: Ash
Kind: Text, Smooth
Weight: 60 (24)
Contains 50% recycled fiber; 20% of total
fiber from postconsumer waste
Acid-free: Yes
Watermarked: NA
InkJet compatible: Yes
Laser compatible: Yes
Copier compatible: Yes

Resume 12

Brand: Beckett Super Smooth Expression
Parent company: International Paper Company
Color: Alabaster
Kind: Writing
Weight: 24 lb.
Contains 20% postconsumer fiber
Acid-free: NA
Watermarked: NA
InkJet compatible: Yes
Laser compatible: Yes
Copier compatible: Yes

Resume 13

Brand: Beckett Concept
Parent company: International Paper Company
Color: Glacier Mist
Kind: Writing
Weight: 24 lb.
Contains 20% postconsumer fiber
Acid-free: Yes
Watermarked: Yes
InkJet compatible: Yes
Laser compatible: Yes
Copier compatible: Yes

Resume 14

Brand: Nekoosa Solutions
Parent company: Georgia-Pacific Papers
Color: Blue Ice
Kind: Text, Smooth
Weight: 70 (28)
Contains 50% recycled fiber; 20% of total
fiber from postconsumer waste
Acid-free: Yes
Watermarked: NA
InkJet compatible: Yes
Laser compatible: Yes
Copier compatible: Yes

Resume 15

Brand: Skytone
Parent company: Georgia-Pacific Papers
Color: Bluestone
Kind: Text
Weight: 24/60 lb.
Contains 50% recycled fiber including 30%
postconsumer fiber
Acid-free: Yes
Watermarked: NA
InkJet compatible: NA
Laser compatible: Yes
Copier compatible: Yes

Resume 16

Brand: Passport
Parent company: Fraser Papers
Color: Moonstone
Kind: Imaging Finish
Weight: 24 lb.
Contains 50% deinked, recycled fiber,
including 20% postconsumer waste
Acid-free: Yes
Watermarked: NA
InkJet compatible: Yes
Laser compatible: Yes
Copier compatible: NA

Accounting/Finance

Resumes at a Glance

PATTY PERKY
3160 Friendly Road
Any City, USA   23332
(804) 444-6666

OBJECTIVE: Customer Service oriented position where excellent supervisory, communication, and problem solving skills can be utilized.

HIGHLIGHTS OF QUALIFICATIONS:

- **Customer Service Skills**: Ability to communicate effectively and establish excellent rapport with clients from diverse socio-economic backgrounds. Serve as liaison between clients and insurance companies to resolve accounts. Handle problems which staff members cannot reconcile.

- **Problem Solving Skills**: Routinely mediate problems concerning financial issues. Negotiate payment plans and resolve account discrepancies to the satisfaction of both the client and the company.

- **Supervisory Skills**: Supervise up to 15 employees including financial counselors, bookkeepers, account representatives, insurance billers, and collectors. Responsible for interviewing, hiring, scheduling, assigning tasks, training, counseling, and terminating. Counsel employees on work performance, infractions of company policy (absenteeism, tardiness, etc.), personal matters, and substance abuse problems.

RELATED EXPERIENCE:

Office Supervisor, Fantastic Company, My Town, USA   1990 - present

Responsible for managing daily activities of a medical practice with a volume of 8,000 accounts monthly. Regularly make on-the-spot management decisions. Supervise and train 15 staff members whose daily tasks include third party and self-pay billing and collections as well as routine clerical functions.

- Handle accounts payable and payroll functions as well as delinquent and accounts receivable reports.
- Monitor efforts of outside collection agencies as well as payments by major 3rd party payors for correctness and timeliness of payment.
- Responsible for weekly updates and revised reports.

Finance Manager, The Best Health Center, This City, USA   1988 - 1989

Responsible for all billing and collection efforts of this 500 bed long-term care facility. Supervised receptionist and bookkeeper (including accounts payable and payroll functions).

- Served as liaison between family members and other healthcare facilities. Position required ability to work with and relate to family members under extreme stress due to illness of loved ones.

Credit Manager, The Local Hospital, My City, USA   1985 - 1987

Responsible for training and supervising of four collectors and three financial counselors. Managed all inpatient and outpatient self-pay receivables. Monitored efforts of three outside collection agencies. Reviewed accounts for possible charity write-off or potential bad debt.

- Utilized excellent interpersonal skills in dealing with family of critically or terminally ill patients. Position required ability to empathize with family members while maintaining a profitable collection department.

Billing Supervisor, In Town Hospital, Any City, USA   1982 - 1985

Began as Billing Clerk and advanced to supervisory position within 1 year. Monitored special service accounts. Responsible for supervision, training, and performance evaluations of one verification clerk and six billing clerks. Coordinated all financial activities of the Unit.

REFERENCES:

Excellent professional and personal references available upon request.

17

Combination. *Susie Brady, Virginia Beach, Virginia*

The Objective statement and Highlights of Qualifications section focus on the individual's dominant skills for customer service, supervision, communication, and solving problems.

JAMES BANKER

P.O. Box 11
Anytown, NY 14141
Home (123) 456-7890   Business (123) 222-2222

SENIOR EXECUTIVE
FINANCIAL / INVESTMENT MANAGEMENT

Focused and profit-driven senior executive with 20+ years experience in commercial banking, investment and business management. Customer-service oriented professional. Proven ability to provide tough, but fair, team-spirited leadership. Maximize productivity and profits by fostering independent decision making and inspiring/developing others to work at their highest level. Skilled at effectively communicating with employees to enable them to see where they fit in "the big picture;" results in attaining company financial and customer relations goals. Proficient at building excellent community banking services without over staffing. Very cost conscious and experienced at negotiating with suppliers.

Areas of expertise include:

- Customer Development
- Maximizing Productivity and Profits
- Team Building and Staff Evaluation
- Budgeting
- Shareholder Communications
- Regulatory Compliance
- Loan/Deposit Operations

- Investment Management
- Policy and Procedure Development
- Data Processing Management
- Asset/Liability Management
- State/Federal Regulatory Reporting
- All Insurance Programs
- Internal Management / Board Reports

Computer Skills: • LAN Installation • Quickbooks • FTS Accounting Package • Lotus 1-2-3
• Microsoft Office • Microsoft Word • Microsoft Excel

PROFESSIONAL EXPERIENCE:

B & D COMPANY, City, NY   1993 to Present
$15 million investment company.

Investment / Business Manager

Manage $15 million investment portfolio (equity and fixed income). Function as CFO and investment counselor to various subsidiaries (including a wholesale seafood company, commercial warehouse, and a race track).

- Automated all companies. Set up and installed LAN and various PC software systems, including Quickbooks and Microsoft Office.

THE BANK OF CITY, City, NY   1985 to 1993
$100 million bank when sold to Rich Savings Bank in 1993.

Senior Vice President / COO / CFO   (1990-1993)

Member of the Senior Executive Management Team responsible for the operations of the entire banking institution. Director and Treasurer of City Mortgage Services, a division of The Bank of City. Served on the Asset/Liability and Compliance Committees. Reported to and communicated with the Board of Directors on a regular basis. Primary liaison to State and Federal Regulatory agencies. Worked closely with the loan work-out officer to collect non-performing assets, OREO properties, and problem loans.

- Restored the Bank back to financial health, resulting in successful sale to Rich Savings Bank in 1993. Reduced non-performing assets from $9.5 million down to $2 million. Reversed losses of $3 million to a $600,000 profit.
- Provided vision and direction to lead and manage a team of 20 employees, including 5 officers.
- Developed and oversaw a successful Asset/Liability and Compliance program. Chaired a Regulatory Compliance Task Force.
- Upgraded and installed various PC based systems, including delinquent loan and charge-off tracking, fixed assets and accounts payable.

- Continued -

18

Combination. *Annamarie Pawlina, location unknown*

This resume illustrates the technique of enclosing within horizontal lines important information that you want the reader to see. In this resume that information is also

JAMES BANKER
Page 2

Treasurer / CFO (1989-1992)

Managed the Bank's Investment Function maintaining a balance between low-risk tolerance and profitability. Coordinated the Bank's Risk Management Program. Oversaw investments in U.S. Treasury and Agency securities. Managed daily cash operations. Bought and sold securities to enhance the Bank's profitability and minimize risk from loss of principal. Served on the Bank's Loan Committee.

- Worked with a Task Force to develop a 5-year Strategic Plan.
- Established a subsidiary Mortgage Company. Managed a team of 15 employees.

Vice President (1985-1989)

Developed the Bank's operational structure from formation to its opening in 3 months. Managed Loan and Deposit Operations, Accounting and Finance. Coordinated renovation of the Bank's main office and operations area.

- Drove the Bank's earnings from -0- to $600,000 in 4 years. Managed a staff that grew from 9 to 15 employees.
- Orchestrated successful opening of the Bank. Hired staff, selected suppliers, computer system and equipment.
- Developed and implemented necessary policies/procedures for productive and efficient operations.

COUNTRY BANK AND TRUST COMPANY, Country, NY 1983 to 1985
$50 million bank with 4 branches.
Vice President of Operations/Finance/Administration

Managed Operations, Finance and Investment areas. Directed strategic planning, policy development, and regulatory compliance (quarterly/annual reporting and exams).

- Built the Bank from $9 million in assets to $50 million in 2 years. Transformed the Bank from $400,000 loss to $80,000 profit in 1 year. Managed a team of 14 employees, including 4 officers.
- Implemented successful completion of holding company's secondary stock offering. Worked with attorneys to write prospectus. Coordinated financial logistics and necessary communications.
- Set up the Bank's Operation department. Established chain of command. Ensured productivity of the Bank and holding company by developing/standardizing policies, procedures and effective control measures.
- Established 2 branch banks. Oversaw site evaluation, hiring, design, scheduling and construction. Maintained tight control over material and labor costs to meet budget goals.

TOWN BANK AND TRUST COMPANY, Town, NY 1983
$150 million bank with 6 branches.
Assistant Vice President (Operations)

Transitioned the Bank from using a service bureau to operating its own in-house computer system. Set up and installed computer system. Managed a staff of 15 employees.

UNITED BANK AND TRUST COMPANY, Town, NY 1974 to 1982
$150 million bank with 12 branches.

Advanced through a series of increasingly responsible positions. Began as a Bank Teller; promoted to Assistant Treasurer and Operations Manager III. Managed a staff of 25 employees.

EDUCATION:

Graduate, **ABA's Stonier Graduate School of Banking,** University of Delaware, Newark, Delaware, 1988.
Focus: Enhancing management skills, including group and incentive management.

B.A., Political Science, **University of Connecticut,** Storrs, CT, 1973.

Continuously update knowledge and skills through professional seminars and **AIB courses**.

positioned at the spot that is most apt to be read in a resume: an area from approximately two inches from the top of the first page to about five inches from the top (a view of Susan Britton Whitcomb in her book *Resume Magic*, JIST Works, 1999).

NATHAN BERNSTEIN
3 Saratoga Street
Needham, MA 02192
617-555-5555

PROFILE

Highly accomplished operations manager with demonstrated success in domestic and international markets. Over 20 years experience in positions of increasing responsibility culminating in Vice President/Controller position. Proven ability to establish and manage financial operations responsive to long-range objectives for growth and profitability. Excellent analytical, communication and interpersonal skills include:

- Contract/Executive Negotiations
- Corporate Vendor Relations
- Inventory Control/Purchasing
- Scheduling/Forecasting/Planning

- New Operations Startup
- Financial Operations
- New Product Development
- Accounts Management

PROFESSIONAL EXPERIENCE

WORLDWIDE WONDERS, Newton, MA   1986-Present
Vice President/Controller

Senior Finance Executive for international manufacturing company (private label food and textile products) with full responsibility for the strategic planning, development, implementation and management of all control and operations systems. Concurrent executive responsibility for corporate vendor relations.
- Increase corporate revenues from $50,000 to $800,000 in seasonal food division.
- Expedite new product creation and development and securing of international patent.
- Design procedures for shipping, purchasing, billing, inventory control.
- Steamline vendor relations by developing office bidding procedures and improving vendor/subcontractor communications, resulting in cost savings which include over $8,000 reduction in transportation costs.
- Predict potential market share for new products based on qualitative and quantitative analyses.

ORLANDO CORPORATION, Hingham, MA   1977-1986
Vice President of Administrative Services

Senior manager responsible for establishing administrative procedures in growing consumer electronics manufacturing company.
- Created purchasing, QC, personnel, and controller departments to help manage growth from $3M to $10M.
- Saved over $300,000 through price negotiations with vendors.
- Interacted with bank executives, UL representatives, and outside vendors.
- Purchased electronic components manufactured abroad.

19

Combination. *Wendy Gelberg, Needham, Massachusetts*

The Profile refers to experience and skills and includes areas of expertise in two bulleted columns. This format is flexible in that you can easily substitute different areas of expertise

TAYLOR LABORATORIES, INC., Winchester, MA   1965-1977
Operations Manager (1972-1977)
Applications Engineer (1969-1972)
Staff Scientist (1965-1969)

Advanced from technical research positions to operations manager for large manufacturing and research company.

- Controlled technical administrative functions.
- Served as company ombudsman, liaison between technical and administrative staff.
- Conducted applied research on single crystal sapphire uses and their application to customer needs.

EDUCATION

MBA — Northeastern University
MS — Northeastern University, Physical Chemistry
BS — Northeastern University, Chemistry

Additional Coursework

Introduction to Windows, Needham (MA) Adult Education, 1995.
Japanese, Japan Society, Boston, MA, 1993.

MILITARY SERVICE

U.S. Army — First Lieutenant.

Excellent References Available Upon Request

for different job targets. In the Professional Experience section the paragraphs for the current and preceding jobs indicate responsibilities, and the bulleted items tell of accomplishments. Whenever possible, these are quantified. This is a strong layout pattern.

GERTRUDE STEIN

Scarborough Manor
Scarborough, NY   10510
(914) 945-1997

INTERNATIONAL FINANCE/CREDIT

Top flight professional career as member of the management team of several high-growth organizations.   Significant contributions in revenue and profit growth through achievements in credit management, operating cost reduction, systems and procedural reengineering and general business management.   Successful in driving solutions to meet the challenges of complex reorganization and high-growth ventures.   Excellent executive presentation and negotiation skills.

PROFILE

- Extensive track record in finance management, bringing a high level of professionalism to the corporate image.
- Organized, take-charge management professional with exceptional follow-through abilities and detail orientation; able to plan and oversee projects from concept to successful conclusion.
- Demonstrated ability to efficiently prioritize a broad range of responsibilities in order to achieve maximum level of organizational operating effectiveness.
- A resource person, problem solver, trouble shooter and creative turn-around manager.
- Versatile; proven ability to manage multiple projects.
- Demonstrated capability to resolve problems swiftly and independently.
- Possess strong interpersonal skills; able to work effectively with individuals on all levels; effective motivator of self and others.
- Adept at developing procedures to maximize efficiency.
- Multi-Lingual; German, English, and French: spoken, written and translated.

AREAS OF
EFFECTIVENESS

Procedural Restructuring - *Revamped* a *chaotic system* and process that *required days and weeks* to complete, *turning* it *into* a *model of efficiency* which *now requires* a *matter of minutes*.
Organizational Streamlining - *Conceived*, *developed* and *implemented informational network*, *linking main branches* coast to coast with a source of up-to-the-minute financial information, *thereby accelerating* credit applications.

EXPERIENCE
August 1981 -
Present

COMMERZBANK, INTERNATIONAL, New York, NY
Coordinator: Credit Administration functioning as Divisional Manager, promoted 1988
- *Direct* the gathering of credit data; personally *oversee financial reporting* to home office.   Report findings to Frankfurt twice yearly.
- *Coordinate complex*, worldwide *data* regarding commercial credit customers and subsidiaries in order to *expedite credit* approval.

Director of Interdepartmental Communication   1993 - 1994
- *Developed* Information Desk and *initiated process* for individual banks to enter group Network and up obtain up to the minute financial data, eliminating the need for postal and fax exchanges, and *resulted in savings* of *over $100K* per year.
- Served as interdepartmental liaison and *built* a *more productive system*, *creating communication connections* between branches.

Marketing Department   1981
- *Initiated* and *negotiated* airline *travel discounts realizing many $10Ks savings* per year.
- *Supervised* the *in-flow* of *Dunn & Bradstreet data*; *negotiated* steep *discounts*.

20

Combination. *Mark D. Berkowitz, Yorktown Heights, New York*

The Profile and Areas of Effectiveness are separate sections. The use of bullets for one and boldfacing of key words in the other helps to distinguish the two sections visually. Such

GERTRUDE STEIN

1967 - 1981	**SENNHEISER ELECTRONIC CORP.,** New York, NY **Assistant to Vice President: Marketing** • Oversaw microphone sales throughout entire United States.
1964 - 1967	**SOPEXI,** Paris, France **Office Manager and Assistant to President** for this importer of agricultural equipment • Maintained heavy sales and customer contact.
1962 - 1964	**TIERFEINKOSTWERKE,** West Germany **Administrative Assistant** for this importer of animal food
EDUCATION	**LYCEUM** (College), West Germany **PRIVATE BUSINESS SCHOOL,** West Germany Associate of Business Administration **SORBONNE UNIVERSITY,** France Professional Diploma: Language and Literature
REFERENCES	Available upon request.

boldfacing appears in most of this writer's resumes because the technique has proved to be helpful to readers who might otherwise gloss over important information. Education is put last even though the institutions are impressive.

Mannatee A. Fish

1234 Any Street • Some Town, State 12345

Office: (000) 555-1234
Home: (000) 555-1234

PROFILE

CPA • Financial Manager • General Manager • MS Accounting/Finance
Results-oriented financial manager seeking senior level general management,
financial management, or business development position.

SUMMARY OF EXPERIENCE

- General manager experienced in operations, finance, and marketing
- Demonstrated abilities to improve profitability
- Comprehensive financial and management experience including financial planning, capital budgeting, internal audits, forecasting and accounting
- Direct control of operations management, asset utilization, operations analysis, management of divested assets
- Initiated, negotiated and closed acquisitions and divestitures
- Controlled financial operations of multi-plant international companies

SIGNIFICANT ACHIEVEMENTS

- Designed and implemented a financial control system and strategic plan for a Fortune 500 company that was instrumental in its turnaround from a loss operation to one of the 20 most profitable in the decade.
- Reduced costs and improved profitability by over 50% for a service company
- Acquired and divested over 30 domestic and international privately-held and NYSE companies ranging in size from $1 million to $700 million.
- Raised funds for working capital, fixed assets, real estate and acquisitions
- Initiated public offerings of wholly-owned subsidiaries in Brazil and Sweden.

EXPERIENCE

General Manager (xxxx - Present)
PERSONAL BUSINESS, INC., Anytown, State/Some Town, State
Reorganized operations and marketing efforts. Since xxxx in Some Town,
opened three satellite units and restructured branch management that resulted in
an 18% increase in sales, increased profits 53% while reducing receivables 40%.

Senior Vice President, Corporate Development (xxxx-xxxx)
COMPANY, Anytown, State
Successfully restructured the Company-owned bank from a significant loss with
severe regulatory problems to a profit and no regulatory restrictions.
Restructured two partnerships, eliminating losses of over $5 million/year.

Staff Vice-President
Director, Operations Analysis Acquisitions & Divestitures (xxxx-xxxx)
LARGE CORPORATION, Another Town, State
Instrumental in downsizing company and restructuring of over $1 billion in debts
while funding $600 million in losses. Conceived and implemented an asset
redeployment program and divested operations with sales of over $1.2 billion;
directed and negotiated the sale of 15 units which generated over $300 million in
proceeds.

21

Combination. *Linda Morton, Lawrence, Kansas*

Achievements appear not only in the Significant Achievements section but also in the statements
about the five positions held. The individual's name and horizontal lines are used as a header

MANATEE A. FISH *Page 2*

Vice President, Administration (xxxx-xxxx)
VERY BIG CORPORATION, Eastern City, State
Directed a program that resulted in acquisition of a major NYSE company and the divestiture of ten divisions constituting over 30% of the company. Stabilized three failing businesses and assisted in privatizing company. Initiated a Washington lobbying effort to bolster defense marketing operations. Reduced corporate administration costs by 17%.

Director of Financial Control (Controller) (xxxx-xxxx)
LARGE COMPANY SYSTEMS, INC., Yet Another Town, State
Developed and implemented an MIS system which reduced reports and provided management with timely, all-inclusive information. Reduced administrative costs by 29%. Created standardized operating procedures in all U.S. and Canadian plants and parts of Europe. Restructured European financial functions in Paris at a savings of $1 million annually.

EDUCATION

B.S. Accounting, University of State
M.S. Accounting and Finance, Some University

LICENSE

Certified Public Accountant

on page 2. Paragraph style is used for these five statements, which display clearly and repeatedly the person's skills in lowering costs, restructuring, eliminating losses, and generating proceeds. Achievements are quantified in percentages and dollar amounts.

JAMES L. GREGG
89 Glenwood Road
Marlboro, New Jersey 07746
(908) 536-7521

SUMMARY OF QUALIFICATIONS

Twenty years of financial management experience encompassing a steady progression of increasing accomplishments and responsibilities and active involvement in many major strategic decisions. Background also includes International Finance and management of a data processing organization. Primary strengths are excellent leadership, analytical, communication, and interpersonal skills.

EXPERIENCE

1975-Present   **H&H CHEMICALS, INC.** - A diversified International chemical company with sales of $500 million.

1986-Present   **VICE PRESIDENT, FINANCE & CONTROLLER**
Responsible for all finance and control functions, including data processing. **CHIEF FINANCIAL OFFICER** and member of the Executive Committee, which sets policies and strategic direction for the Corporation. Supervises several departments including 65 employees.

1979-1985   **CORPORATE CONTROLLER**

1977-1978   **DIRECTOR OF COST ACCOUNTING AND DATA PROCESSING**

1975-1976   **MANAGER OF COST ACCOUNTING**

ACCOMPLISHMENTS

- Significantly upgraded the Company's information systems (EDP) capabilities while at the same time reducing data processing costs by more than 20%.

- Initiated and led a program that reduced working capital by 5% of sales, thereby lowering interest and operating expenses by $3 million.

- Analyzed and participated in negotiation of many major acquisitions and divestitures which enhanced the strategic thrust of the Company.

- Significantly reduced accounting errors, accelerated the monthly closing cycle, and eliminated "surprises". Consistently had clean audit reports.

- Implemented financial statement reporting by major product line. This enhanced decision-making and focused business managers' attention on the "bottom line" for their products.

- Streamlined and enhanced the Corporate budgeting process and made it the cornerstone upon which the Company's operations are measured.

22

Combination. *Beverly Baskin, Marlboro, New Jersey*

The individual wanted his promotions within the current company to stand out. Putting an extensive Accomplishments section after these promotions calls attention to them. The 10

JAMES L. GREGG   Page 2

<u>**ACCOMPLISHMENTS**</u> (Continued)

- Restructured foreign subsidiaries' balance sheets and updated transfer prices and management fees so that the Corporation's tax payments were reduced by over $1 million.

- Significantly improved the financial reporting systems to make them more responsive to the needs of the Business.

- Standardized cost accounting practices at all locations. This greatly enhanced controls and aided in decision-making.

- Developed and conducted financial seminars for Business Management to aid them in the use of financial concepts for decision-making.

<u>**1973 - 1975**</u>   **LONDON CORPORATION - ESSEX DIVISION**

> **MANAGER OF FINANCIAL PLANNING & ANALYSIS** - Supervised a department of eight. Responsible for preparation and review of the annual budget and long-range plans; operational analysis of monthly results and trends; preparation and analysis of capital expenditure requests; monthly closings.

<u>**1966 - 1973**</u>   **STAMCO, INC.**

> **SENIOR FINANCIAL ANALYST (1970-1973)** - Analyzed and prepared all major capital expenditure requests for submission to the Board of Directors; learned both Fortran and Basic programming languages and developed timesharing computer models such as plant production simulation studies and Monte Carlo investment risk analysis.

> **CHEMICAL ENGINEER (1966-1969)**

<u>**EDUCATION**</u>

MASTER OF BUSINESS ADMINISTRATION, 1975 - Rutgers University

BACHELOR OF CHEMICAL ENGINEERING, 1966 - City College of New York (CCNY)

- Captain of City College Tennis Team
- President of Omega Tau Alpha Fraternity

<u>**PERSONAL**</u>

Married, two children, excellent health, likes to participate in athletic activities.

items in the Accomplishment section exhibit careful use of parallel verb forms. Although usually omitted nowadays, the Personal section ends the resume on a light note. The use of boldface with all-uppercase characters in a sans serif font makes this resume look strong.

STACY GARCIA
1414 Elm Lane • Staten Island, New York • 10314
(718) 222-2255

LETTERS OF CREDIT / COLLECTIONS SUPERVISOR

OVERVIEW
- Highly experienced administrator in Letters of Credit and Bank Collections.
- Track record of setting-up new departments and improving operating efficiency.
- Spearhead departmental growth by millions of dollars annually.
- Outstanding skills in presentations, project management, and strategic planning.
- Excellent interpersonal relations with customers, businesses, and employees.
- Effective communicator; Bilingual English-Spanish, written and verbal.

EXPERIENCE

1990 to present AMERICAN BANK, New York, NY
Operations Officer/Manager of Documentary Services Department
- Supervise the processing of all letters of credit, including:
  - · issuances   · amendments   · negotiations acceptances
  - · discounts   · reimbursements   · assignment of proceeds
  - · advices   · transfers   · finance
- Plan and implement operations for Documentary Services Department.
- Establish departmental policies and procedures to maximize efficiency.
- Train and supervise 35 employees in letters of credit and collection methods.
- Establish a rapport with business contacts to enhance customer relations.
- Negotiate and process issuance of Commercial and Stand-By Letters of Credit.
- Handle issuance of steamship guaranties and airway bill releases.
- Complete process of import and export clean and documentary collections.
- Calculate pre- and post-export finance and issue Trust Receipts.
- Enforce Bank operating procedures and controls to maintain auditory compliance.
- Monitor workflow to ensure that all work is completed within deadlines.
- Prepare reports related to the production of the department.

1985 to 1990 NATIONAL WESTMINSTER BANK, New York, NY
Letters of Credit/Collection Specialist
- Received and processed letters of credit and collection items for 50 accounts daily.
- Logged and checked documents and reviewed for accuracy.
- Traced unpaid items and handled transfer of funds.

1982 to 1985 WINTHROP TRUST COMPANY, New York, NY
Collection Specialist/Supervisor
- Performed collections and supervised four Collection Clerks.

COMPUTERS Advanced user of Microsoft Word, Excel, PowerPoint, Access, WordPerfect, Lotus 1-2-3, and dBASE.

EDUCATION **Bachelor of Business Administration - Finance,** 1990
WAGNER COLLEGE, Staten Island, NY
Financed education 100%

23

Combination. *Kim Isaacs, Jackson Heights, New York*

Horizontal lines enclose occupation information so that the reader can see it immediately. The Overview is both a Profile and a Summary of Skills with an indication of achievements.

Administrative Support

Resumes at a Glance

Susan Hernandez-Koegeboehn

805 S. County Line Road
Hebron, Indiana 46341
(219) 996-6110

OBJECTIVE

Entry-level management position involved in logistics and global transportation utilizing my human relations and decision-making skills to strengthen a company's business operations that values and rewards results.

PROFILE

♦ Certification, *Fundamentals of International Marketing*, **ABC University Calumet**, 05/99.
♦ Instructed *ZAPP* a tool to improve employee satisfaction, quality, and productivity; and Initiated competitive business strategies and measures for continuous system improvements.
♦ Effective interpersonal skills; Organized, detailed-minded problem-solver; and Cross-trained staff.
♦ Self-motivated and positive attitude to meet/exceed goals unsupervised as well as in team role.
♦ Fluent in Spanish.

PROFESSIONAL EXPERIENCE

Administrative Assistant
05/99-05/99

The ABC Corporation, Gary, Indiana ♦ RESPONSIBILITIES: Organized and prepared *IDEM* and *OSHA* requirements for company's certification of asbestos removal; Initiated and implemented a bilingual accident packet for company vehicles; Researched, reviewed, and prepared legal contracts, documents, and forms; and Attended crisis management seminar.

Tele-Services Administrative Assistant
05/99-05/99

XYZ Brothers, Inc., Pittsburgh, Pennsylvania ♦ RESPONSIBILITIES: Managed headset and telephone inventory for 15 telemarketing offices; Reduced costs 40% on product inventory; Streamlined productivity reports for top management; Conducted data management for productivity levels; and Cross-trained Tele-services Department.

Accounting Clerk
05/99-05/99

ABC Industries, Inc., Wichita, Kansas ♦ RESPONSIBILITIES: Development of Strategies and Measures, Team member; Trained Accounting Department on receivable system; Provided customer service to Canadian/U.S. sales teams; Prepared invoices and monthly financial statements; and Assisted Credit Department with collection procedures.

EDUCATION

Bachelor of Business Administration (International Business)
05/99-05/99

The Wichita State University, Wichita, Kansas ♦ MINOR: Economics, MINOR: Spanish ♦ G.P.A.: 3.3/4.0

International Business/Studies Projects:

Environmental Analysis of Lodging Industry, (i.e., East Asia: *Tokyu Hotel*; Europe: *Forte Plc.*; and North America: *Marriott Corporation*), Team Member, 1999

Environmental Analysis of Multinational Trading Companies, (i.e., *C. Itoh & Company, Ltd.*; *Mitsui & Company, Ltd.*; and *Sumitomo Corporation*), Team Member, 1999

European Communities Trade Conference, Extensive Study of European Economic Communities, Wichita, Kansas, Delegate, 1999

United North American Conference, Extensive Study of NAFTA, Denver, Colorado, Delegate, 1999

Exporting Corn to Mexico, Individual International Market Study, 1999

Achievements:

Dean's List, Spring 1999 and Spring 1999

Earned 100% of academic & living expenses by working 35-40 hours per week, 1999-1999

The World Trade Council of Wichita, Inc., International Business/Studies Scholarship, Recipient, 1999

American G.I. Forum Kansas State Scholarship, Recipient, 1999-1999

Organizations:

Association of International Students in Business and Commerce (AIESEC), 1999-1999

MEMBERSHIP

Northwest Indiana World Trade Council, 1999-
The World Trade Council of Wichita, Inc., 1999-1999

24

Combination. *Susan K. Schumm, Carmel, Indiana*

Type resembling printing for the person's name, plus a decorative horizontal line, makes this resume distinctive from the top. Embedded diamond bullets pull the eye to responsibilities.

BARBARA MORRIS

Smith Avenue
Mount Kisco, NY 10550
(914) 666-6666

Clerical • Word Processing • General Office Support • Data Entry Position

PROFILE

- More than 15 years administrative / clerical / word processing experience; type 65+ wpm.
- Dedicated, conscientious, detail-oriented and dependable.
- Can work well independently, and enjoy contributing to team effort.
- Excellent organizational, and oral and written communication skills.
- Able to take responsibility for implementing a project, to achieve goals and meet deadlines.
- Proficient in WordPerfect 5.1, Lotus 123, Microsoft Word for Windows 6.0 & 6.1.

RELEVANT EXPERIENCE

General Office Support
- Typed and proofread business correspondence, financial and year-end reports, invoices, legal contracts, and statistical information.
- Prepared new employee personnel folders, calculated time sheets, and maintained accurate employee attendance records.
- Provided office support in residence for mentally retarded, disabled, and senior adults. Interacted with residents, typed medical evaluations and diagnoses, updated patient records, and ordered supplies.
- Operated variety of office machines, including fax, copier, TTY, postage meter.
- Maintained filing systems, and generated reports from files created.
- Opened mail, dated and distributed to staff.
- Supervised typists, distributed work, scheduled vacations, recorded time sheets.

EMPLOYMENT HISTORY

Temporary Typist / Office Support	Manpower, Elizabeth James, Harbrowe Employment Agencies, Westchester, NY	1995-Present
Mental Health Counselor	Futura House, White Plains, NY	1994-1995
Billing Clerk	Fire-End & Croker, Elmsford, NY	1992-1993
Typist	Temporary Agencies in Westchester	1990-1992
Word Processing Supervisor	Keyboard Communications, White Plains	1989-1990
Word Processing Operator	PepsiCo, Law Dept. Purchase, NY	1987-1989
Word Processor / Desk Clerk / Cashier		*1981-1987*

EDUCATION AND TRAINING

Westchester Community College, Certificate in Word Processing, 1995
Career Blazers, Certificate in dBase III
Keyboard Communication, Inc., Supervisory Skill Training
National Seminars Workshop, How to Supervise People
New England Conservatory of Music, Boston, MA

25

Combination. *Linsey Levine, Chappaqua, New York*

Center-aligned contact information and center-aligned data in the Education and Training section help to direct the reader's attention down the page through the centered headings.

Kirk Laker

9 Paris Parkway
Edison, New Hampshire 07728
(877) 949-3148

SUMMARY

Increasing responsibilities in the following areas:

- Clerical Administration
- Research and Writing
- Billing
- Customer Service
- Statistical Analysis
- Insurance Procedures

PROFILE

Known as a hands-on helper and professional with excellent mathematical and analytical skills.....develop rapport with people in all age groups.....additional functions include researching and collecting data, problem solving, and working in a team atmosphere.

EDUCATION

BS in Psychology
University of Maryland, College Park, MD

ADMINISTRATION

Served as the **lead file clerk** in a large computer company. Knowledge of the following computer software packages: **Word 6, WordPerfect 5.1, Excel, Fox Pro, Claris Works, and SAS. IBM and Macintosh computers; familiar with DOS and Windows operating systems.**

Served as an **Receptionist for the Advanced Back Care Center** in Metuchen, New Hampshire. Educated patients about back care exercises and communicated instructions concerning home care treatments. Performed additional **duties, filing, and insurance functions.**

Worked two years while attending college as a **Field Technician** and **Medical File Clerk** for **Dr. Frances and Dr. Tony**, Board Certified Ophthalmologists. Assisted patients in Visual Field Testing; **responsible for all confidential records including billing and insurance**. Received extensive training in medical terminology.

EMPLOYMENT

■ Lead File Clerk
EGI, Inc. - Computer Manufacturer, East Brunswick, NH
Summer 1994

■ Receptionist
Advanced Back Care Center, Metuchen, NH Summer 1993

■ Field Technician and Medical File Clerk
Dr. J. Frances and Dr. F. Tony, Edison, NH 1990-1994
(Full time and part time)

VOLUNTEER

■ University of Maryland, Physical Therapy Department
■ South Health Rehabilitation Center, Edison, NH
■ Johnson Children's Hospital, Washington, DC

26

Combination. *Beverly Baskin, Marlboro, New Jersey*

A resume for an entry-level billing/clerical worker. The bold horizontal line, bold side section headings, boldfacing for key words in text, and filled square bullets give this resume weight.

LINDA J. JONES

101 Thomas Court   Tulsa, Oklahoma 70000   (918) 000-0000

PROFESSIONAL STRENGTHS

Excellent people skills; enjoy assisting clients from all socioeconomic levels; comfortable dealing with media. Thrive as team player and coordinator of special events and programs. Self-starter who meets program deadlines and requirements while performing multiple tasks. Proficient at handling all support staff functions. Computer skills: Wordperfect 5.1, File Express, Print Shop Deluxe, specialized test scanning programs.

PROFESSIONAL EXPERIENCE

VOCATIONAL-TECHNICAL SCHOOL, Tulsa, Oklahoma   1994 - Present
Student Services Secretary/Assessment Facilitator
- Sign up clients for assessment; administer, electronically grade and record tests. Provide information concerning enrollment, financial aid and assessment.
- Maintain student records and reports per state and district requirements. Assist with compiling statistical reports. Notify students of absences and implement excessive absence procedures.
- Answer phones; generate and file correspondence.
- Special accomplishments include organizing in-house seminar on suicide; as member of Safety Committee, ordering safety films for in-house viewing.

Secretary, Single Parent/Displaced Homemakers/Single Pregnant Women Program (SP/DH/SPW) and Student Services
- Assisted clients and maintained program database per rules of U.S. Department of Education.
- Composed correspondence and handled bulk mailing of newsletter.   Oversaw program library.
- Represented school at health fairs; assisted organizing campus career fair. Managed campus clothes closet.

CRISIS CENTER, Tulsa, Oklahoma   1992 - 1993
Volunteer Coordinator
- Recruited, trained and scheduled volunteer staff in six different programs: Crisis Line; Sexual Assault Advocates; Kids Group; Sunshine Squad; Office Volunteers; Donation Distribution Center.
- Organized and directed community awareness special events: recruited panelists, speakers, and other participants; handled publicity with print media and community organizations and businesses.
- Coordinated content and publishing of quarterly newsletter.
- Provided crisis intervention over telephone and face to face.

INSTITUTE FOR PETROLEUM AND ENERGY RESEARCH, Tulsa, Oklahoma
Secretary and Property Specialist   1985 - 1990
- Conducted complete inventory of equipment and set up inventory plan and files.
- Tracked company contracts and proposals (approximately 500 outstanding at any time); handled Department of Energy reports; expedited purchase orders; filed; assisted with property sales.

EDUCATION & TRAINING

Associate of Arts degree, concentrating in Behavioral Science, Secretarial Science, and Journalism. Tulsa College, Tulsa, Oklahoma, 1982.

Ongoing computer training courses.

COMMUNITY INVOLVEMENT

Member, Board of Directors, Tulsa County Association for Mental Health.
Certified child caregiver with the Cooperative Disaster Childcare Organization.
Deacon and member of Administrative Board, First Christian Church, Tulsa, Oklahoma.

REFERENCES AVAILABLE UPON REQUEST

27

Combination. *Laura C. Karlak, Bartlesville, Oklahoma*

This individual was unsure of her career goals, so the writer emphasized in the Professional Strengths section general skills that would be useful in any support/administrative position.

Susan D. Wilson
5 South End Avenue
Palisades, FL 55555
(550) 505-0005

Summary

- Strong interpersonal skills; possess the ability to work effectively with all people
- Highly organized and resourceful; work very well under pressure
- Excellent communication capabilities
- Dependable and responsible; thrive in challenging situations requiring ability to learn new skills

Professional Experience

Clinical Administrative Assistant, Miami Dental Lab • Miami, FL   Apr. 1988–Present
- Provide administrative support to busy dental lab serving 150+ private dental practices and clinics throughout Florida (primary geography covered includes Broward, Sarasota, and Miami counties) with customized preparation and fabrication of crowns, plates, bridges, and dentures. Handle out-of-state work through overnight courier services.
- Prepare cases and arrange for transport through staff of seven couriers.
- Provide heavy telephone support, working extensively with dentists, nurses, and dental practice office support personnel.
- Utilize personal computer for logging in and monitoring status of cases.
- Maintain extensive filing system for each dental practice, with detailed sub-files for each of their respective patients.
- Expedite billing process, provide detailed explanation of charges as necessary, and assist with reconciliation of statements.
- Maintain schedule of in-office visits to dentists by Dental Lab staff.
- Over course of eight years, position responsibilities have been progressively enhanced as familiarity with operations has developed.
- Promoted from Office Clerk to Clinical Administrative Assistant (1993).

Retail Sales Associate, Lighting and Fabrics by Design • West Palm Beach, FL   1986–88
- Worked directly with clientele in selection of fabrics for custom-ordered furnishings.
- Displayed variety of lines available within client budgets.
- Assisted with planning for overall color scheme and "look" clients were seeking.
- Provided retail sales assistance to ancillary custom curtain, drapery, and accessory shop on the premises.
- Held position on part-time basis while pursuing studies.

Education

Broward County Community College • Miami, FL
- A.S., Business Administration (1988)

Miami Art Institute • Miami, FL
- Pursued studies in Interior Design (1984–86)
- Successfully completed numerous courses related to all aspects of interior design.

28

Combination. *Jan Melnik, Durham, Connecticut*

This individual never had a resume and had gotten previous work through word-of-mouth contacts. This resume surprised her: she hadn't realized that she had done this much.

SARA J. JENNINGS

SS No.: 000-00-0000

21344 SW Birch Street, Bellevue, WA 00000

555-555-5555

Previous Federal Employment:	NA
Citizenship:	United States
Veterans Preference:	NA

Objective: ADMINISTRATIVE SERVICES CLERK (CHILD DEVELOPMENT SERVICES)

QUALIFICATION SUMMARY

ADMINISTRATIVE SUPPORT

- Typed letters, memorandums and forms using various computer systems. Ensured accuracy of grammar, punctuation, spelling and format.
- Set up, reorganized and maintained alphabetical and chronological filing systems.
- Experienced in the use and basic troubleshooting of most office equipment: computers, facsimile machines, copy machines, ten keys and electronic cash registers.
- Extensive experience scheduling package/product deliveries, client appointments, business meetings and travel accommodations.

ORAL AND WRITTEN COMMUNICATIONS SKILLS

- More than ten years of experience working successfully with the public, as an employee and as a volunteer.
- Consistently receive customer commendations for excellent service.
- Researched, authored, edited and newsletters.
- Managed multi-line phone systems: coordinated incoming calls, took messages and referred callers to appropriate party.
- Successfully hosted recreational outings for Travel Club members. Recognized for promoting friendly environment as well as creative and interesting agenda.
- Speak Spanish and know basics of American Sign Language.
- Worked as a volunteer with developmentally disabled children.

COMPUTER EXPERIENCE

- Performed extensive word processing, including newsletters and advertising brochures, using WordPerfect 5.1, WordPerfect 6.1 and MS Word.
- Created newsletters and promotional materials.
- Processed accounts payable/receivable and payroll using Quicken and Peachtree.
- Developed spreadsheets using Excel.
- Experienced in using IBM PCs and IBM compatibles running DOS, Windows 3.1 and Windows '95 operating systems.
- Developed simple housing floor plans using APEX.
- Tracked location of UPS shipments/packages by computer.

29

Combination. *Lonnie L. Swanson, Poulsbo, Washington*

A resume for Federal processing. The resume includes a Social Security number, hours worked, salary history, previous supervisors and their contact information, citizenship

Sara J. Jennings, SS No.: 000-00-0000   Page 2

RELATED WORK EXPERIENCE

Customer Service Representative (Temporary), 2/96 - Present
United Parcel Service (Thru VOLT Temporary Services)   20 hrs per wk
2134 Southern Highway, Suite 302, Hawthorne, NV 00000 $8.00 per hr
Supervisor May Be Contacted: Charlene Lawrence, 555-555-5555

- Performed routine office functions: operated facsimile machine, copy machine, multi-line phone
  system, 10 key and electronic cash register.
- Provided courteous, friendly and professional customer service. Successfully resolved customer
  concerns, ensuring return business.
- Dispatched drivers and scheduled package pickups.
- Received packages from customers and processed packages for national and international
  mailing/delivery. Repacked when necessary, determined charges and accepted payment.
  Completed necessary paperwork for each transaction. Received and recorded COD packages.

Driver Helper (Seasonal/Temporary), 10/95 - 2/96
United Parcel Service, 54321 West Sagebrush, Sparks, NV 00000   25 hrs per wk
Supervisor May Be Contacted: Roger Devers, 555-555-5555 $8.00   per hr

- Delivered packages to homes and businesses. Volume of holiday business was exceptional and
  duties were accomplished with speed and accuracy.
- Continually commended by customers and management for providing excellent service.

Office Manager, 3/92 - 9/95
South Center RV Travel Club, 3621 Waaga Court, South Center, WA 00000   40 hrs per wk
Supervisor May Be Contacted: Larry Bradley, 555-555-5555 $9.50 per hr

- Typed correspondence, reports, memorandums, letters and billing material. Ensured correct
  format, grammar, punctuation, and spelling. Developed spreadsheets.
- Screened clients, scheduled appointments, maintained office tickler file.
- Managed purchasing, inventory, accounts payable/receivable, timekeeping and payroll.
- Produced, edited, and distributed monthly newsletter with circulation of more than 1,500.
  Developed and distributed advertising brochures.
- Planned, organized, coordinated and acted as guide for monthly overnight Club outings.
- Maintained alphabetical and numerical filing systems for correspondence, billing, etc.

Office Manager, 1/90 - 3/92
King County Appraisal, P.O. Box 9001, Seattle, WA 00000   40 hrs per wk
Supervisor May Be Contacted: Hank Jefferson, 555-555-5555 $7.50 per hr

- Performed all office support functions, including: preparation of correspondence on computer
  from rough draft and dictaphone, scheduling of clients and meetings, reception services,
  maintenance of filing systems, and processing of accounts payable/receivable.

status, veteran status, and so on. Applications without this information will be returned.
Note the lack of underlining, bold, and italic. The type is from 10 to 12 pitch (characters
per inch) "to accommodate the scanning equipment used by some installations."

Sara J. Jennings, SS No.: 000-00-0000   Page 3

RELATED WORK EXPERIENCE
(Continued)

Customer Service Representative (Seasonal), 3/87 - 1/90   Varying hrs
Sweetheart Florist, 20976 Pacific Highway, $5.00 per hr
South Center Shopping Center, South Center, WA 00000
Supervisor May Be Contacted: Mary Anderson, 000-000-0000

- Provided service to walk in, phone, and facsimile customers.
- Assisted customers in selection and design of appropriate home decor items and gifts.
- Prepared flower arrangements, wreaths, and floral gift baskets to customer specificiations.
- Operated an electronic cash register.
- Scheduled and tracked merchandise/product delivery.

EDUCATION

1992   Office Assistant Certification
        Eton Business School, Tacoma WA

1990   Olympic College, Bremerton, WA
        Completed course work in Early Childhood Education and Nutrition.

1989   Graduate, North Kitsap High School, Poulsbo WA 98370
        Graduated in TOP TEN of graduating class of 160+.
        Consistent Honor Roll Student, GPA 3.8.

PERSONAL PROFILE

- Take pride in reputation for dependability and integrity.
- Committed to treating people with respect and dignity.
- Experienced and successful working with people from a wide range of cultural backgrounds.
- High energy employee, adept at managing changing priorities in a fast paced environment.
- Effective and efficient working independently and as a team member.

REFERENCES AVAILABLE UPON REQUEST

The Qualification Summary comprises three groups of responsibilities, skills, and experience, making an impressive first page. Square bullets tie together visually the resume's three pages. Unlike most resumes, this resume ends with a Profile.

Animal Care

Resumes at a Glance

SPOTSWOOD BRAVO

265 Charlotte Street
Asheville, NC 28801
704/254-7893

Office Cat

Seeking a career of challenge and service in professional environment. Documented competence and initiative; promotion to high visibility position on executive desk (in Out-Box) gained through merit and softness of fur. Highly unusual markings. Dedicated; often asleep.

EXPERIENCE

GATEHOUSE BUSINESS SERVICES, Asheville, NC
Supervisor/Mouse Patrol
• Initiated and implemented program of systematic reduction of staff in mouse department; 75% reduction in record time.
• Enthusiastic purring, adaptability, and open-door accessibility resulted in marked improvement in office morale.

JOHN JONES HOUSEHOLD, Asheville, NC
House Cat
• Consistently met mouse quota while maintaining appearance of complete ease.
• Liaison to dog, successfully representing 2 other much-older cats in difficult negotiations.
• Communications ability, far-sightedness (can see in the dark), combined with excellent climbing and decision-making skills, led to rapid promotion as Top Cat.

HUMANE SOCIETY, Asheville, NC
Kitten
• Instrumental in bringing record number of potential adopters to kitten section during open house.
• Outstanding good looks resulted in adoption of mother as well as siblings.

EDUCATION

Graduate, The Silent Miaow, Paul Gallico course on how to become an indispensable member of a human household.

REFERENCES

Excellent, perhaps overly enthusiastic references available on request.

30

Combination. *Dayna J. Feist, Asheville, North Carolina*

This easy-to-read resume, making good use of white space, is for a real cat that probably couldn't care less about relocation or a new career.

BARBARA S. SHERR

OBJECTIVE	12121 Northlane Drive ❙ Cloverdale, Washington 00000 ❙ **(555) 555-5555**

Veterinary Technician position where I can use my training, documented communications skills and lifelong love of animals to help your organization provide high-quality and compassionate animal care.

EDUCATION & TRAINING

Veterinary Assistant Certificate, 1993   *Associate of Science,* 1990
Pima Medical Institute   Chaminade University
Seattle, Washington   Honolulu, Hawaii

CPR and First Aid Medic Certified

QUALIFICATION SUMMARY

EXPERIENCE WITH ANIMALS
- Lifelong experience feeding, grooming, bathing, exercising, medicating when appropriate and generally ensuring the well-being of pets, including rabbits, cats, and dogs.
- Worked in a professional capacity with trained drug dogs and their handlers during site inspections.
- Current volunteer at Kitsap County Humane Society.

EMERGENCY RESPONSE
- Documented success working in emergency situations with rapidly changing priorities. Examples of incidents include domestic violence, injury/non-injury accidents, natural disasters, and burglary.
- Noted for maintaining composure and using sound judgement in responding to injury and crisis situations.
- Recognized as efficient/effective problem solver who takes control and initiates appropriate action, working without direct supervision.

COMMUNICATION SKILLS
- Experienced in dealing successfully with people of diverse cultures.
- Effective in calming victims/witnesses who have been traumatized by accident/assault, while taking appropriate action at the scene.
- Excellent written communication skills as demonstrated by documentation and reporting of accidents and injuries in compliance with governing regulations.
- Dedicated to treating others with respect and dignity.

ADMINISTRATIVE SKILLS
- Experienced in accurate and detailed report preparation.
- Managed busy multi-line phone system.
- Reorganized and maintained alphabetical/numerical filing systems.
- Computer literate.

EMPLOYMENT HISTORY

1991 - 1996   *Security Patrol Officer,* Naval Submarine Base, Bangor, WA
1987 - 1991   *Police Officer,* Security Investigative Services, Cincinatti, OH

DETAILS OF EDUCATION INCLUDED AS ADDENDUM

31

Chronological. *Lonnie L. Swanson, Poulsbo, Washington*

Thick-thin lines at the bottom of both pages mirror the thin-thick lines at the top. Lines are named as if they were the lower edge of a rectangular frame. That is why, in reading from

BARBARA S. SHERR

12121 Northlane Drive ▌Cloverdale, Washington 00000 ▌(555) 555-5555

ADDENDUM TO RÉSUMÉ

Veterinary Assistant Program, Pima Medical Institute, Seattle, Washington

Course work included:

Medical Terminology
Medical Ethics and Law
Anatomy and Physiology

Nursing Skills, including:
Canine & Feline Behavior and Restraint
Bandaging/Medication/Injections
Vital Signs/Physical Exams
Care of Hospitalized Animals
Blood Collection/Transfusions/Fluid Therapy
Obstetrics/Neonatal Care

Pharmacology, including:
Drug types
Dosage/Labeling

Radiology, including:
Safety Precautions
Machine Operation
Positioning
Loading and Developing Film

Surgery Skills, including:
Instrument Care and ID
Glove and Gowning
Animal Preparation
Monitoring of Anesthesia/Intubation
Post Operative Care

Laboratory Skills, including:
Operation of Microscope & Centrifuge
Parasitology
Fecal Flotations/Direct Smears
Urinalysis
Hematology
Blood Smears & Staining
CBC, RBC Morphology, WBC Counts, Differentials
Microbiology/Cytology/Histopathology

Emergency Medicine
Front Office Skills

the outside in, you mention the thick line first for this bottom pair and the thin line first for the top pair. In the Addendum on the second page, center-alignment helps to distinguish this page visually from the first page.

Lola A. Mueller

_____Professional Profile

6893 Shenley Drive
Erie, Pennsylvania 16505
(814) 457-2811

Summary of
Qualifications:

Administrative Skills:
Recruit volunteers, write subpermits, inventory control, organize and conduct fund-raising events, coordinate and schedule staff

Communication Skills:
Prepare and design hand-outs, write news releases, sales experience and receptionist duties

Educational Skills:
Prepare and conduct training sessions, work with interns perusing the wildlife field

Writing Skills:
Grant writing for a non-profit organization, file year end reports and request up to date permits

Professional
Highlights:

10/91 - present

Erie Animal Hospital, Erie, Pennsylvania
Veterinarian Receptionist
Responsible for extensive Receptionist duties. Handle incoming calls, direct calls, assist customers with situations, file, type, data entry, dispense medicines and bill patients. As a Veterinarian Technician, restrain animals, draw blood, assist doctors, check laboratory specimens and perform various other duties as assigned.

03/90 - 09/91

Canine Control Division, Woodbridge, Connecticut
Canine Control Officer
Responsible for pet therapy at nursing homes, daily record keeping, license survey, issue infractions for dog law violations and answered dog complaints. Also impound stray dogs, handle dog adoptions, euthanize dogs and attend special educational / training programs.

10/88 - 03/90

Bethany Veterinary Hospital, Bethany, Connecticut
Veterinary Technician Assistant
Responsible for prescription dispensing, prepare vaccines, assist surgeons during surgery, clean cages, feed animals and autoclave surgical instruments. Also assume all Receptionist duties.

06/86 - 06/88

Connecticut Audubon Society, Fairfield, Connecticut
Educator / Assistant
Responsible for the environmental education for K-6 grade. Also wildlife rehabilitator, fund-raiser for wildlife program, coordinate volunteers and oversee the Foster Family Program.

Education:
08/85

The Pennsylvania State University, State College, Pennsylvania
Master of Science in Recreation and Parks

06/82

Mercyhurst College, Erie, Pennsylvania
Bachelor of Arts in Environmental Studies

References:

Available upon request

32

Combination. *Wendy A. Lowry, Edinboro, Pennsylvania*

A difficult resume for a multitalented person who, with education and experience in one field, wants to expand into some other field but hasn't chosen it yet. Boldfacing is effective.

Career Change

Resumes at a Glance

Colin M. Amaros

Castle Avenue #17
St. Louis, MO 63110
(314) 555-0337

Successful background in medical recruiting and staffing for a major Midwest healthcare services company. Interested in helping a company increase sales, profits, and market share.

- Maintain close working relationships with hospital administrators, nursing directors, and a network of physicians in Kansas, Nebraska, and Missouri. Consistently staff about 1500 hours per week (office average is less than 1000 hours).

- Accustomed to scheduling quarterly visits with participating hospitals to facilitate long-term account development and introduce new client services. Learned to work effectively with difficult personalities and handle details in a strictly regulated environment.

- Excellent crisis management, customer service, and communication skills.

RELATED EXPERIENCE

Staffing Coordinator/Physician Recruiter, 1995-Present
Coastal Physician Services of the Midwest, St. Louis, Missouri
- Schedule and recruit primary care physicians for emergency departments in 12 client hospitals scattered throughout Kansas (primary territory), Missouri, and Nebraska.
- Negotiate hourly pay rates to satisfy both physician needs and company profit margins.
- Serve as primary liaison between physician and client hospitals. Make quarterly visits to build long-term relationships and educate clients about value-added services.
- Prepare monthly physician payroll for all client hospitals.
- Analyze markets and gather competitive information to provide leads and help coordinate start-up contracts.

Additional background includes three years experience in educational program development and independent sales experience with a major cosmetics company. Built clientele within a specific territory, coordinated promotional events, tracked sales, and targeted growth areas. Regularly updated product knowledge and additional customer services.

EDUCATION

Anatomy & Physiology Coursework, Washington University, St. Louis, Missouri, 1996
Bachelor of Arts Degree, Webster University, St. Louis, Missouri, 1992

References Available Upon Request

33

Combination. *John A. Suarez, location unknown*

The white-on-black initials capture attention immediately. The opening content displays information often found in a Profile. Limited boldfacing draws the eye to the job position.

JANE R. SMITH

123 Cumberland Street
Anytown, Tennessee 00000

Home: 000-000-0000
Work: 000-000-0000

OBJECTIVE

Position in **Sales Management** capitalizing on successful retail sales and management experience and leading to major responsibilities in store operations.

QUALIFICATIONS

- Operations Management
- Customer Relations
- Cash Management
- Personnel Training
- Inventory Control
- Merchandising

MANAGEMENT EXPERIENCE

Operations Assistant • 1994 - Present
Men's Clothing Store • Anytown, Tennessee
- Assist manager with day-to-day operations and store activities
- Design in-store and window displays, accent lighting, and seasonal floor changes
- Train new personnel in procedures for operating computer cash register
- Control and maintain extensive merchandise inventory
- Prepare bank deposits, balance daily sales receipts, perform stock transfers
- Direct overall back room organization, including supplies and maintenance

SALES EXPERIENCE

Sales Associate • Junior Miss Department • 1993
Major Department Store • Anytown, Tennessee
- Demonstrated exceptional sales abilities
- Consistently achieved monthly sales quota
- Acquired detailed knowledge of clothing and accessories

Sales Associate • 1991 - 1992
Specialty Boutique • Anytown, Tennessee

Sales Associate • 1990 - 1991
Men's Store • Anytown, Tennessee

EDUCATION

Local State Community College • Somewhere, Tennessee
1992 - 1993 • Major: Retail Merchandising

References and Additional Information Available Upon Request

34

Combination. *Carolyn S. Braden, Hendersonville, Tennessee*

After some job-hopping, this individual wanted a career in sales management. The writer separated management experience from sales experience in this easy-to-read resume.

STEVEN JON HANSEN

9 Bellita Drive ✦ Vail, Colorado 86205 ✦ (719) 510-3333

———————————————— PROFILE ————————————————

SALES AND MARKETING PROFESSIONAL

Successful four year sales and management career building and developing a small business within emerging and highly competitive business markets. Outstanding presentation, negotiation and leadership qualifications. Demonstrated achievements in:

- ★ Customer Relationship Management
- ★ Strategic Sales and Market Planning
- ★ New Business Development

- ★ Recruitment and Training
- ★ Consultative Solutions Selling
- ★ Team Building and Leadership

———————— PROFESSIONAL EXPERIENCE ————————

MORRISON PEST CONTROL, Conroe, Texas   1992 - Present
Co-founded pest control business upon college graduation, targeting commercial, industrial and residential clientele. Quickly cultivated and maintained an extensive, loyal client base. Bought partner out in 1994; diversified marketing strategy to focus on Integrated Pest Management.

President/Owner
As initial partner of a start-up operation, responsibilities included business planning, new business development, recruitment, training and supervision, marketing and sales strategies, advertising, purchasing, inventory control, finance and banking relationships. Developed and monitored daily, weekly and monthly sales/production goals for technicians. Established yearly budget and business plan. Manage a staff of five technicians and administrative personnel.

- Built and maintained customer base exceeding 500 businesses/individuals.
- Drove sales from a zero base to $250,000 annually.
- Successfully negotiated and sold company to prominent industry leader in August of 1996.

———————————————— EDUCATION ————————————————

University of Houston, Houston, Texas
B.S., Industrial Distribution 1992
Specialized in Sales, Marketing and Engineering

———————————— COMPUTER SKILLS ————————————

CAD/CAM ✦ Auto/CAD ✦ Lotus 1-2-3 ✦ Word Perfect

———————— PROFESSIONAL ASSOCIATIONS ————————

Professional Association of Industrial Distributors
Montgomery County Chamber of Commerce
State Pest Control Association

———————————— HOBBIES--INTERESTS ————————————

Golf (Handicap 12) ✦ Weight Training ✦ Skeet

35

Combination. *Cheryl Ann Harland, The Woodlands, Texas*

This person started his own firm after college. He later sold his business to search for a sales and marketing position. Lines enclosing the headings make the sections easy to see.

MELINDA M. TYLER

9 Bellita Drive ✦ Pueblo, Colorado 81001 ✦ (719) 564-3213

PROFILE:	Ten years of broad-based professional experience in areas of sales, marketing, advertising, operations and facilities management within property management, retail, and fashion design industries. Strong general management qualifications in employee recruitment, training and supervision, budgeting and financial reporting.
PROFESSIONAL EXPERIENCE:	**HORIZON GROUP**, Muskegon, Michigan 1992 - Present

(A subsidiary of Horizon/Glen Outlet Centers L.P.)
<u>General Manager</u>, Conroe Outlet Center
High profile senior level executive responsible for the leasing, maintenance, operations and profitability of 281,000 s.f. retail center, currently at 98% occupancy with 81 tenants. Scope of responsibility is diverse and includes recruitment, training and supervision of office support and facility maintenance department; developing, coordinating and facilitating promotional events through extensive community relations activity; conducting traffic report and market analysis studies; directing facility maintenance operations, including landscaping, security, trash removal and routine building maintenance; monitor CAM operating budget and negotiate/procure equipment, supplies and subcontractor/vendor services. Dual responsibility for creating and orchestrating promotional events for tenants to generate traffic through the center. Design flyers, promotional materials and newspaper advertisements; worked directly with community service groups in coordinating the events. Key events include: Sidewalk Sales, On Site Fashion Shows, Chamber of Commerce After Hours, Community Blood Drive and Kids Check Program.

- Successfully generated 32% more traffic through marketing efforts
- Received Visual Merchandising Award 1995
- Obtained 100% property inspection rating from corporate headquarters for property aesthetics and internal controls
- Earned "Center Operations Team Award" 1996

LERNER NEW YORK, New York   1989 - 1992
<u>Store Manager</u>, Arlington, TX
Originally hired as Associate Manager and within seven months, was promoted to manage the fourth largest store in the Dallas region ($2 million, 12 employees). Scope of responsibilities included sales recruitment and training, employee development, scheduling, visual merchandising, inventory management, pricing, advertising, customer service and financial reporting.

- Drove sales volume up 121% within six months.
- Successfully brought inventory shrinkage level below company average (2%).
- Trained and developed two store managers for other store locations.

COSTUME WORLD AND INCOGNITO COSTUMES   1986 - 1989
<u>Designer</u>, Houston and Dallas, Texas
Created and designed theatrical costumes and custom specialty clothing for the public. Managed a staff of seamstresses.

EDUCATION:	Texas Tech University Lubbock, Texas 1986 **B.S.**, *Fashion Merchandising and Design*
COMPUTER SKILLS:	- MS Word - Word Perfect - Lotus 1-2-3

36

Combination. *Cheryl Ann Harland, The Woodlands, Texas*

A resume for an individual with a background in property management and retail sales. She wanted a position in sales and marketing. Square bullets point to quantified achievements.

Angela S. Elbert

977 Ivy Trail
Rosedale, NY 00000
(000) 000-0000

Objective: To obtain a position in Human Resources administration that would enable me to contribute to business success through the utilization of my strong administrative and supervisory skills as well as my experience in customer service and project management.

Professional Skills/Knowledge

Leadership	Quality
Project management	Interpersonal skills
Documentation	Methods and procedures
Supervisory skills	Customer service

Applications: Word Perfect 6.0 for Windows, CPI, Lotus 1-2-3

PROFESSIONAL EXPERIENCE

People's Savings Bank, Rosedale, NY   1992-present
Have played key leadership roles in managing quality improvement programs, creating and chairing an Employee Committee and working with senior management to improve customer satisfaction and employee morale.
Assumption processor
- Created, chaired and served as secretary for Employee Committee. Solicited representatives from each department. Represented the Assumptions department. Implemented quality improvements, cut costs, boosted employee morale via recognition luncheons, interdepartmental competitions, casual days and flex time. Briefed senior management on an on-going basis.
- Administer both qualifying and non-qualifying assumptions. Handle all correspondence. Insure completeness of documentation.
- High customer contact with much emotional interaction. Heavy interface with attorneys, title companies, closing agents, other departments to ensure problems are resolved expeditiously.
- Conduct extensive research on documents and client histories.

Document administrator
- Heavy telephone interaction with investors, custodians, title companies to ensure file completion and accuracy.
- Self-starter responsible for setting own project goals.
Special Project: Solely responsible for all documentation needs for three new company start-ups. Reported directly to senior management.

Payoff technician
- Utilized CPI to determine mortgage payoff amounts. Interfaced with customers to ensure satisfaction.
- Promoted to head of department. Supervised and trained staff of two to five payoff clerks.
- High levels of customer contact and interaction with customer services, attorneys, companies and individual customers.

County College of New York, Adult Education department, Rosedale, NY   1990-1992
Student aide
- Customer contact in person and by phone.
- Heavy interaction with all departments of the College.

Ace Oil Company, Rosedale, NY   1989-1990
Office manager
- Administered all aspects of billing, dispatching and customer satisfaction.
- Supervision and training of part time staff.

EDUCATION
Bachelor of Arts, Oneida State, Oneonta, NY   December, 1995

VOLUNTEER ACTIVITIES
Alcohol & Drug Education Program, Rosedale, NY
- Coordinated participation in fund-raisers for Fetal Alcohol Syndrome.
- Organized and participated in walks and community days.
- Attended seminars and manned information booths.

Combination. *Fran Kelley, Waldwick, New Jersey*

This individual had no human resources experience but wanted to move into an HR position. The writer used narrower margins and smaller type to fit more information onto one page.

EDMUND C. FERRIS

2378 Snowfall Circle
Anytown, VA 23460
804 • 439 • 2947

JOB OBJECTIVE: Sales position in an insurance environment with an opportunity to produce top sales results, develop excellent customer relations, and advance to higher sales levels.

SUMMARY OF QUALIFICATIONS: Have exemplary customer relations and excellent interpersonal skills. Work well with people at all levels. Am self-motivated, able to work independently and have a proven outstanding record as a consistent top producer. With a quick grasp of problem solving am able to meet deadlines promptly.

PROFESSIONAL EXPERIENCE: U.S. NAVY, Norfolk, VA. 1991-Present
Special Assistant to Command Fearless Leader. Schedule meetings and apprise supervisor of daily events. Assist with ceremonial events and award ceremonies. Write thank you notes, letters of appreciation and ghostwrite a monthly column.

AWG-1 Radar Technician, AIMD, Naval Air Station Oceana, Virginia. Troubleshooter and technician for F21 weapons control radar. Interpreted manuals and tracked source of equipment failure.

TURNPIKE AUTO PARTS, Northville, New York.
Outside sales and customer relations director. 1989-1991 including summers 1986-1989. Duties included calling on customers and developing selling skills. Increased sales by approximately $30,000/month. Had the ability to settle employee and customer related problems.

A variety of other positions leading to experience in dealing with the general public.

EDUCATION: **Happy Days University**, Somewhere, Oklahoma, B.S. 1989. Telecommunications and Journalism.

Dows College, Smalltown, NewYork, 1984-1985. Liberal arts courses.

U.S. Navy F14 Weapons Control Radar School. 1992
U.S. Navy Aviation Electronics Class "A" School, Memphis, Tn. 1991

EXTRA CURRICULAR ACTIVITIES:
- Active in POW/MIA Foundation.

- College activities included sports editing for yearbook, staff writer for Oracle - university newspaper, on-air personality for KORU college radio staff, athletic chairman college fraternity, member University Telecommunications Association, and active in all intramural sports and tournaments.

- Selected to Society of Distinguished High School students, 1985.

38

Combination. *Anne G. Kramer, Virginia Beach, Virginia*

This resume helped the individual gain a second interview. The resume is easily read with side headings, selective use of boldfacing, limited use of bullets, and adequate white space.

BILL CHESTER

600 Little Pan Place
Virginia Beach, VA 23456

604 • 470 • 1700

OBJECTIVE

To obtain a food service position with an establishment that encourages professional growth and offers opportunities for responsibility and advancement.

SUMMARY OF QUALIFICATIONS

Competent leadership and management abilities developed while serving as a Mess Management Specialist in the U.S. Navy • Responsible for food preparation for more than 1200 personnel • Able to oversee and supervise good usage of kitchen equipment, sanitation, and maintenance • Supervised and arranged work schedules of approximately twelve employees • Able to handle problem calls involving cleanliness, maintenance, and repairs.

Capable of managing and operating a small hotel/motel complex • Completed studies and training involving check in/checkout system on a Marlboro computer • Able to supervise effective front desk management and maintain accurate records • Well trained in providing prompt, courteous service and information to residents.

Am a versatile individual with the ability to adapt to new duties and situations • Abilities include being a strong team player, high achiever, task and people oriented • Able to execute effective plans maximizing utilization of scarce assets.

MISCELLANEOUS

• Recipient of numerous medals, badges, citations and campaign ribbons.
• Honorable discharge June 1990.

39

Functional. *Anne G. Kramer, Virginia Beach, Virginia*

The writer indented "every other paragraph" and used full-justification to make this resume look different. Other features are centered headings and lines to separate the sections.

ANDREW T. SALESMAN

111 Wide Heaven Street • Bestown, NJ 00000 • (123) 555-5555

CAREER SUMMARY

Experienced professional with a solid 15-year work history. Proven skills in increasing the bottom line through the development of new accounts while maintaining existing accounts.

SKILLS/QUALIFICATIONS

Sales/Marketing

- Solid grasp of demographics, marketing, and competitive bidding.
- Made face-to-face sales calls on current and potential customers and initiated service orders.
- Secured new accounts by cold-calling; developed sales strategies for various accounts.
- Built strong business partnerships, maximized account retention, and improved customer loyalty.
- Strong vendor relations.
- Effectively handled customer complaints and inquiries.
- Knowledgeable in product comparison and salvage value.

Community/Public Relations

- Instrumental in setting up and organizing product for trade shows.
- Strong interpersonal and communication skills; quick grasp of technical products and services.
- Assisted in the coordination of safety meeting including training and certification; experience with OSHA and environmental regulations.
- Key contact person for United Way Campaign.
- Volunteer at International Museum.

Organization/Administrative

- Operational management including advertising, program development, and inventory control.
- Strong verbal and written communication skills; adept at report writing.
- Proficient with custom software.

EMPLOYMENT HISTORY

BEST ELECTRIC COMPANY, Bestown, NJ
Material Recovery Technician, Technical Services   1/87 - Present
Inspection and Reseal Representative   9/85 - 12/86

RELATED PROFESSIONAL EMPLOYMENT

THE BEST LANDSCAPING, Anywhere, NJ
Owner/Manager   1979 - 1982
OWNER'S LANDSCAPING, Anywhere, NJ
Owner/Manager   1983 - 1994
TIME, Anywhere, NJ
Owner/Operator   1984 - 1992

EDUCATION

The Best College, Bestown, NJ
Major: Business Management/Human Resource Management   1993 - Present
Junior College, Bestown, NJ
Major: Mass Communications/General Business   1977 - 1981
Community College, Bestown, NJ
Major: General Business/Pre-Law   1978 - 1981

CERTIFICATIONS

Certified Emergency Medical Technician   1976 - 1977

40

Combination. *M. Carol Heider, Tampa, Florida*

The individual was making a career change and seeking a position in sales and marketing. The writer therefore grouped Sales/Marketing skills first under Skills/Qualifications.

AMY J. KING
1044 Wickham Road North
Melbourne, FL 32935
(404) 555-1212

OBJECTIVE

To secure a position as a Marketing/Public Relations Representative utilizing outstanding corporate sales management skills

CREDENTIALS

Outstanding Sales Ability

» 9 years corporate sales and sales marketing experience

» Organize entire sales process from appointment setting through consultation, deadline maintenance, delivery, billing and collection

Excellent Communication Skills and Customer Relations

» Received several letters from satisfied corporate clientele, including Perrier, attesting to "customer service attitude" and desire to "do what it takes to get the job done"

» Accomplished and comfortable as a public speaker and company/promotional representative; assisted in promoting the Dallas Grand Prix

» Ability to function both independently or as a "team member"

Strong Management Skills

» Personnel Management: successfully supervise and motivate personnel to reach projected sales goals

» Operation/Project Management: oversee product production from design concept to completion

» Quality Control: meet regularly with manager and supervisors to create a more streamlined and highly motivated professional atmosphere

EDUCATION

Bachelor of Arts in Graphic Art - UNIVERSITY OF NEW ORLEANS, New Orleans, Louisiana

WORK HISTORY

Corporate Sales and Supervisor - July 1986 to Present - MJDesigns, Metro Dallas, TX.   Responsible for handling corporate sales, design, and production of picture framing for corporate needs
• Set appointments and deadlines, visit clients at their office, oversee framing process, perform billing and collection
• Supervise and motivate up to seven production personnel, motivating them to reach projected goals
• Assist management in determining personnel reviews
• Attend management meetings to brainstorm new ideas
• Certified Picture Framer
• Member, Professional Picture Framer's of America

Model - 1983 to 1986 - "Stars Over Texas" Modeling Agency, Dallas, TX
Modeled for numerous promotional assignments promoting various products such as clothes, foods, perfumes, and events including the Dallas Grand Prix

Food Server - 1978 to 1982 - The Roman Noodle, Old Spaghetti Factory, New Orleans, LA

41

Combination. *Laura A. DeCarlo, Melbourne, Florida*

This person had a background in sales and customer service and wanted to move into marketing and public relations. Chevron bullets point to sales and communication skills.

Daniel Hartman

111 Crandall Avenue ▪ Center Moriches, New York 55555 ▪ (555) 555-5555

- **Successful business owner and operator**
- **Skilled sales and management professional**
- **Innovative entertainment and event coordinator**
- **Accomplished presenter and communicator**

Career Profile

Twenty years professional background in profitable business ownership and general management. Consistently achieve and surpass objectives through a dynamic combination of creative, organizational, communication and leadership abilities.

- Known for a contagious passion for excellence, a talent for resourceful business solutions and a capacity for motivational leadership. As a trained educator, possess outstanding communication and presentation abilities.

- Dedicated far beyond conventional expectations; committed, responsible and unusually organized. Demonstrated ability to combine efficiency with creativity to produce bottom-line results.

- Effectively market tangible/intangible products or services; skilled in persuasive presentation and profitable negotiation. Offer excellent customer relations skills; consistently develop a loyal, often multi-generational following.

- Understand and utilize the dynamic of personal and collective interaction. In business, entertainment and education, recognized for ability to merge dissimilar numbers of people into cohesive groups with a common focus.

Business Ownership

Owner and operator of SURROUND SOUND, Inc. a company providing the highest standard in creative recorded musical entertainment and peripherals as well as private and corporate event coordination services. (1976 to present)

- Perform as disc jockey, master of ceremonies, and event organizer for private, charity, government and corporate functions for up to 2,000 participants. Representative clients include Coca Cola, NYNEX, General Electric, Liberty Mutual, AHRC, Three Village Schools, and Suffolk County National Bank.

- Receive numerous referrals and maintain 90% client retention rate. Recognized by clients and colleagues as a consummate professional with the utmost creativity and personal integrity. Perceptive, patient and persistent; nurture trust and confidence, relax tension and create animated party atmosphere.

- Utilize extensive knowledge of consultative sales techniques, music and the arts to determine perspective clients' entertainment preferences and to profitably educate clients in the nuances of fine event planning and musical presentation. Complete customer satisfaction is a primary goal; have never received a letter of complaint or threat of litigation.

- Control daily administration of business: planning, marketing, advertising, sales and bookkeeping. Carry no business debt.

42

Combination. *Deborah Wile Dib, Medford, New York*

After 20 years of business management and ownership in entertainment, this candidate wanted a corporate position. Thick horizontal lines and bold, sans serif type for the individual's name,

Daniel Hartman page two

General Management

General Manager for Metro Electronic Supply, one of the largest distributors of licensed replacement parts for major electronics manufacturers. (1972 to 1984)

- Learned business from hands-on experience working part-time and full-time operations positions. Promoted to General Manager with staff of fifteen. Controlled all ordering, shipping, inventory and sales support operations.

- Held inventory control responsibility for ordering and tracking millions of parts. Known for ability to memorize, recognize and locate thousands of parts and part numbers by description alone.

- Handled daily ordering and service interface for over 250 contracted accounts plus additional sales to nationwide service centers and international affiliates. Processed orders, oversaw proper shipping standards, and resolved service issues. Conducted extensive correspondence.

- Negotiated lucrative licensing contracts with major global vendors as member of company sales team. Learned nuances of profitable negotiation with executives of different cultures. Represented Metro at national electronics trade shows.

Teaching

Art Teacher (NYS certified K-12) with creative abilities in all media. Worked as preferred building substitute covering leave replacements, long-term assignments, sabbaticals and daily substitute teaching for Center Moriches schools. (1977 to 1980)

- Took mental ownership of each classroom and conducted class as if it were sole responsibility. Developed lesson plans, schedules, special projects and generated innovate ideas for other substitute art teachers. Maintained professional attitude toward substitute teaching commitment.

- Offered permanent teaching placement in 1980 but position was cut before beginning of school year. Discontinued substitute teaching in 1980 to change career focus to business and music.

Business Philosophy

Sell yourself, or your product, from conviction and integrity; recognize that without communication, there can be no understanding, cooperation or accomplishment.

Education

Bachelor of Science in Art Education, Pratt Institute, New York, NY

Professional and Civic Affiliations

Member American Disc Jockey Association. Effective fund-raiser for community and school organizations. Active in children's educational and sports activities.

opening profile points, section headings, descriptive paragraph under each heading, and academic degree make this resume strong. Square bullets throughout tie together the two pages visually.

RECREATIONAL RUTH

1982 GOPHER DRIVE ■ SACRAMENTO, CA 99959 ■ (777) 555-1212

PROFILE

- ► Diverse experience in the field includes therapeutic recreation services applied in psychiatric, rehabilitation, and preschool settings. Knowledgeable in documentation of case progress from initial assessment interviews to discharge summaries.

- ► Approach to therapeutic recreation is characterized by enthusiasm and a strong commitment to the field as an evolving profession.

- ► Skilled in working with all age groups; particular strengths interacting with children.

- ► Proven organization and time management skills utilized to achieve goals for the client, team, and myself.

RELEVANT EXPERIENCE

CALIFORNIA SCHOOL DISTRICT, Sacramento, CA
Diagnostician
Administer and score battery of academic tests to children in ten elementary, middle and high schools who have been identified for possible placement in the Exceptional Children program. Assist psychologists with written behavioral observations and parent interviews.

Work Site Specialist
Prepared mentally handicapped high school students for employment utilizing a variety of training techniques. Trained employers in supervision encouraging a successful transition from teaching program to independent employment. Assessed and documented student performance through interviews with parents, teachers, and employers.

LOS ANGELES REGIONAL MEDICAL CENTER, Los Angeles, CA
Earthquake Rehabilitation Hospital & The Pines (psychiatric facility)
Therapeutic Recreation Specialist
Filled in for staff Therapeutic Recreation Specialists on leave. Provided programs on exercise, leisure education, horticulture, pottery, needlework, woodwork, as well as community outings for patients. Conducted initial assessment interviews, counseled patients and documented their progress, participated in treatment team meetings, wrote treatment plans, and prepared discharge summaries.

Earthquake Rehabilitation Hospital
Volunteer

CALIFORNIAN DEVELOPMENT CENTER, Los Angeles, CA
Therapeutic Preschool Teacher
Designed and implemented a new program for developmentally delayed preschoolers. Adapted class activities to the changing needs of both mainstreamed, normally-developing students and delayed students. Promoted mainstreaming concept to parents, other professionals, and the community.

43

Combination. *Sandy Adcox Saburn, Wilmington, North Carolina*

This job seeker did not go into her field immediately after she earned her degree. "Family matters and a stint in real estate 'distracted' her from her profession." The writer emphasized

RECREATIONAL RUTH
■ PAGE TWO ■

RELEVANT EXPERIENCE (CONTINUED)

WESTERN HEALTH CENTER, Sacramento, CA
Support Teacher
Programmed and led activities for classroom of students ages three to six with behavioral disorders. Taught movement class incorporating physical education and play therapy. Designed and led weekly workshop series for parents and day care providers on topics that included self-esteem, communication, and discipline.

CALIFORNIA RECREATIONAL DEPARTMENT, Sacramento, CA
Camp Director
Camp Counselor
Performed duties of camp counselor for groups of children, both with and without disabilities. Responsible for pre-camp planning, including design of program structure, distribution of registration materials, purchasing supplies, and hiring and training 19 employees. Developed camp manual.

CALIFORNIA MEMORIAL HOSPITAL IN HOLLYWOOD
Intern
Full time internship position on acute psychiatric unit. Documented initial assessments, treatment team plans, and discharge summaries for fifteen adolescents and adults. Planned and led individual and group programs on stress management, relaxation therapy, exercise, horticulture, games, and leisure education. Facilitated patient meeting to plan weekly community outings.

EDUCATION

UNIVERSITY OF SOUTHERN CALIFORNIA
Teacher Certification in Special Education (all but Student Teaching)

Bachelor of Arts in Parks and Recreation
Option in Therapeutic Recreation

CERTIFICATION

Certified as a Therapeutic Recreation Specialist
Administered by the National Council for Therapeutic Recreation

PROFESSIONAL AFFILIATIONS

- American Therapeutic Recreation Association

- Californian Therapeutic Recreation Association

- Californian Recreation and Parks Society

REFERENCES

Provided upon request

experience relevant to a target position and left out dates to grab the reader's attention. Questions about dates and other experience were left to the interview. Notice in this resume the use of bullets (two kinds) and boldfacing as unifying devices.

MANAGEMENT / COMMUNICATIONS

JASON T. PARKER
44 North Jones Street
Melbourne, FL 32934
(407) 752-6000

SUMMARY OF QUALIFICATIONS:
- Commitment to quality assurance with zero errors toleration
- Provide outstanding training, management, and motivation to personnel
- Extensive knowledge on the installation, maintenance, testing, and troubleshooting of hardware, satellite, microwave, high frequency and single band radios, line-of-sight radios, tropospheric radios, cables, televisions, computers, and various other electronics, analog and digital circuits
- Possess Top Secret Clearance since 1985

PROFESSIONAL EXPERIENCE:
UNITED STATES ARMY - 1980 to Present

Communications and Electronics
- Set up video teleconferencing system and e-mail system; ensured daily operations of a dial central office and outside plant facilities, military affiliated radio station, and telecommunications center. 1992.
- Personally organized and activated the first Computer help desk at Ft. Mason. 1993-1994.
- Directed, coordinated, and managed the installation, operation, and maintenance of satellite vans, line-of-sight radio vans, switch vans, vehicles, and generators valued in excess of $20 million. 1988-1991.
- Supervised daily operations of tactical signal company which provided satellite, tropospheric, and hf radio operation to both U.S. and United Coalition forces; ensured operation and maintenance of communication assemblages and auxiliary equipment worth over $17 million. 1990-1991.

Management and Training
- Maintained 100% accountability of property/equipment in excess of $12 million. 1992.
- Provided guidance within all areas of communications systems employment, maintenance, and logistical support to up to 180 personnel both military and civilian. All positions.
- Outstanding quality control resulted in zero injuries, workman's compensation cases, or investigations. 1991.
- Provided training on signal operations and maintenance to all National Guard and Reserve units throughout the State of Georgia. Provided defense coordination element support for disaster relief operations. 1995.

AWARDS:
- Army Commendation Medal for maintaining a 98.6 reliability time on a triple microwave relay which covered 150 miles. September 1985.
- Army Achievement Medal for leading platoon to highest skill qualification test score of any cable section in 11th Signal Brigade. 1987.
- Meritorious Service Award for improving standard of platoons and initiating first organized evaluation of transmission teams in 505th Signal Company. 1989-1991.
- Meritorious Service Award for developing and implementing a company inspection program enabling company to obtain highly successful ratings on all inspections. Developed a safety program resulting in Company having zero vehicle accidents despite average 30,000 miles driving per year. 1990-1995.

EDUCATION:
Radio Teletype Course, Tactical Satellite/Microwave
Radio Operations, Radio Service & Repair, Military Science - Georgia State University

44

Combination. *Laura A. DeCarlo, Melbourne, Florida*

For this person with 25 years of experience in communications management with the military, the writer omitted job titles because they did not resemble civilian job goals.

Communications

Resumes at a Glance

ROBERTA REPORTER

85 Alameda Avenue • Winston, California 95498
(707) 555-1212

OBJECTIVE   A position as City Reporter.

PROFILE

- Over 10 years experience in newspaper reporting, writing and editing.
- BA in Communication/Print Media including newswriting and publication.
- Excellent public and written communicator, skilled in expository style.
- Held different progressive positions to increase professional experience.
- Proficient in Microsoft Word, WordPerfect, PCWrite for IBM, and QuarkXPress.

EDUCATION

BA - Communication/Print Media, University of the West, Stanton, CA, 1994

RELEVANT EXPERIENCE AND ACCOMPLISHMENTS

REPORTER
- Gathered and wrote news and feature stories for The Winston News front page.
  - Interviewed public officials and reported events at weekly City Council meeting.
- Assembled and composed news stories for two-page business section.
- Produced black and white photographs to accompany stories.
- Organized, created and designed layout and paste-up copy for printing.

EDITOR AND WRITER
- Assigned stories, wrote and edited articles, reviews and copy for weekly campus newspaper at The Pacifican.
  - Created tabloid style magazine insert published once per semester.
- Supervised up to 10 staff members and students, scheduled assignments, and coordinated production of campus-wide circulation.

BROADCAST JOURNALISM
- Performed as radio host at campus AM station, KPAC, Stanton.
  - Read news hourly and played selected music.

EMPLOYMENT HISTORY

1994-present   **General Assignment Reporter and Business Editor** • The Winston News, Winston, CA
Gather and write news and feature stories with accompanying black and white photographs, when applicable, for twice-weekly city newspaper.

WORK HISTORY

1993-1994   **Managing Editor and Writer** • The Pacifican, Stanton, CA
Served as managing editor for weekly university newspaper. Created headlines, designed and laid out news pages.

1992-1993   **Page Editor and Senior Staff Writer** • Pacific Tide Magazine, Stanton, CA
Wrote articles and reviews, and edited copy for campus newspaper magazine insert. Edited health page, reported general features, and reviewed restaurants.

1989-1991   **Page Editor and Senior Staff Writer** • La Madrone Community College, Pittstown, CA
Edited and designed sports page, reported and edited general news for newspaper.

1985-1987   **Staff Writer** • The Liberty, San Juan, CA
Wrote and edited feature and news articles for monthly high school paper. Gained first experience as reporter.

PROFESSIONAL AWARD

Best Media Coverage and Fair Photo, Redway Empire Fair Board of Directors, 1995

45

Combination. *Nancy Karvonen, Galt, California*

This individual was hired at her first interview the day after her resume was completed. Relevant Experience and Accomplishments are grouped according to three categories.

HEES A. WRITER

1234 Any Street • Anytown, State 12345 • (000) 555-1234 (h) • (000) 555-1234 (w)

SUMMARY OF QUALIFICATIONS

- **Over five years professional experience** holding a variety of responsible positions in communications.

- Experienced in **both national and international public contact roles**; able to cultivate and maintain relationships with a wide variety of individuals.

- **Conversant with federal and state regulatory agencies**; proven ability to establish and maintain important professional relationships with key personnel.

- Extensive **oral and written communication skills**.

- **Perform well under pressure**; accustomed to working with deadlines.

- **Creative and innovative professional**; prepared to adapt a variety of talents toward a new challenge.

PROFESSIONAL EXPERIENCE

A BIG GROUP ASSOCIATION OF PEOPLE, Anytown, State
Manager of Government Relations (x/xx-Present)
- Coordinate with counsel and Director of Communications to analyze and summarize information on federal regulations, administrative rules and environmental initiatives. Write/produce Government xxxxxxxx, bulletins, position papers and presentations to keep membership apprised of new laws, administrative regulations, government relations policies and relevant environmental topics. Create key contacts with EPA, OSHA, Labor, congressional offices. Formulate and recommend courses of action for association.

Staff Writer (x/xx-x/xx)
- Researched, developed and wrote original feature material for Group Association magazine, both on assigned and enterprise basis. Written material also ranged from straight news stories and departmental material to complex feature articles covering such subjects as association activities, something operations and management methods and current technology.

ANYTOWN DAILY PAPER, Anytown, State
Area Reporter (x/xx-x/xx)
- Covered a four-county area that included: 10 city councils, 9 school districts, 1 four-year college, sheriff and police departments. Reported agriculture, weather, general assignments, and spot news.

ANOTHER COUPLE OF NEWSPAPERS, Sometown, State
Reporter (x/xx-xx/xx)
- Reported all newsworthy activities and events in county and city government, courts, community corrections, county hospital and school district. Photographed events for news stories and wrote a bi-monthly column.

UNIVERSITY PAPER, Anytown, State
Columnist (x/xx-x/xx)
- Researched and created a weekly humor and entertainment column.

Reporter (x/xx-xx/xx)
- Established and implemented beat coverage of physical operations at the University. Additionally covered general assignments.

EDUCATION
B.S., Journalism; B.A., English (xxxx), University, Anytown, State

46

Combination. *Linda Morton, Lawrence Kansas*

The Summary of Qualifications emphasizes breadth (national/international, federal/state, oral/written). The Experience section shows job growth from college reporter to manager.

Profile: Presenting an extensive experience as a COMMUNICATIONS SPECIALIST, with expertise in:
- PROMOTIONS & SPECIAL EVENTS
- PUBLIC & GOVERNMENT RELATIONS
- PRINT & ELECTRONIC MEDIA
- MARKETING & SALES
- BUSINESS DEVELOPMENT
- PRODUCTION COMPANY ORGANIZATION
- STAFF TRAINING & MANAGEMENT

Achievements:
- Created Special Interest Women's Expo (Two local counties), enlisted sponsorship, exhibitor/advertiser/major media/corporate interest.
- Devised sales plan to promote Sailing Prize '92.
- Developed sponsorship for the Aerobat Air Show.
- Increased corporate sponsorship 100% for the "Accolades '92" Some Branch military honors presentation.
- Secured noted personalities for keynote addresses (e.g., noted actors/actresses).
- Produced three annual Congressional Technology Conferences Conferences on Global Interests and North American Trade Alliance (featured high-level government officials).
- Planned and assisted Presidential and Congressional candidate fund raising planning and development.
- Served House and Senate subcommittees on Education and the Department of Education.

Mary Anne Smith

1212 East Street
Some City, California 90000
111/555-1212

Career History:

1989-Present	**President & Founder - Interest Concepts International, Some City, CA**
1988-1989	**Director, Public Relations - Congressman Jim Smith, Some City, CA**
1987-1988	**Special Assistant, Administration & Program Services - Center in the National Interests, Major University Program, Near the Nation's Capitol.**
1984-1986	**Congressional Aide - Congressman John Smith, Washington, D.C.**

Education:

1987	M.A., International Affairs, Major University, East Coast, USA
1984	B.A., Political Science, Good College, City of Honors, PA
1984	University of Florence, Florence, Italy
1983	Universite Francois Language, Provence, France

Memberships: Big World Trade Organization; Big World Affairs Council; Fund raising Chair, United Nations Association, San Diego; Meeting Planners International; Some County Convention & Visitors Bureau, Membership Committee.

References: Available upon establishment of mutual interest.

47

Combination. *Nita Busby, Orange, California*

Placement of the name below center gives prominence to Profile and Achievements sections. All-uppercase letters and oval bullets make the Profile stand out further.

JIM T. ANNOUNCER

(000) 555-1234 Business
(000) 555-1234 (Home)

EDUCATION

B.S., Journalism (xxxx-xxxx), *University,* Anytown, State
Major: Broadcasting; Minors: English, Political Science, Economics
Relevant coursework included:

Broadcast Newswriting	Composition I and II
Mass Media	Broadcast Programming
Music Theory	Private Voice Lessons
Music History	Participation in top choirs

Honors: Alpha Epsilon Rho (Broadcast honorary)

State College, Another Town, State (xxxx-xxxx)
Major: Communications; Minor: Music
Relevant coursework included:

Music Theory	Private Voice Lessons
Music History	Participation in top choirs

Received training in WordPerfect Computer Software (xxxx)

**PROFESSIONAL
EXPERIENCE**

Classical Radio, Some City, States (xxxx-Present)
Morning Show Host and Production Director.

The Bird, Anytown, State (xxxx-Present)
Writer and Reporter.

A Philanthropy, Anytown, State (xxxx-xxxx)
Consultant/Supervisor to groups needing to raise money.

XXXX Radio, Anytown, State (xxxx-xxxx)
**Acting News Director, news writer, reporter, morning
anchor/personality.**

KLIN Radio, Place, State (xxxx-xxxx)
News writer, reporter, announcer, and disc jockey.

University Radio & TV, Place, State (xxxx-xxxx)
News writer and reporter.

Telemarketing, Place, State (xxxx-xxxx)
Sales Operator

ORGANIZATIONS

President, Knights of Columbus Council xxxx; Church Pastoral
Council; Announcer at University of State, former member of
Association of News Broadcasters of State, former Associated Press
Stringer, Member of Toastmasters.

48

Chronological. *Linda Morton, Lawrence, Kansas*

Clean design and white space make this resume easy to read. Courses in two columns display
the person's music background and suitability for hosting a morning classical radio show.

On-Air Talent
Program Director

PATTY SMYTH

Main Street ✦ Pleasantville, New York 12569
Home: (914) 555-4181 ✦ Work: (914) 555-5555

On-Air Radio Personality/Station Programming with seven years experience encompassing multi-track production, studio and live broadcasts, talk show production and editing, and commercial voice-overs. Expert in consistently entertaining large audiences with tireless enthusiasm.

QUALIFICATION HIGHLIGHTS:

* Knowledgeable in operations of state-of-the-art production studios
* Talent for generating creative ideas and organizing projects
* Outstanding record of excellence, reinforced by several letters of recognition
* Highly organized; strong in planning and implementing programs
* Proven ability to develop and cultivate a wide range of community contacts
* Sociable, personable; communicate easily with a broad range of personalities
* Enthusiastic, committed, resourceful; can be counted on to get the job done

SUMMARY of EXPERIENCE:

- Local producer of nationally networked and local talk radio shows
- Public appearances include:
  - ✦ Stage Announcements
  - ✦ Public Service/Charity Events
  - ✦ Concerts
  - ✦ Happy Hour
  - ✦ Live Broadcasts
- As intern to program director:
  - ✦ Listen To Air Checks
  - ✦ Participate in Interview Process of Radio Personalities
  - ✦ Prepare Program Schedule
- Assist in the production of national, regional and local commercials
- Update client sponsored weather phone network
- Own and operate professional DJ entertainment business

PROFESSIONAL EXPERIENCE:

WXYZ/WEAR/WRNV Broadcasting, Pleasantville, NY   *1992-Present*
    ASSISTANT PRODUCTION DIRECTOR
    OVERNIGHT AIR PERSONALITY
    SWING SHIFT AIR PERSONALITY
    INTERN TO PROGRAM DIRECTOR

WHVW/WIRE Broadcasting, Poughkeepsie, NY   *1989-1992*
    WEEK-END AIR PERSONALITY
    TALK RADIO SHOW PRODUCER
    BOARD OPERATOR

EDUCATION:

    Bachelor of Arts, Communications/Public Relations   *May, 1996*
    Marist College   *Poughkeepsie, NY*

49

Combination. *Marian Kozlowski, Poughkeepsie, New York*

The career goal above the contact information ensures that this goal will be seen easily in a quick look at a stack of resumes. Note the bold uppercase letters under Experience.

Laura T. Smith

324 E. Franklin Street ▸ Appleton, Wisconsin 54911 ▸ (414) 787–8714

Summary of Attributes	▸ Exceptional written and verbal communication skills.
	▸ Strong organizational and facilitation abilities; efficiently meet deadlines.
	▸ Proven track record in successful project development.
	▸ Effective sales and presentation skills; poised and confident addressing groups of all sizes.
	▸ Speak Spanish; able to assimilate/quickly learn languages.
	▸ Highly motivated to learn.

Experience

S & T Construction Company, Green Bay, Wisconsin
International construction company primarily focused on commercial building and highway projects.

February 1988 to Present

Manager of Public Relations and Advertising

Sales

▸ Coordinate the design and layout of sales proposals for the Wisconsin operating group; consultant for outlying offices.
▸ Coauthor of corporate sales proposals; copy edit proposals for all divisions.
▸ Orchestrate the design and production of presentation boards.
▸ Coach staff members to deliver effective, persuasive presentations.
▸ Generate and qualify sales leads.

Public Relations

▸ Developed and implemented Public Relations program from ground–zero.
▸ Administer media relations, ad design and placement.
▸ Facilitate public/community relations in regard to construction disruptions.
▸ Generate external and internal communications and collateral materials.

Design Work

▸ Execute production of internal and external corporate photography utilized in brochures and newsletters.
▸ Design and produce promotional items, awards, and job site signage.

Authorship

▸ Coauthor, editor, and production/distribution coordinator of quarterly corporate newsletter; editor of corporate biweekly newsletter.
▸ Author of two published articles in *Construction News* (May and July 1992).

Accomplishments:
▸ Directed enhancement of corporate logo.
▸ Developed corporate image, promotion announcement, media management,and crisis management policies.
▸ Authored various brochures and directed photography for same.
▸ Designed, coordinated production, and administered corporate Total Quality Management incentive program including program logo, gift selection, program catalog, achievement certificate, and recognition pins.

50

Combination. *Kathy Keshemberg, Appleton, Wisconsin*

This candidate was exploring opportunities in a number of areas, including her current field and sales/marketing in particular. Areas of responsibility and details of her wide range of expertise

Laura T. Smith

Experience *(Continued)*	Famous Retail Store, Minneapolis, Minnesota August 1985 — January 1988

Store Manager, Fox River Mall, Appleton
- Managed operations of $500,000 retail clothing store. Recruited at high schools, state colleges, and technical colleges; conducted employee security profile testing; developed and implemented training program; conducted district sales meetings on topics including sales techniques, management, motivation, security, and maximizing sales volume.

Training Assistant
- Hired and trained personnel for new stores in the Chicago area. Upon completion of construction, coordinated merchandise layout and display, and grand opening events.

Accomplishments:
- Instrumental in increasing the store's sales volume nearly 78% in 1.5 years; consistently surpassed corporate sales quotas.
- Store was awarded Regional Security Award five consecutive quarters.

Community Involvement

American Cancer Society — Community 5K Walk/Run
- Co–Chair, 1994–1996; Committee member, 1989–1994

American Heart Association — Annual Campaign, 1992–1993; 1995

Girl Scouts of the Bay–Lakes Council
- Annual Golf Outing, 1992–1995; brochure design and distribution
- Business Olympics, 1992–1993; committee member, brochure design and distribution, public relations coordinator.
- Annual Council Recognition Dinner, 1994 Chairman
- 20th Anniversary Encampment, 1993; designed, authored, produced commemorative book; directed advertising sales; solicited donations of pre–press, press services, and paper supply

Chamber of Commerce
- Intensive Training Program, 1995 Program Graduate
- Youth Internship Project; chairman

Professional Business Womens' Association
- First Vice President, 1994-1996; brochure development and design
- District President, 1996

Education

University of Wisconsin—Madison, Wisconsin
- Bachelor of Arts — Spanish/Marketing, 1985

Failes Management Institute
- Certified Facilitator of Total Quality Management in Construction, 1993

were grouped under the current position because of her multiple interests. The writer included an extensive list of community activities because many of them were career-related. Subheadings for Accomplishments help these to be conspicuous.

SUE A. SMITH

67 North Summerstorm Circle ♦ The Woodlands, Texas 77382 ♦ (409) 237-1032

PROFILE:

ADVERTISING AND MEDIA DIRECTOR
Self-directed professional with 20+ years experience developing, planning and implementing advertising and media campaigns for highly competitive automotive industry. Effective public speaker and presenter with strong communication skills, both verbal and written. Successfully combines astute marketing research and analysis with sound business operating and management practices to position agencies for long-term growth and profitability. Extensive experience working with independent dealers and dealer associations, and at the national level. Qualifications include:

★ Marketing & Media Research	★	Client Relationship Management
★ Media Budgeting & Planning	★	Executive Presentations & Negotiations
★ Competitive Analysis & Strategies	★	Commercial Creation & Production
★ Promotional Campaign Development	★	Meeting Management

PROFESSIONAL EXPERIENCE:

BOZELL WORLDWIDE, Houston, TX   1994 - Present
International advertising agency employing over 2,000 people worldwide.   1985 - 1992
Account Manager
A nine year career history highlighted by a series of promotions to increasingly responsible positions throughout the country. Originally hired to assist Senior Vice President of Advertising Operations. Quickly promoted to Account Executive responsible for identifying effective advertising vehicles to promote Chrysler-Plymouth Associations and their products. Created and developed media programs in Washington, DC, Boston, Dallas and Minneapolis with budgetary responsibilities exceed $10 million.
- Significantly increased budgets/expenditures in the Dallas and Minneapolis zones.
- Designed and produced a series of innovative campaign strategies to establish identity and strengthen market presence.

After accepting a one year assignment as Senior Account Executive supporting H. Lee Galles' automotive dealership and advertising agency, returned to Bozell Worldwide as Account Manager with total advertising and marketing responsibility for Jeep and Eagle Dealer Advertising Association consisting of 70 dealers generating over $10 million in annual revenues. Direct responsibility and accountability for media planning and development, goal setting and attainment, budgeting, forecasting and financial analysis reporting.
- Within 2 years of spearheading the redesign of the Houston Zone Jeep and Eagle marketing operation, income increased 100%.
- Successfully increased Houston's market share by 1% and doubled the media budget.
- Worked extensively with Board of Directors in cooperation with dealers to establish a mutually beneficial relationship between the parties.
- Designed promotional programs resulting in increased dealer participation and enthusiasm.
- Developed annual media plan for Association, increasing media placement by 20%.

THE SMOOTH EDGE, Albuquerque, NM   1993 - 1994
Senior Account Executive
Senior Advertising Manager assisting H. Lee Jones in business development initiatives and executive presentations to several key automotive dealerships throughout New Mexico.
- Negotiated and secured Stockton Auto Center account.
- Restructured and revamped Burt Chevrolet, Ford, Nissan, Subaru campaigns and advertising strategies.

MARITZ COMMUNICATIONS COMPANY, Detroit, MI   1972 - 1985
Associate Writer and Producer
Created and produced training, marketing and sales materials for GM Parts, GMC Truck, Chrysler Corporation and Ford Motor Company. Total project responsibility included print, layout, music selection, video on/off line, film location, budgeting, administration and cost control.

EDUCATION:

Oakland College, Farmington Hills, Michigan
Business Management 1981

51

Combination. *Cheryl Ann Harland, The Woodlands, Texas*

The writer uses smaller print to fit more information onto one page—a technique often used in resumes for executives. Underlining is used to make the job positions stand out.

Consultant

Resumes at a Glance

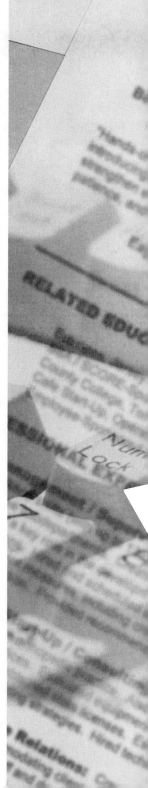

PROFESSIONAL PROFILE

CHARLES B. RILEY, CEI/CES

BACKGROUND

Charles B. Riley has had over 25 years of diversified experience in the technical and engineering field. His qualifications include having worked in Manufacturing/Industrial Management, Engineering Sales and Management; in addition to his positions as a Management Consultant Engineer, Safety Director, and more recently, Environmental Consultant.

PROFESSIONAL EXPERIENCE

A Professional Environmental Consultant since 1988, Mr. Riley specializes in the marketing of services related to:

- Contamination Assessments and Remediation at Hazardous and Non-hazardous sites.
- Underground Storage Tank (UST) Evaluations.
- Phase I, II and III Assessments.
- Asbestos Abatement/Radon Testing.
- OSHA 40-Hour Haz-Met School.
- Personnel Placement of Engineers and Technicians.

Mr. Riley's professional background includes prior employment with the following companies:

Donahue Groover & Associates, Staff Engineer/Consultant. Coordinated financial budget (P&E); marketing and logistics; Industrial Relations; general overall monitoring of organizational activities.

INA Insurance Company of North America (now Cigna), Senior Marketing Technical Representative. Responsible for monitoring total loss control, in conjunction with 30 insurance agencies. Instructed insurance officials, their insureds, and prospective clients on the OSHA Regulations and the implementation of safety programs to insure governmental compliance.

Hayes Aircraft, Senior Project Engineer. Supervised eight engineers. Coordinated research and design problems on Saturn V Swing Arms. Worked closely with NASA Engineers in reviewing and resolving problem areas.

Bendix Corporation, Supervisor of 50 personnel at John F. Kennedy Space Center, Florida. Coordinated refurbishment of Saturn V Swing Arm. Supported NASA Contractors and directed all operations. Training instructor for mechanical and pneumatic personnel involved in Swing Arm project. Instructor at Ground School for Heavy Equipment and Launch Control Systems.

Honeywell, Inc., Industrial Engineer/Cost Estimator. Worked on various "classified assemblies" and military electronic devices. Prepared cost estimates for bidding.

EDUCATION

Mr. Riley studied Industrial Engineering at Ohio University and is also a graduate of the International Safety Academy. In July, 1992, he received a 40-Hour OSHA Certification from the Technical Environmental Training Institute. During his career, he has participated in a variety of certified, specialized training and management programs; together with being an instructor for a Welding School and the Saturn V Ground Support School. He has conducted seminars and given speeches on OSHA Regulations and Procedures; Safety Programs to Insure Compliance with OSHA; Environmental Work - Air Quality, Smoke Stack Emissions, and Water Contamination.

PROFESSIONAL MEMBERSHIPS/AFFILIATIONS

- Environmental Asssessment Association (EAA)
- Environmental Conservation Organization (ECO)
- Lifetime Member - Methods Time Management Association (MTM)

52

Professional Profile. *Diane McGoldrick, Tampa, Florida*

The whole document is billed as a profile rather than a resume. Nevertheless, the profile contains some traditional resume sections (Professional Experience, Education, and so on).

Marie L. Traveler

1945 Springdale Avenue • Cincinnati, Ohio 45236
(513) 555-5555

Profile

Experienced travel consultant with diverse travel background. Trained and experienced with WORLDSPAN and TRAMS systems. Proficient in a variety of computer applications.

Background in teaching and training; exceptional organizational skills; flexible and adaptable.

Travel Experience

Travel Consultant
VOYAGERS TRAVEL, INC., Cincinnati, Ohio • 1994-Present
- Support agency operations using TRAMS (TRavel Agency Management Systems) to prepare weekly reports, invoices, profiles, payments, and other documentation and record-keeping.
- Assist clients with personal and business travel arrangements.

Extensive travel experiences — Highlights of business and personal travel:
- Washington and Oregon (1995-96, 1994, 1993, 1992)
- Atlanta, Georgia (1995)
- California (1994, 1991, 1967)
- Canada (Alberta, 1994; British Columbia, 1993, 1992; Ontario, 1991, 1987)
- Ohio, Pennsylvania, Washington DC, Virginia — hosting Russian exchange teacher (1994)
- Beloretsk, Bashkortostan, and Moscow, Russia — teacher exchange program (1993)
- London and Scandinavia (1993)
- Colorado (1991, 1989)
- Hawaii, New Zealand, Australia (1991)
- Southern United States (1989, 1967)
- Wyoming (1988, 1967)
- Italy and Greece (1983)
- Florida (1979-82)
- Switzerland and Germany (1972)
- Numerous additional trips throughout the United States

Other Experience

Consultant/Co-Teacher, "Hands-on Connected Math and Science"
NORTHERN KENTUCKY UNIVERSITY, Highland Heights, Kentucky • Summers 1994, 1995, 1996
- Instrumental in the design and presentation of this teachers' workshop focusing on teaching science principles through experiments and hands-on activities rather than textbook learning.

Teacher
SYCAMORE SCHOOL DISTRICT, Cincinnati, Ohio • 1976-Present
- Full-time classroom teaching responsibilities (grades 3, 5 and 2).
- Leadership role in numerous initiatives and committees.

Education

Travel Consultant training, Voyagers Travel, Inc., Cincinnati, Ohio • 1993-94
- Reservations systems training, WORLDSPAN, Atlanta, Georgia • 1994
- Travel Agency Management Systems training, TRAMS, Atlanta, Georgia • 1994

M.Ed., University of Cincinnati, Cincinnati, Ohio • 1979

B.A., University of Michigan, Ann Arbor, Michigan • 1976

53

Combination. *Louise M. Kursmark, Cincinnati, Ohio*

This part-time travel agent wanted to work full time. She had limited agency experience but much travel experience. This was played up, as well as her leadership skills as a teacher.

GAIL ROBERTS
55 Brighten Road
Coral City, NY 10555
(914) 333-4444

Objective: **Creative Position in Corporate or Wholesale Travel**

PROFILE

- **Twenty-three years of proven successful experience in the Business and Leisure Travel Industry.**
- **Expertise in designing Foreign Independent Tours. Sabre-trained.**
- **Special skills in advising, counseling, planning, organizing, and prioritizing.**
- **Detail-oriented, dependable, enthusiastic, with excellent interpersonal skills.**
- **Creative and cost-conscious problem solver; responsive to customers' needs and desires.**
- **High-energy, efficient professional; comfortable in dynamic and fast-paced environment.**

RELEVANT EXPERIENCE

SKYWAY TRAVEL, Clinton, NY   1990-Present
TAYLOR TRAVEL, Utica, NY   1973-1988

Travel Consultant
- Provide international and domestic travel assistance to individuals, groups, families, and businesses, building client base through referrals from satisfied customers.
- Conduct firsthand comparative evaluations of worldwide travel markets and services.
- Assess client needs and advise customers on details of:

travel accommodations	sight-seeing	restaurants
costs & services	ambiance	reputable merchants and best buys
unusual things to do	planning itineraries	special packages

- Coordinate air/ticketing requests and tour departures; issue tickets and provide typed itineraries.
- Resolve client problems and special requests.
- Verify international and domestic regulations, and advise clients of all necessary information.
- Assist clients in using mileage awards to best advantage.
- Special areas of international expertise include France, England, Italy, and Israel.

OTHER EXPERIENCE

President of two volunteer community organizations:
- Directed special events to engage membership excitement and enthusiasm
- Conducted fundraising efforts, raising $75,000.
- Created and directed promotional activities.

EDUCATION

B.A. William Smith College, Geneva NY

54

Combination. *Linsey Levine, Chappaqua, New York*

This resume displays a pleasing mix of center-aligned components (contact information, Objective, headings, and Education section) and left-aligned information with indentation.

Sally B. Johnson

660 Fountain Avenue   (504) 345-6392
Hillsdale, CA 94108

OBJECTIVE

Customer Service Specialist:
- Sensitive to the needs, wants and concerns of customers and prospects.
- Quick to resolve problems.
- Provides assistance in selection and use of appropriate products and services.
- Takes the initiative in anticipating needs and providing "service plus."

QUALIFICATIONS

- Outstanding career in the hospitality and travel industries focusing on the building and maintenance of a high level of customer satisfaction.
- Excellent communication and interpersonal skills.
- A strong personal commitment to service and a rich foundation in organizing and perpetuating a wide variety of community enhancing projects.
- Attentiveness, patience and enthusiasm.

KEY SKILLS

- Listening/Clarifying
- Trouble-Shooting
- Communicating
- Coaching

- Investigating/Tracking
- Problem-Solving
- Following-up
- Analyzing

- Advising
- Supervising
- Word Processing
- Spreadsheeting

PROFESSIONAL EXPERIENCE

- *Rosebud Catering Service*   Catering Consultant   Rosebud, CA
- *Sierra Nevada Airlines*   Senior Flight Attendant   Fresno, CA
- *Hertiage Church Diocese*   Vice-Pres. - Women's Affairs Hillsdale, CA
- *Children's Welfare Association* Vice President - Publicity   Hillsdale, CA

PERFORMANCE PROFILE

- **Quick to analyze** and solve problems; investigative, logical and clear thinking.
- **Performs confidently** and effectively under pressure, and thrives on challenge.
- **Excellent Communicator**, a good listener and a valued contributor.
- **Skilled with people**, enthusiastic, sense of humor, motivational, tactfully direct.
- **Visionary and goal oriented**; inspires trust, cooperation and teamwork.

ACCOMPLISHMENTS

- Handled all travel and function arrangements for corporate Board of Directors, organizing luncheons, dinners, conferences and meetings, and making all reservation, ticketing, function room and speaker/entertainment arrangements.

- Took charge of flight attendant teams, with responsibility for the safety and comfort of thousands of airline travelers during intra-continental flights, catering to health needs and special menus, providing quality efficient service. all within tight time constraints.

EDUCATION

- Mt. Heritage College   *Certificate in Office Automation Systems*   Sunnydale, CA

"Sally Johnson is an exceptionally service-oriented individual who has done much to strengthen relations with our customers".
- Jane Seymour, President, Rosebud Catering Services

55

Functional. *David Newbold, location unknown*

After a free-form presentation of contact information, the resume, beginning with the Objective, becomes tightly structured to the end. The testimonial is a strong ending.

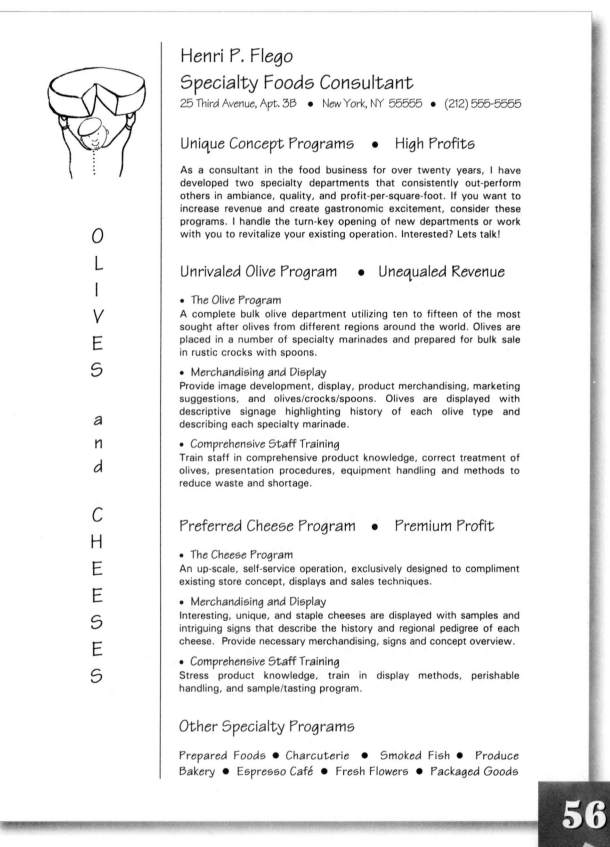

Henri P. Flego
Specialty Foods Consultant

25 Third Avenue, Apt. 3B • New York, NY 55555 • (212) 555-5555

Unique Concept Programs • High Profits

As a consultant in the food business for over twenty years, I have developed two specialty departments that consistently out-perform others in ambiance, quality, and profit-per-square-foot. If you want to increase revenue and create gastronomic excitement, consider these programs. I handle the turn-key opening of new departments or work with you to revitalize your existing operation. Interested? Lets talk!

Unrivaled Olive Program • Unequaled Revenue

• *The Olive Program*
A complete bulk olive department utilizing ten to fifteen of the most sought after olives from different regions around the world. Olives are placed in a number of specialty marinades and prepared for bulk sale in rustic crocks with spoons.

• *Merchandising and Display*
Provide image development, display, product merchandising, marketing suggestions, and olives/crocks/spoons. Olives are displayed with descriptive signage highlighting history of each olive type and describing each specialty marinade.

• *Comprehensive Staff Training*
Train staff in comprehensive product knowledge, correct treatment of olives, presentation procedures, equipment handling and methods to reduce waste and shortage.

Preferred Cheese Program • Premium Profit

• *The Cheese Program*
An up-scale, self-service operation, exclusively designed to compliment existing store concept, displays and sales techniques.

• *Merchandising and Display*
Interesting, unique, and staple cheeses are displayed with samples and intriguing signs that describe the history and regional pedigree of each cheese. Provide necessary merchandising, signs and concept overview.

• *Comprehensive Staff Training*
Stress product knowledge, train in display methods, perishable handling, and sample/tasting program.

Other Specialty Programs

Prepared Foods • Charcuterie • Smoked Fish • Produce
Bakery • Espresso Café • Fresh Flowers • Packaged Goods

56

Functional. *Deborah Wile Dib, Medford, New York*

A stand-alone sheet profiling a special program. Note the graphic, the use of fonts and vertical type, the two sizes of bullets, and the specialty programs at the end—inducements.

John System

2991 Computer Lane
Brighton, NY 11111

555-555-1212 (w)
555-555-1212 (h)

PROFILE

SYSTEMS ANALYST/CONSULTANT/PROGRAMMER

A pragmatic and creative business executive strongly rooted in both entrepreneurial and highly diverse corporate environments. Special expertise lies in problem solving, work flow systems analysis, procedures redesign and user training. Highly effective combining Industrial Engineering techniques with computer hardware/software knowledge to gain quick insight into user needs and problems.

PROFESSIONAL EXPERIENCE

Computer Consultant

Urgent Data, NY, NY   **2/96 - present**

Responsible for the design and implementation of enterprise database systems to control and integrate division-wide information.

- Converted existing system to Windows.
- Designed and implemented links with other corporate systems.
- Designed an enhanced tracking system that monitors a project both strategically and tactically, from inception through production and transportation/traffic.
  - System contains costs, production schedules, sizes, dimensions and colors.
  - Provides instantaneous status of any project.
  - Automatically inputs data to finance, production, forecasting, bar code and shipping.

Computer Consultant

Teledata, Inc., Invest, NJ   **10/92 - 2/96**

- Designed/developed OPR/SPECTRAK/STRAT PRO System in conjunction with Information Management standards and data structures.
- Devised the system criteria for the migration from an OS/2 environment to NOVELL 3.11.
- Established the workstation and server set-up for database serviceability at four sites.
- Instrumental in the set-up and maintenance of both on-site and remote workstations.
- Helped formulate/institute changes to ensure easier and more efficient work flow.
- Innovated to improve the throughput and validity of data.

General Manager

New Jersey News, Invest, NJ   **1970 - 1984/1988 - 10/92**

Carried overall P&L responsibility for this newspaper distribution business which included finance, marketing, operations and workforce administration.

- Achieved sales of $625,000.
- Directed the activities of a workforce of 30.
- Established delivery routes, trained personnel and created a payroll and billing system.
- Installed NOVELL network and Multi-user hardware for efficient use of personnel.
- Designed and instituted a series of management reports and computerized programs that monitor worker efficiency, billing, routing, payroll and account delinquency.

57

Combination. *Fran Kelley, Waldwick, New Jersey*

Center-alignment of the Profile and Education sections gives the resume an evident beginning and ending. Dashes are used for a second level of bullets. Controlled use of boldfacing directs

John System

555-555-1212 (w)
555-555-1212 (h)   *page two*

Manager/Systems Analyst/Programmer
Data bases, Data, NJ   **1985-1991**
Responsible for operation of this computer consulting and software/hardware sales company.
- Analyzed business/information flow and designed/selected suitable operational systems to maximize operations for clients.
- Customized, designed and implemented database systems in multi-user environments. to control inventory and process payroll, receivables and payables.
- Managed client 'Hotline' for hardware/software problems.
- Installed/managed NOVELL networks for various clients.

Manager/Systems Analyst/Programmer
Love My Data Corporation, Data, NJ   **1978-1984**
Created and operated all phases of this computer service bureau: planning, sales, marketing, proposal development, negotiations, administration and billing.
- Developed expertise in marketing, making presentations and negotiations.
- Formulated methodology for the evaluation of computer solutions through the analysis of business/information flow for the multitude of business challenges the bureau addressed for its various clients.
- Created a unique receivables system for physicians' groups to accommodate third party billing. The system also scheduled appointments, maintained patient histories, and performed normal physician billing/invoicing.

Computer Liaison Specialist
Aerospace Corporation, Data, NY   **1969-1970**
Served as the interface between manufacturing and computer personnel. Evaluated and translated manufacturing needs to computer personnel for the creation of appropriate systems.
- Developed and installed user manuals.
- Learned mainframe operations (OS-360/75), JCL/HASP and different protocols.
- Programmed in assembler, COBOL and RPG.

Industrial Engineer
Datascopic, Data, NY   **1966-1968**
- Conducted Special Staff studies.
- Initiated Capital evaluations and requests.
- Managed company cost reduction program.

EDUCATION
BSIE - Industrial Engineering - College of Engineering

Wang MVP 2200 school
NOVELL Authorization Certificate
NOVELL Network 386 Certificate
Data Access - Dataflex migration from 2.3 to 3.0
Data Access - Dataflex 3.0 Level III

the eye to the individual's name, the Profile, the headings, the job positions and dates, and the degree in the Education section. Thin, horizontal lines delineate the sections and the header at the top of page 2.

Mary L. Howard

123 Riverdale Road • Anytown, Tennessee 00000 | (000) 000-0000

• PROFILE

Provide **PRODUCTION SUPPORT** with abilities in coordinating location shoots and related production activities, staff training and management, operations and logistics planning, and hair and make-up artistry and design. Able to establish and maintain relationships with key personnel. Successfully meet production schedules and accustomed to working with deadlines.

• PRODUCTION EXPERIENCE

- As Production Coordinator for *Youth Challenge* with the USA Network, had total responsibility for organizing and coordinating daily location shoots, including talent, technical crew, and other personnel.

- As professional ice skater with Lorimar Telepictures *(Thundercats Live National Tour),* Space Concerts, and MTM Productions *(Masters of the Universe National Tour),* assisted the director with choreography, costuming, and related production activities, as well as hair styling and make-up artistry.

• WORK HISTORY

1993 - Present	**INDEPENDENT CONSULTANT • Majestic Hair Salon •** Nashville, TN
	• Responsible for personnel development, advertising and promotions, and product inventory
	• Color educator for Redken Laboratories line of hair color products
1991 - 1993	**PRODUCTION COORDINATOR • USA Network/Youth Challenge •** Dallas, TX
	• Used planning skills to organize daily location shoots
	• Worked closely with producers, directors, and technicians to ensure production continuity
1989 - 1991	**COLOR SPECIALIST • Belmont International •** Nashville, TN
	• Taught basic and advanced color techniques in salons and at trade shows
1988 - 1989	**MANAGER/HAIR STYLIST • Studio 54 Hair Salon •** Nashville, TN
	• Directed all aspects of organizing the set-up and opening of new hair salon
	• Trained new salon manager and ensured smooth operation of salon during transition period

• EDUCATION

Local State Community College • Somewhere, Tennessee
Major: Television Production • 1992 - 1994

Professional School of Beauty • Los Angeles, California

• *References and Portfolio Available Upon Request* •

Combination. *Carolyn S. Braden, Hendersonville, Tennessee*

This person had experience in hair and beauty care, and she wanted a position with a TV or movie production company. The writer plays up related professional skating experience.

Education/Training

Resumes at a Glance

DONNA L. GILBERT
55 North Main Street
Augusta, ME 55555
(550) 555-0050

PHILOSOPHY AND ATTRIBUTES

Highly motivated and dedicated teaching professional with empathy and compassion toward young children and their individualized strengths and needs. Advocate for hands-on, student-centered learning which fosters an appreciation for multiculturalism and integrates a Whole Language approach. Possess an energetic, enthusiastic, and creative style; performance characterized as loyal and hard-working. Proficient in various computer software packages for Macintosh and IBM systems, including WordPerfect and Microsoft Works. Financed 100% of undergraduate education.

EDUCATION

University of Maine • Orono, ME
- *Bachelor of Science* in Elementary Education; Concentration: Sociology (1991)

University of Massachusetts • Amherst, MA — Concentration: Liberal Arts (1986–88)

CERTIFICATION

- Maine Teacher Certification (K-6) — Infant and Child First Aid/CPR

PROFESSIONAL EXPERIENCE

Mountain Magic Children's Center • Waterville, ME   June 1990–Present
Preschool Teacher (promoted from Childcare/Assistant Preschool Teacher in 1994)
- Plan exciting, developmentally appropriate, child-focused activities for group of 10 children.
- Utilize thematic-based instruction, including implementation of such innovative, hands-on units as The Feeding and Caring of Ourselves (nutrition), We Grow as the Seasons Change (a year-long look incorporating science, weather, and human growth), and Our Gardens Teach Us (environment, commitment, and outdoor activities).
- Conduct annual parent conferences; provide individualized learning summaries based on observation of each child's progress.
- Maintain observation-based anecdotal records; developed and implemented a systematic program for evaluating student development and growth.
- Regularly attend workshops presented by NAEYC to ensure skills are fully up to date and professional education is ongoing.

Orono Nature Center • Orono, ME   Summers, 1993–Present
Summer Camp Naturalist
- Instruct summer camp four days per week to preschoolers (8–12 attendees); program emphasis is on protecting and understanding the wonders of nature. Thematic program includes focus on insects, trees, birds, and animals.
- Conduct programs on habitats, adaptations, and "KIDS CARE" at local schools, community centers, churches, and day care facilities.

Before/After School Program • Waterville, ME   Spring/Summer 1991
Assistant Program Director
- Initiated recreational opportunities for 25 school-age children, grades kindergarten through six.

STUDENT TEACHING EXPERIENCE

John Smith Preschool • Winslow, ME   Feb. 1991–May 1991
- Planned and implemented hands-on mathematics, science, and language arts units, gradually assuming all classroom teaching responsibilities in a classroom for 15 preschoolers.
- Developed age-appropriate, integrated units and lesson plans in introductory chemistry, multiplication, and poetry.

Winslow Elementary School • Winslow, ME   Fall 1989, 1990
- As kindergarten bilingual tutor, formulated creative learning techniques for non-English speaking students.

59

Combination. *Jan Melnik, Durham, Connecticut*

This individual had no resume. The writer gleaned the information from one-to-one consultation. The applicant became manager of eight teachers at a corporate preschool.

Julie Anne O'Rourke ▪ *6309 Sunset Drive* ▪ *Kalamazoo MI 49007* ▪ *000-222-2200*

"Instill Self-Confidence - And The Learning Never Stops"

Summary
Demonstrated competencies in child and activities supervision:
- Knowledge of instructional strategies, educational goals, learning principles.
- Experienced in curriculum development and procedures administration.
- Ability to establish rapport with diverse individuals; caring, friendly, committed.
- Possess strength of character and sincere sensitivity to all segments of the community.
- Excellent writing and presentation skills.

Education
1989: Bachelor of Arts; Major: *Practical Writing*. Minor: *English*.
Western Michigan University, Kalamazoo, MI.

Background
7+ years in a private classroom setting as Teaching Assistant with the Montessori School:
- Employs a positive approach to group learning for approximately 35 children ages 2-5.
- Excellent knowledge of and experience in the significant trends in pre-school education.
- Strong understanding of the basic principals of Montessori pedagogical methods.
- Utilizes an activity-centered learning program combining group and individual guidance.
- Provides instruction in reading comprehension, writing, spelling, and geography.
- Exceptional time management skills for constantly changing priorities and work loads.

Professional Experience
1989-Present: *Teaching Assistant*, Montessori School, Kalamazoo, MI.

Strengths
Noted for my ability to:
- Interact effectively with people of all ages on a one-on-one and group basis.
- Detect problem areas and explain material in an interesting and clear manner.
- Research a subject thoroughly and prepare well-documented reports.
- Evaluate and draw inferences through careful listening and observing.
- Organize and coordinate a multitude of assignments and responsibilities.
- Perform amiably under chaotic conditions and maintain a sense of humor.

Other Employment
1986-1989: *Customer Service Representative*, Cablevision of Michigan, Kalamazoo, MI.
1985-1987: *Floor Clerk*, Pets Plus, Kalamazoo, MI.
1984:   *Housewares Stock Clerk*, Meijer, Inc., Kalamazoo, MI.

Values Statement
"I view myself as a loyal, responsible employee with a superior work ethic - The Montessori School
satisfies my creative side, and I strive each day to provide a unique and challenging learning
environment for my children. My work has been an excellent training ground in my ongoing
quest as a lifelong learner. I have come far since graduation and my communications and
interpersonal skills are so much sharper than they were only 5 years ago. My superiors have
commended my zeal, my reliability and conscientiousness, and my determination for excellence.
As I pursue new avenues for employment, I will carry these learning outcomes with me and the
self-esteem born from them."

60

Combination. *Randy Clair, location unknown*

A resume for a private school teacher. The quotation below the contact information expresses succinctly the person's teaching philosophy—of interest to school principals.

Colleen J. Smith

E-mail: cjs@ohiou.edu

Current Address	**Permanent Address**
1 North Lancaster Street	2188 Gibbs Road
Athens, Ohio 45701	Shade, Ohio 45776
(614) 592-0000	(614) 696-0000

OBJECTIVE: ELEMENTARY TEACHER

EDUCATION + HONORS

OHIO UNIVERSITY, Athens, Ohio - June 1997
Candidate for Bachelor of Science in Education • Minor in Science
Major GPA: 4.0 • Overall GPA: 3.47 • Dean's List • Kappa Delta Pi - national education honorary organization

CERTIFICATIONS

Certified in Science Programs "Project Learning Tree" and "Project Wild"
Certified in Community First-Aid and Child Abuse

FIELD EXPERIENCE

Teacher Assistant   9/95-6/96
THE PLAINS ELEMENTARY/OHIO UNIVERSITY PROFESSIONAL DEVELOPMENT PARTNERSHIP, The Plains, Ohio
One of 56 educational programs honored as Ohio's BEST (Building Excellent Schools Together) Practices in Education
- Completed over 600 hours hands-on experience in various classrooms
- Acquired valuable pedagogy theory and extensive classroom experience while completing junior level methods classes
- Gained experience working with special education students and teachers in inclusion classrooms
- Studied a curriculum incorporating Venture Capital Professional Development Model Initiatives, cooperative learning and action research

Multicultural Field Experience   12/95
SHADE ELEMENTARY SCHOOL, Shade, Ohio
- Observed classes in an Africentric/Multicultural Immersion Community Model School
- Interviewed students, teachers and administration to gain additional insight

ADDITIONAL RELATED EXPERIENCE

Child Care Assistant — OHIO UNIVERSITY CHILD DEVELOPMENT CENTER, Athens, Ohio   9/96-present
- Assisted teachers in providing care for children in a developmentally appropriate environment

Day Camp Counselor — YMCA OF GREATER SHADE, Shade, Ohio   6/96-present
- Coordinated weekly activities, games and art projects around the camp curriculum
- Monitored activities and facilities ensuring the safety of all children
- Recorded camper progress and implemented a positive reinforcement system

Day Care Teacher — RACINE CHILD CARE CENTER, Racine, Ohio   6/95-9/95
- Developed age appropriate activities for children in a preschool setting
- Monitored children with special needs and behavior handicaps

ACTIVITIES

Alpha Beta Gamma Sorority - Ohio University
- Pledge Educator on Executive Board — Prepared 50 new members for full-fledged membership
- Member at Large on Executive Board — Maintained effective communication between executive board and chapter members

61

Combination. *Melissa L. Kasler, Athens, Ohio*

The special font simulates characters written by an elementary school student badly in need of handwriting lessons and of learning the difference between upper- and lowercase letters.

SANDY SUE CLARK
1999 Wilmington Street
Wilmington, North Carolina 28000
(910) 555-0000

SUMMARY

Committed to quality in every task from personal interaction with co-workers and customers to any services provided to the company or customer.

Possess excellent interpersonal skills and have a strong commitment to customer service. Experienced in working with individuals of many backgrounds, cultures, and age groups.

Demonstrated ability as a supervisor with experience hiring, training, and motivating employees as well as conducting performance reviews.

Dependable and hard working employee.

SKILLS AND ABILITIES

Customer Service and Sales:
- Arrange and conduct tours of facilities. Provide information regarding company policies and procedures and answer questions.
- More than four years experience in retail sales and customer service through full-time positions during college.

Supervision:
- Directly supervised up to 15 employees including all responsibility for ongoing training and performance reviews.
- Interview applicants and conduct orientation for new employees.

Policy and Regulation Compliance:
- Ensure teachers are in compliance with company policies and state regulations include OSHA and health regulations as well as regulations relating to center's certification with childcare agencies.
- Conduct monthly team meetings. Prepare agenda and materials. Present new company business and/or policies and answer questions the group may have.

Computer Skills:
- Computer skills include word processing and basic desktop publishing on IBM compatible PCs.

EDUCATION AND TRAINING

UNIVERSITY OF NORTH CAROLINA AT WILMINGTON
Bachelor of Arts - Elementary Education   1991
North Carolina Teaching Certificate - K-6
Infant & Child CPR Certified

EMPLOYMENT HISTORY

BIG KID'S DAY CARE CENTER, Wilmington, NC   1992 - Present
Assistant Director
Head Teacher - Infants and Toddlers
Infant Teacher

62

Combination. *Sandy Adcox Saburn, Wilmington, North Carolina*

This applicant was trying to overcome the "babysitter" stigma that often accompanies the day care field. The writer therefore focused on skill areas rather than employment.

KERRY A. SMYTH

285 Main Street ♦ White Plains, NY 10598 ♦ (914) 555-5555

Elementary Education Diversified background in all phases of elementary education.

QUALIFICATION HIGHLIGHTS:
- BA in Education, with a concentration in Psychology; elementary teaching certification pending
- Firm, positive attitude; excellent rapport with faculty, administrators and students
- Skilled in selecting and adapting appropriate teaching materials for classroom presentation
- Deeply committed to high quality education for young children

PROFESSIONAL EXPERIENCE:
Curricula Development & Course Evaluation
- Development of "Celebration of Learning Through Dance" in collaboration with New York City Ballet
- Exceptional ability to quickly master new software and incorporate it into class instruction
- Develop and implement lesson plans in Math, Reading, and Social Studies
- Methods and procedures to monitor lesson effectiveness include:
  - Observation   • Test Taking   • One-on-One Interaction With Student

Classroom Presentation
- Successful and self-confident in classroom presentation and team teaching
- Teaching techniques include whole language approach and cooperative group activity
- Utilize reciprocal teaching strategy (read and comprehend content related text)

Parent Contact & Staff Relations
- Meet with parents at parent/staff meetings, inviting their input into all phases of program planning and generating a cooperative atmosphere
- Participate in staff and PTA meetings; address problem issues with children and community involvement
- Implement Parent/Teacher/Student journals to encourage and improve communication

EMPLOYMENT HISTORY:
Long-Term Substitute Teacher	Mount Pleasant Central Schools, Thornwood, NY	*1994-Present*
Student Teacher	Mount Pleasant Central Schools, Thornwood, NY	*1993*

EDUCATION:
Graduate Candidate, Education
Western Connecticut State University, Danbury CT   *(anticipated completion 1997)*

Bachelor of Science, Education/Psychology
Pace University, Pleasantville, NY   *(1993)*

COMPUTER SKILLS:
Microsoft Word / WordPerfect / Lotus 1-2-3 / Excel

PROFESSIONAL DEVELOPMENT SEMINARS:
In-Service Training Workshops in Reading, Writing and Mathematics

LICENSE/CERTIFICATION:
New York State Provisional Certification for Kindergarten through 6th Grade

63

Chronological. *Marian Kozlowski, Poughkeepsie, New York*

The challenge was that few jobs were available and the person did not meet requirements for full state certification as a substitute teacher. The task was to make every fact look good.

JANE HALE

39-11 Briarwood Lane • Marlboro, MA 01752
(508) 624-7349

OBJECTIVE	To obtain a position as an *Elementary School Teacher* in which a strong dedication to the total development of children and a high degree of enthusiasm can be fully utilized.
EXPERIENCE 9/90 to Present	Mary Finn School, Southboro, MA *First Grade Teacher*

- ✏ Participated in the design and development of a **Whole Language Reading** curriculum that included large and small group instruction. Participated in the development of assessment tools to evaluate Whole Language.
- ✏ Adapted the Whole Language Program to meet individual needs by using elements of a basal and/or a phonetic reading program.
- ✏ Implemented DMP (**Developmental Math Process**) which is a hands on approach to problem solving through the use of math manipulatives.
- ✏ Developed learning centers based on the needs of a heterogeneous class. Utilized a **thematic approach** to the curriculum.
- ✏ Have stressed an individual approach to learning by providing enrichment as well as modification based on a particular student's needs.
- ✏ Participated in organizing curriculum units including Chinese New Year, Ecology, and Weather.
- ✏ Fostered ongoing communication with parents through the use of a monthly newsletter detailing thematic units.
- ✏ Involved parent volunteers to assist the children in classroom enrichment activities such as the use of computers and numerous whole class projects.
- ✏ Contributing member of Building Based Support Team pilot program, a 3 year grant funded by the State Department of Education.

COLLEGE RELATED TEACHING ASSIGNMENTS

Fall 1989	Mary Finn School, Southboro, MA *First Grade--Student Teacher.*

- ✏ Developed teaching units on the seashore and trees, and utilized advanced teaching methods including Whole Language and math manipulatives. Developed and implemented learning centers.

Spring 1989	Warren School, Ashland, MA *Second Grade--Field Study II.*

- ✏ Developed plans for individual and group use on Time and Money.

Fall 1988	Framingham State College Nursery School, Framingham, MA *To Fulfill Requirements for Curriculum I.*

- ✏ Developed extensive observation and management skills.

Spring 1988	Lilja Elementary School, Natick, MA *First Grade--Field Study I; Teachers Aide*
EDUCATION	Framingham State College, Framingham, MA **B.S.,** Early Childhood Education. Minor: Psychology. 1990. Workshop: American Sign Language. Sponsored by Mary Finn School.

AWARDS AND ACHIEVEMENTS

Dorothea J. Kunde Memorial Award For Excellence In Teaching 1989-1990.
President's List, 1989-1990; **Dean's List,** 1988-1990.

64

Combination. *Steven Green, Northboro, Massachusetts*

Pencil-shaped bullets call attention to this innovative teacher's achievements as she looks for her second teaching position to implement her new Whole Language Reading curriculum.

BESS T. TEACHER

Box 123 ● Samson, New York
(201) 234-2344

PROFESSIONAL GOAL

As an Educator (Grades 1-8) my goal is to embrace the uniqueness, dignity, and worth of each individual and provide for instructional achievement conducive to the mental, physical, social and ethical growth of the student.

PROFESSIONAL EXPERIENCE

- Eight years' teaching experience in elementary grades working with at-risk, special needs, learning disabled, and multicultural students including limited-English proficient, second language learners.

- Planned and implemented team teaching program with rotations in Language Arts, Math, and Science; taught Language Arts using blend of phonics and whole language.

- Utilize an integrated, thematic curriculum with cooperative learning, peer tutoring, and cross-age tutoring to increase learning, cross-cultural understanding, and self-esteem. Emphasize an active, positive learning environment, high student expectations, and hands-on activities in a student-centered classroom.

- Experienced measurable successes with at-risk and "problem" students: through inventory and nurturing of child's gifts and employing classroom management techniques, improved on-task behavior, eliminated negative comments among peers, and reduced administrative involvement for disciplinary actions.

- Increased parent involvement through regular communications (minimum of one telephone call or note daily) and invitations to participate in classroom language arts activities and special events.

- Comments from principals: "promote[s] a positive awareness of multi-cultural diversity" ... "development of a positive school image and parental communication" ... "proactive management of classroom" ... "flexible, cooperative."

PROFESSIONAL SUMMARY -- Elementary teacher with the U.S. Department of Defense (DoDDS)

1st & 2nd Grades, Pizzolo Elementary School, Pizzolo, Italy	9/92-6/93
3rd Grade, Petersham Elementary School, Petersham, England	8/89-6/91
3rd Grade, Cappezzio Elementary School, Cappezzio, Italy	9/83-6/86
3rd Grade, Luthenhaggen Elementary School, Luthenhaggen, Germany	9/82-6/83

EDUCATION, CREDENTIALS

Elementary Teaching Credential, Grades 1-8 -- U.S. Department of Defense Schools
B.A. Degree, Liberal Arts -- University of Somewhere
Advanced Education Seminars and University Courses:
- Math & Science in the Elementary School
- Early Childhood Academy (classroom environment portfolio assessment, instructional strategies)
- Math Our Way (manipulatives)
- Teachers Studying Teaching (TST)
- Creative Writing

ACTIVITIES

Travel: United States, United Kingdom, Germany, Austria, Spain, Italy, Czechoslovakia, Holland
Interests: Theater, music, cooking, history, exploring life in all its delights and sharing it with my students!

References Upon Request

65

Combination. *Susan Britton Whitcomb, Fresno, California*

This teacher had gaps in her teaching because her husband moved a great deal in the military and she took time off to raise children. Her experience helps to offset these gaps.

KAREN SMITH
123 N. West
Modesto, CA 93456
(209) 234-2345

PROFESSION

Elementary Educator, Grades 2-5 -- highlights of 15-year career with Allied Unified School District include:

- Three years experience as Mentor Teacher.
- Five years as Master Teacher for University of California School of Education.
- Strengths in science and math; effective classroom management skills; excellent rapport with multi-cultural, LEP, special needs, and at-risk students.

EDUCATION, CREDENTIAL

Language Development Specialist Certificate
Multiple Subject Teaching Credential -- University of California
B.S., Education / Biology Minor -- University of Florida

PROFESSIONAL EXPERIENCE

ALLIED UNIFIED SCHOOL DISTRICT   1980-Present

Teacher, Grades 3 and 3/4 Combination -- Bush Elementary (1983-Present)
Certificated Math Tutor -- Reagan Elementary (1980-1983)
Summer School Teacher -- Clinton Demonstration School (1990)

- Create an engaging, positive learning environment featuring integrated curriculum, hands-on lessons, computer applications, and use of portfolios to document students' growth and talents.

- Structure whole group, small group, and individual instruction to accommodate the needs of different academic levels and learning styles.

- Apply cooperative learning and cross-age tutoring to increase learning, self-esteem, and cross-cultural understanding.

- Employ C-SIN and AIMS activities in science and math to develop students' critical thinking skills and improve overall comprehension.

- Utilize SDAIE, Natural Approach, Language Experience Approach, and Total Physical Response to overcome language barriers.

- Selected by principal to develop and implement special programs, such as Margaret Smith's MTA, TRIBES conflict resolution, and DBAE.

- Wrote and received community partnership mini-grant "Walk Through California."

CONTINUING EDUCATION -- Received training in and implemented the following:

Multi-Sensory Teaching Approach (MTA)   Tribes (self-esteem/conflict resolution)
C-SIN (CA Science Implementation Network)   True Colors
Lee Canter's Assertive Discipline   Math Camp
Lee Canter's Beyond Assertive Discipline   Grade 3 Math Replacement Project
DBAE (Discipline-Based Art Education)   Cooperative Learning

CO-CURRICULAR INVOLVEMENT

Served on District-wide Program Quality Review Team, Technology Team, Math Adoption Committee, and Science Adoption Committee.

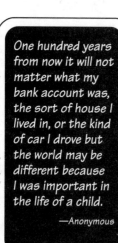

One hundred years from now it will not matter what my bank account was, the sort of house I lived in, or the kind of car I drove but the world may be different because I was important in the life of a child.

—Anonymous

66

Combination. *Susan Britton Whitcomb, Fresno, California*

A resume for an experienced teacher with a solid employment record with one district. Blank lines before and after sections and data clusters ensure adequate white space.

FELICIA R. SMITHERS

Current Address:	*Permanent Address:*
23455 S.W. Main Street	P.O. Box 705
Beaverton, Oregon 97005	Puma, Arizona 99546
(503) 432-9066	(907) 423-9088

Profile
Innovative school counselor with a well-rounded combination of experience, clinical knowledge and therapeutic skills.
- Highly self-motivated with ability to develop programs and procedures to meet objectives.
- Comfortable handling a high level of responsibility.
- Strong leadership and "focusing" skills; able to work cooperatively with others.
- Experienced working with children from diverse ethnic and economic backgrounds.

Education

M.A. Counseling Psychology / School Counseling (3.8 GPA) 1991
Portland State University, Portland, Oregon

B.S. Psychology (4.0 GPA) 1989
Southern Oregon State College, Ashland, Oregon

B.S. Elementary Education (3.75 GPA) 1988
Southern Oregon State College, Ashland, Oregon

Experience

School Counselor 1994-Present
Tigard School District, Tigard, Oregon
- Provide individual and group counseling.
- Consult with administrators, teachers and parents.
- Facilitate parenting groups and family counseling programs.

Intern 1992-1993
Lake Oswego School District, Lake Oswego, Oregon
- Facilitated individual and group counseling.
- Developed and implemented new group strategies.

Summer Youth Counselor 1989-1992
Kodiak Area Native Association, Kodiak, Alaska
- Provided counseling for Alaska native youth.
- Hired and supervised 14 students.
- Worked with outside agencies to develop employment opportunities for Alaskan youth.

Substitute Teacher 1991
Ashland School District, Ashland, Oregon
- Managed classroom and provided individual and group instruction.
- Adjusted and modified teaching style to facilitate effective learning.

Affiliations
Kappa Delta Pi Honor Society; Iota Omicron Chapter (Secretary)
Association for Supervision and Curriculum Development
Psi Chi National Honor Society

References Attached

67

Combination. *Pat Kendall, Aloha, Oregon*

Balanced format is used for the contact information. Education is strategically put near the top because of the degrees and high grade-point averages at two different institutions.

Suzanne P. Keating
22 Branford Street
Needham, MA 02192
(617) 444-9282

Objective	To obtain a position as a *Principal* utilizing demonstrated expertise as an educational leader and effective organizer.
Summary	• Demonstrated ability as an effective educational leader and manager. • Excellent knowledge and experience of the significant trends in education including Whole Language, Process Writing, Cooperative Learning, Learning Centers and the use of techniques promoted by the National Council of Teachers of Mathematics. • Outstanding parent, staff and student communication skills.

Experience
1992 to Present

DOVER ELEMENTARY SCHOOL, Dover, MA
Principal
• Effectively manage a school with almost 500 students in grades 1-5, and a professional staff of 40.

Curriculum Innovation
• Instituted quarterly curriculum updates to evaluate effectiveness of all programs.
• Developed new math curriculum to meet the recommendations of the National Teachers of Mathematics national agenda.
• Pioneered a multi-age classroom for first and second grade.
• Integrated a variety of disciplines including art/music/library and gym.
• Initiated the "Poetry Corner" to promote literature and poetry.
• Brought in enrichment programs including expanded use of computers.

Communication
• Created the concept of "The Principal's Coffee" to encourage greater community/parental participation in the school.
• Regularly publish a newsletter called "It's Elementary" to keep parents informed about school activities, events and general information.
• Developed good working relationships with the local news media and regularly issue press releases to assure positive and recurring coverage of the school.

Staff Development
• Hired a number of new staff including specialists.
• Conduct regularly scheduled performance reviews using the Skillful Teacher model.
• Work closely with new teachers to instill the confidence necessary to perform effectively.
• Use site based management principles to have teachers feel a part of the decision making process and take ownership for school results.
• Providing common planning time for staff to better coordinate curriculum.

School Organization
• Eliminated a punitive discipline program and replaced it with a conflict resolution approach that gives each student responsibility for their actions.
• Reorganized bus schedules to allow children more quality time while awaiting the beginning of the day and the time for dismissal.
• Revamped the PTO in an attempt to revitalize the program.

Plant Management
• Managed the process of installing a new $125,000 roof.
• Redefined performance standards for custodial staff.

68

Combination. *Steven Green, Northboro, Massachusetts*

Side subheadings in italic in the Experience section are useful categories for grouping the individual's many achievements in her current position. The bullets across two pages help to

Suzanne P. Keating Page Two

1985 to 1992 **MARLBORO PUBLIC SCHOOLS**, Marlboro, MA
Director - STEP Program
Head Teacher
First Grade & Fourth Grade Teacher

Administrative
- Organized and supervised teachers and students in an after school program.
- Member, Teacher Interview and Selection Committee.
- Organized and implemented Professional Development Program for staff.
- Successfully implemented Whole Language Program in first grade, developed method of evaluation and collected data for the assessment.
- Chairperson, School Based Support Team (SBST) Pilot Program. Wrote handbook entitled, "Helping Teachers Help Children".
- Designed parent survey focusing on language development in kindergarten for Chapter I grant.
- Designed and delivered science workshop for MESPA (Massachusetts Elementary Schools Principals Association).
- Developed effective relationship with local newspaper to publicize school events.
- Supervised Student Teachers.

Classroom
- Utilize activity-centered learning.
- Integrated Whole Language throughout curriculum.
- Implemented DMP (Developmental Math Process) which uses a hands-on-approach to problem solving and emphasize process in math.
- Organize cooperative groups in a heterogeneous self-contained class.

1975 to 1985 **FOXBORO PUBLIC SCHOOLS**, Foxboro, MA
Grade Leader - Third Grade
Kindergarten & Third Grade Teacher
- Successfully organized an intergenerational Thanksgiving Dinner involving students and senior citizens.
- Developed an integrated day curriculum using contracts (scheduled programs of classwork) to foster student independence.
- Member of Grant Writing Committee that acquired funding for the integration of arts in the curriculum.
- Created new curriculum units based on student interests including Poetry, Genealogy, Endangered Species, and Outer Space.
- Participated in organizing a Gifted Committee consisting of parents, teachers, and administrators. The systems first Gifted Program resulted from this effort. Approached by the Superintendent to accept the directorship of the program.

1970 to 1975 **NEW YORK CITY PUBLIC SCHOOLS**, Brooklyn, NY
First Grade Teacher, Bilingual
Kindergarten Teacher

Education
City University of New York, Queens College
M.S., Early Childhood Education. 1975
B.S., Early Childhood Education. 1970.

Worcester State College, Worcester, MA
Principal Certification Program. 1990.
C.A.G.S., Leadership and Educational Administration. 1991.

Other
- **Selected**, Steering Committee, Principals Center, Worcester, MA
- *Business Advisor* for Junior Achievement.
- **Appointed**, Board of Directors, Learning Experience School, Marlboro, MA.

unify this resume visually. The dates of employment show no gap and display steady progress from kindergarten teacher to school principal. Bold italic for the job positions makes them easy to see at a glance.

JOHN C. CAUSELAND

4 Savoy Court
Iowa City, Iowa 52246
(319) 777-3289

TEACHING EXPERIENCE

THE UNIVERSITY OF IOWA, Iowa City, IA
    Visiting Assistant Professor - Theater Department   1974 to Present
       Courses (undergraduate)
          Acting with Verse
          Acting I

MIDDLEBURY COLLEGE, BREAD LOAF SCHOOL OF ENGLISH, Middlebury, VT
    Professor of Theater - Summers   1965 to Present
       Courses (graduate)
          Actor's Perspective: Embodying the Text
          Introductory Acting
          Connections: Improvisation and Writing
       Honors
          Named 1975-76 Merino Professor of Literature

PRINCETON UNIVERSITY, Princeton, NJ
    Guest Director - Program in Theater and Dance   1963 to 1973
    Lecturer - Program in Theater and Dance   1963 to 1972
    Lecturer - Department of English   1962 to 1973
       Courses (undergraduate)
          Women in American Theater
          Modern Drama
          Introductory Acting
          The Processes of Theater
       Honors
          Profiled in Ken Macrorie's *Good Teachers Good Deeds* (Oxford University Press,
            1967) as one of twenty outstanding teachers in the United States and Great Britain.

WESTMINSTER CHOIR COLLEGE, Princeton, NJ
    Lecturer - Theater   1964 to 1971
       Courses (undergraduate)
          Improvisation and Movement for Singers
          Introductory Acting for Singers

RUTGERS UNIVERSITY, MASON GROSS SCHOOL OF THE ARTS, New Brunswick, NJ
    Graduate Teaching Assistant   1963
       Courses (undergraduate)
          Beginning Acting

NEW HAMPSHIRE SCHOOL SYSTEMS
    English and Drama Teacher   1956 to 1962
       Honors
          Pacesetter Award: Teacher of the Year, New Hampshire State Department of
            Education, 1961.
          Highest Teaching Award, New Hampshire Council for Better Schools, 1961.

69

Chronological. *Elizabeth J. Axnix, Iowa City, Iowa*

Prominence is given to the names of the prestigious institutions where this theater professor has taught or is teaching, rather than to the ranks or positions held at these institutions. Centered

JOHN C. CAUSELAND
Page Two

DIRECTING EXPERIENCE

Equity Theater
McCarter Theater, Princeton, New Jersey, Director's Laboratory
House of Bernarda Alba
Lorca, 1970
Theater of the Open Eye, New York City, New York
The Sixteen Appropriate Steps For Viewing Your Grandfather In An Open Coffin
Billy Aronson, 1969

University Theater

The Scarlet Letter	Carol Easton	The University of Iowa, 1976
	Ellen Laver	
The Emperor of the Moon	Aphra Behn	The University of Iowa, 1975
Sean, The Fool, The Devil	Ted Hughes	The University of Iowa, 1974
The Pregnant Pause	George Feydeau	Rider College, 1974
A Doll House	Henrik Ibsen	Princeton University, 1973
Rococo	Harry Kondoleon	Princeton University, 1971
Cloud Nine	Caryl Churchill	Princeton University, 1970
Measure for Measure	Wm Shakespeare	Princeton University, 1969
Miss Furr and Miss Skeene	Gertrude Stein	Bread Loaf, 1969
The Rover	Aphra Behn	Princeton University, 1968
Love's Labor's Lost	Wm Shakespeare	Princeton University, 1967
Vinegar Tom	Caryl Churchill	Princeton University, 1967
A Midsummer Night's Dream	Wm Shakespeare	Princeton University, 1966
Ethel and Julie: The Rosenbergs	Alec Baron	Princeton University, 1966
The Fifteen Minute Hamlet	Tom Stoppard	Princeton University, 1965
The Seagull	Anton Chekhov	Princeton University, 1964
Everyman	Anonymous	Princeton University, 1964
The Imaginary Invalid	Moliere	Princeton University, 1963
The Good Person of Setzuan	Bertolt Brecht	Princeton University, 1962
Aeneas In Flames	Billy Aronson	Princeton University, 1962
Play Without Words II	Samuel Beckett	Princeton University, 1961
The Bear	Anton Chekhov	Princeton University, 1961
On The Harmfulness of Tobacco	Anton Chekhov	Princeton University, 1961
No Trifling With Love	Alfred de Musset	Rutgers University, 1961
Killer's Head	Sam Shepard	Princeton University, 1960
Crocodiles (adapted: Pynchon's *V*)	Alan Mokler	Princeton University, 1960
Offending The Audience	Peter Handke	Bread Loaf, 1960

Edinburgh Festival Fringe, Scotland

Action	Sam Shepard	1965
Delearium	Billy Aronson	1965
Christopher Columbus	Michel deGhelderode	1964
Three Pieces By...	Gertrude Stein	1963

headings—all uppercase, underlined, and in italic—tie together this four-page curriculum vitae. The extensive list of plays, playwrights, places, and years is impressive. (At the Edinburgh Festival each August, Fringe events are not main events at main venues but

GUEST ARTIST ROLES

Role	Work/Playwright	Company
Regan	*King Lear*/Shakespeare	Bread Loaf, 1974
Various Roles	*Caucasian Chalk Circle*/Brecht	Bread Loaf, 1973
May	*Footfalls*/Beckett	Princeton, 1972 ·
Sonnerie	*Red Noses*/Barnes	Bread Loaf, 1971
Lady Macduff	*Macbeth*/Shakespeare	Bread Loaf, 1970
Hermione	*A Winter's Tale*/Shakespeare	Bread Loaf, 1969
Edward/Betty	*Cloud Nine*/Churchill	Bread Loaf, 1968
Joyce	*Top Girls*/Churchill	Princeton, 1968
Olivia	*Twelfth Night*/Shakespeare	Bread Loaf, 1967
Chorus leader	*Oedipus the King*/Sophocles	Princeton, 1966
Maggie	*American Days*/Poliakoff	Princeton, 1965
Varya	*The Cherry Orchard*/Chekhov	Bread Loaf, 1964
Amy	*The War Widow*/Perr	Princeton, 1963
Nina	*The Seagull*/Chekhov	Bread Loaf, 1962

RELATED THEATER ACTIVITIES

National Endowment for the Humanities Institute: Visiting Artist, 1976.

National Endowment for the Humanities Institute: Master Teacher of Acting, Bread Loaf School of English, Middlebury, Vermont, 1975.

Children's Theater of The University of Iowa: Founded, organized, produced, and directed, 1975.

National Endowment for the Humanities Institute: Visiting Fellow, led workshops and taught classes at high schools through the United States, 1972 to 1973.

The Acting Ensemble: Member of this Equity company which performs at Bread Loaf and whose members assist in course in literature, writing, and theater, 1968 to Present.

Princeton to Edinburgh Project: Founded, organized, produced, and directed productions which represented Princeton University at the Edinburgh Fringe Festival, 1963 to 1965.

BBC 2: Filmed and aired *Three Sisters Who Are Not Sisters,* 1963.

ARTS (Arts Recognition and Talent Search): Theater Adjudication Panel, National Level, 1963 to 1968.

Educational Testing Service: Theater Consultant, 1962 to 1969.

Children's Theater: Founded, organized, produced, and directed original theater pieces for children performed by high school students. These pieces toured the state of New Hampshire and were presented on New Hampshire educational television, 1957 to 1959.

smaller groups at peripheral sites to attract some of the attendees. "Beyond the Fringe" was a 1960s group with Dudley Moore that later became well known in Britain and the United States.) The equally impressive lists of Guest Artist Roles and Related Theater Activities

JOHN C. CAUSELAND
Page Four

PROFESSIONAL TRAINING

Acting and Directing	Joseph Cates, Robert Smith, Bill Enson
Improvisation	Bill Ashes, Steve Cayan
Dance and Movement	Adam Zeller, Eva Cahen
Voice	Joan Smooth
Set Design	Doug Fein

EDUCATION

Master of Arts degree in **English and Dramatic Arts**   1966
MIDDLEBURY COLLEGE
Middlebury, Vermont

Bachelor of Arts degree in **English** with Honors   1956
NOTRE DAME COLLEGE
Manchester, New Hampshire

sustain interest and help to display a high level of expertise and accomplishment throughout. By the time you get to the fourth page, the smaller amount of material is acceptable as a fitting conclusion to the first three substantial pages.

MICHAEL P. STEPHENS
3128 Lake Washington Road
Melbourne, FL 32934
(401) 752-0881
email: stephens@ucon.net

Objective: To secure a position as Director of Training with NexCorp.

TRAINING EXPERTISE

- Instructional System Design
- Training Section Management
- Course Development
- Training Program Management
- Technical Instructor
- Total Quality Management

CREDENTIALS

Training
- 15 years experience in training development with extensive knowledge and experience in Instructional System Design (ISD) and On the Job Training principles.
- 17 years experience as an Instructor.
- Specialized training including: Command Instructor Certification Program, Total Quality Management, Train the Trainer course, and Resident Instructor Skills Training Course.

Computer Skills
- Extensive knowledge and experience with Microsoft Word, PowerPoint, Excel and PerformPro document software.
- Limited knowledge and use of Dbase III and Microsoft Access database software.
- Skilled with electronic mail, internet programs, and html programming.

Professional Memberships
- Member, American Society for Training and Development.
- Member, Society for Technical Communications.

TRAINING ACHIEVEMENTS

United States Air Force - 1978 to Present

- Provided policy and guidance in development and implementation of organization training which included lectures, presentations, performance-demonstrations, and OJT sessions.
- Developed, coordinated, and facilitated table-top training sessions saving an estimated $45,000.00 per session.
- Restructured and refocused instructor certification program which reduced time to certify instructors from 30 days to one week.
- Revamped and streamlined training program using ISD concepts which reduced training time by 4 months and saved an estimated $21,250.00 per student per year.
- Rewrote 14 organizational instruction manuals and consolidated them into one operating instruction which saved approximately 45 man hours per year.
- Developed 1500 question master knowledge test bank which saved approximately 100 man hours per month in instructor research.

EDUCATION

Bachelor of Science Degree in Instructional Systems Design
University of Central Florida, Orlando, FL - GPA: 3.3

70

Combination. *Laura A. DeCarlo, Melbourne, Florida*

The challenge was using civilian language to fit 17 years of trainer experience in the military onto one page. The writer used scannable categories and chose top achievements.

Britain J. Walker

1108 Fox Run Drive • Chicago, Illinois 60606 • 555-757-0422

Highlights of Qualifications
- ✎ Master's degree in mathematics with major in statistics
- ✎ Specialties in statistics and actuarial science
- ✎ Subspecialties in calculus, algebra, and trigonometry
- ✎ Ten successful years of applied mathematics in actuarial applications
- ✎ Five years' experience as an effective corporate actuarial trainer
- ✎ Proven ability to communicate technical data and theory to non-technical people
- ✎ Outstanding management, analysis, and interpersonal skills; highly creative

Experience
Actuarial Supervisor • 1991-present
Polysystems of Chicago, Chicago, Illinois
- ✎ Trained coworkers and outside clients in CMO modeling techniques
- ✎ Headed team of six on CMO Project, reporting directly to vice president
- ✎ Supervised writing, editing, and production of CMO software instruction manual

Actuarial Assistant • 1986-1991
Capital Investments, Inc., St. Louis, Missouri
- ✎ Trained actuarial students, utilizing Tillinghast software

Graduate Math Teaching Assistant & Tutor for Athletic Department • 1983-1986
University of Nebraska, Lincoln, Nebraska

Education
- ✎ Master of Arts and Teaching in Mathematics
  University of Nebraska at Lincoln • GPA 3.27
  Major: Statistics • Minor: Educational Psychology

- ✎ Bachelor of Fine Art
  University of Nebraska at Lincoln • GPA 3.25
  Teaching Certification in Math an Art

- ✎ Actuarial Exams Passed: 100, 110, 120, 130, 135, 140 (110 hours)

Affiliations and Memberships
- ✎ Pi Mu Alpha, Math Honorary Fraternity
- ✎ Chicago Actuarial Association
- ✎ Business Professional Association
- ✎ Art Institute
- ✎ Goodman Theatre

71

Combination. *Barbie Dallmann, Charleston, West Virginia*

Notice a number of distinctive features: a thin page border, an extra thick thick-thin line in the contact information, partial lines after bold italic headings, and two kinds of bullets.

Charles Parker

2543 Elm Street
Cabrillo, CA 93157

Tel: (318) 579-9876

Objective	**Hospitality Management Trainer**

Summary
- *Front Desk Manager* and *Shift Supervisor* for 8 years with the Sunshine Hotel.
- High volume hotel Sales Agent responsible for major commercial and business accounts.
- Extensive experience in training staff in most effective and efficient use of the *Zodiac Reservation System*, thereby achieving maximum productivity.
- Extensive *classroom experience* with Cabrillo Unified School District, teaching students to score highly on ASAT tests.
- Proven record in training highly effective hotel managers and staff
- Total fluency in English and Spanish - written and spoken.

Performance Profile
- **Strong leadership qualities**, with a winning attitude that positively affects others.
- **Organized and efficient**, resourceful, bottom-line oriented, with a strong drive to excel.
- **Performs confidently** and effectively under pressure, and thrives on challenge.
- **Excellent Communicator**, a good listener and a valued contributor - English & Spanish.
- **Quick to analyze** and solve problems; investigative, logical and clear thinking.
- **Skilled with people**, enthusiastic, sense of humor, motivational, tactfully direct.
- **Visionary and goal oriented**; inspires trust, cooperation and teamwork

Key Skills

Leadership	Communications	Training & Development	Flexibility
Organization	Team Building	*Zodiac Computer System*	Creativity
Management	Sales/Marketing	Bilingual - English/Spanish	Public Speaking

Previous Professional Experience

Front Desk Manager	Sunshine Hotel	Cabrillo, CA
Sales Agent	Beach Front Hotel	Cabrillo, CA
Special Education Technician	Cabrillo School Dist.	Cabrillo, CA
Pre-School Teachers' Assistant	Johnson Child Dev. Center	Cabrillo, CA
Reading Tutor	West End Community Center	Cabrillo, CA

Achievements
- Supervised shifts and Front Desk employees, handling customer complaints, finding best solutions to problems, and creating friendly atmosphere and long term customer relations.
- Generated new accounts through convincing telemarketing techniques and emphasis on features and benefits, achieving outstanding results in increased business.
- Trained numerous Front Desk employees in effective use of the *Zodiac Reservation System*, resulting in excellent level of staff competence and expertise.
- Trained hotel personnel in marketing techniques, providing substantial increase in repeat business.
- Supervised employees, emphasizing friendliness and efficiency, resulting in exceptional level of customer satisfaction and increased hotel profitability.
- Instructed hotel staff in conversion from micro computers to upgraded hotel registration computer system, resulting in improved level of customer service and staff productivity.

Education

Peterborough High School	General Studies	Graduated	1985
Northern State College	1) Administration of Justice (Emphasis on Education)	To Graduate	1995
	2) Law Enforcement	Certificate	1995
	3) Corrections	Certificate	1995

"Every age needs men who will redeem the time by living with a vision of things that are to be." - Adlai Stevenson

72

Combination. *David Newbold, location unknown*

A well-designed resume integrated with decorative paper. The drop cap in the contact information is unusual but successful, as is the famous quotation at the end of the resume.

Graduating/Graduated Student

Resumes at a Glance

KIMBERLY J. BROWN
40-A Washington Avenue • Lodi, New Jersey 00000
(555) 555-5555

CAREER OBJECTIVE:

Seeking a position as a Physical Educator, Health Instructor and/or Coach that will utilize strong academic credentials and hands-on experience.

PROFILE SUMMARY:

AN EXPERIENCED AND DEDICATED INDIVIDUAL WITH STRONG INTERPERSONAL SKILLS AND THE ABILITY TO INTERACT EFFECTIVELY WITH STUDENTS WITH VARIOUS DISABILITIES. EXCELLENT MOTIVATIONAL AND COACHING SKILLS. ABILITY TO DEVISE AND IMPLEMENT LESSON PLANS TO ENSURE PEAK LEVELS OF EDUCATION. EASILY DEVELOPS A POSITIVE RAPPORT WITH STUDENTS.

ACADEMIC CREDENTIALS:

MASTERS OF EDUCATION: Adapted Physical Education (1996)
University of Virginia • Charlottesville, Virginia
Federal Fellowship from Office of Special Education

BACHELOR OF SCIENCE: Physical Education and Health (1994)
George Mason University • Fairfax, Virginia
Dean's List • Full Athletic Basketball Scholarship
Athletic Directors Honor Roll • Colonial Athletic Association Scholar Athlete Award

New Jersey Teacher's Certification (K-12) • Virginia Teacher's Certificate (K-12)

PROFESSIONAL EXPERIENCE:

GEORGE MASON UNIVERSITY, Fairfax, VA   **Assistant Basketball Coach, 1996 - Present**
- Travel throughout the country as the main recruiter for a 15 member NCAA Division I women's team.
- Implement drills to emphasize all aspects of the game.
- Serve as summer camp organizer and planner.
  - *Led team to a 21-11 record.*
  - *Top contenders for C.A.A. Championship; competed in the finals.*

BROADUS WOOD ELEMENTARY SCHOOL, Earlysville, VA   **Adapted Physical Educator, 1994 - 1995**
- Served as a part time instructor for regular physical education and adapted physical education classes, grades K-5.
- Implemented and personalized programs for students with a variety of serious health impairments.
- Served as an active member of an interdisciplinary team.
  - *Coached T-ball team which included 3 students with disabilities; modified rules and obtained approval from Commissioner.*
  - *Successfully taught a child with cerebral palsy to ride a modified bicycle.*
  - *Evaluated 2 girls with mental retardation and made recommendations for day camp placement.*

OLDE CREEK ELEMENTARY, Fairfax, VA   **Student Teacher, 3/94 - 5/94**
ROBERT FROST INTERMEDIATE SCHOOL, Fairfax, VA   **Student Teacher, 1/94 - 2/94**

PROFESSIONAL AFFILIATIONS:

American Alliance for Health, Physical Education, Recreation and Dance
Virginia Alliance for Health, Physical, Education, Recreation and Dance
Women's Basketball Coaches Association

73

Combination. *Alesia Benedict, Rochelle Park, New Jersey*

The master's degree in Education was recent, so the writer centered on the page the Academic Credentials section "for maximum effect." The border is the "final visual touch."

Tommy Therapy
1999 Therapy Lane
Recreationland, VA 55555
(910) 000-5555

PROFILE

Goal: Therapeutic Recreation Position

From volunteer and field work have gained exposure to all facets of the field of therapeutic recreation in long-term, community, and rehabilitation settings. Dedicated professional with strong desire to learn and build skills.

Experienced assisting individuals from many backgrounds, of all age groups, and of varying educational levels through teaching, coaching, and volunteer activities.

EDUCATION

University of Therapy at Virginia
Bachelor of Art in Parks & Recreation Management
Concentration in Therapeutic Recreation, December 1996

Recreation Therapy Community College
Bachelor of Art Degree in Physical Education, Minor in History, 1988

Combat Lifesaver Certified

PIC [Protective Intervention Course] Training

RELEVANT EXPERIENCE

Therapy Related Medical Hospital   Summer 1996 - Present
Shadowed therapeutic recreation and other professionals in assessment, treatment planning, treatment, and discharge planning in an inpatient state-of-the-art facility. Knowledge of Critical Pathways methodology.

Holiday Haven Healthcare Center   Spring 1995 - 1996
Observed interdisciplinary team with activities and outings. Awarded responsibility of making patient assessments, planning activities, and participating in community outings. In addition, completed relevant paperwork and assisted in preparation for state inspections.

Special Olympics Coach, Virginia Middle School   Spring 1996
Worked with autistic students both individually and in small groups helping them prepare for Special Olympics competition.

Special Projects   Spring & Summer 1996
Conducted thorough, in-depth study and analysis of therapeutic recreation's history and its current philosophy and practices. Developed a written and oral presentation delivered to faculty. Worked closely with two other students to develop a working program of therapeutic horseback riding. Interviewed professionals involved in this area of treatment from across the country and developed a proposal which is currently being implemented.

74

Combination. *Sandy Adcox Saburn, Wilmington, North Carolina*

A strong Profile gives this recent graduate an edge and the start of a readable resume. Evident throughout are firsthand experience and a drive to succeed in the chosen field.

Tommy Therapy
Page Two

101st Airborne, United States Army	**1991 - 1994**

Teacher, Virginia State Schools   **1990 - 1991**
Led physical education, health education, and weight training classes for students in grades 9-12. Assisted in coaching boys and girls sports teams.

Teacher, Southeastern County Schools   **1989 - 1990**
Taught physical education to more than 1200 students in three elementary schools in the county. Developed lesson plans to meet the needs of each class and in keeping with each school's goals and priorities. Coached sports teams.

Virginian Parks Association   **1988 - 1989**
Planned and led recreation activities for the community. Participated in the maintenance and improvement of facilities.

ACTIVITIES

Virginian Therapeutic Recreation Annual Conference
Committee Member, 1997
Participant, 1996

Community Involvement
In conjunction with the Recreation Majors Club, participated in community service activities including United Way's Woodlot project, Adopt-A-Highway, and other programs.

International Travel
Traveled throughout Europe, Canada, Africa, Korea, Somalia, Haiti, and the United States. Speak Spanish on a basic level; read Korean minimally.

Member of American Therapeutic Recreation Association (ATRA) and Virginia Parks & Recreation Society

COMPUTER SKILLS

Rec-Ware, WordPerfect, Excel, DOS, and the Internet

REFERENCES

Provided upon request

The thin-thick-thin horizontal lines after the contact information appear again as part of the header on page 2. Education is put near the top of the first page because the person has *two* bachelor's degrees. Exceptional military service stands out at the top of page 2.

PAUL A. ROBERTS

Telephone:
(555) 555-5555
E-mail: rober@mail.OIT.OSSHE.EDU

Oregon Institute of Technology
P.O. Box 0000
Klamath Falls, OR 97601

Laser Systems • *Visual Imagery* • *Interferometry* • *Holography* • *Electronics*

Fiber Optic Sensor & Communication Systems • *Audio-Engineering* • *Computer Optic Interfacing*

PROFILE

- Imaginative, curious, and creative Laser Optical Engineering Technology student with particular interests in special effects, visual imagery, and virtual reality
- Background as musician and performer, with recording studio equipment experience
- Additional skills include electronics, mechanics, creative and technical writing, and computers
- Hands-on experience designing real time fingerprint scanner using pulsed laser holography
- Built optical computer using lasers capable of addition, subtraction, multiplication and division
- Senior project in process involving Virtual Reality
- Hobbies include audio production, pyrotechnics, laser light show production.

EDUCATION

OREGON INSTITUTE OF TECHNOLOGY, Klamath Falls, OR
Laser Optical Engineering Technology Program.
  Bachelor of Engineering Technology Degree expected 1997

  Physics and mathematics used in studies include Differential and Integral Calculus,
Differential Equation Solving, Fourier and LaPlace analysis, Classical and Quantum Physics, Quantum
Electro-dynamics, Tenser Physics, Spinner Theory, Basic Chemistry (as applied to Laser Engineering)

TECHNICAL SKILLS

Trained and experienced in, design, setup & alignment, information gathering, troubleshooting and
analysis, safety procedures, and physics of many types of **Laser Systems**, including:
• **Helium-Neon** • **Argon** • **CO_2** • **Neodymium Yag** • **Dye pumped laser** • **Semi-conductor solid state**
Application systems include, but are not limited to:
- **Interferometry**
- **Fiber Optic Systems**
- **Optical and IR Detection Systems**
- **Holographic Systems**
- **Laser Projection Systems**
- **Optical Component Testing**

COMPUTER SKILLS

Hands on experience with PC and Macintosh. Experience coding RS232 and IEEE488 interface.
Qualified in the use of leading edge information technologies for data acquisition and analysis, numerical
problem solving, 3-D graphic design, animation, and presentations. Software includes spreadsheets, databases,
word processors, mathematics software, CAD, CAM, Windows, DOS. Proficient in Borland c+ and basic
programming, and LabView and Igor (Mac).

75

Functional. *Linsey Levine, Chappaqua, New York*

This resume was written for a student applying for an internship with Walt Disney Imagineering.
Partial horizontal lines point to the section headings and help them stand out.

LARRY BROZART
15 Scott Avenue ♦ Ames, Iowa 50014 ♦ (515) 555-2664

- Fine Arts Student seeking an internship involving versatile visual and graphic design skills. Demonstrated leadership in organizations and projects requiring visual planning, development, and display within strict budgetary and time restraints.

- Familiar with two- and three-dimensional media, including computer-aided art and design. Learning Photoshop, Adobe Illustrator, Pagemaker, and Auto CAD software applications, with emphasis on concept development and problem solving.

- Solid foundation in drawing, painting, illustration, color concepts, art history, and sources of visual design.

EDUCATION

<u>Bachelor of Fine Arts Degree Program</u> *(Current status: Senior)*
Iowa State University, Ames, Iowa
- Member, Delta Tau Delta Fraternity

KEY DESIGN PROJECTS:

<u>1995 Veishea Co-Chair</u> *(largest student run organization in the country)*
- Worked on a 3-person design team. Organized work crews and delegated assignments. Participated in all design and construction phases of a 50' x 16' x 15' float. Purchased supplies and solicited business sponsorships to cover costs.
- Raised money to offset float construction costs totaling $14,000.

<u>1994 Homecoming Committee Co-Chair</u>
- Designed and built a 40' x 20' x 15' lawn display for homecoming.
- Purchased supplies and solicited business sponsorships to cover costs.
- Raised money to offset lawn display costs totaling $3,500.

EXPERIENCE

Marketing Research, Champaign-Urbana IL area, Summer 1995
Semi-Trailer Repair/Inspection, Summer 1995
Equipment/Car Maintenance, 1993
Office Worker/Computer Operator, 1992-1993

References Available Upon Request

76

Combination. *John Suarez, location unknown*

Shading, graphics, and unusual font selection make this resume visually strong and unique. The writer emphasized teamwork and design skills in Key Design Projects under Education.

Kristiane G. Kristophe

309 West Candlestyck #129 ◆ Kalamazoo MI 49001 ◆ 555-000-2222

SELF-IMAGE ◆ COMMUNICATION ◆ CUSTOMER RELATIONS ◆ BUSINESS DEVELOPMENT

Current Objective

Entry-level Sales or Public Relations involving international travel.

Strengths

- Friendly, outgoing, charismatic; easily adapts to new environments and changing priorities.
- Ability to learn new procedures and material quickly as demonstrated by volunteer experience; superior memory and attention to detail.
- Career-committed with outstanding *"people skills;"* articulate and professional; qualified for customer interaction; demonstrated drive and skills needed for successful progression in field.
- *Multilingual*; speak/write fluent Polish; studied German 4 years; lived in Japan.

Summary of Experience and Accomplishments

UNIQUE OPPORTUNITIES IN DOMESTIC AND FOREIGN ENVIRONMENTS:

- 1995-1996. **Student/English Major**: Western Michigan University, Kalamazoo, Michigan.
- 1995. **Graduate**: Dearborn High School, Dearborn, MI. Honorable Mention: *Who's Who In American Students*, Grade Point Average: 3.65.
- 1994-1995. **Model**: John Robert Powers Modeling School & Agency, Detroit, MI. Trained in: *Etiquette, Public Relations, Personal Conduct, and Self-Image.*
- 1994-1995. **Videographer**: Back Porch Video Music Show, Dearborn, MI. Served as: *Floor Manager, Announcer, Assistant Script Editor.*
- 1994. **Volunteer Editor/Translator**: RFM Radio, Krakow, Poland. Responsibilities included: *computer-related translating and editing of news broadcasts.*
- 1993. **Exchange Student**: Nara, Japan. Lived with host family for 6 weeks; learned Japanese culture from a family perspective.

College-related Work History

- 1996. **Waitress**: Paid 100% of college expenses through part-time employment in area restaurants and nightclubs. Demonstrate excellent team skills and provide superior service through enthusiastic interaction - recognizing always the importance of a sense of humor.

Values Statement

In addition to my experiences in area dining establishments - *where I have learned the importance of a positive mental attitude as it relates to customer service and satisfaction* - my exposure abroad has instilled in me: self confidence, independence, and heightened self-reliance. I view my life experiences as *Seminars-in-Learning*. I am thankful that I have been afforded these opportunities, therefore, I strive for excellence in all tasks and I perform my duties with professionalism and diplomacy. My many achievements, coupled with a solid work ethic, will allow me to continue as a forward thinker and team player with a strong commitment to my customers and the organizations I work for.

References

Excellent references will be forwarded upon request.

Combination. *Randy Clair, location unknown*

Bold double-underlining of the person's name in the contact information and of the section headings is the key visual feature in this resume for an entry-level public relations worker.

PHILIP M. MORRIS

1038 E. Wedgemere Circle ♦ The Woodlands, Texas 77381 ♦ (713) 277-6300

PROFILE: Highly motivated professional offering a **Bachelor of Arts in Business Administration** with a specialization in **Environmental Studies** and two years experience in sales and sales management, marketing and environmental assessment work. Outstanding presentation, negotiation and public speaking qualifications.

EDUCATION: Baylor University
Waco, Texas
B.A., Business Administration 1995
Specialization in Environmental Studies

COMPUTER SKILLS:
- ★ MS Word
- ★ Excel 5.0
- ★ File Maker Pro

COLLEGE-RELATED WORK EXPERIENCE:

♦ Conducted Phase 1 site assessment for Baylor's new school library involving extensive interaction with the EPA, federal and state agencies, consumer groups, water municipalities and local city officials. Completed title search, documented all findings and presented report to Board of Regents.

♦ Participated in epidemiological study investigating probable link between electromagnetic fields from high tension wires and increased rates of cancer in City of West Texas. Interviewed victims' families and physicians, researched medical records and compiled all statistical and research data.

PROFESSIONAL EXPERIENCE:

EQUINOX INTERNATIONAL, Austin, Texas   1995 - Present
Director

Recruited as an Independent Representative for this multi-level sales organization marketing water and air filtration systems and other home care products through extensive cold calling and networking strategies. Enrolled in intensive sales training and development workshops on recruitment, networking, presentation, leadership training and building a successful sales organization.

- Recruited and developed a 40-man sales force generating over $25,000 a month.
- Promoted from Independent Representative to Manager, Supervisor and finally Director within a 60 day period.
- Chosen to establish McAllen branch office and recruit sales force while managing branch office in Austin.
- Awarded "Top Manager, Group Sales Volume" for Dallas office January, 1996

AIR TOUCH PAGING, Fort Worth, Texas   1995
Sales Associate

Sold/Marketed pagers, voice mail and other wireless communication products to local businesses throughout the Dallas/Fort Worth Metroplex. Directed entire selling cycle, from initial client consultation and needs assessment through proposal presentation, price negotiation and sales closing.

- Consistently achieved sales quota each month.
- Secured account of a large dispatch and delivery services company generating over $37,000 in sales revenue.

78

Combination. *Cheryl Ann Harland, The Woodlands, Texas*

This college graduate without environmental experience wanted a position in the Environmental Industry. The writer played up transferable skills. Note the different bullets.

John Doe

Permanent Address

123 Anywhere Court
Montgomery Alabama
36117
Telephone (205)555-9466

Career Objective

Immediate :	An entry level Programmer / Analyst position
Long term :	Progression to System Annalist responsible for creation and maintenance of information systems.
Education ;	Auburn University , Auburn Alabama Bachelor of Science in Business Administration Major : Management Information Systems G.P.A. in major - 2.75 / 4.0 Date Graduated March 19 , 1993
M.I.S. Classes :	Analysis and Design of Computer - based Systems Telecommunications Management Information Resource Management Survey of Current Technologies in M.I.S. Business Computer Applications
Experience :	Installed hardware and software on P. C.-compatible computers ; am familiar with several Word Processors ,Database programs , CASE tools , COBOL , and Windows. Group leader for three project teams.

79

Combination (Before). *Provided by Don Orlando, Montgomery, Alabama*

A student's stab at resume writing. Evident weaknesses are extra character spaces, a misspelling in the long-term objective, and a lack of development throughout.

John Doe

123 Anywhere Court
Montgomery, Alabama 36117   ℘ [205] 555-5566

Objective:	To add to the profitability of XYZ Manufacturing Company by improving or designing customers' computer systems and offering topnotch training for their employees.
Strengths:	◆ The ability to *listen* ◆ Natural grasp of how information is organized and processes work ◆ Knack for turning irate consumers into understanding clients
Education:	Central University, Central, Alabama
degree	Bachelor of Science in Business Administration (Management Information Systems) – 1993
courses	◆ Analysis and Design of Computer-Based Systems ◆ Telecommunications Management ◆ Information Resource Management ◆ Survey of Current Management Information Systems Technologies ◆ Business Computer Applications
Experience:	◆ Installed variety of PC hardware and software. ◆ Convinced businessman to hire me. Reworked his computer system. In only three months, updated his inventory control by entering 10,000 records in my spare time. ◆ Analyzed independent company, found key problems, designed solutions and persuaded tough audience to approve my plan. ◆ Led a team of four to complete 10-week software project despite tight schedule. Turned general guidelines into specific solutions that worked.
Special Qualifications:	◆ Know DOS 6.0, Windows, BASIC, COBOL, C, word processing, data base and CASE ◆ Widely traveled in European Economic Community countries ◆ Fluent in French; speak Spanish ◆ Hands-on experience with mainframes, VAX, PCs and Ethernet

80

Combination (After). *Don Orlando, Montgomery, Alabama*

The resume after development. The resume, accompanied by a cover letter and followed up within 24 hours by a thank-you note, helped the student acquire a hard-to-get job.

JEFFREY D. ACTOR
(000) 555-1234   *1234 Any Street   •   Anytown, State 12345*

OBJECTIVE
A full time position in TV that will offer opportunities to develop well-rounded knowledge in all aspects of television production, augmenting my education and experience in broadcasting.

PROFILE
- Excellent **on-camera and behind-camera experience**
- Hands-on training and operation of **video cameras, video editing** equipment, sound equipment and lighting
- **Radio announcer** for 4 years
- Professional background in live theatre including **writing, directing, performing,** set construction and lighting
- Highly professional; work well under pressure
- Strong communication skills

PROFESSIONAL EXPERIENCE

Host, *TV Show* (May 1993-Present)
LOCAL CABLEVISION, Anytown, State
Research and write material for one-hour live production. Interview a wide variety of guests on camera and elicit audience participation. Requires ability to control flow of conversation and "think on my feet."

Announcer (October xxxx-August xxxx)
AUDIO READER, Anytown, State
Provided both live and taped announcing at radio station for the visually impaired. Ran sound board and monitored taped material.

Actor (Summer xxxx)
THE FARM PLAYERS, Resort Area, State
Performed 3 shows weekly in melodramas, playing different role in each play. Wrote radio advertising promoting shows.

Carpenter/Properties Assistant (May xxxx-May xxxx)
UNIVERSITY THEATRE, University of State, Anytown
Built scenery for all University Theatre productions, as well as purchasing and creating stage props.

ADDITIONAL EXPERIENCE

Sales Associate (xxxx-Present)
SPORTSWEAR STORE, Anytown, State

EDUCATION

B.G.S. Theater and Film (May xxxx), *University of State*, Anytown
- Responsible for *100*% of college finances
- Performed in 30 productions, directed 10
- Author of play chosen for production at Inge Theatre...directed and produced play

81

Combination. *Linda Morton, Lawrence, Kansas*

A pair of thin-thick lines encloses the contact information, making it easy to spot. Distinctive "reel" bullets call attention thematically to items in the Profile and Education section.

Gavin D. Derrick

154 Hawthorne Drive #120   Moscow, ID 83843   (208) 555-5555

OBJECTIVE

To obtain a full-time position in Development with the ABC Bread Company of Dalton, Montana.

SKILLS AND ABILITIES

MANAGEMENT

- ▸ <u>Experienced</u> in supervision of employees. <u>Served</u> as training supervisor.
- ▸ <u>Coordinated</u> and <u>accompanied</u> 10-15 newsboys on cold-call selling trips to neighboring communities to initiate new sub-scriptions.
- ▸ <u>Responsible</u> for closing of the tills and daily reports.
- ▸ <u>Performed</u> closing procedures, making sure all security measures were followed.

CUSTOMER RELATIONS

- ▸ <u>Excellent</u> communication and people skills.
- ▸ <u>Thorough</u> understanding of "needs satisfaction" and other selling techniques.
- ▸ <u>Adept</u> at handling customer complaints; able to defuse the most complicated of situations.

PERSONAL

- ▸ Enthusiastic, energetic and goal-oriented.
- ▸ Works well on individual and team projects.
- ▸ Enjoys challenging tasks; quick learner.

EDUCATION

UNIVERSITY OF ULSTER, Jordanstown, N. Ireland
BACHELOR OF ARTS - HONORS (1993)

UNIVERSITY OF IDAHO, Moscow, ID
Exchange Student (1991-1992)

EMPLOYMENT HISTORY

1993 - Present   CAMBRIDGE MORNING TRIBUNE, Moscow, Idaho
ASSISTANT DISTRICT MANAGER

1992 - 1993   GENERAL'S FRIED CHICKEN, Ballyhackamore, Belfast, N. Ireland
1989 - 1991   **TRAINING SUPERVISOR/ NIGHT AUDITOR/ COUNTER SERVICE/ COOK**

1986 - 1989   RON'S FOODS - BAKERY DEPT., Bloomfield, Belfast, N. Ireland
FOOD PREPARATIONS/ BAKER/ COUNTER SERVICE/ NIGHT CLOSE

References Furnished Upon Request

82

Combination. *Kathlene Y. McNamee, Butte, Montana*

Skills and abilities are grouped according to three categories (management, customer relations, and personal). Key words are underlined. The original was on decorative paper.

CARL P. MORGAN

7644 McIntyre Way
Saginaw, MI 48602
(517) 555-2591

PERSONAL SUMMARY

- Motivated self-starter
- Flexible and adaptable
- Enjoy interacting with others
- Eager to learn

EDUCATION

BAKER COLLEGE OF BUSINESS • Flint, MI   *Degree Anticipated:* 1998
Pursuing **Bachelor of Business Administration**
Major: Marketing

EMPLOYMENT HISTORY

HEATHER'S HERBS & MORE • Flint, MI   1992-Present
Inventory Control
- Monitor inventory of several hundred products including dried herbs, potpourri, dry food mixes and related supplies.
- Based on visual assessment and experience, maintain stock levels to support six retail outlets across the state.
- Rotate stock to ensure freshness of all products.
- Perform shipping and receiving duties; fill and deliver orders to retail outlets as instructed.

ABC WAREHOUSE • Flint, MI   1990-1992
Receiving Clerk
- Maintained inventory of incoming merchandise via company and vendor trucks.
- Coordinated return of damaged merchandise.
- Loaded merchandise into customer vehicles.

BEST LAWN CARE • Flint, MI   1989-1990
Landscaper
- Performed general landscaping of clients' lawns.

COMPUTER SKILLS

- ✓ Windows
- ✓ Microsoft Word
- ✓ Lotus 1-2-3
- ✓ Microsoft Excel

COMMUNITY INVOLVEMENT

Volunteer as basketball and baseball coach at Genesee Recreation Little League.
Represented employer as participant in Operation Brush-up.

References available on request.

83

Combination. *Janet L. Beckstrom, Flint, Michigan*

A horizontal line under the person's name and under each section heading makes it easy to spot the resume's sections at a glance. Three kinds of bullets add variety to the lists.

JAMES F. LEWIS ▪ 422 Clayborne Avenue ▪ Walker MI 49544 ▪ 444-777-0044

- Master of Science, *Physical Therapy*, Grand Valley State University - April 1996.
- Bachelor of Science, *Health Science*, Grand Valley State University - April 1994.
  Achievements: Dean's List: G.P.A. 3.65 3 years: as Junior, Senior, 1st year Master studies.

Professional Objective: Position as Physical Therapist.

✓ **SUMMARY OF QUALIFICATIONS**

Educated, articulate concerned professional with hands-on experience and knowledge in providing rehabilitative and health-related services to patients in the areas of *orthopedic, neurologic, geriatric, and acute care.*
Excellent foundation and learning ground as Physical Therapist Technician and Student Intern. Proven effectiveness in developing and implementing treatment plans consistent with the needs and resources of individuals and families.

✓ **CAREER-RELATED STRENGTHS**

Compassionate, good listener and very supportive; excellent people skills: experienced and effective in maintaining excellent rapport with patients; ability to work with patients and professionals from a variety of backgrounds and disciplines.

✓ **PERSONAL PROFILE**

Outstanding communication skills; proficiently utilizes interpersonal skills in relating to others; ability to effectively handle difficult situations by negotiating, developing, and implementing both short- and long-term solutions.
Exceptional management skills; ability to coordinate multifaceted activities within an unsupervised environment; effective problem solver and decision maker; excellent planning and organization skills; detail oriented; prepares timely charting and patient reporting for accurate assessment of progress; solid understanding of P.T. processes and procedures.

✓ **RELEVANT EXPERIENCE**

Physical Therapist Technician:

1992-Pres.	• Holland Community Hospital, Holland, MI.
1991-1992.	• Mid Michigan Regional Medical Center, Midland, MI.
1991.	• Holmes Regional Medical Center, Melbourne, FL.

▪ **Related Accomplishments:**

<u>As Physical Therapist Technician</u>: primary responsibilities include providing individualized in-patient care for orthopedic and neurologic patients; monitoring and balancing patient activities; preparing and assisting with exercise and gait training techniques; assisting in debridement and dressing changes in the Hydrotherapy Unit; providing in-patient treatment of orthopedic patients; scheduling, filing, and recordkeeping. Other responsibilities include providing exercise programs for in-patient/out-patient populations; and participating in treatments for geriatric patients at local nursing homes.

Student Intern:

10/95-12/95.	• Lakeland Regional Medical Center, St. Joseph, MI.
08/95-10/95.	• Saginaw General Hospital - North, Saginaw, MI.
01/95-02/95.	• William Beaumont Hospital, Royal Oak, MI.
05/94-06/94.	• Hurley Medical Center, Flint, MI.

▪ **Related Accomplishments:**

<u>As Student Intern</u>: primary responsibilities involved providing in-patient orthopedic and neurologic treatments; developed and implemented individual treatment plans; held family conferences; interacted with interdisciplinary staff; led in-service presentation for hemiplegic shoulder management. Additional primary responsibilities included evaluating and assessing orthopedic patients; participated in Quality Assessment Program; supervised treatment of patients and delegated duties to support staff; monitored patient progress from initial assessment through daily improvement and discharge.

Excellent professional references available upon request.

84

Combination. *Randy Clair, location unknown*

Education information and the Objective are included with the contact information. The result: Qualifications, Strengths, and the Profile are where they will more likely be read.

Heather McNamera
1313 W. Nugget Ave.
Butte, Montana 59701
(406) 555-5555

Job Objective	*To secure a job which allows for me to save for college while gaining practical knowledge.*
Education	***Butte High School,*** *Butte, Montana - Graduate 1993* • *College Preparatory Classes*
Honors & Awards	• *Girls State Delegate 1992* • *National Honor Society 1992* • *DARE Role Model to Elementary Schools 1991* • *George Herbert Walker Bush Representative Band, July 4, 1991, Washington, D.C.* • *Butte High Speech Team - Memorized Public Address*

Experience

October 1991 to Present	***Janet Gallsington,*** *Butte, MT* • *Housekeeper*
September 1989 to July 1991	***United American Presbyterian Church,*** *Butte, MT* • *Church Nursery Attendant*
December 1990	***Holder & Associates,*** *Butte, MT* • *Substitute Receptionist*

Other Positions Held

• *Nannie*	• *Pet Sitter*
• *Babysitter*	• *Gardener*
• *Painter/Laborer*	

• *Continued on Reverse Side* •

85

Chronological. *Kathlene Y. McNamee, Butte, Montana*

A resume for a young student prospecting for a job by "cold calling." The original resume had references listed on the reverse side—a format adults might use without a cover letter.

Insurance/Real Estate

Resumes at a Glance

Tony E. Sharpe

49 Turner Way
Belle Mead, New York 08604-5825
(808) 392-5734

Profile

*Thorough, dedicated insurance professional with
in-depth industry knowledge.....considered an excellent
negotiator.....utilizing extensive skills in underwriting and marketing.*

Experience

1986-Present   SHERWIN B. MELVIN INC., Warren, NY
(Wholesale and retail agency/brokerage services)

1986-1989   Broker/Underwriter

- Achieved consistent profitable performance over nine years
- Initiated and designed procedures necessary for the underwriting program.
- Established and expanded client base resulting in increased revenue.
- Accompanied agents on large and medium size accounts to provide technical and problem solving support service.
- Obtained an in-depth knowledge of all lines of insurance which broadened the scope of services provided.

1984-1986   CROWLEY CUSTOM MANOR, Warren, NY
(Wholesale division)

Eastern Branch Casualty Manager

- Responsible for management of $10 million in premium volume that represented significant growth while reducing expenses and exposure.
- Performed commercial underwriting, marketing, and administrative duties including establishing and exceeding budget projections, overseeing underwriting and support staff, and underwriting training.
- Responsible for sister branch audits, arranging territory structure and assignments, appointing and terminating brokers
- Elevated the level of interaction between the legal, actuarial, loss control, and underwriting departments in order to maximize underwriting profit.
- Obtained brokers license.

1982-1984   DRYERN AND COMPANY, Chatham, NY
(Prudential Reinsurance Subsidiary)

Senior Excess and Surplus Lines Underwriter

- Initiated, negotiated, and administered a lucrative semi automatic facultative reinsurance arrangement.

1979-1982   KAMPIN INSURANCE COMPANY, Summit, NY

Casualty Underwriter

Education

BS, Business Administration, 1979, Susquehanna University, Selinsgrove,
PA Licensed Insurance Broker for Property, Casualty, and Health, 1985

86

Combination. *Beverly Baskin, Marlboro, New Jersey*

Reduced font size and less "leading," or line spacing, make it possible to fit more information on a page and still provide an adequate amount of white space for an airy look.

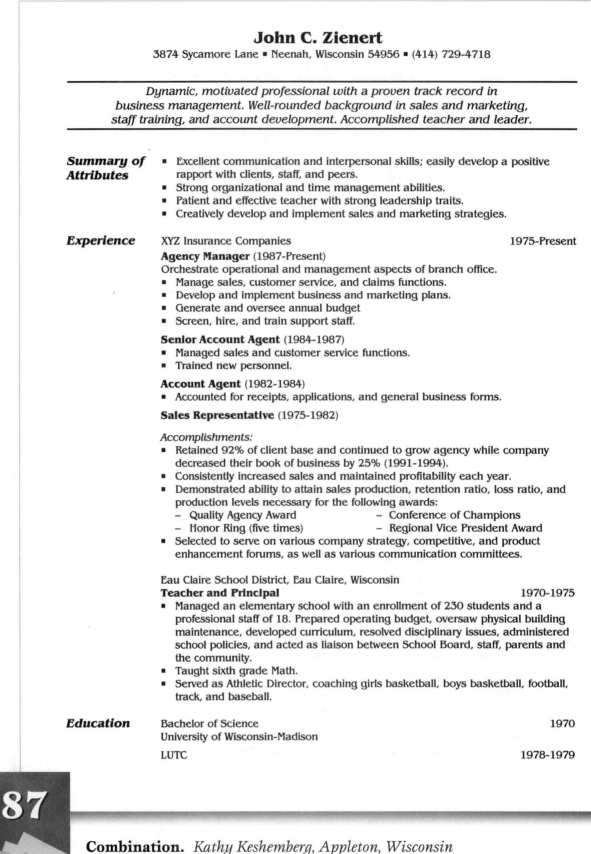

John C. Zienert

3874 Sycamore Lane ▪ Neenah, Wisconsin 54956 ▪ (414) 729-4718

Dynamic, motivated professional with a proven track record in business management. Well-rounded background in sales and marketing, staff training, and account development. Accomplished teacher and leader.

Summary of Attributes
- Excellent communication and interpersonal skills; easily develop a positive rapport with clients, staff, and peers.
- Strong organizational and time management abilities.
- Patient and effective teacher with strong leadership traits.
- Creatively develop and implement sales and marketing strategies.

Experience

XYZ Insurance Companies   1975-Present

Agency Manager (1987-Present)
Orchestrate operational and management aspects of branch office.
- Manage sales, customer service, and claims functions.
- Develop and implement business and marketing plans.
- Generate and oversee annual budget
- Screen, hire, and train support staff.

Senior Account Agent (1984-1987)
- Managed sales and customer service functions.
- Trained new personnel.

Account Agent (1982-1984)
- Accounted for receipts, applications, and general business forms.

Sales Representative (1975-1982)

Accomplishments:
- Retained 92% of client base and continued to grow agency while company decreased their book of business by 25% (1991-1994).
- Consistently increased sales and maintained profitability each year.
- Demonstrated ability to attain sales production, retention ratio, loss ratio, and production levels necessary for the following awards:
  - Quality Agency Award
  - Honor Ring (five times)
  - Conference of Champions
  - Regional Vice President Award
- Selected to serve on various company strategy, competitive, and product enhancement forums, as well as various communication committees.

Eau Claire School District, Eau Claire, Wisconsin
Teacher and Principal   1970-1975
- Managed an elementary school with an enrollment of 230 students and a professional staff of 18. Prepared operating budget, oversaw physical building maintenance, developed curriculum, resolved disciplinary issues, administered school policies, and acted as liaison between School Board, staff, parents and the community.
- Taught sixth grade Math.
- Served as Athletic Director, coaching girls basketball, boys basketball, football, track, and baseball.

Education

Bachelor of Science   1970
University of Wisconsin-Madison

LUTC   1978-1979

87

Combination. *Kathy Keshemberg, Appleton, Wisconsin*

Lines enclose information that is like a Profile. Square bullets pull the reader's attention down the page to the beginning of each item. A heading introduces accomplishments.

ROBERT SMITH

1800 Rolldown Terrace	Atlanta, Georgia 30033	(404) 331-0000

SUMMARY OF QUALIFICATIONS

Comprehensive knowledge of Sales, Management, and Transportation Operations. Record of consistent achievement, proven P/L management skills, personal commitment, and positive corporate growth. Ability to execute multiple projects simultaneously, communicate ideas to others, and bring functional groups together to achieve a common goal. Dedicated to professionalism; determined to succeed. Excellent organizational skills, well developed sales techniques, and detail oriented.

Management

- Supervised 80 employees, established training programs, instituted efficient procedures, and coordinated daily operations.
- Directed development of new business and implemented effective methods of account management.
- Total P/L responsibility; negotiated leases, materials, and contracts in various work environments to ensure cost effectiveness.

Sales

- Skilled at recognizing buying patterns, designing market strategies, and developing geographic sales territories; knowledge of highway networks and major cities throughout the Eastern United States.
- Directed all aspects of sales transactions from initial implication of interest, through all negotiations to consummation of sale; effectively assessed and verified financial documentation of potential customers.
- Developed and implemented canvassing techniques to build client base.

Received Numerous Sales Awards
from the National Association of Home Builders
and the National Board of Realtors

Completed Tom Hopkins Sales Seminar

Transportation

- Administered fleet of 26 trucks for both short and long distance hauling.
- Generated sales and coordinated movement of fleet to transport diverse materials efficiently.
- Full knowledge of DOT regulations, truck maintenance, and industry requirements.

CAREER HISTORY

Broker / Residential Sales, ROBERT SMITH REALTY
Salesperson, ANOTHER REALTY SALES
Associate Broker, NATIONAL HOMES, INC.
Manager of Housekeeping, ST. JOSEPH'S HOSPITAL
Office Manager, FIDELITY ACCEPTANCE CORPORATION OF AMERICA
Transportation Manager, SMITH TRUCKING

EDUCATION

ANYTOWN COLLEGE, Anytown, Pennsylvania *Bachelor of Science*

88

Functional. *Carol Lawrence, Savannah, Georgia*

Notice the design of this resume. It is mostly a Summary of Qualifications with a brief Career History (without dates) and an Education line. Notice also the centered awards information.

DOUGLAS S. MITCHELL
2920 Cypress Tree Court
Brandon, Florida 33511
813-675-7292

OBJECTIVE

Seeking a **Marketing/Sales** position where I can utilize my related experience and management background to contribute to the expansion of business development, productivity, increase revenues, and achieve career enhancement.

SUMMARY OF QUALIFICATIONS

- Proven performance record in progressively responsible positions; skilled in both **service and product-related sales.** Consistently increase productivity and sales revenues. Grew business approximately 125%.

- Design and implement creative marketing and sales techniques responsible for generating new business accounts. Achieved **Top Salesperson** recognition.

- Well-developed analytical and organizational skills; goal-directed and results-oriented; able to assimilate goals in conjunction with profit objectives, cost effectiveness, and budget awareness. Decreased marketing expenses while simultaneously increasing profits.

- Excellent written and verbal communications . . . strong "people" skills. Successfully manage and motivate employees, stimulate maximum levels of sales achievement, and provide high standards of service to customer/clients resulting in repeat business that expanded profit margins.

- "Team Player" with the self-motivation, initiative, and business savvy necessary to meet the challenges of today's competitive marketplace.

PROFESSIONAL EMPLOYMENT HISTORY

PRUDENTIAL INSURANCE AND FINANCIAL SERVICES, Tampa, FL   **1989-Present**
District Agent

- Market and sell a full range of financial products including life insurance, property and casualty insurance, mutual funds, and annuities.

- Successfully developed a detailed bulk mail system and referral network resulting in effective expansion of client base by 100%.

- Provide assistance to businesses and individuals seeking to supplement existing benefit plans; coordinate financial planning focussed on comfortable retirement programs.

- Consistently maintain a high-standard performance record via exceptional service, follow-through, and specific attention to detail which resulted in higher sales.

<u>Accomplishments:</u>

- Consistently rank in the top 10% of sales for the Company.

- Created a book of business exceeding premiums of $490,000 annually.

- Recipient of **Quality Service Award** and **National Sales Achievement Award.**

Combination. *Diane McGoldrick, Tampa, Florida*

The Objective statement is supported by statements in the Summary of Qualifications and by comments about the two work experiences. Special accomplishments are listed separately.

DOUGLAS S. MITCHELL   **Page Two**

EXECUTIVE PHONE SYSTEMS, Tampa, FL   **1987-1989**
Sales Representative

- Initiated and designed strategic marketing plan which included telemarketing and referral systems to generate new business.

- Directly oversaw customer's installation requirements.

- Provided customer service follow-up and promoted sales of additional equipment.

Accomplishments:

- **Top Salesperson for 2 quarter periods.**

- Increased productivity 150% in the first year.

EDUCATION

MISSISSIPPI UNIVERSITY, Columbus, MS   **Graduated 1986**
B.S. Degree - Business Administration

   Worked full time to earn 100% of college tuition/expenses and support my family.

PROFESSIONAL TRAINING/SEMINARS

Participated in several Seminar Training Programs relative to the following topics:

- Internal Sales and Servicing
- Financial Planning
- Tom Hopkins Sales Seminars
- Keystone Selling Skills
- Time Management
- Effective Progressive Discipline
- Discovering Your Management Style
- Fast Track Sales Techniques

LICENSURE

Licenses held in the State of Florida

- Health Insurance
- Variable Annuity
- NASD - Series 6
- Life Insurance
- Property Insurance
- Casualty Insurance

MILITARY

AIR NATIONAL GUARD (Honorable Discharge)   **1979-1985**
Photo Intelligence

AFFILIATIONS/MEMBERSHIPS

   Tampa Association of Life Underwriters
   National Association of Life Underwriters
   Masonic Lodge
   Shriners

REFERENCES AVAILABLE UPON REQUEST

The inclusion of professional training/seminars, licenses, military experience, and affiliations justifies the use of a second page. Notice the use of two columns for short, bulleted items. Boldfacing directs attention to key information throughout the resume.

Michael E. Human Resources

29 Helpful Lane
Humanitarian, NJ 00000

555-555-1212 (w)
555-555-1212 (h)

PROFESSIONAL EXPERIENCE

Technologies Company, Inc., NY, NY   **1974 - present**

*Played key leadership roles with increasing responsibilities which contributed value-added expertise and
demonstrated continuous professional development during this period.*

HR Business Partner - Real Estate   **Present**

Provide strategic Human Resources initiatives to this internationally deployed organization of 2,500 real estate
professionals. Report to the VP Real Estate.

- Create and implement a skills and competency process linking Real Estate business strategy with current
  performance management practices.
- Designed measurement processes for employee and customer satisfaction linked to the cultural reinvention
  of the organization.
- Created a career potential assessment tool for middle and upper managers.

CIO HR Leader - Lucent CIO Organization   **1996 - 1997**

Responsible for ensuring seamless delivery of human resources services and programs to an organization of 4,000
employees. Responsible for ensuring the consistent application and implementation of hr policies during the
transition from the Telecommunications Company to the Technologies Company, Inc. Reported to the VP and CIO.

- Spearheaded the outsourcing of 1,500 employees.
- Led a team to transition transactional hr services to a central hr organization.
- Directed and managed the activities of a team of five direct reports.
- Counseled and advised senior management on hr concerns including performance management, compensation,
  employee survey results, skills and competencies and coaching skills.
- Led a team in developing an intranet web site for the deployment of hr information and services.

Human Resources Leader - CIO Organization   **1994 - 1996**

Responsible for the management and support of human resources processes and services for an organization of
1,100 employees nationwide.

- Created a strategic CIO people plan using performance management as the organizational change model.
- Analyzed employee survey results using statistical correlations to identify key drivers to People Value Added
  (PVA) and performance management improvement
- Created and project-managed the production and deployment of a video tape that emphasized customer
- views and expectations.
- Created PVA improvement teams to ensure strategic linkage with overall CIO people improvement strategy.
- Led the development and implementation of a people re-skilling plan.
- Projected managed a macro level skills assessment of CIO people..
- Led the creation, design and implementation of a CIO selection process for appointment to Distinguished Member
  of Technical Staff (DMTS).

Human Resources Generalist   **1993 - 1994**

Responsible for the design and deployment of a model that identified key drivers to PVA improvement using
correlation analysis of employee survey results.

- Created data packages with action statistical models and issued counter measure registers for each
- executive level organization.
- Translated drivers of PVA improvement from statistical model to implementation.
- Developed and implemented action plans regarding employee survey results. Result: overall improvement in
  PVA index of 47 percent from 1993 to 1994.

90

Chronological. *Fran Kelley, Waldwick, New Jersey*

A resume that displays a stable career with one company for an individual's working life—a rarity
nowadays. Chronological format makes evident the unbroken progression of job positions

Michael E. Human Resources

555-555-1212 (w)   555-555-1212 (h)
page two

Human Resources Generalist, cont'd.   **1993 - 1994**
- Utilized correlation model as the basis for 1994 Leadership Forum presentation on PVA improvement.
- Project-managed an employee survey process and facilitated focus groups for a 1,000 employee organization.
- Led the implementation of an employee communication process.
- Led a cross organizational team to create, develop and pilot an upward feedback process.

Human Resources Generalist   **1992 - 1993**
Responsible for the implementation of HR processes: performance management, career development and training, staffing, selection, succession planning and compensation.
- Designed and delivered diversity awareness seminars in partnership with Anti-Defamation League.
- Led and designed a team to create an informal recognition award process.

International HR Manager   **1987 - 1992**
- Researched, benchmarked and designed a pay plan for installers on short-term international assignments.
- Participated on a team to create a compensation plan for expatriates on short term international assignments.
- Benchmarked with consulting firms and companies with similar universes of employees (General Dynamics, Bechtel Construction, Texas Instruments, Grumman Aircraft).
- Researched and created a model for recruiting Japanese college students, using key stakeholder and subject matter expert input from Hill and Knowlton-Japan, J. Walter Thompson Company-Japan, Texas Instruments-Japan, The Sanwa Bank Ltd, Dallas, AT&T Jens Corp., Yoshi Nakada, Bell Labs; Mo Iwama, Bell Labs. (*Basic model later implemented and used by AT&T Japan, Ltd.*)
- Initiated and project managed a 1991 cross cultural "bias check" of Dimensions of Leadership, using the work of Dr. Geert Hofstede, to demonstrate that current US notions of leadership are not exportable.
- Created a prototype computerized model for self assessment of cross cultural adaptability, using research work of Daniel J. Kealey, PhD, *Cross Cultural Effectiveness-A Study of Canadian Technical Advisors Overseas* in conjunction with the Canadian International Development Agency and Queens University.

EDUCATION
BA - Political Science - A Liberal Arts College

CERTIFICATIONS
Hay Job Evaluation Certification

PROFESSIONAL RECOGNITION
- Recipient of HR Star Award for "Dedication to Helping Customers"   **1995**
- Recipient of Process Improvement Excellence Award for "Exceeding Customer Expectations" and "Engaging Our People"   **1994 and 1995**
- Recipient of "Spot Cash" recognition award in support in PVA improvement model   **1994**

within the same company. Boldfacing helps to make the various positions stand out.
Relatively small type and narrower margins are characteristics of executive resumes and make it possible to fit much information on two pages.

Michael A. McNamera, Jr.
1313 West Nugget Ave.
Butte, Montana 59701

RESUME OF QUALIFICATIONS

Telephone: (406) 555-5555

SUMMARY OF QUALIFICATIONS

MANAGEMENT

Served as Adjuster-In-Charge of the Butte, Montana ABC Adjusting Company office for the past 13 years. Supervised clerical support and adjusters. Last year produced $110,000 billable hours.

MARKETING

Contacted area insurance agencies and national companies on a regular basis to promote ABC Adjusting Company. Developed strong, loyal client base through top quality, timely service. Took over office in 1980 with 5 claims per month, now average 50 claims per month. (An experienced adjuster normally handles 35 claims per month).

EDUCATOR

Taught photography classes to bachelor degree candidates at Warren Air Force Base through Los Angeles Community College.

Currently developing a photography course for adjusters to be published by ABC Adjusting Company for world-wide distribution.

Instructed photography adult classes for the Arts Chalet. Conducted numerous seminars for area 4-H groups. Judged local and area 4-H fairs. Facilitated parliamentary procedure workshops for local service clubs and 4-H clubs.

COMMUNICATION

Demonstrated oral and written communication skills. Ability to be personable, yet remain succinct. Experience in commercial photography and public relations including public speaking and media appearances.

COORDINATION

Numerous commendations for the efficient and professional coordination of contractors, consultants and employers on complex projects.

ACADEMIC GROWTH

Continually pursued postgraduate and technical courses to maintain personal standards of excellence. Received Chartered Property and Casualty Underwriter designation 10/92.

ORGANIZATION

Adept at handling complicated cases, keeping focused despite interruptions and distractions.

PROMOTION OF EXCELLENCE

Served as a technical adviser to other ABC Adjusting Company adjusters to assure quality service to clients.

REPUTATION

Business community reports satisfaction over honest and fair dealings.

COMMUNITY

Dedicated to the growth and enhancement of Butte through local service clubs, boards and church.

91

Combination. *Kathlene Y. McNamee, Butte, Montana*

A Summary of Qualifications taking up a whole page is impressive. Categories in the left column make it easy for the reader to find quickly qualifications of particular interest. Underlining of

EXPERIENCE

November 1977 to Present	**ABC Adjusting Company,** Butte, Montana **Adjuster-In-Charge** (October, 1980 - Present)

- <u>Licensed</u> and <u>bonded</u> as an independent adjuster in the State of Montana.
- <u>Experienced</u> in multiline property and casualty insurance adjusting.
- <u>Analyze</u> complex coverage issues.
- <u>Interpret</u> financial statements for business interruption losses.
- <u>Coordinate</u> independent experts, such as arson investigators or accident reconstruction experts.
- <u>Communicate</u> with policyholders or claimants who have suffered a loss and are therefore anxious, angry, and otherwise stressed.
- <u>Negotiate</u> settlements with attorneys, including structured settlements.
- <u>Mediate</u> disputes between policyholders and their insurers.
- <u>Report</u> succinctly, factually and timely to insurance companies.
- <u>Estimate</u> the cost of repairs for damaged vehicles or buildings.
- <u>Receive</u> and <u>disperse</u> settlement funds--millions of dollars per year.
- <u>Advise</u> self-insured clients regarding liability claims handling, risk management and loss control.
- <u>Travel</u> to other locations to handle specific, complex losses, i.e., railroad explosion in Helena (1989).
- <u>Decide</u> complex issues within settlement authority provided by principals, many times under adverse conditions, i.e., scene of a truck wreck involving perishable cargo, liability exposure, hazardous spills, and bodily injuries.

Adjuster, Cheyenne, Wyoming   (January 1979 - October 1980)
- Multiline adjuster, including the handling of catastrophic level storms involving hail and tornadoes. Concluded 2,000 vehicle estimates and 50 houses in a two-month period.

Adjuster, Cody, Wyoming   (November 1977 - January 1979)
- Multi-line adjuster. Handled a fatality the first day on the job.

January 1979 to January 1980	**LOS ANGELES COMMUNITY COLLEGE,** Cheyenne, Wyoming **Instructor** (part-time) - Warren AFB • College instructor of photography for bachelor degree candidates.
June 1976 to October 1977	**DON DORRS, MASTER PHOTOGRAPHER,** Sheridan, Wyoming **Wedding and Portrait Photographer**
1971 to June 1976	**UNIVERSITY OF WYOMING PHOTO/NEWS SERVICE,** Laramie, Wyoming **Photographer/Writer**

key words is combined with bullets to call attention to work activities. Dates show continual employment from 1971, as well as work as a part-time instructor. Boldfacing is used for the employers and the job positions since both are important.

EDUCATION

Chartered Property and Casualty Underwriter Designation (CPCU) 1992

Five year, postgraduate degree program. Only two percent of insurance professionals complete all 10 parts of this coursework. Designed to provide a thorough understanding of risk management and insurance. Segments include:

- Principles of Risk Management
- Personal Risk Management and Insurance
- Commercial Property Risk Management and Insurance
- Commercial Liability Risk Management and Insurance
- Legal Environment of Risk Management and Insurance
- Business Management
- Accounting and Finance
- Macro and Micro Economics
- Insurance Company Operations
- Ethics

Montana College of Mineral Science & Technology, Butte, Montana
Real Estate Appraisal

University of Wyoming, Laramie, Wyoming
Bachelor of Science Degree in Public Relations-Journalism
- Emphasis in Advertising, Photography, Layout and Design

Corporate Training

- I-CAR Collision Repair 1991
- Error and Omission Loss Prevention 1988
- Advanced Property Adjusting 1986
- Time Element Coverages 1986
- Accounting Fundamentals 1986

Volunteer Activities

- Butte Junior Achievement, Board Member 1991 - 1994
- Butte Junior Achievement, Treasurer 1991
- Butte Junior Achievement, Company Advisor 1984
- Butte Executive Club (275 members), President 1990
- Butte Exchange Club (250 members), Member 1980 - 1992
- Butte Exchange Club, Program Chairman 1987
- Unite American Presbyterian Church (300 members), Elder 1983 - 1986, 1993 - 1996
- United American Presbyterian Church, Treasurer 1981 - 1986
- Arts Chalet, Member 1988 - Present
- Arts Chalet, Photography Instructor (200 students) 1984 - 1993
- Montana Adjusters Association, Convention Chairman 1991

The wealth of information in the Education, Corporate Training, and Volunteer Activities sections justifies the use of a third page. Bullets unify the second and third pages visually. This page portrays a person who believes in self-development and being of help to others.

Maintenance and Material Handling

Resumes at a Glance

ROBERT McGLAUGHEN
780 Westwood Avenue . Huntingdon, Pennsylvania 17764
(814) 635-4201

OBJECTIVE	Heavy Equipment Operator for Brown Lime and Stone Company
CERTIFICATION	Certified Heavy Equipment Operator/ Driver Category C Class 4 Certified Welder CDL License (Pending)
SPECIALIZED TRAINING	Equipment Operator: Cranes, RT 58, RT 400, AT 400, RT 500, RT 600, RT 745, RT 990, Scissor Lift, Manlift, Fork Lift, Overhead Industrial Crane (10 Ton and 20) Completed two "Company sponsored" courses on Hazardous Waste Handling and Removal
WORK EXPERIENCE	WILTON COMPANY - Huntingdon, PA **Maintenance** . February 1993 to Present Maintain/repair bands of conveyor belt used to transport leather hides for painting. ACE SERVICES - Willow Park, PA **Mechanic Assembler** . March 1989 to February 1993 Assembled cranes from frame to completion. Welded, wired, and lubricated equipment. Started, performed troubleshooting procedure **Shipping/Receiving** Handled incoming parts for distribution throughout the plant. Computerized inventory utilizing IBM computer. KENTUCKY FREIGHT - Pittsburgh, PA **Dock Worker** . September 1992 to January 1993 (part-time) Loaded and unloaded 8000 lbs. freight per hour. SPRINGFIELD FARM - Huntingdon, PA **Dairy Herd Manager** . June 1980 to March 1989 Milking, feeding, general care of herd. Maintained/repaired equipment and buildings. Operated farm machinery: Farm Tractor, Skid Loader, Dump Truck, Combine, Corn Planter, Grain Drill, Chisel Plow, Post Driver, Hay Baler.
EDUCATION	**Diploma** in Heavy Equipment Operation June 1980 Huntingdon Area Vocational Technical School - Huntingdon, PA Maintenance, repair and operation of construction equipment Recipient of "Outstanding Senior" Award
REFERENCES	Available upon request

92

Combination. *Margaret M. Hilling, Huntingdon, Pennsylvania*

Skills and abilities are evident in certifications and in the kinds of equipment the person can operate (see the Specialized Training section). Boldfacing help the work positions stand out.

ROB MATTISON

3240 N. 42nd Drive
Phoenix, AZ 85019   (602) 272-2159

Objective: Position in maintenance and repair.

HIGHLIGHTS OF QUALIFICATIONS

- Enthusiastic, dependable, self-motivated; assumes responsibility necessary to get the job done.
- Work cooperatively with a wide range of personalities.
- Equally effective working alone or as a member of a team.
- Skilled in handling the public with professionalism and diplomacy.
- Strong skills in organizing work flow, ideas, materials, people.
- Hired, trained and supervised work crews.
- Takes pride in achieving the best possible results.

WORK HISTORY

1992-Present	**Engineer,** SCOTTSDALE PLAZA RESORT, Scottsdale, AZ
9/91-11/91	**Engineer,** OMNI HOTEL (formerly PHOENIX SHERATON), Phoenix, Arizona
8/90-6/91	**Engineer,** CROWN STERLING SUITES HOTEL (formerly EMBASSY SUITES BILTMORE), Phoenix, Arizona
8/88-8/90	**Chief Engineer,** WOOLLEY'S PETITE SUITES HOTEL, Tempe, Arizona
5/87-8/88	**Owner,** MAINTENANCE AND REPAIR, Phoenix, Arizona
6/85-5/87	**Maintenance Worker,** J.P.H. ENTERPRISES, Indio, California

MAINTENANCE SKILLS

Appliances, Carpentry, Electrical, Fencing, Flooring, Locks, Painting, Plumbing, Pools & Spas, Roofing
Irrigation and Sprinklers
Air Conditioning, Refrigeration and Heating

EDUCATION

Air Conditioning & Refrigeration
College of the Desert, Palm Desert, California

Electronics
DeVry Institute of Technology, Phoenix, Arizona

PROFESSIONAL EXPERIENCE

Building Repair
- During a monsoon storm in Phoenix, climbed hotel roof to check drains; upon discovering six inches of water and drains patched over with roofing cement, immediately cut through patches and cleared the drains.
- Within three hours, completely rebuilt apartment complex stairs that collapsed after two heavy tenants moved in; added joist hangers and extra supports underneath to meet legal specs and ensure future stability.
- When a four-inch copper pipe burst and flooded a ground-floor room, removed all furniture, pulled up carpet and dug four feet deep to repair the pipe; after drying, filled in hole, poured concrete, installed carpet and put back furniture.
- Replaced broken windows, made screens, hung doors and jambs, hung and patched drywall, textured and painted walls, installed electrical switches and outlets, moved phone jacks, rewired disconnect and breaker panels, installed and repaired lighting.

Mechanical Repair
- During breakfast rush hour, quickly removed stuck soda dispenser solenoid, which caused Dr. Pepper to flood the entire waitress station; temporarily adjusted unit until Coca-Cola repairman arrived.
- Repaired chillers, boilers, water softeners, ice machines, washers, dryers, motors, pumps and other equipment for various establishments; also troubleshoot elevators and escalators.
- Fixed hotel restaurant equipment, including grills, ovens, refrigerators, dishwashers, etc.

Customer Service
- Regularly earned commendations for diplomacy and courtesy toward hotel guests and apartment tenants during work-related encounters.
- Developed cooperative working relationships with management, staff and contracted help; was left in charge of operations of Woolley's Petite Suites for a week when managers and staff went to Florida to participate in a hostile takeover of three hotels.
- Resolved wide range of customer problems, including patiently and diligently working to pry a broken key from a hotel room lock, earning a letter of commendation from the guest who "appreciated his control in a trying situation."

93

Combination. *Sallie Young, Riverton, Utah*

An imaginative design to help a maintenance person stand out. Notice the use of brief stories in the Professional Experience section to show how the individual solved problems.

Joseph A. Bluecollar

Rt. 1 Box 5E
Shade, Ohio 45776
(614) 696-0000

---

*" ... a top paid, top rated **building technician** for GTE with a superb attendance record."*

" ... excellent working knowledge of carpentry, electrical and plumbing areas."

" ... produces excellent results and meets all schedules and time limits."

*" ... highly skilled, highly trained individual who is always striving to improve himself ." **

OBJECTIVE

Seeking a position in building maintenance or HVAC/Refrigeration which will utilize my extensive experience and training in these areas.

SKILLS ANALYSIS

- Over eight years experience as building technician
- Extensive experience and training in HVAC/Refrigeration
- Highly knowledgeable in all areas of building maintenance
- Supervisory experience; ability to motivate employees to work at peak efficiency levels
- Experience in installation of uninterrupted power source for large computer systems
- Experience with Sleeve Units to 700 ton chillers–Liebert A/C

RELATED EXPERIENCE

Building Technician - GENERAL TELEPHONE COMPANY	1988-present
Maintenance/HVAC Repair - CENTRAL OHIO COAL COMPANY	1982-1988
Owner - BLUECOLLAR REFRIGERATION & HEATING	1980-1982
Maintenance Supervisor - SOUTHERN OHIO COAL COMPANY	1973-1982
Production Supervisor - LOCKHEED AIRCRAFT	1967-1973
Diesel & Gas Mechanic Welder - U.S. ARMY	1964-1967

TRAINING & CERTIFICATION

Universal Technician Certification No. 277423951 - Refrigerant Transition & Recovery

Commercial Trades Institute - Training in HVAC & Refrigeration

---

Excellent References Provided Upon Request

*Excerpts from Performance Evaluations & Letter of Recommendation by Al Supervisor, Coord. of Bldg. Administration, GTE

94

Combination. *Melissa L. Kasler, Athens, Ohio*

Lines enclose and make readily seen four winning testimonials. They are winning in that the reader is won over to the individual without having seen anything else in the resume.

MICHAEL MAINTAINER

123 Main Street   Somewhere, MA 00000   (555) 555-5555

HANDS-ON PROFESSIONAL with diverse areas of expertise, encompassing technical, mechanical, construction, medical, communications, public relations, and more. Over 15 years of comprehensive experience in maintenance, maintenance supervision, carpentry, firefighting, and mechanical repair. Licensed Class 1 driver; certified EMT. Skills include vehicle maintenance, Advanced Life Support, electronic troubleshooting / repair. Public service includes civic duty as elected city official.

SKILLS

MAINTENANCE
Professional skills in office machinery and sound system maintenance, usage and repair, automobile maintenance, basic plumbing and electrical upkeep /repair. Journeyman carpenter with design, bidding and construction experience (commercial and heavy construction). Cable and telephone installation/repair.

BUSINESS / MANAGEMENT
Demonstrated leadership ability in the training, motivation and development of staffs. Experienced in all phases of business management, including cost/job estimation, ordering, vendor communications, scheduling and employee relations. Thrives in an environment demanding a wide range of competencies.

PUBLIC RELATIONS
Successful at establishing excellent public relations in the community. Experienced public speaker and campaign manager, with the ability to interact effectively at all levels, both public and partisan. Advocate for children; co-founder and Vice-President of Child Protection Network, and teacher's assistant in local regional school.

TECHNICAL
State Firefighter I and II certification. Certified in firefighting techniques, vehicle maintenance, Advanced Self Contained Breathing Apparatus Techniques, Rescue Tool Operation (Jaws of Life), pumper operations. EMT-IV-D qualified. Certificate in Advanced Life Support.

ACCOMPLISHMENTS:

- Elected member: Board of Selectmen, Anywhere, MA
  Officer, local volunteer fire department
  Co-secretary, Anywhere Democratic Town Committee
- Co-founder: Child Protection Network
  Member: Board of Directors
  Vice-President
- State certified voting machine mechanic
- First Anywhere Artillery Regiment
  Member: American Artillery Association

95

Combination. *Debra O'Reilly, Bristol, Connecticut*

Similar lines enclose what amounts to a Profile. This use of lines is a powerful device for capturing attention. For some reason, the reader wants to read first what appears between

Michael Maintainer   Page 2

PROFESSIONAL EXPERIENCE

REGIONAL SCHOOL DISTRICT #6, Anywhere, MA   1991 - Present
Head Custodian/Maintenance
Maintains entire physical plant; runs and maintains office equipment and sound system. Designed and constructed three new offices, utilizing spare classroom space. Assists teaching staff with students; provides medical care during absence of part-time school nurse.

   ◆ Earned awards for school appearance and cleanliness, and for reworking faulty equipment.

UNION LOCAL #24, Anywhere, MA   1987 - 1991
Journeyman Carpenter
Commercial and heavy construction projects in southern region.

XYZ COMMUNICATIONS, Anywhere, MA
Supervisor and Project Coordinator   1978 - 1980, 1983 - 1987
Directed eight employees for telephone wiring subcontractor. Performed site surveys, researched job costs and prepared estimates. Installed systems, procuring materials and overseeing completion of each project. Rehired at higher wage and upgraded from previous position as Cable Installer / Service Technician.

ABC OLDSMOBILE-CADILLAC, Anywhere, MA   1980 - 1983
Auto Mechanic/Assistant Service Manager

EDUCATION / CERTIFICATIONS

State Certification: Voting Machine Mechanic
Emergency Medical Technician Defibrillation Certification
Emergency Medical Technician / Intravenous Technician Certification
State Fire Training School
     Firefighter I Certification
     Firefighter II Certification
     Advanced Self Contained Breathing Apparatus Techniques: Certificate

ZYX INSTITUTE, Anywhere, MA
One-Year Auto Mechanics Program: Certificate

COUNTY SCHOOLS, Anywhere, MA
Tractor Trailer Driving Program: Certificate

ANYWHERE HIGH SCHOOL, Anywhere, MA
Graduated

EXCELLENT PROFESSIONAL REFERENCES FURNISHED UPON REQUEST

lines. Skills are grouped according to four categories, making it easier for the reader to spot an interest. Accomplishments complete a powerful first page. Boldfacing on the second page makes the job positions stand out. A diamond bullet signals another achievement.

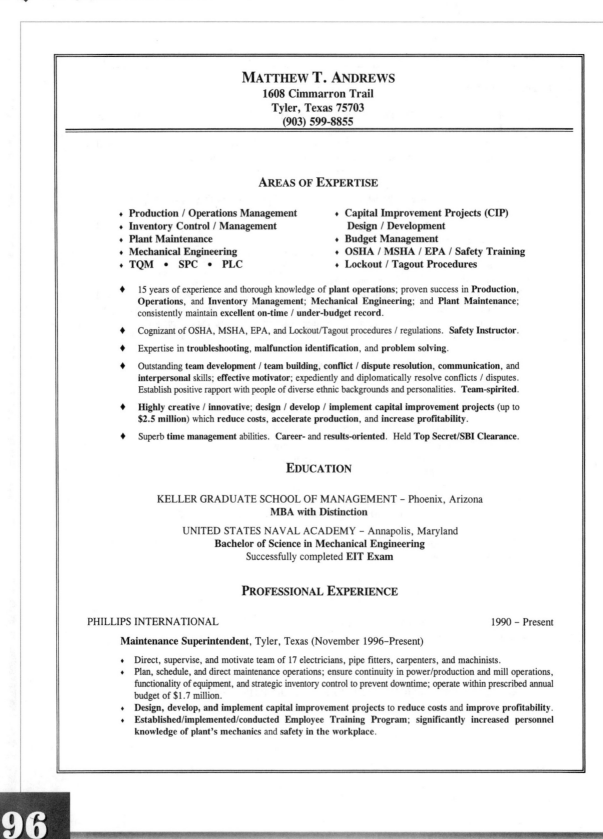

MATTHEW T. ANDREWS
1608 Cimmarron Trail
Tyler, Texas 75703
(903) 599-8855

AREAS OF EXPERTISE

- Production / Operations Management
- Inventory Control / Management
- Plant Maintenance
- Mechanical Engineering
- TQM • SPC • PLC

- Capital Improvement Projects (CIP)
  Design / Development
- Budget Management
- OSHA / MSHA / EPA / Safety Training
- Lockout / Tagout Procedures

- 15 years of experience and thorough knowledge of **plant operations**; proven success in **Production, Operations,** and **Inventory Management; Mechanical Engineering;** and **Plant Maintenance;** consistently maintain **excellent on-time / under-budget record.**

- Cognizant of OSHA, MSHA, EPA, and Lockout/Tagout procedures / regulations. **Safety Instructor.**

- Expertise in **troubleshooting, malfunction identification,** and **problem solving.**

- Outstanding **team development / team building, conflict / dispute resolution, communication,** and **interpersonal** skills; **effective motivator**; expediently and diplomatically resolve conflicts / disputes. Establish positive rapport with people of diverse ethnic backgrounds and personalities. **Team-spirited.**

- **Highly creative / innovative; design / develop / implement capital improvement projects** (up to **$2.5 million**) which **reduce costs, accelerate production,** and **increase profitability.**

- Superb **time management** abilities. **Career-** and **results-oriented.** Held **Top Secret/SBI Clearance.**

EDUCATION

KELLER GRADUATE SCHOOL OF MANAGEMENT – Phoenix, Arizona
MBA with Distinction

UNITED STATES NAVAL ACADEMY – Annapolis, Maryland
Bachelor of Science in Mechanical Engineering
Successfully completed **EIT Exam**

PROFESSIONAL EXPERIENCE

PHILLIPS INTERNATIONAL   1990 – Present

Maintenance Superintendent, Tyler, Texas (November 1996–Present)

- Direct, supervise, and motivate team of 17 electricians, pipe fitters, carpenters, and machinists.
- Plan, schedule, and direct maintenance operations; ensure continuity in power/production and mill operations, functionality of equipment, and strategic inventory control to prevent downtime; operate within prescribed annual budget of $1.7 million.
- **Design, develop,** and **implement capital improvement projects** to **reduce costs** and **improve profitability.**
- **Established/implemented/conducted Employee Training Program; significantly increased** personnel knowledge of **plant's mechanics** and **safety in the workplace.**

96

Combination. *Ann Klint, Tyler, Texas*

A resume for a person wanting a plant management position. The person has substantial experience in production and plant maintenance but limited experience in overall plant

MATTHEW T. ANDREWS   Page Two

PHILLIPS INTERNATIONAL (Continued)

Maintenance Supervisor, Superior, Arizona (October 1993–November 1996)

♦ Supervised maintenance crew of 12; managed production, operations, and inventory of entire plant.
♦ Established and efficiently managed $2 million annual budget.
♦ Conducted safety training program; ensured compliance with OSHA, MSHA, EPA regulations.
♦ **Designed, developed, and implemented pumping system** for solar salt production which **reduced costs by $50,000 per month** and **increased production by 30 tons per hour**.

Project Engineer, Superior, Arizona (February 1992–October 1993)

♦ Designed, developed and installed capital improvement projects.
♦ Responsible for **complete installation of plastic membrane liners** in solar ponds which **drastically reduced brine costs** and resulted in **$100,000 savings annually**.

Project Engineer, Kansas City, Kansas (April 1990–February 1992)

♦ **Designed, established, and implemented capital improvement projects of up to $2.5 million** from conceptualization through completion.
♦ **Replaced obsolete steam boilers with state-of-the-art equipment**; resulted in **significant natural gas savings**.

UNITED STATES NAVY   1982 – 1990
Lieutenant / Warfare Officer / Quality Assurance Officer

Advanced to rank of **Lieutenant / Antisubmarine Warfare Officer** directly responsible for operation, planning, maintenance, and security of a nuclear-powered attack submarine and training, supervision, and safety of a division with 28 personnel. Served as **Qualified Officer of the Deck / Ship's Duty Officer; assumed total responsibility of ship** during Captain's absence.

♦ **Devised/implemented Quality Assurance System; authored/implemented QA program** and **safety procedures for the entire ship**.
♦ **Implemented ship's Radiological Control Program**; managed the chemistry control of the ship's nuclear power plant.
♦ Directed all mechanical and electrical operations of Sonar, Fire Control, and major mechanical systems (nuclear pumps, valves, turbines, generators, and reactor).

♦ ♦ **Professional References Furnished On Request** ♦ ♦

management. The writer's task is to play up leadership experience and managerial skills that the individual could draw on as a manager. Page borders, horizontal lines, diamond bullets, and use of the person's name on the second page tie the two pages together.

A. MICHAEL TRUCKER

P.O. BOX 000 • WESTVIEW, MARYLAND • 11111
(000) 000-0000

Self-motivated businessman with nine years operating experience in U.S. trucking industry. In-depth knowledge about the operation and maintenance of Class 8 vehicles. Recognized for outstanding road safety record. Seeking new career challenges in the trucking industry or a related field.

EXPERIENCE

A.M. TRUCKER & SON, (TRUCKING BUSINESS) RIDGELY, MD   1988 to present
Owner and Operator
- Experienced in the hauling of numerous commodities including dry van freight, bulk liquids, oversize flat beds, refrigerated foods and other temperature-sensitive freight.
- Performed routine maintenance and repair on vehicles.
- Experienced in the loading and unloading of trailers by hand, pallet jack and fork lift.
- Experienced in all aspects of operating a trucking business.
- Experienced in processing all required paperwork including logs, bills of lading, vehicle inspections, etc.
- Logged 1 million, accident-free miles. Consistently recognized for outstanding safety record by the American Trucking Association. (Have received awards each year, 1991-1995).
- Experienced in providing instruction for Class "A" CDL license.

PEP-UP SERVICE STATION (T/A WIN/WIN CORP.) WESTVIEW, MD   1985 to 1988
Co-Owner of family business
- Supervised 23 full time and/or part-time employees.
- Responsible for all financial/administrative aspects of business including accounting, bookkeeping, ordering, and inventory.
- Filed all applications including tax forms, workers compensation and insurance forms.
- Maintained all mechanical equipment.
- Handled all bills and correspondence for business account.

BRICE HOME CENTER, BALTIMORE, MD   1984 to 1985
Department head
- Responsible for the sales of all lumber and building materials.
- Supervised five full time and/or part-time sales associates.
- Worked with outside vendors.
- Resolved customer problems.
- Filled-in, as needed, in other departments.
- Ordered and stocked merchandise.

Z&X BOATING SUPPLY CO., BALTIMORE, MD   1982 to 1983
Warehouse Supervisor
- Ordered and stocked merchandise.
- Worked with outside vendors.
- Maintained warehouse in neat and orderly fashion.
- Followed cost-effective and profitable inventory procedures.
- Assisted on sales floor as needed.

EDUCATION

SUSSEX COMMUNITY COLLEGE, BALTIMORE, MD   1984
Associate of Arts, Criminology

AMERICAN TRUCKING ASSOCIATION
Attended seminars on Safety in the Trucking Industry, DOT/regulations, CDL Licensing, Drug and Alcohol Abuse, Hauling Hazardous Materials, etc.

COMMUNITY

Participate in community sports activities, coaching Westview Little League (2 Years), and Westview Soccer Team (1 Year).

97

Chronological. *Thomas E. Spann, Easton, Maryland*

Frames around contact information and section headings are distinctive. Shadowed, unfilled square bullets complement the frames. Italic makes the job positions more visible.

Timothy A. Beckman
4937 Blue Lake Drive
Bayville, Michigan 48555
(810) 555-3266

HIGHLIGHTS OF QUALIFICATIONS

- Comprehensive knowledge of quality control, shipping & receiving, and just-in-time delivery of inventory.
- Complete understanding of General Motors' requirements and procedures relating to inventory control.
- Fluent in the use of General Motors computerized parts handling and ISP systems.
- Thorough product knowledge.
- Respected reputation among customers, suppliers and co-workers.

EMPLOYMENT EXPERIENCE

MILLER AUTO TRANSPORT CO. • Saginaw, MI
Inventory Specialist and **Quality Supervisor** • 1993-Present
- Coordinate shipping and receiving of $2.5 million inventory from over 390 suppliers to General Motors (GM) plants utilizing just-in-time inventory practices based on 2-hour pull system.
- Act as liaison and develop working relationship with quality control personnel at GM's Truck plant.
- Coordinate pilot program for new model year (including identifying, sequencing and loading parts).
- Monitor inventory for parts shipped in error and OSD (overages, shortages and damages); process CMR (credited material return) for Truck plant and return damaged parts to suppliers.
- Conduct annual random checks of all suppliers to verify accuracy of shipments.
- Identify unmarked parts through investigation, product knowledge, and contact with quality control personnel.
- Coordinate work assignments of two quality control employees.
- Promoted from position as dock worker.

YMCA • Pontiac, MI
Lifeguard (seasonal) • 1992

BUILDERS SQUARE • Lansing, MI
Material Handler and **Forklift Truck Driver** • 1990-1991

EDUCATION

BAKER COLLEGE • Owosso, MI
Pursuing **Bachelor Degree in Management**

References available on request.

98

Combination. *Janet L. Beckstrom, Flint, Michigan*

This person wanted a job with General Motors. The writer therefore emphasized in his current job any involvement with GM. The bottom line echoes the top line.

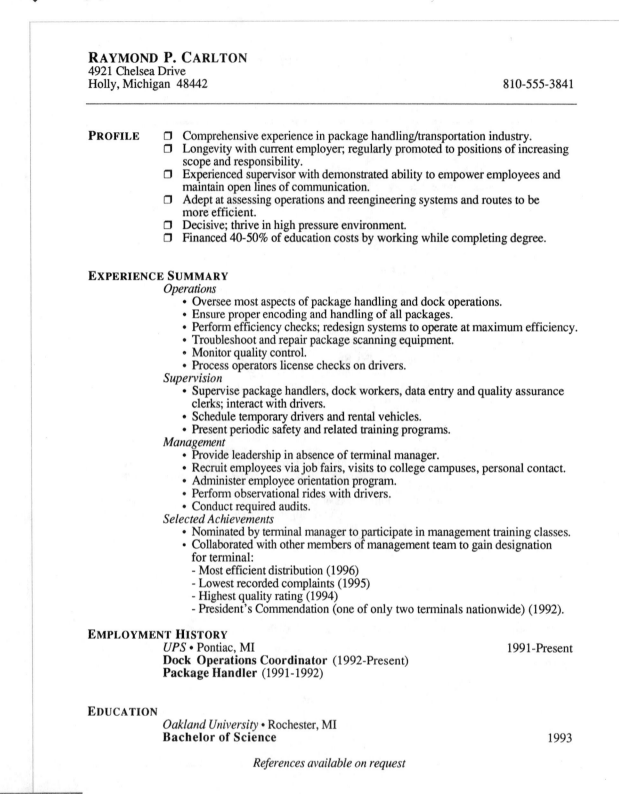

RAYMOND P. CARLTON
4921 Chelsea Drive
Holly, Michigan 48442

810-555-3841

PROFILE
- ❏ Comprehensive experience in package handling/transportation industry.
- ❏ Longevity with current employer; regularly promoted to positions of increasing scope and responsibility.
- ❏ Experienced supervisor with demonstrated ability to empower employees and maintain open lines of communication.
- ❏ Adept at assessing operations and reengineering systems and routes to be more efficient.
- ❏ Decisive; thrive in high pressure environment.
- ❏ Financed 40-50% of education costs by working while completing degree.

EXPERIENCE SUMMARY

Operations
- Oversee most aspects of package handling and dock operations.
- Ensure proper encoding and handling of all packages.
- Perform efficiency checks; redesign systems to operate at maximum efficiency.
- Troubleshoot and repair package scanning equipment.
- Monitor quality control.
- Process operators license checks on drivers.

Supervision
- Supervise package handlers, dock workers, data entry and quality assurance clerks; interact with drivers.
- Schedule temporary drivers and rental vehicles.
- Present periodic safety and related training programs.

Management
- Provide leadership in absence of terminal manager.
- Recruit employees via job fairs, visits to college campuses, personal contact.
- Administer employee orientation program.
- Perform observational rides with drivers.
- Conduct required audits.

Selected Achievements
- Nominated by terminal manager to participate in management training classes.
- Collaborated with other members of management team to gain designation for terminal:
  - Most efficient distribution (1996)
  - Lowest recorded complaints (1995)
  - Highest quality rating (1994)
  - President's Commendation (one of only two terminals nationwide) (1992).

EMPLOYMENT HISTORY

UPS • Pontiac, MI   1991-Present
Dock Operations Coordinator (1992-Present)
Package Handler (1991-1992)

EDUCATION

Oakland University • Rochester, MI
Bachelor of Science   1993

References available on request

99

Combination. *Janet L. Beckstrom, Flint, Michigan*

Shadowed, unfilled square bullets make the Profile seem substantial. Four categories of experience in the Experience Summary are much easier to read than a long list without them.

ANDREW P. HOLDEN
4307 Maplewood Dr.
Vassar, Michigan 48768   (517) 555-6756

PROFESSIONAL SUMMARY

Highly motivated, focused, and goal-oriented. Familiar with all aspects of warehouse and inventory control operations through hands-on experience in positions of increasing responsibility. Strong communication skills demonstrated on a daily basis. Decisive and respected. Committed to mutually beneficial company and personal ideals. Ready and eager to meet new challenges.

HIGHLIGHTS OF RESPONSIBILITIES

- Empower and motivate employees by creating desirable working atmosphere where employee feedback is encouraged.
- Train employees in many aspects of warehouse operations.
- Recruited to participate in Future Planning Committee.
- Contributed to creation of *Receiving Operations Manual*.
- Manage operations in receiving dock; anticipate needs and demands, troubleshoot as necessary.
- Coordinate inter-company shipments.
- Monitor inventory control utilizing company-developed computer system.

EMPLOYMENT HISTORY

MEYER FOODS • Port Huron, MI   1988-Present
    Lead Man - Receiving Dock
    Receiving Dock Checker
    Lead Man - Turret Drivers
    Turret Driver
    Merge Operations
    Selector

FORD HOSPITAL • Plymouth, MI   1984-1988
    Storekeeper - Head of Receiving for Dietary Department

EDUCATION and TRAINING

MANAGEMENT TRAINING I & II (Meyer Foods)   1995-1996

DALE CARNEGIE COURSE   1995

KIRKWOOD COMMUNITY COLLEGE • Bayville, MI   1986-1987
    Business and general coursework

ACHIEVEMENTS

- Received *Highest Award for Achievement* from the Dale Carnegie course.
- Awarded Meyer Food's *Outstanding Warehouse Production Award*.

COMMUNITY INVOLVEMENT

- Annually participate in *World's Largest Garage Sale* which benefits American Tuberous Sclerosis Foundation.
- Serve as *Deacon* and active member of Vassar Community Church.

References available on request.

100

Combination. *Janet L. Beckstrom, Flint, Michigan*

The Professional Summary and the Highlights of Responsibilities appear where they are most likely to be read—in the zone from two to five inches down from the top edge of the page.

MICHAEL R. WIRT
4321 Milton Avenue
Bothell, Washington 00000

555-555-5555

Material Movement Equipment Specialist

QUALIFICATION SUMMARY

- Trained and licensed company personnel in the use of an extensive range of material moving equipment.
- Frequently selected to organize and coordinate special/short-used material movement projects because of extensive knowledge of supply system and equipment.
- Routinely accomplish projects and assignments prior to scheduled deadlines.
- Certified to operate most material moving equipment used in the industry.
- Experienced and effective working with people of diverse cultures and backgrounds.
- Computer literate: Windows, Quattro Pro, WordPerfect, and NISTAR material movement software.

WORK HISTORY

US Fleet & Industrial Supply Center, Freight Terminal Department, Guam   1992 - 1995
Command License Examiner/Marine Cargo Specialist, 1994 - 1995
- **Personally selected by activity Commander** to develop lesson plans and teaching aids and provide classroom instruction to all employees in use and safe operation of all heavy equipment/materials handling equipment in use at facility.
- Issued, renewed, and checked currency of licenses for all material handling equipment.

Material Handler, 1992 - 1994
- Provided material movement services for facilities on Guam, Japan, Phillippines, and East and West Coasts of United States.
- Managed documentation of material movements through Naval Integrated Storage, Tracking, and Retrieval (NISTAR) computer system, checking for quantity, orders, receipts, and destination. Experienced in use of computerized automated carousels and computerized hand-held terminals.
- Experienced and when appropriate, certified, in safe and efficient use of an extensive range of warehousing equipment, such as:

  - Forklift (2&4K)
  - Pallet Jack
  - Hand Tools
  - Order Pickers
  - 10 Ton Truck
  - Banding Machines
  - Reach Trucks
  - Standard Pick Up
  - Picks & Stows

- Assigned to manage Medical Storage Warehouse for six-month period to conduct surveys and cleanup after Typhoon Omar. Coordinated rotation of materials and constant changing of shelf-life codes. Ensured security of syringes and other controlled items. Monitored refrigerators and freezers for temperature and break down to safeguard vaccine and other perishable items.

101

Combination. *Lonnie L. Swanson, Poulsbo, Washington*

The pages of a two-page resume can appear unrelated without unifying devices. Such devices in this resume include the use of a thin-thick line at the top of each page, partial dual lines after

MICHAEL R. WIRT   **Page 2**

Naval Underwater Warfare Engineering Station, Keyport, WA   1989 - 1992
Torpedo Branch
Mechanic Helper
- Procured submarine assemblies and conducted testing of components.
- Completed documentation of all test procedures, discrepancy reports, and material route sheets, with accuracy and attention to detail.

Vitro Corporation, Keyport, WA   1986 - 1989
Supply Clerk
- Inventoried, ordered, and issued parts and equipment for MK48 torpedoes.
- Issued and maintained records of printed circuit boards and gyros.
- Used electronic bar graph machine to track parts throughout the maintenance cycle.

U.S. Army   1983 - 1986
Fire Control Instrument Repairer - Honorable Discharge
- Troubleshot, maintained, and repaired fire control instruments, maintaining appropriate records of procedures and repairs.

EDUCATION & CERTIFICATIONS

1991 - **Associate of Technical Arts**, Olympic College, Bremerton, WA

Hazardous Materials Training Program	Transportation of Hazardous Materials
Naval Explosives Forklift Operation	Tractor Trailer: 25 Ton Training
Bus Gas/Diesel: 40 Pax Training	Stake Truck: 10 Ton Training
Forklift, Gas, Diesel, and Electric: 25,000 Tons	Material Handling Equipment Training
Silent Hoist and Crane Container Handler: 72K	Lansing Container Handler: 60-67K
Clark Container Handler: 60K	John Deere Forklift: 10K
Order Pickers: 3K	Lift Truck: 3K
DockMule w/4Trailers	Certified Diver
CPR/First Aid	

PERSONAL PROFILE

- Physically fit.
- Perform effectively in a stressful environment.
- Efficiently accomplish goals despite rapidly changing priorities.
- Take pride in documented reputation as excellent worker. *Consistently rated "Outstanding"* for job performance, individually and as team member.
- Received *Special Service* and *Time Off* Awards for quality of performance.

REFERENCES AVAILABLE UPON REQUEST

each section heading, square bullets throughout the resume, columnar lists on each page, and bold italic for job positions on each page. Sometimes throw-away information is put last. In this resume some of the best information—like dessert—is put last.

James S. Robertson

1928 Blye Road
Mt. Morris, MI 48458
(810) 555-8332

HIGHLIGHTS OF QUALIFICATIONS

Areas of Expertise
- Extensive experience and knowledge of beverage manufacturing/bottling operations, warehouse operations, inventory control and route sales.
- All aspects of supervision including scheduling and resolving employee disputes.
- Skilled in operating standard warehousing and shipping/receiving equipment.
- Familiarity with applicable governmental regulations (OSHA, FDA, MDA).

Personal Attributes
- Leadership style adaptable to situation and diverse personalities.
- Strong motivator who coaches others to work effectively as team members.
- Well developed organizational skills and attention to detail.
- Forward-thinking and eager to meet new challenges.

ACCOMPLISHMENTS

- Originated concept for and designed month-end inventory process, significantly reducing time involved and increasing accuracy.
- Established procedures to minimize misloads during truck loading operations.
- Consistently achieve *Highest Efficiency* rating for truck loading.
- Revised inventory control system to minimize excessive use of raw materials.

EMPLOYMENT HISTORY

VERNOR'S GINGER ALE • Detroit, MI   1982-Present
Longevity with company in positions of increasing responsibility.
Operations Dock Foreman
Production Sanitation Foreman
City Routes Supervisor
City Routes Dispatcher
OTR Dispatcher

COCA COLA BOTTLE GROUP • Saginaw, MI   1978-1982
Route Sales Driver

Additional experience in beverage distribution and retail management.

EDUCATION/TRAINING

Continuing Education seminars *(complete list available on request)*

Mott Community College • Flint, MI

Clio High School • Clio, MI

References furnished on request

102

Combination. *Janet L. Beckstrom, Flint, Michigan*

This person had been in soft drink bottling for almost 20 years and had worked mainly for one of his employers. The writer needed to make this person appealing to any employer.

Management

Resumes at a Glance

CHANNON L. JACOBS, III
109 Maple Court
Orlando, Florida 32703
(407) 000-0000

CAREER FOCUS: Cosmetic Manager / Retail Industry

PROFESSIONAL SUMMARY

- **Highly motivated, self-directed individual** oriented to a fast-pace and maintaining a pivotal role in a retail sales environment; proven ability to capitalize on opportunities that increase profit margins.

- **"Top Producer" who excels in augmenting sales**, training personnel, launching promotions, product development and customer service. Traveled nationwide to initiate "turnaround" of faltering product sales in other regions.

- **Accomplished cosmetician** with a comprehensive portfolio encompassing a prolific career as a make-up artist in the entertainment industry. Special talent for color coordinating and blending make-up, skilled in application techniques and exhibit high-level expertise in enhancing appearance.

- **Successfully orchestrated start-up** of an exclusive salon's private label for skin care products and color lines inclusive of total department set-up and designing visual displays to market products.

- **Pioneered opening** of personally owned salon providing a complete line of cosmetician services to a select client base.

- **Experienced in business management**, general accounting procedures, supervising personnel and contract negotiations.

- **Demonstrated strengths** in tracking industry trends, implementing innovative ideas, organizational management and coordinating special events/trade shows.

- **Very outgoing and personable** with excellent communication and "people" skills; possess conscientious work ethic, willingness to accept challenging roles and commitment to job performance.

COMPUTER SKILLS

DOS/Window-based programs, Corel Draw, Microsoft Word, Access, Adobe Photoshop, Apollo *(travel industry program)*

EMPLOYMENT HISTORY

1995 - Present	**Administrative Manager**	UPSCALE TRAVEL AGENCY	Orlando, FL
1989 - 1995	**Owner/Cosmetician**	STUDIO WEST	West Hollywood, CA
1986 - 1989	**Make-up Artist**	LaCAGE AUX FOLLES	Hollywood, CA
1985 -1986	**Make-up/Skin Care Specialist and Merchandiser**	REUBEN SALON	Beverly Hills, CA
1983 - 1985	**Pacific Region Make-up Artist and Merchandiser**	NATURAL COSMETICS	Philadelphia, PA

EDUCATION

Cosmetician/Cosmetologist Diplomas Yamano Beauty School
Art Major University of Southern California
Telecommunications Oral Robert University

103

Combination. *Diane McGoldrick, Tampa, Florida*

A nicely designed resume that is easy to size up at a glance. Narrower margins and smaller type ensure that the resume presents much information with white space on one page.

WARREN D. WATERS
59 Spruce Road • Clayton, NJ 55555 • (555) 111-1111

RETAIL MANAGEMENT
• Cruise Industry •

SUMMARY

Innovate, successful **Retail Manager** with over **15 years** of experience in Operations Management, Merchandising, Sales and Customer Service, Staff Recruiting and Supervision, Product Selection, and Facility Maintenance. Proven ability to increase revenues by creating an inviting shopping environment offering **friendly, personal attention.** **Avid ship historian and cruise passenger with extensive knowledge of the maritime industry.**

EDUCATION / PROFESSIONAL DEVELOPMENT

A.A.S., Retail Management and Merchandising, 1983 • Middlesex County College, Edison, NJ
Attended employer-sponsored seminars on Sales and Customer Service.

RETAIL MANAGEMENT EXPERIENCE

STORE MANAGER, Sam Goody, Inc./Sun Coast Motion Picture Co., Clayton, NJ   1991 - Present
Manage daily operations of a music and entertainment retail location with over $1 million in annual sales. Supervise a staff of five. Scope of responsibility includes sales and customer service, cash management, financial reporting, facility maintenance, employee relations, merchandising, and promotions. Manage an inventory of $200,000.

- Drove up revenues from $400,000 to over $1 million, in a four-year period, through strong focus on customer service, excellent merchandising, and team work.
- Formally recognized for highest increase in special orders throughout the region (150 stores) in 1996.
- Reduced shrink from 1.96% to .94%, consistently surpassing company standards.
- Received corporate recognition for developing innovative, attention-getting merchandising strategies.
- Achieved one of the lowest turnover rates in the company by creating a cohesive team environment.
- Recognized potential of staff; played a key role in their development and promotion to managerial positions.

CO-MANAGER, Sizes Unlimited/The Limited, Inc., Eatontown, NJ   1987 - 1990
Supervised a staff of 10 in a 9000 sq. ft. women's apparel store, specializing in large sizes. Analyzed market and selected merchandise, coordinated all merchandising activities, created fresh displays, hired and trained staff, enforced store security, managed shipping / receiving, and maintained inventory records.

- Significantly increased sales, leading to a planned store expansion/renovation.
- Expanded customer base by offering a wide range of stylish ensembles and creating a trendy, warm atmosphere that increased the comfort level of patrons.
- Achieved a high volume of add-on sales by suggesting fashionable accessories.
- Received frequent requests from customers to personally assist with their selections.

STORE MANAGER, Signature/Capezio (Ascot Shoes, Inc.), Woodbridge, NJ   1981 - 1987
Managed a high-end retail women's footwear store, with average prices between $170-$250. Served an eclectic customer base from N.Y. and N.J.; competed successfully in a large mall with numerous shoe businesses. Was one of the youngest store managers in the company; promoted from sales associate.

- Selected by regional director to evaluate new locations in P.A. and N.J., and provide guidance in layout, decorating, display design, and merchandising.
- Accompanied executives on buying trips to high-profile vendors; made product recommendations.
- Innovated and introduced successful promotions; initiated promotional collaborations with an affiliated mall store to broaden customer base at both sites.

104

Combination. *Rhoda Kopy, Toms River, New Jersey*

The wheel graphic as a symbol of the cruise industry is eye-catching. Because of smaller type and narrower margins, this one-page resume can contain much information.

Raymond H. Wilson

832 Newport Rd., Newport, MI 48166
(313) 555-3130

Summary

Retail Manager

- 16 years experience in retail, 12 in retail management for a major chain.
- Experienced in operations, budgeting, merchandising, customer service, purchasing, and inventory control.
- Strong customer service orientation; work well with the public.
- Excellent leadership skills–can communicate effectively with employees and motivate them to perform at their best. Can set direction for the team. Hands-on approach to training.
- Can effectively manage budget and save costs.
- Flexible–proven ability to adapt to corporate changes in operations or personnel.
- 16-year record of dependability and loyalty to the company.

Experience

WAL-MART, Monroe, Michigan   1980-Present

Replenishment Manager, 1994-Present
Operations Assistant Manager, 1992-1994 (Promotion)
Customer Service Manager, 1990-1992
Merchandising Assistant-Hardlines, 1987-1990 (Promotion)
Store Assistant Manager, 1984-1987 (Promotion)
Floor Supervisor, 1981-1984 (Promotion)
Stock Person-Patio, 1980-1981

- Assist in overseeing day-to day operations of entire store.
- Have managed up to 40 employees, including scheduling, training, supervising daily assignments, and evaluating performance.
- Monitor expenditures of all store supplies, ensuring that they are within budget.
- Increase profits through effective displays and merchandising.
- Numerous customer service awards.

Education

EASTERN MICHIGAN UNIVERSITY, Ypsilanti, Michigan
Three Years of Credits towards BA in Mathematics

MONROE HIGH SCHOOL, Monroe, Michigan
Graduate

105

Combination. *Deborah L. Schuster, Newport, Michigan*

This person's experience was all at one company. The writer listed all positions together and then indicated the promotions. The rest were lateral moves or reorganizations.

Daniel T. Phillips

123 Country View Circle • Anytown, TN 00000   Home/Message • (000) 000-0000

Professional Background

Over 15 years of problem solving, troubleshooting, professional advancement, and increased responsibility. Extensive experience in a hands-on manufacturing environment, including production, machine operations, maintenance, powder coating, health, safety, and environmental inspections, and hazardous materials transportation.

Qualifications Summary

- ☒ People-oriented, machine-friendly individual with strong technical expertise and problem-solving skills
- ☒ Quality-conscious manager with the ability to detect design flaws and recommend changes to facilitate production, prevent errors, and save time with a constant eye to safety
- ☒ Strong record of compliance with all safety regulations and guidelines, including OSHA, EPA, and DOT
- ☒ Highly effective in organizing work flow, ideas, materials, and personnel
- ☒ Computer and software skills include *DOS, Microsoft Windows, Lotus 1-2-3, Lotus Smart Suite, AmiPro, Harvard Graphics,* and *Auto CAD*
- ☒ Special interest and ability in developing powder coating process and spraying techniques

Employment History

XYZ AUTO PARTS, INC. • Anytown, Tennessee
Store Manager • 1995 - Present / *Assistant Manager* • 1994

- Direct and monitor daily store operations, including customer service, inside and outside sales staff, inventory, shipping and receiving, and recordkeeping
- Personally service 75 established accounts and generate new business through cold calling and maintaining extensive network of prospective customers
- Prepare bids for state, county, and city government agencies

EQUIPMENT SUPPLY COMPANY • Anytown, Kentucky
Inside Sales Representative • 1994 - 1995

- Represented and sold hand tools, electric and pneumatic power tools, safety equipment, and other industrial-related merchandise
- Researched and prepared 80% of all quotes for Major Aluminum Company, as well as quotes for other area companies

ABC PERFORMANCE PARTS • Anytown, Tennessee • 1982 - 1994
A remanufacturer of automotive carburetors and a division of Technical Industries.

Maintenance Supervisor/Environmental Project Technician • 1991 - 1994
- Implemented and monitored various safety programs, such as Health and Safety Inspections, Fire Prevention, Hazardous Waste Handling and Storage in accordance with federal, state, and local agencies and insurance regulations
- Designed and developed computerized checklist to track potential OSHA violations by plant location, department, and individual item
- Coordinated maintenance repairs with production personnel to eliminate production down time

106

Combination. *Carolyn S. Braden, Hendersonville, Tennessee*

The individual was a victim of corporate downsizing two years earlier and was seeking to return as a mid-level manager to manufacturing. His area of expertise was powder coating, and he

Daniel T. Phillips   **Page 2**

Employment History (continued)

Industrial Engineering Project Technician ● 1987 - 1991
- Developed powder coating process for ABC Custom Shop from start-up through application of finished product
- Maintained powder coating equipment, substrate preparation, and spraying techniques
- Assisted in the development of projects involving fuel injectors, stand-alone fuel injection, O.E. replacement throttle body injection, and development of test equipment and procedures for fuel injection components

Production Engineering Technician ● 1984 - 1987
- Provided assistance and on-the-spot engineering advice to correct production problems
- Supervised all flow test procedures and production flow masters

Development Engineering Technician ● 1984
- Developed Bill of Materials and specification data sheets for remanufactured carburetors

Development Engineering Flow Technician ● 1982 - 1984
- Developed flow test procedures for LPG carburetors and production flow masters for Development Engineering

ACME CORPORATION ● Anytown, Tennessee
Electronics Technician ● 1981 - 1982
- Performed maintenance, troubleshooting, and repairs of digital circuits on wire-guided mobility forklifts (6502 and 6800 computer systems used on the mobility forklifts)

Education and Professional Training

Hazardous Materials Training Course ● HMT Technology, Inc. ● March 1993

CF MotorFreight Hazardous Materials Seminar ● July 1992

Nashville State Technical Institute ● Emphasis on *Electronic Engineering* ● 1975 - 1976

───

● **Additional Information Available Upon Request** ●

had developed a new process and spraying technique. The writer emphasizes the person's strong manufacturing background and commitment to production and quality standards. Bold italic helps the various job positions stand out.

TIMOTHY P. WILSON

10 W. 5th Street ▪ Troy, MI 48000
(313) 555-1234

Objective

A Logistical/Maintenance Management Position.

Summary of Qualifications

Seventeen years training, education, and practical experience in **maintenance and transportation operations management**–in both military and civilian environments–with a detailed working knowledge in:

- Managing transportation, logistics and maintenance of military vehicles and weapons systems.
- Overseeing transportation operations.
- Overseeing repair and maintenance of heavy semi-tractor/trailer vehicles; and managing the parts department to support that maintenance.
- Project management and organizational development.
- Recruiting, staffing, training, supervising, and managing personnel.
- Creating a synergistic work environment–maximizing productivity of personnel and equipment.
- Administering safety and security programs and risk assessment.
- Managing budgets and records, including computer-generated tracking systems.

Experience

PK TRUCKING, Ann Arbor, Michigan   February, 1993 - Present
(One of the nation's leading transport companies)

Parts Manager (Promotion) (8/94 - Present)

- Manage Parts Department with $100,000 base parts inventory, supporting maintenance for 7,600 trucks and 12,500 trailers.
- Oversee five employees, including day-to-day supervision, hiring, training, scheduling, and promotions.
- Manage inventory, including cost analysis of vendor-supplied items.
- Order, receive, and inspect parts; and return obsolete or defective items.
- Instituted vigorous housecleaning program to reorganize storage rooms for greater efficiency. Purged and reorganized filing system.
- Developed comprehensive training and retraining program for both new and old employees, which increased productivity.

Shop Foreman (Promotion) (9/93 - 8/94)

- Oversaw all aspects of maintenance, preventive maintenance, and repair of heavy over-the-road semi-tractors.
  Region Covered: Upper Midwest and parts of Canada. **Volume:** 75-200 Vehicles per day.
- Scheduled, assigned, and monitored repair activities; directly supervised twelve mechanics.

107

Functional. *Deborah L. Schuster, Newport, Michigan*

The applicant had strong backgrounds in maintenance management and logistics. He also had equally strong civilian and military experience. The challenge was to summarize his extensive

Timothy P. Wilson

Resume/2

PK TRUCKING (Continued)

Driver Supervisor/Yard Control (2/93 - 9/93)

- Scheduled and supervised incoming and outgoing freight.
- Coordinated assignment of equipment, preplanning and dispatching.
- Handled high volume paperwork, including customs requirements.

Military Experience (1977 - 1992)

US ARMY   1977 - 1992

Warrant Officer (86 - 92)

- Directed battalion-sized transportation, logistics, and maintenance operations, including: Driver/Operator training and testing; Automated parts supply and maintenance management systems; Motor vehicle dispatch and utilization; Scheduling; All mechanical repair, maintenance, and quality control for a wide variety of machinery, equipment, vehicles, and weapons systems; and Records Management–both manual and computer, including (TAMMS).
- Formulated policies and procedures for transportation, logistics, and maintenance, including timetables, assignment of drivers/cargo, and procedures for monitoring movement.
- Conducted assessment studies of facilities configuration, maintenance operations, actuaries, equipment/personnel utilization. Initiated improvements based on the analysis. *Result: Improved efficiency of operations.*
- Trained, directed, and supervised mechanics and technicians.

1977-1986: Received consistent promotions from Private to Staff Sergeant, and ultimately to Warrant Officer.

Military Awards:
Excellent personal and professional evaluations with numerous awards, honors, and recognition for outstanding technical skills, exemplary performance, outstanding achievement, meritorious service, individual initiative, professionalism, and proficiency.

Education

A.A. Degree - Technical Education:
Piece Community College, Tacoma, Washington   1990

U.S. Army Warrant Officer Training School
Aberdeen Proving Grounds, Maryland   1986

**Basic, Advanced, and Senior Leadership/Management Training, and
NCO/Enlisted Technical Training**
U.S. Army Institute for Professional Development   1977 - 1986

---

civilian and military backgrounds with equal emphases. The writer added a Summary of Qualifications to merge the person's civilian and military backgrounds and "to provide a comprehensive 'snapshot' of his abilities."

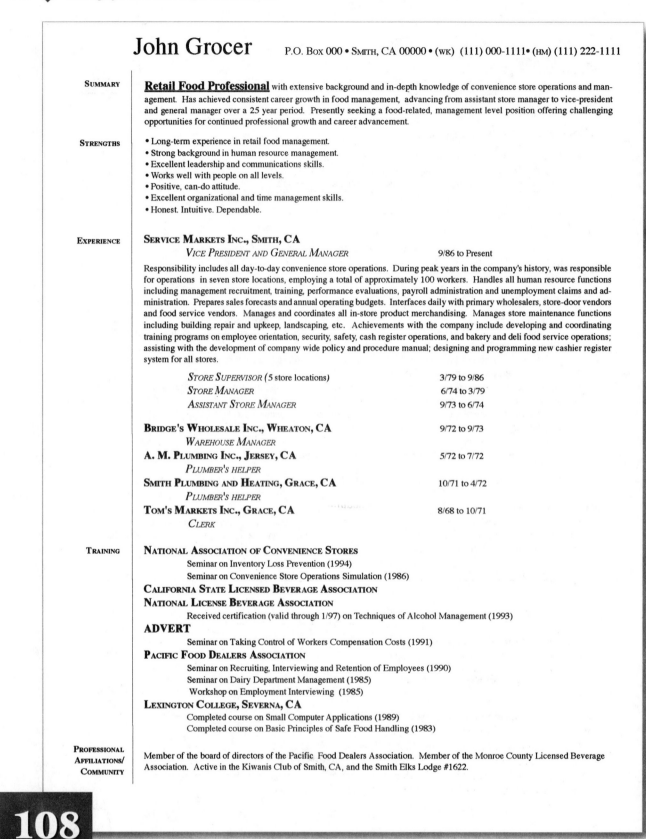

John Grocer
P.O. Box 000 • Smith, CA 00000 • (wk) (111) 000-1111• (hm) (111) 222-1111

SUMMARY

Retail Food Professional with extensive background and in-depth knowledge of convenience store operations and management. Has achieved consistent career growth in food management, advancing from assistant store manager to vice-president and general manager over a 25 year period. Presently seeking a food-related, management level position offering challenging opportunities for continued professional growth and career advancement.

STRENGTHS

- Long-term experience in retail food management.
- Strong background in human resource management.
- Excellent leadership and communications skills.
- Works well with people on all levels.
- Positive, can-do attitude.
- Excellent organizational and time management skills.
- Honest. Intuitive. Dependable.

EXPERIENCE

SERVICE MARKETS INC., SMITH, CA

VICE PRESIDENT AND GENERAL MANAGER   9/86 to Present

Responsibility includes all day-to-day convenience store operations. During peak years in the company's history, was responsible for operations in seven store locations, employing a total of approximately 100 workers. Handles all human resource functions including management recruitment, training, performance evaluations, payroll administration and unemployment claims and administration. Prepares sales forecasts and annual operating budgets. Interfaces daily with primary wholesalers, store-door vendors and food service vendors. Manages and coordinates all in-store product merchandising. Manages store maintenance functions including building repair and upkeep, landscaping, etc. Achievements with the company include developing and coordinating training programs on employee orientation, security, safety, cash register operations, and bakery and deli food service operations; assisting with the development of company wide policy and procedure manual; designing and programming new cashier register system for all stores.

STORE SUPERVISOR (5 store locations)	3/79 to 9/86
STORE MANAGER	6/74 to 3/79
ASSISTANT STORE MANAGER	9/73 to 6/74

BRIDGE'S WHOLESALE INC., WHEATON, CA   9/72 to 9/73
WAREHOUSE MANAGER

A. M. PLUMBING INC., JERSEY, CA   5/72 to 7/72
PLUMBER'S HELPER

SMITH PLUMBING AND HEATING, GRACE, CA   10/71 to 4/72
PLUMBER'S HELPER

TOM'S MARKETS INC., GRACE, CA   8/68 to 10/71
CLERK

TRAINING

NATIONAL ASSOCIATION OF CONVENIENCE STORES
Seminar on Inventory Loss Prevention (1994)
Seminar on Convenience Store Operations Simulation (1986)

CALIFORNIA STATE LICENSED BEVERAGE ASSOCIATION

NATIONAL LICENSE BEVERAGE ASSOCIATION
Received certification (valid through 1/97) on Techniques of Alcohol Management (1993)

ADVERT
Seminar on Taking Control of Workers Compensation Costs (1991)

PACIFIC FOOD DEALERS ASSOCIATION
Seminar on Recruiting, Interviewing and Retention of Employees (1990)
Seminar on Dairy Department Management (1985)
Workshop on Employment Interviewing (1985)

LEXINGTON COLLEGE, SEVERNA, CA
Completed course on Small Computer Applications (1989)
Completed course on Basic Principles of Safe Food Handling (1983)

PROFESSIONAL AFFILIATIONS/ COMMUNITY

Member of the board of directors of the Pacific Food Dealers Association. Member of the Monroe County Licensed Beverage Association. Active in the Kiwanis Club of Smith, CA, and the Smith Elks Lodge #1622.

108

Combination. *Thomas E. Spann, Easton, Maryland*

An executive resume with very small type and narrow margins to present much information and still keep the resume to one page with adequate white space.

Mark T. Bradley, B.S.

9275 Catalpa ● New Holland, Michigan 48337
(612) 555-9617

PROFILE:

Background of proven success in *Hospitality Management* including food and beverage control in various hotel and resort establishments. Experience features involvement with fine dining facilities in a 4 star, 4 diamond hotel, banquet facilities, and corporate fast food operations. Customer service a priority.

EDUCATION:

College of Business, B.S. Hospitality Management, A.A.S. Diversified Business
Ferris State University, Big Rapids, Michigan

SUMMARY OF SKILLS AND TRAINING:

- Hire, train, schedule, and supervise up to 25 employees
- Develop advertising/marketing strategies
- Assist in determining menu selections stressing variety and utilizing seasonal foods
- Handle cost controls (food and labor), inventory controls, pricing, and purchasing
- Ensure all sanitation standards are being met including city, state, and federal codes
- Prepare and submit forecasting for financial and management matters
- Define goals for day to day operations
- Assist guests with room registration providing personalized service maximizing revenue and customer satisfaction
- Perform room service operations
- Set up and served banquets to 600 people
- Utilize computer for audits, reports, scheduling, etc.

PROFESSIONAL EXPERIENCE:

Manager
Pizza Hut, South Haven, Michigan

Internship
Amway Grand Plaza Hotel, Grand Rapids, Michigan (Front Desk)
Marriotts Marco Island Resort, Marco Island, Florida (Room Service and Banquets)

Bellhop/Room Service
Clarion Hotel & Conference Center, Big Rapids, Michigan

RELATED PROFESSIONAL ACTIVITIES:

- Purchasing Committee Chairman 1994 Annual Gala
- Training Intervention Procedures by Servers of Alcohol (TIPS)
- Front Office Procedures Certificate
- SYSCO Frost Pack Food Show, New Holland, Michigan

109

Functional. *Patricia L. Nieboer, Fremont, Michigan*

The food-related graphic is eye-catching and draws the reader into the resume. The Summary of Skills is centered vertically, and Experience displays three categories.

DIANE MARKS
22 West 256th St.
Riverdale, NY 10463
Voice/Fax: (718) 796-5534 (H)

PROFILE

Extensive knowledge of the wine industry including supplier, distributor, on and off premise, and consumer levels. Ability to develop an "instant rapport" with both the trade and public. Extensive product knowledge. Demonstrate a high level of motivation and enthusiasm in all aspects of work.

EXPERIENCE

REGIONAL MANAGEMENT

- Actively manage extensive Northeast distribution network for Winestock Valley Vineyards.
- Responsible for programming and key account management.
- Directly supervise, train, and evaluate distributor sales force regarding product knowledge, current media coverage, and special promotions.
- Participate regularly in trade tastings, shows, and vintner dinners.

DISTRIBUTION

- Successfully opened up new accounts and increased sales by 40% during a one year period for two major fine wine distributors in Massachusetts.
- Served as exclusive agent on Two Wales Island.
- Trained restaurant staff in product knowledge, service, and food and wine pairing.
- Utilized expertise of exclusive resort area in developing and servicing accounts.
- Provided a high level of customer service by going the extra mile.

RESTAURANT MANAGEMENT/SOMMELIER

- Managed front house operations in high volume restaurant (American Cuisine Restaurant) specializing in American regional foods and wines.
- Maintained, upgraded, and promoted wine list of 140 selections in same.
- Expanded wine selections from 80 to 230 and wine revenues by 25% as Sommelier.
- Brought The Massachusetts Inn wine list to national recognition with 1989 *Wine Expert Award of Prominence.*
- Responsible for ordering, pricing, inventories, and rotation of wines offerings by the glass.
- Instrumental in the planning/execution of six vintner dinners.
- Functioned in numerous capacities utilizing a solid understanding of restaurant management.

WORK HISTORY

Winestock Valley Vineyards, Sonoma Valley, CA
Northeast Regional Manager (1993 - Present)

Boston Wine Inc., Boston, MA
On and Off Premise Sales Consultant (1991-1993)

TUC Wine Corporation, Sommers, MA
On and Off Premise Sales Consultant (1989-1991)

American Cuisine Restaurant, Two Wales Island, MA
Floor Manager (1991-1992)

The Massachusetts Inn, Two Wales Island, MA
Sommelier (1989-1990)

EDUCATION

Boston University, Boston, MA
Completed four years of undergraduate study

References on request.

110

Combination. *Etta R. Barmann, New York, New York*

The value of grouping Experience entries under categories instead of presenting them in one long list is that the reader can get a quick overview of a range of experience.

Ronald W. Eastwood ────────────

Objective: A management position in the Food or Food Service Industry.

Profile:
- 13 years of experience in the Food Service Industry; 4 years in Restaurant Management.
- Strong record of cutting costs, increasing sales, and reducing waste.
- Excellent employee management skills. Improve morale and motivate staff through incentives, employee training, and improving the work atmosphere.

Experience: **Wallabey's**, Detroit, Michigan   January 1991-Present
Dining Room Manager (6/94-Present)
Beverage Manager (7/92-6/94)
Bartender (1/91-7/92)

Manage dining room for one of the top grossing restaurants in Michigan. Supervise an average of 50 employees per shift. Handle hiring, training, scheduling, and labor tracking. Control inventory and order front-of-the-house supplies. Oversee guest service and handle any customer complaints. Accountable for all monies, including cash drawer and bank deposits.

- **Cost Controls:** Reduced inventory by tracking a year's worth of sales and planning accordingly. Reduce payroll by careful employee scheduling. Reduced liquor costs through improved security, bartender retraining, and inventory control.
- **Sales:** Increased sales by training waitstaff in suggestive selling and by educating them about the products. Also introduced waitstaff sales incentives.
- **Awards:** Won "House of Seagrams" cocktail award, and was featured in an article by the <u>Michigan Beverage Journal</u>.

East Side Charley's, Harper Woods, Michigan March 1986-December 1991
Bartender (12/86-1/91)
Server (3/86-12/86)

- Trained for and earned in-house certification to train new employees.

L-Bow Room, Mt. Clemens, Michigan   July 1983-March 1986
Room Service, Bussed Tables

Education: *Graduate (1985)*
Clintondale High School, Mt. Clemens, Michigan

Additional Training: Attended numerous in-house seminars on management, sales, and employee training.

─────────────────────────────── 23 Elm Street, Monroe, MI 48161
(313) 555-3344

111

Combination. *Deborah L. Schuster, Newport, Michigan*

Here, achievements are grouped by categories. The writer put the contact information at the bottom so that the reader's eye could move directly from the name to the Objective.

DAVID LEE WILSON

65432 SE Buthler Court ■ Reddin, South Dakota 00000 ■ **555-555-5555**

PROFESSIONAL PROFILE

Results-oriented self-starter with more than twenty years of experience in restaurant management. Documented record of highly developed management, supervisory and training skills. Proven commitment to team-building, demonstrated by the ability to lead and motivate staff to perform at top efficiency levels.

QUALIFICATION SUMMARY

MANAGEMENT AND ADMINISTRATION

- Monitor in-restaurant controllable costs, including: product line variance, waste control, labor percentage, cash variance, customer service, food safety and quality, and cleanliness/sanitation of facilities.
- Contract vendors based upon research to determine cost and quality of service and product.
- Consistently achieve projected profit and loss objectives through effective budget management. Developed personnel audit form and conducted audits at five locations.
- Analyzed voluminous records/documentation on prior performance of restaurants in order to assist in development of, and make recommendations for, new Business Plan for Arby's Corporation.
- Coordinated opening of two new McDonalds restaurants. Oversaw progress of contractors, received and verified delivery of equipment and supplies, initialized all equipment and verified calibration, secured funds for and acquired local advertising, and acquired required health permits.

SUPERVISION AND TRAINING

- Staff restaurants through implementation of goals and objectives of Equal Opportunity and Affirmative Action. Coordinate with South Dakota State Employment Security Office on staffing issues.
- When acting for my supervisor, monitor performance, training and development of intermediate managers and crews of *five restaurants*, through delegation and daily follow-up.
- Coordinate cross training among staff to ensure efficient operation under all circumstances.
- Provide advice/assistance to managers and crew, when required and appropriate, on 24 hour a day basis.

SELECTED ACCOMPLISHMENTS

- Earned *Best Restaurant Traveling Award* over all other South Dakota Arby's in the first quarter 1995, from Arby's Corporation. This award recognized quality, service and cleanliness inspected on an unannounced schedule.
- Under my management the Rapid City Arby's was recognized in June 1993 by the County Health District as one of *top ten food service facilities* in Oacoma County, based on inspection scores.
- Prepared restaurant for corporate audit while assisting managers of four other restaurants with preparation for their audits.
- Performance Summary in 1989, which covered concurrent management of two Mcdonalds restaurants, stated, "*David is an excellent manager*. Every market could use a manager like him. David opened up two company restaurants in a year's time. Both were very organized and ready to open on schedule."
- Tasked with running a struggling McDonalds in the White Center business district, completely staffed restaurant and *increased sales by 19%* in eight months.
- Recognized for maintaining *outstanding cash control* for Tacoma Arby's.
- Honored as *Manager of the Year* in 1984 for management of Gig Harbor McDonalds.

112

Combination. *Lonnie L. Swanson, Poulsbo, Washington*

Thick-thin lines at the bottom of each page mirror thin-thick lines at the top. Partial lines after each section heading make the design of the resume evident at a glance. The lines and the

DAVID LEE WILSON

EMPLOYMENT HISTORY

Arby's Restaurant, Rapid City, South Dakota **1991 - Present**
Restaurant Manager

Oversee the daily operation of an Arby's restaurant serving over 20,000 customers each month. Total management responsibility, personally or through intermediate managers, covers staff placement, development and training; quality of product and service; budget administration; and documentation and analysis of business volume. In addition to daily responsibilities:

- Conduct Assistant Manager meetings attended by 20 or more to discuss pending product promotions, corporate policy issues, and individual store performance.
- Conduct weekly in-restaurant management meetings and quarterly crew meetings in order to maintain and improve the level of service and product.
- Set long term goal and objectives for restaurant and develop weekly and monthly restaurant performance reports to track the progress of objectives.

McDonalds Corporation, Seattle, Washington **1986 - 1991**
Restaurant Manager

Managed several restaurants for McDonalds Corporation during this time period. Supervised up to five intermediate managers and 30 - 40 crew members per store. Daily responsibilities included staffing, training and performance reviews for management and crew; daily, weekly and monthly reports; budget management; equipment calibration and repair; and quality of service and product. In addition to daily responsibilities:

- Simultaneously coordinated the construction, set-up and opening of two restaurants. After successful restaurant openings, tasked with concurrent management of both stores which was accomplished through effective delegation.
- Through hard work and effective management, dramatically improved the profit/loss ratio of a White Center McDonalds which was previously poorly controlled and severely understaffed.

Various Bay Area Fast Food Restaurants - Details Available **1973 - 1986**
Progressive Promotions from Crew Person to Head Manager

EDUCATION AND TRAINING

Salmon Center Community College
Suquamish, Washington
- Course work in Hotel/Motel Management

South Shore College
Graham, Washington
- Course work in Basic Computer Skills

CONTINUING EDUCATION COURSES

Intermediate Management Training
Basic Management Training
People, The Winning Edge

Applied Food Service Sanitation
Industrial First Aid Certification
CPR Certification

---

square bullets unify the two pages visually. Across the two pages boldfacing attracts the eye to important information, achievements, and job positions. For each position a paragraph indicates responsibilities, and bulleted items show notable activities.

Claudette Ford-Worthy

3388 Oakwood Road • Charleston, WV 25311 • (304) 555-4447

Qualifications Summary

- Six years small business management experience, with specialization in personnel management, staff development, and team building
- Highly articulate with a natural instinct for creative marketing strategies
- Adept at designing new systems and procedures to maximize workplace efficiency
- Respected, affable team leader with a record of inspiring high morale and productivity
- Well versed in many computer programs, including DOS and Windows applications
- Highly energetic professional; a life-long learner with a reputation for welcoming challenge and overcoming adversity

Professional Experience

PROTECTED PROPERTY COMPANY, Charleston, West Virginia   1990-Present
Operations Manager

Areas of Responsibility:
- ▶ Managed team of 17, coordinating service schedules and interacting with clients to arrange for over 100 technical calls per day
- ▶ Purchased all company supplies, equipment, fleet vehicles, and resale merchandise
- ▶ Served as safety director, evaluating work environment and coordinating training
- ▶ Edited *The Safety Voice*, the monthly newsletter of the West Virginia Safety Council
- ▶ Managed credit and collections functions, keeping annual write-offs to less than 1%

Major Accomplishments:
- ▶ Directed the relocation and merger of two companies, including the consolidation of inventories, personnel, administrative procedures, and accounting functions
- ▶ While safety director, company received the Governor's Safety Award for its outstanding safety record
- ▶ Researched and wrote company's OSHA hazardous material communication plan; implemented the program and conducted the training company wide
- ▶ Achieved company's highest inside sales for 1995

Education

- **Business Administration,** San Antonio College, San Antonio, Texas, 1988-1990
- **Associate of Applied Sciences in Business,** National Education Center, San Antonio, Texas, 1988, GPA 4.0
- **Continuing Education,** 1990-1995, topics included:
  - ▶ Hazardous Communications
  - ▶ Americans with Disabilities Act
  - ▶ Managing Multiple Projects
  - ▶ Confined Space Training
  - ▶ Skill Path Career Development
  - ▶ Team Building

Affiliations

- West Virginia Safety Council
- National Association of Female Executives
- Charleston YWCA, active with community volunteer programs
- Shaolin martial arts

113

Combination. *Barbie Dallmann, Charleston, West Virginia*

Experience was with only one family-owned business. After a large company bought the business, her new job was a demotion. The focus is on past duties and achievements.

Sheryl Lerlin
7 Jester Court
Marlboro, New York 07746
808-777-1777

Objective

To continue my career in the areas of recruitment, staffing, and human resources. Broad-based responsibilities in areas including:

Training and Recruitment	Interviewing, Screening, Testing
Marketing, Sales, Advertising	Payroll and Accounting Functions
Branch Operations	Client Relations/Troubleshooting

Experience

1995-Present

Emerson Staffing, (*Formerly One Temps, Inc.*), Manalapan, NY
Operations Manager
- Responsible for client contact and customer service for all new and existing accounts.
- In charge of all recruiting and staffing for exempt and non-exempt employment positions. Interview, screen, and place all applicants.
- Serve as payroll supervisor for approximately 65 temporary employees per week.
- Manage the advertising for Ewing Staffing newspaper advertisements and other forms of media advertising.

1989-1995

One Temps, Inc./One Management Resource Group, Freehold, NY
General Manager (1993-1995)
- Increased sales by 60%, including inside and outside sales.
- Oversaw a staff of five employees.
- Placed, screened, and interviewed all applicants for a variety of positions.
- Prepared payroll for average billing of $25,000 per week.
- Held power of attorney for all banking functions. Authorized to sign checks.
- Handled all advertising and public relations for the temporary business.
- Provided customer service to all new and existing accounts.

Additional Positions: (1989-1993)
One Temps, Inc./One Management Resource Group, Freehold, NY
Permanent Placement Counselor/Accountants and MIS Personnel

- Worked with Big 10 Accounting Firms and Fortune 500 financial institutions.

Former Employment

Howard E. Ruth & Co., Inc., New York, NY (4 years)

- Worked as an Administrative Assistant to the President of RE Management Company. Handled correspondence with state and city housing authority.
- Sold and rented apartments and condominiums. Submitted necessary papers for low-income housing projects to various governmental agencies.
- Interfaced with superintendents of major high-rise apartment buildings.
- Made court appearances on behalf of the company against tenants.

Education

Hunter College of New York - completed 20 credits
AAS Degree Bronx Community College

114

Combination. *Beverly Baskin, Marlboro, New Jersey*

The Objective includes areas of expertise in two columns. This format makes it easy to substitute expertise areas to create a new resume for each new job target.

H. Beaumont Lower MBA

655 Sierra Madre • Yuma, Mexico 88888 • (888) 555-5973

PROFILE

FINANCE & BUSINESS DEVELOPMENT MANAGER

- *Specializing in:* Acquisitions Management, Financial Analysis, Strategic Planning, and Financial Reporting.
- *Focused on:* Generating increased profitability, reducing operating costs, and controlling inventory expenditures.
- *Computer proficiencies:* Excel, Access, MS Word, PowerPoint, Harvard Graphics, SPSS, ExecuStat, SAS, Lindo, Lotus 1-2-3

CAREER DEVELOPMENT

FOREIGN DATA SYSTEMS, Mesa, Arizona   **199x to Present**

Publicly-held, $360MM supplier of data collection systems and services serving primarily financial services, healthcare, government, and business entities worldwide.

Manager—Business Development

Identify, evaluate, and negotiate niche acquisitions. Lead process of integrating acquired companies into operational structure. Introduce strategic plans, financial controls, information technologies, and growth initiatives which improve revenues, strengthen business practices, and enhance reporting and forecasting capabilities.

Key Contributions

- Formulated and executed new market niche joint venture which captured 10% market share within 1 year.
- Directed due diligence reviews and financial negotiations for 3 strategic acquisitions resulting in maximized market share and allowing for penetration into new markets.
- Spearheaded drive to identify and evaluate growth opportunities more efficiently by developing growth model based on strategic planning, competitor analysis, and trend forecasting.
- Authored 5-year strategic plan which focused on domestic and international acquisitions, joint ventures, and partnerships.

ALLIED CORPORATION, Morris, New State   199x

$14 billion Fortune 100 manufacturing company featuring over 100 subsidiaries globally, employing 86,000, and serving the aerospace, automotive, and engineered materials markets.

MBA Associate—Operations Analysis Group

- Researched and analyzed potential merger/divestiture candidates.
- Maximized local and foreign tax credits by analyzing foreign subsidiaries' debt capacity and determining optimal debt/equity mix.
- Analyzed joint venture opportunity to facilitate entry into emerging market with existing technology while minimizing associated risk.
- Developed cash flow tracking system which optimized cash management and foreign exchange processes.

115

Combination. *Elizabeth J. Axnix, Iowa City, Iowa*

"An MBA resume for an individual who served in another country's armed forces." The partial horizontal lines point to the section headings and therefore help to make visible the overall

H. Beaumont Lower MBA

Page Two

CAREER DEVELOPMENT, cont.

XYZ FUND, Chicago, Illinois   199x to 199x

Financial consulting group which provided services to mid-sized companies within the Midwest.

Consultant

- Performed financial analyses implementing proforma models which included cash-flow analyses, P/E ratios extrapolations, multiples, and dividends models.
- Performed marketing analyses designed to enhance businesses' market share and allow for diversification into new niches.
- Pioneered structure and implementation of group's TQM program which achieved higher productivity levels and strengthened overall communications and teamwork.

EDUCATION

THE MANAGEMENT SCHOOL—UNIVERSITY OF MEXICO, Yuma
MBA—Finance & Risk Management (199x)
Joseph C. Smith Achievement Award

THE UNIVERSITY OF UTAH, Utah City
BBA—Accounting & Finance (199x)
Summa Cum Laude

MILITARY SERVICE

AIR FORCE   198x to 198x

Operations and Logistics Officer

Led electronic lab team of 120 professionals to achieve greater efficiency and higher quality levels on a daily basis; identified and capitalized on cost reduction opportunities. Trained over 150 officers in leadership skills and conducted Efficient Management Workshops required to attain rank of Captain.

Key Contributions

- Managed design, execution, and implementation of $300MM electronic warfare system within budget and on schedule.
- Supervised acquisition and integration of US Navy electronic warfare system; led on-site implementation and directed staff of 44 technicians and engineers.

arrangement of the resume. Note the use of italic in this resume: in Profile groups, in subtitles for Key Contributions for the current employer and during military service, in company-name explanations, and for impressive academic achievements.

JEFFREY W. HOLT

- 100 Harvest Road   • Galt, California 95632   • (209) 555-1212

OBJECTIVE   A position in Transportation and Logistics Management.

SUMMARY

- Over 15 years experience in logistics and transportation management.
- Proficient in surface, air, rail and linehaul systems coordination and development.
- Employ straightforward management approach for motivating cooperation.
- Strong record of providing personable and professional customer service.
- Knowledgeable in Procom, Microsoft Word, LAN, and HP mainframe.

EXPERIENCE AND ACCOMPLISHMENTS

LINEHAUL COORDINATION AND SCHEDULING
- Increased monthly truck mileage by 10%.
- Reduced driver turnover rates and raised employee retention level.
- Developed software solutions to ease management of linehaul system.
- Established time-efficient nationwide linehaul schedules.
  - Ensured JIT delivery and maximized volume capacity.
- Administered system for Qualcomm Satellite Tracking System.

VENDOR MANAGEMENT
- Reduced mileage rates by implementing newly developed software program.
- Redefined optimum carrier program to increase vendor performance.
- Review vendor performance and negotiate rates with national account managers.

SUPERVISION AND TRAINING
- Conduct ongoing multi-site computer training for over 100 employees.
- Coordinate with Fleet Services on linehaul and personnel issues.
- Encourage team efforts and collaboration to attain goals and objectives.

EMPLOYMENT HISTORY

1995-present   **Divisional Linehaul Coordinator** • Skyway Freight Systems, Inc., Sacramento
Coordinate linehaul activities within division, ensuring on-time service in the most cost effective manner. Manage truckload vendor services and negotiations.

Truck Dispatch/Lead Linehaul Agent   1990-1995
Managed daily linehaul operations. Interviewed, hired, trained, supervised, and reviewed truck dispatch agents.

Central Operations Agent   1989-1990
As first linehaul operations specialist, set up truck dispatch and linehaul group.

PU&D Dispatch Supervisor   1986-1989
Managed local PU&D operations and coordinated daily operations for 20 drivers.

1976-1985   **Linehaul Coordinator** • Viking Freight System, San Jose
Coordinated daily efficient linehaul operations for 32 terminals and over 200 drivers.

EDUCATION AND RELATED TRAINING
Foothill College, Business and General Education, Los Altos Hills
Watsonville Adult Education, Computer Science, Watsonville

- Hazardous Materials • Front-Line Leadership • Zenger Miller Management Course
- Interpersonal Communications • Route-It-Right • Earthquake preparedness
- Hold CDL with doubles/triples, tankers and hazardous materials endorsements.
- CHP/DOT Hours of Service/Log Book Requirement.

116

Combination. *Nancy Karvonen, Galt, California*

Horizontal lines slightly shorter than line width make it easier to spot the beginning of each section heading. If the lines indicate sections, the Objective and Summary are in one section.

Matthew C. Hatson

653 River Road, Grosse Ile, MI 48138
H: (313) 555-7654 ◆ W: (313) 333-1324

Career Highlights

Manager with extensive background in Engineering, Logistics, and Human Resources. Skilled troubleshooter, leader, negotiator, and communicator with a proven ability to increase profitability, productivity, efficiency, and morale.

Engineering	Directed UPS staff in job planning, workload/workforce balancing, and documentation control. Developed and maintained long-range plans for operations, training, and inspections. Developed a "Master Operating Plan" (M.O.P.)–a standardized procedure for processing Canadian shipments through Customs–for Detroit Area. The plan streamlined procedures and resulted in improved productivity and a decrease in errors. The M.O.P. was used as a nationwide model, and I was sent to Seattle, Buffalo, Minneapolis and Montreal to implement the program. Served as mediator with Customs. Increased pieces per hour by 300%, reduced fines, and improved morale.
Logistics	Set up UPS facilities to handle package flow. Successfully managed Midwest shipping and distribution of the Diet Pepsi "Gotta Have It" promotion. Midwest operation was the most efficient in the U.S. Brought consistency to Time-in-Transit nationwide.
Management	Trained in operations, logistics, personnel management, customer service, production management, inventory control and shipping. Successfully set up Customer Service Export Hold Center as a troubleshooting center for problem packages. Currently manage a restaurant, and a $35,000/per month budget. Experienced with negotiating union contracts; work well with Teamsters.
Human Resources	Excellent leadership skills with the ability to motivate and direct staff. Have supervised staff of up to 150–both hourly employees and salaried supervisors. Developed training video for pre-work communication meeting. As Hub Training Supervisor, hired and trained 69 people in two months, with no turnover during the Christmas rush. Opened Madison Heights UPS facility and trained Management on hiring and keeping employees.

Professional History

ST. MARTIN'S, La Salle, MI Owner/Manager	1994 - Present
UNITED PARCEL SERVICE Volume Reconciliation Supervisor, Livonia Hub Supervisor, Night Sort Supervisor	1985 - 1994

Education

UNIVERSITY OF MICHIGAN Computer Science/Marketing	1983 - 1988
GROSSE ILE HIGH SCHOOL, Grosse Ile, Michigan	Graduated in 1978

117

Combination. *Deborah L. Schuster, Newport, Michigan*

This person had been a logistics manager for a major shipping company but had purchased a restaurant and was its full-time manager. He now wanted to get back into logistics.

POLLY PRODUCTION
4711 Cologne Street
Best City, New State 55555
(888) 555-6059

SUMMARY

Qualified production manager offering 10+ years' experience in NCS backend operations with particular management and leadership expertise in:

√ 2nd shift packaging
√ output processing
√ computer operations

PROFESSIONAL DEVELOPMENT

NATIONAL CAN SYSTEMS, Best City, New State   **197x-Present**
Operations Representative, Output Processing—199x-Present
Challenged to manage resources and assure quality in meeting internal and contractual commitments for this educational testing and information management company.

√ Lead the process of developing assumptions, generating schedules of estimated resources and conducting pre / post project reviews. Manage direct reports of 6 senior work group coordinators.
√ Set project rate standards. Monitor process flow to attain highest level of quality.
√ Liaison with management, non-exempt staff, and product line staff to assertively manage temporary employee assignments.
√ Identify potential improvements to process control system. Suggest enhancements to management and vendors relevant to interdepartmental schedule concerns, priority requests or failure to meet customer requests.
√ Direct schedules involving multiple shifts; frequently called upon to assume acting manager responsibilities.

Critical Contributions
Seasonal Manager, 2nd Shift Packaging—1/9x-3/9x; 12/9x-5/9x

√ Maintained optimal use of resources to meet schedule commitments and shipping deadlines in processing test materials for shipment.
√ Selected 3 acting senior coordinators and managed up to 74 full-time and temporary employees.

Senior Processing Coordinator, Packaging—199x-199x
Senior Computer Operator, Computer Operations—198x-199x
Computer Operator, Computer Operations—198x-198x
Production Clerk, Pre-Mailing—197x-198x

COMPUTER PROFICIENCIES

MVS/XA Operation
Word ... Excel ... PowerPoint
DOS ... Win95 ... Macintosh

... Production Management ... 2nd or 3rd Shift ...

118

Combination. *Elizabeth J. Axnix, Iowa City, Iowa*

Check mark bullets stand out in this resume for a production manager with much experience. Boldfacing for job positions makes them easy to see at a glance.

MARTIN C. GRENNER
14 Albright Avenue • Dunston, NJ 00111 • (555) 555-5555

TRUCKING INDUSTRY MANAGER

Results-driven management professional with over 14 years of experience in key facets of the trucking industry with domestic and international carriers. Exceptional track record of increasing terminal operating efficiency, boosting profitability, and unifying employees through knowledge and expertise in:

Trucking / Air Freight / Rail Operations ... Terminal Management ... Warehousing / Distribution ...
Customer Service ... Scheduling / Routing ... Systems Analysis ... Cost Containment ... Equipment
Purchasing ... Service Costing / Pricing ...... Staff Supervision ... Employee Relations ... Labor Relations

Versatile, dedicated manager who leads by example, thrives on challenge, and is determined to excel.

PROFESSIONAL EXPERIENCE

Fralcot Trucking, Summit, NJ   1992 - Present
(A regional LTL common carrier, with 90 terminals, servicing the East and Midwest. Strong focus on quality service. Client base includes large food warehouses, discount chains, automotive parts suppliers, and electronic companies.)

OPERATIONS MANAGER (1994 - Present)
Manage all aspects of a 75-door terminal operation (inbound/outbound, dispatching, and administration) with full responsibility for all three shifts. Schedule and supervise 50 drivers, 25 dock workers, and office staff in a union environment. Plan and oversee 300-400 daily deliveries, and handle 600-700 bills of lading during evening operation. Use automated system for planning, tracking, and analysis. Challenged to enhance operating efficiency, reduce costs, and unify staff. Promoted to position based on strong performance as **Inbound / Outbound Supervisor** (1992 - 1994).

- Significantly increased profitability by reducing operating ratio from 1.20 to .97.
- Restructured routing system and consolidated routes, which resulted in more deliveries, in less time, with fewer staff.
- Established excellent business relations with prospective and existing clients by remaining attuned to their needs.
- Unified and motivated staff; clarified goals and expectations, and held workers accountable for actions.
- Drastically improved hostile relationships between managers and union members.

K.S. International, Pawsten, NJ   1988 - 1992
(Domestic and international air freight / LTL trucking company; nonunion environment.)

OPERATIONS MANAGER
Oversaw operation of a 40-door terminal and supervised a 30-person work force (dock workers and drivers). Maintained constant contact with terminals and airlines, and insured timely trucking/air freight shipments and deliveries. Assisted with costing/pricing of services.

- Played a key role in the tremendous growth of the operation, which expanded from a 15-door to a 40-door facility, and more than doubled its client base and freight volume.
- Developed an effective operations plan which increased efficiency and productivity.
- Evaluated equipment needs and purchased new equipment and vehicles.
- Revamped entire work force and hired qualified staff; enhanced the screening / hiring process.
- Improved the work environment to induce good workers to stay.

Barcley Beverages., So. Kearny, NJ   1987 - 1988

WAREHOUSE SUPERVISOR
Multifaceted position involving supervision of truck loading/routing operations, dock/warehouse operations, and security. Responsible for an inventory of 500,000 - 1 million cases of soda. Researched and implemented effective cost-cutting measures. Reduced daily shrink losses from $3000 to under $200. Increased team spirit among workers.

From 1984 - 1987 held a union dock worker position with Lilcante Freight, which provided an excellent introduction to the transportation industry and strengthened my ability to relate effectively with managers and laborers.

CERTIFICATION

Hazardous Materials Handling

119

Combination. *Rhoda Kopy, Toms River, New Jersey*

Lines enclose an opening section that is the equivalent of a Profile and a section exhibiting areas of expertise separated by ellipses. Underlining helps to make company names visible.

Hunter A. Lawrence

121 Hardscrabble Road ▪ Chappaqua, New York 10514 ▪ (914) 555-0000

Administrative and Customer Service ▪ Human Resources ▪ Travel Services Management

Professional Profile

Diversified and solid management career with particular expertise in multi-site operations management. Focus on planning of major conventions. Significant experience as outside travel agent and coordinator of corporate travel plans. Highly visible manager with superior communication skills critical in providing quality customer service. Innovative style used in support-staff recruitment, hiring and training. Personal travel throughout the United States, Europe, South America and Russia.

Management Accomplishments

OUTSOURCE COMPANY, INC.   1992–present

Long-term assignments for management services firm supporting corporations in the major markets.

TOP-TIER COMPANY   1993–present
Manager of Administrative Operations at three locations: Montvale, New Jersey, Westbury, New York and New York City. Oversaw customer-service centers in Montvale and Westbury.

- Currently manage nine full-time contract employees, directing mailroom shipping and receiving functions, reproduction and copy services.

- Manage budget, payroll and personnel requirements. Allocate resources and meet with regulatory compliance, including safety standards.

- Employ persuasive and thorough communication and research skills to recruit and interview new hires. Interpret specifications of positions, define culture of each site and evaluate employees' skills and abilities to fit company's needs.

- Created concept for, and implemented, customer-satisfaction surveys in response to company commission to study economic feasibility of copy centers. Client evaluation of services resulted in a 90% approval rating, surpassing the mark of previous service supplier by more than 25%.

- Adept at purchasing and inventory management, evaluated bids on copier leases to achieve cost savings of $150,000 over previous year's contracts.

- Facilitated workflow through development of site-specific procedural manuals. Translated technical language into clear, readily usable terms.

ABC CORPORATION, INTERNATIONAL HEADQUARTERS, White Plains, New York   1992–1993
Site Manager in charge of American Express contract for travel services. Directed Customer Centers supporting client education, video conferencing, audio-visual services and graphic arts control. Maintained telecommunications system, internal assets and capital equipment.

- Collaborated with department managers in reviewing travel reports, resulting in a reduced travel budget and a company-wide $275,000 increase in surplus operating revenue.

- Instituted a program rewarding video conference usage that contributed to further reductions in travel costs.

- Selected as Team Leader for Travel Quality Council, representing staff from Outsource, ABC and American Express. Council monitored services, customer satisfaction and cost control for travel provided to ABC.

120

Combination. *Phyllis B. Shabad, Ossining, New York*

A font with rounded characters for the person's name, section headings, and side subheadings in the Related Activities and Achievements section warms this resume and gives it an aura of

Hunter A. Lawrence page two

ABC CORPORATION, VARIOUS U.S. AND INTERNATIONAL DIVISIONS   1979–1992

*Held increasingly responsible positions in **Management, Personnel, Recruiting, Accounting** and **Customer Service**. Broad experience in facilities management, including food and travel services, secretarial support, education enrollments and internal asset security.*

- Detail-oriented travel manager who ensured swift resolution of problems arising from corporate travel policy. Reconciled discrepancies and implemented cost controls. Thorough knowledge of reservation transactions, including booking and ticketing. Interfaced with brokers and assembled packages. Finalized plans with on-line reservation systems.

- Successfully managed logistical planning of arrivals, departures and dining accommodations for over 1,200 attendees at each of four Latin American Sales Recognition Conventions held in Nashville, Orlando, New Orleans and Miami.

- Directed $500,000 site renovation of cafeteria, accompanied by a facilities upgrade of food preparation and refrigeration equipment.

- Spearheaded team effort to initiate customer promotion program, bringing food service operations to a break-even point and eliminating need for corporate subsidy.

- Streamlined expenses of sales unit and held down costs through attrition and consolidation.

- Progressive human resource manager in entry-level recruiting, interviewing and hiring. Maximized staff performance and boosted morale through career development, focusing on coaching, training and skills assessment.

- Recognized for accuracy, organization and thoroughness in financial records management, accounting and international billing processing. Coordinated monthly salary compensations for American ABC employees on assignment in Europe. Monitored accounts receivable collection operations for 8 ABC branches.

Related Activities and Achievements

Awards	In recognition of exceptional performance for contributions to quality service, received ABC Customer Service Award. Also earned Regional Managers and District Managers Awards.
Professional Development	Certified by NYU Travel Management Program. Coursework included managing business and personal travel.
	Attended Pitney-Bowes workshops on mailroom operations.
	Regularly attend series of National Postal Forum seminars on new products, services and government regulations.
	Participated in numerous ABC management training programs.
Computer Literacy	Utilize Lotus 1-2-3 and AmiPro, as well as internal corporate systems, for accounting solutions.

friendliness. Bulleted items include achievements as well as responsibilities. When the individual was downsized from "ABC," he subcontracted his services to an outsourcing firm and "never had a gap in his employment record."

JOHN APPLETON

2314 SW 7th Place
Panama City, Florida 32401
(904) 889-2315

BACKGROUND

Over 12 years of broad-based business management experience with a proven record of accomplishment in operations, human resources, merchandise management, construction management, and franchise services.

BUSINESS MANAGEMENT EXPERIENCE

THE GAP, INC   November 1981 to present

Initially hired as a **Manager Trainee** at the national headquarters in Tampa, Florida. Promoted to **Manager** of 4,000 square foot store in Raleigh, North Carolina in 1982 where I received Manager-of-the-Year Award. Promoted to **District Manager** in 1983. Promoted to a corporate position at the national headquarters in Tampa, Florida in 1984 with responsibility for directing the following administrative functions:

- **Operations** -- Direct all operational activities for 35 corporate stores with a total annual sales volume of $17 million. Supervise 4 District Managers, 35 Store Managers, 25 Manager Trainees, and 250 Sales Associates. Monitor company-wide expenses and inventory. Implement and enforce operational procedures (e.g., security, point-of-sale, check guarantee, credit cards, employee policies) at the store level. Administer a $2.1 million payroll. Direct all activities associated with new store openings. Accomplishments include development of a company operational manual and a mystery shopper program.

- **Human Resources** -- Recruit, interview, hire, and train company personnel. Coordinate relocation arrangements for manager trainees. Developed a comprehensive employee policy manual. Accomplishments include the creation of an in-store training program and the development and implementation a "recruiting center" program at state universities to identify and recruit promising new graduates for the company's management training program.

121

Combination. *Steven M. Burt, location unknown*

A well-organized resume with ABCDE A+B+C+D+E structure. Five areas of accomplishment are indicated in the Background section. Each is described in turn in the Experience section. Notice

BUSINESS MANAGEMENT EXPERIENCE (continued)	■ **Merchandise Management** -- Responsible for coordinating a corporate-wide inventory of $3.9 million. Monitor specific shoe categories to determine best sell-thru vs. worst sell-thru. Coordinate shoe stock rotation among the corporate stores. Determine product mix and inventory stock levels. Oversee and develop the apparel buying programs on a seasonal basis. Accomplishments include the development and implementation of The Gap's college contract printing program. Strong background and practical experience in the operation of IBM computer equipment and Island Pacific Management System software.

■ **Construction Coordination** -- Responsible for store design. Review construction bids and select general contractor. Work closely with the project architect. Oversee store set-up upon completion of construction. Monitor all leasehold improvements and individual store fixture requirements. Negotiate and maintain all vendor contracts (i.e., HVAC, electrical, plumbing, pest control, carpet cleaning, etc.) at the store level as well as for the home office.

■ **Franchise Services Management** -- Serve as company liaison to over 100 franchise stores. Coordinate and negotiate buying programs for the franchisee. Direct all activities associated with the start-up of new franchise stores including preparing the initial purchase orders, setting up merchandise accounts, and personnel training. Contribute to the monthly franchise newsletter. Select the Franchise-of-the-Month. Coordinate the annual franchise meeting and participate in the semi-annual Franchise Advisory Committee meeting.

EDUCATION

Florida State University
Tallahassee, Florida
Bachelor of Science in Physical Education, 1981

PERSONAL BACKGROUND

Available to begin work immediately
Willing to travel
References available on request

that the descriptions of the five areas of responsibility are in block paragraph style and that each paragraph is preceded by a filled square bullet, unifying the two pages. Relatively large print helps to make the two pages easy to read.

Michael J. Morris

8475 Main Avenue
Appleton, Wisconsin 54915

Office: 414 / 729–3478
Home: 414 / 832–1742

*Results-oriented professional with excellent skills in developing,
motivating, training, and coaching employees in a team environment.
Effectively analyze programs and implement procedure changes to
achieve cost savings. Strong leader who pays close attention to details
and quickly formulates solutions to problems.*

Experience

XYZ Corporation — Main Street Production Plant   1980–Present

Operations Supervisor (1993-Present)
Supervise 30 employees directly, 52 indirectly, in this unionized facility. Promote decision-making and efficiency improvements on a team level. Specific areas of responsibility include:

Manpower: Devise short- and long-term manpower forecasts. Conduct weekly audits to monitor actual versus forecasted labor. Direct weekly staff meetings.
- Instrumental in designing a computerized vacation scheduling program.
- Oversee hourly administrative teams in the development of work schedules to alleviate manpower shortages.

Material Handling: Administer the allocation of raw materials to and removal of waste from the operating floor. Regulate recyclable and hazardous waste handling methods. Recommend procedure improvements.
- Stage raw material to guarantee zero down time on grade changes; analyze incorrect distribution and initiate corrective actions.
- Streamline material and floor lay-out; create collection methods to minimize use of floor space and segregate recyclables.
- Facilitate compliance with outside vendors' recycling requirements.

Emergency Safety Procedures: Review facility policies to ensure continued effectiveness with current work situations.

Housekeeping: Oversee both in-house and contract service personnel in maintaining a high level of housekeeping plant-wide.
- Conduct regular plant inspections to identify and eliminate unsightly areas.
- Transitioned handicapped personnel into previously non-restrictive positions.

Facility Security: Verify compliance to pedestrian access and property movement policies. Investigate security violations.

122

Combination. *Kathy Keshemberg, Appleton, Wisconsin*

This candidate was Operations Supervisor at the production facility of a large international paper-manufacturing corporation. Many changes were occurring, and he wanted a resume

Michael J. Morris

Internal Control Coordinator (1992-1993)

Orchestrated system audits of 176 mill procedures, implementing changes as warranted. Acted as liaison between area managers, department supervisors, and top management.

- Originated a quick reference "User's Guide" summarizing procedures routinely used in specific departments.
- Identified weaknesses in plant access procedures; established an added level of security.
- Revised property pass procedure to limit authorization to appropriate personnel.

Plant Safety Manager (1990-1992)

Initiated OSHA-mandated training programs, investigated accidents, and recognized safety hazards. Assessed new projects for potential OSHA violations. Conceptualized and executed plant-wide safety promotion programs.

- Reduced accident incident ratio by 50%.

Line Supervisor (1980-1990)

Team leader with direct supervisory responsibility for 45 employees.

- Successfully transitioned two operating crews from supervisor-led status to a self-managed team concept.

Education

University of Wisconsin-Madison
Bachelor of Business Administration   1976

Seminar Attendance:
Environmental Laws & Regulations Compliance
DOT-Hazardous Material, Waste and Substances Training
Interactive Management Programs-Managing Performance
Indispensable Assistant
Managing Multiple Projects, Objectives and Deadlines
Wisconsin Workers' Compensation
Time Systems Workshop
National Safety Council Workshop
Participative Leadership
Working with People
Deming - Quality Management Process

ready should a need for it arise. The resume shows the person's range of responsibilities and his career progression. "A narrative description of each position is followed by specific accomplishments. The opening paragraph profiles the candidate's strengths."

MATILDE KHAN

114 Meadows Drive • Brooklyn, New York • 02222
Phone: (718) 222-4243 • E-mail: BMatt1@aol.com

SUMMARY	· Nine years of hands-on and supervisory experience in the jewelry industry. · Expertise in design, product development, appraisal, sales, and buying. · Creative and artistic with superior attention to detail. · Results-oriented leader; Self-motivated to produce high-level work. · Extensive experience with gemstones and a talent for discerning quality.
EMPLOYMENT **1991 to present**	**Parker Fine Jewelry Company,** East Islip, NY **Product Development Supervisor** · Develop new programs for national home shopping television shows. · Coordinate product development for department that produces 75 to 100 designs per month. · Supervise 5 Jewelry Designers and 3 Stone Setters. · Selected to head seven member Color Product Development team. · Use leadership role to encourage creativity among team members. · Facilitate departmental communication and assist team with product-line decisions. · Review artist designs to determine feasibility for production. · Create new designs and present specifications to designers. · Implement cost-cutting measures while maintaining quality products.
1988 to 1991	**Midtown Jewelry,** New York, NY **Manager, Colored Stone Division,** Precious Gems Department · Supervised and evaluated a team of 12 Lapidaries. · Coordinated work flow between Lapidaries and Stone Setters. · Negotiated prices and purchased colored stones. · Used organizational methods that doubled the department's output. *Previous Positions/Promotions:* Assistant to Diamond and Colored Stones Buyer, Assistant Shop Supervisor, Jeweler's Apprentice · Crafted fine jewelry in 18 karat gold and platinum. · Evaluated newly cut stones for proper shape and color quality. · Estimated size, weight, and color specifications based on designer drawings and customer request.
COMPUTERS	· Proficient in Microsoft Word, Excel, Access, and PowerPoint. · Knowledge of Lotus 1-2-3 and WordPerfect. · Experience using commercial on-line services and the Internet.
EDUCATION	**Bachelor of Business Administration,** Major in Marketing Brooklyn College, Brooklyn, New York, 1987 *Professional Courses:* - Stone Setting - Polishing - Design - Casting - Identifying Gems

123

Combination. *Kim Isaacs, Jackson Heights, New York*

Table format was used for this resume. The five-row, two-column table had a thick-thin border, but the left and right borders have been eliminated. The first column is shaded.

Johnson C. Charles

3501 Anystreet Avenue, Southtown, LA 0000 (318) 111-2222

OBJECTIVE

A management position with a progressive, established company with opportunity for professional growth.

SUMMARY OF QUALIFICATIONS

- Highly polished managerial skills with excellent organization skills. Integrate strong leadership skills with a positive, optimistic style that effectively motivates staff.
- Successfully managed and marketed a corporation in both public and private sector.
- Experienced in Human Resource management duties; recruited, trained, and evaluated staff.
- Excellent communication, leadership, negotiations, and troubleshooting skills that interact with clients, staff, and management.
- Creative in formulating special projects and developing program designs.

EXPERIENCE

President/Owner
C.J.'S TENNIS ASSOCIATION, INC., Southtown, LA (1993 - Present)
Successfully manage an association that contracts tennis pros for club activities in the North Louisiana region.
- Work with board of directors on a regular basis; manage pros' schedules; organize leagues and teaching clinics.
- Schedule events with special pros (including internationally known).
- Set up and manage entire computer system for AP/AR, payroll, taxes and inventory for business.
- Successfully developed and implemented competitive sales and marketing driven management strategies.

Tennis Manager/Pro
BAYSIDE COUNTRY CLUB, Bayou, LA (1991 - Present)
Managed Pro Shop, increasing yearly profits by utilizing selective buying and creative merchandising techniques.
- Implemented computerized billing system for Pro Shop for AP/AR and financial statements.
- Successfully organized leagues and increased the percentage of teaching lessons.
- Cut expenses by developing a realistic and workable budget.
- Performed Human Resource management duties, i.e., recruitment, selection, training, and evaluation of staff.

Tennis Manager/Pro
CITY OF BAYOU, Bayou, LA (1987 - Present)
Manage two separate facilities of 16 courts as well as one Pro Shop.
- Organized leagues of approximately 420 members.
- Prepared schedules for two full-time pro's. Set up entire computerized billing system for Pro Shop.

President/Owner
DOPSON & PETERSON, INC., Anytown, LA (1993)
Co-owner of wholesale convenient store with $56,000 in retail inventory.
- Inventory control; purchasing.
- Hiring, training, and evaluating of all employees.

Assistant Manager-Tennis Department
NEVADA BOB'S DISCOUNT GOLF AND TENNIS, Bayou, LA (1985 - 1987)
- Responsible for buying inventory, arranging displays, and sales.

EDUCATION AND TRAINING

NORTHTOWN LOUISIANA UNIVERSITY, Anytown, LA
B.A. (1992)
Focus: Business and Management

REFERENCES AVAILABLE UPON REQUEST.

124

Combination. *Melanie Douthit, West Monroe, Louisiana*

A resume that displays a person's ability to manage separate facilities simultaneously. Small type ensures both the inclusion of much information and the preservation of white space.

RICHARD B. STEIN

| 1931 Smith Street | Peekskill, NY 10566 | (914) 736-1997 |
| | | (914) 734-1996 |

OBJECTIVE

A management position in the print industry which will benefit from my technical expertise and strong leadership skills, utilizing my proven twenty plus year track record maximizing productivity and profitability.

PROFILE

☑ Versatile management professional with twenty plus year track record in the computer graphics industry; proven ability to manage multiple projects.

☑ Detail-oriented graphic artist with exceptional follow-through abilities and excellent management skills; able to plan and oversee projects from concept to successful final product.

☑ Demonstrated ability to efficiently prioritize a broad range of responsibilities in order to consistently meet deadlines. Effective in getting cooperation of staff.

☑ A resource person, problem solver, trouble shooter and creative turn-around manager. Proven ability in determining what the customer is doing wrong and minimizing expenditures.

☑ Demonstrated strength in resolving problems swiftly and independently.

☑ Possess comprehensive, diversified expertise in the print industry; knowledge of pricing, prep, and press.

☑ Strong computer skills; expertise in state of the art computerized graphics, scanning, layout, photo retouching and word processing programs.

AREAS OF EFFECTIVENESS

☑ Documented *consultative skills*; proven ability in suggesting methods to *increase project efficiency* and enhance esthetic quality.

☑ Proven customer service skills, achieved *high levels* of customer satisfaction *generating significant repeat business.*

Management	✓ Production scheduling
	✓ Oversee Production; estimate time and costs
	✓ Produce imposition and lay-out dummies
	✓ Monitor work flow; ensure efficiency

| *Training and Development* | ✓ Instruct prep people on methods to optimize variety of jobs |

| *Electronic Stripping and Imposition* | ✓ Four color process |
| | ✓ Flat color creation |

| *Scanner Work* | ✓ Optical character recognition, 4-color, duotone and B/W illustration |

PROFESSIONAL EXPERIENCE

March 1994 - Present

M T M PRINTING, College Point, NY
Manager: Electronic Pre-press

♦ *Established electronic pre-press department* thereby *increasing billable in-house production by 31%.*

♦ Recommended software and hardware to enable in-house production of proofs and film for 4-color process printing.

♦ Set up network and trouble shoot conflicts.

♦ Train staff.

125

Combination. *Mark D. Berkowitz, Yorktown Heights, New York*

The stacked initials catch the eye immediately. The staggered lines—one dark, the other light—recur beside the Professional Experience and Education headings and in the headers at the top

RICHARD STEIN   *page 2*

April 1992- March 1994	**COLOR GRAPHIC PRESS,** Long Island City, NY **Manager: Graphic Services** ♦ Hired, trained and supervised staff of two. ♦ *Re-engineered work-flow* to take advantage of electronic image processing *resulting in a near doubling of revenues* from process color preparation work. ♦ Bought and *set up network* server using Novell Netware to *link PCs* and *MACs*.
June 1986 - July 1992	**ENHANCE-A-COLOR,** North White Plains, NY **Shift Supervisor: Color Correction/Re-toucher** ♦ Operated film setters and proprietary image manipulation systems for film out-put service. ♦ Implemented procedures which *increased production capacity by 71%*. ♦ Managed introduction of routines to process new customers' electronic files into plate-ready film. ♦ Analyzed and altered customer-supplied art work to achieve proper integration of parts into plate ready film.
October 1980 - June 1986	**XEROX CORPORATION,** Armonk, NY **Production Manager, Slide System Division** (sold October 1985 to MAGI Inc.) ♦ *Established successful profit center,* a service group designing and producing slide presentations on the MAGI slide system. ♦ *Managed production facility* with staff of 5 persons servicing country-wide customer base. ♦ *Instituted production and quality control procedures* and enlisted staffing to *effectively control a tripling of product volume.* ♦ *Provided continuity of management* during transfer of production facility from Xerox to MAGI after sale by Xerox to the system developer. ♦ *Supervised* and *documented* the commercial introduction of six new hard-copy products.
September 1979 - October 1980	**INTERACTIVE GRAPHICS, INC.,** Wayne, PA **Graphic Designer** Designed and produced slide presentations for major corporations on second generation computer graphics system, "Genigraphics."
June 1977 - June 1979	**AMERICAN SIGN & INDICATOR,** Spokane, WA **Manager: Systems Graphic Services** ♦ Established graphic services department to service customers for computer-controlled animating public display systems. ♦ Designed and produced magnetically encoded advertising and entertainment graphics for San Diego Stadium, RFK Stadium, Pontiac Stadium, Phoenix and San Antonio coliseums among others. ♦ Supervised acceptance testing of systems. ♦ Wrote and produced instruction manuals; acted as customer advocate in design of operator interface for development graphic system. Wrote service programs, planned and implemented computer graphics marketing procedure. ♦ Publlished article on original research in optics, <u>Journal of Illuminating Engineers Society</u>, October, 1978.
October 1976 - May 1977	**SPECTACOLOR,** New York, NY **Vice President and Director of Graphic Services** ♦ Designed and produced animated advertising graphics for computer-controlled four color display on Times Square. ♦ Assembled and trained staff. ♦ Prepared presentations and acted as liaison with advertising agencies and direct advertisers. ♦ Developed concepts, graphic settings and wrote copy. ♦ Accepted position with manufacturer of sign system.

of pages 2 and 3. Checked-box bullets tie together visually the Profile and the Areas of Effectiveness. Check marks in the Areas of Effectiveness contrast with diamond bullets throughout the rest of the resume. These areas are grouped according to four categories.

RICHARD STEIN *page 3*

| October 1975 -
October 1976 | **GENERAL ELECTRIC COMPANY, New York, NY**
Computer Graphics Designer
◆ Designed color slide presentations for Fortune 500 clients, and executed slides on GE's "Genigraphics" computer graphics system.
◆ Trained and supervised three new designers. |

EDUCATION

PARSONS SCHOOL OF DESIGN (THE NEW SCHOOL), New York, NY
Courses in color and design   1972 - 1973

COLUMBIA UNIVERSITY, New York, NY
Woodrow Wilson Fellow   1960 - 1961

ILLINOIS INSTITUTE OF TECHNOLOGY, Chicago, IL
Bachelor of Science   1960
Major: English
Minor: Graphics (Institute of Design)

REFERENCES   Available upon request.

This writer likes to boldface key words and achievements to make them more visible to the reader. The use of all-uppercase letters for the various employers makes them stand out. This technique is of value when firms are as well known as Xerox and General Electric.

Dale B. Young

7777 La Jolla Avenue • San Jose, CA • 95124 • (408) 555-7777

Professional Experience

Management/Trouble Shooting
- Designed software that enabled real time analysis of worker productivity, scheduling, job cost and production.
- Handled all corrective action requests, including trouble-shooting, customer relations, writing corrective actions, developing tools to solve problems and implementing new procedures.
- Engineered software to control specialized printing equipment.
- Developed competency evaluations for new job applicants.

Quality Administration
- Developed quality control manual for large printing company.
- Inspected incoming components and materials per military specifications for defense contractor.
- Wrote procedures for new and current processes.

Technical Expertise
- Troubleshot and repaired various tools and equipment; designed and installed new equipment.
- Developed software for chemical analysis and retail sales applications.
- Oversaw installation of IBM and Macintosh network computer systems and their software applications.
- Supervised and worked with union and non-union crews on theater/film lighting, sound and set construction.

Employment History

Quality Assurance Manager/Bar Code Supervisor
MABI LABELS, San Jose, CA, 1990-Present

Air Conditioning Technician
THERMAL SERVICE, San Jose, CA, 1990

Quality Receiving Inspector
FRONTIER ENGINEERING, Stillwater, OK, 1989

Repair/Service Manager
BLUE RIDGE POOLS, Atlanta, GA, 1986-1989

Shop Foreman
Various theatrical and film productions in California and Utah, 1976-1986

RÉSUMÉ OBJECTIVE
Position as
Quality Control Supervisor
with progressive company.

Qualification Highlights

✓ Wide range of experiences with technical equipment, tools, materials and processes.
✓ Solid background in physics, chemistry, mathematics and material science.
✓ Ability to pinpoint problems and initiate creative solutions.
✓ Able to read specifications and technical drawings.
✓ Resourceful, innovative, quick learner; able to adapt quickly to a challenge.
✓ Remain calm and work well under demanding conditions.
✓ Ability to prioritize, delegate and motivate.

Technical Skills

Equipment: Comparators, reticles, Rockwell hardness tester, tensile strength press, various electrical and electronic meters, calipers, scales.
Processes: Welding (gas and arc), plastic fabrication (thermoplastics and thermosetting plastics), photography (motion and still).
Computers: IBM, Macintosh, Atari
Programming Languages: Fortran, C, Basic
Databases: dBase IV, FileMaker II, FirstChoice
Spreadsheets: Lotus123, Supercalc, Microsoft Excel, VIP, First Choice
CAD: Drafix, Draft Plus

Education

B.A., *Technical Theater - Magna Cum Laude,* **1982**
(Minor in Chemistry)
Southern Utah State College

Additional studies in
Engineering
Oklahoma State University, 1989
University of Utah, 1988

© *THE WORDSMITH, Sallie Young, 1991*

126

Combination. *Sallie Young, Riverton, Utah*

The monogram, the shadowed text box, and the horizontal and vertical lines are the design features of this imaginative resume. Italic headings match the person's name in italic.

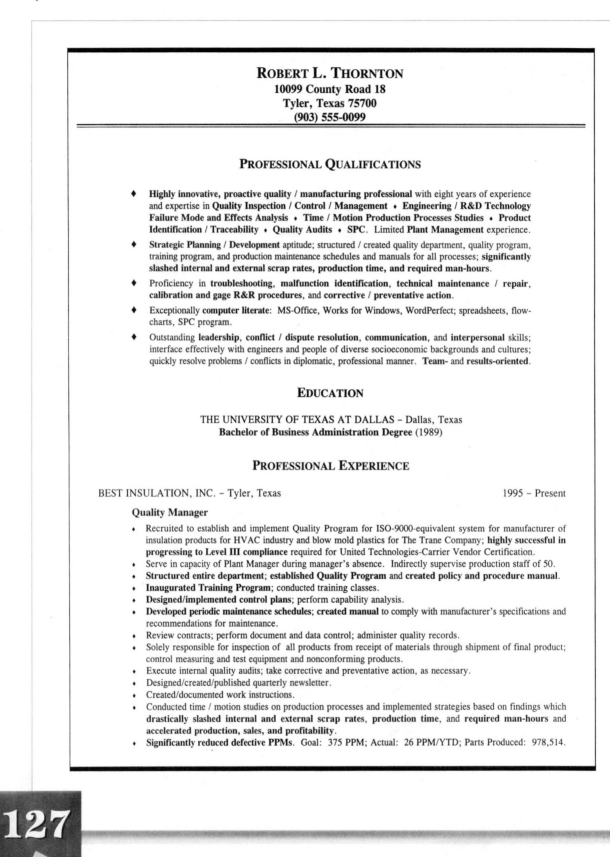

ROBERT L. THORNTON
10099 County Road 18
Tyler, Texas 75700
(903) 555-0099

PROFESSIONAL QUALIFICATIONS

◆ **Highly innovative, proactive quality / manufacturing professional** with eight years of experience and expertise in **Quality Inspection / Control / Management** ◆ **Engineering / R&D Technology Failure Mode and Effects Analysis** ◆ **Time / Motion Production Processes Studies** ◆ **Product Identification / Traceability** ◆ **Quality Audits** ◆ **SPC.** Limited **Plant Management** experience.

◆ **Strategic Planning / Development** aptitude; structured / created quality department, quality program, training program, and production maintenance schedules and manuals for all processes; **significantly slashed internal and external scrap rates, production time, and required man-hours.**

◆ Proficiency in **troubleshooting, malfunction identification, technical maintenance / repair, calibration and gage R&R procedures,** and **corrective / preventative action.**

◆ Exceptionally **computer literate:** MS-Office, Works for Windows, WordPerfect; spreadsheets, flow-charts, SPC program.

◆ Outstanding **leadership, conflict / dispute resolution, communication,** and **interpersonal** skills; interface effectively with engineers and people of diverse socioeconomic backgrounds and cultures; quickly resolve problems / conflicts in diplomatic, professional manner. **Team- and results-oriented.**

EDUCATION

THE UNIVERSITY OF TEXAS AT DALLAS – Dallas, Texas
Bachelor of Business Administration Degree (1989)

PROFESSIONAL EXPERIENCE

BEST INSULATION, INC. – Tyler, Texas   1995 – Present

Quality Manager

◆ Recruited to establish and implement Quality Program for ISO-9000-equivalent system for manufacturer of insulation products for HVAC industry and blow mold plastics for The Trane Company; **highly successful in progressing to Level III compliance** required for United Technologies-Carrier Vendor Certification.
◆ Serve in capacity of Plant Manager during manager's absence. Indirectly supervise production staff of 50.
◆ **Structured entire department; established Quality Program** and **created policy and procedure manual.**
◆ **Inaugurated Training Program;** conducted training classes.
◆ **Designed/implemented control plans;** perform capability analysis.
◆ **Developed periodic maintenance schedules; created manual** to comply with manufacturer's specifications and recommendations for maintenance.
◆ Review contracts; perform document and data control; administer quality records.
◆ Solely responsible for inspection of all products from receipt of materials through shipment of final product; control measuring and test equipment and nonconforming products.
◆ Execute internal quality audits; take corrective and preventative action, as necessary.
◆ Designed/created/published quarterly newsletter.
◆ Created/documented work instructions.
◆ Conducted time / motion studies on production processes and implemented strategies based on findings which **drastically slashed internal and external scrap rates, production time,** and **required man-hours** and **accelerated production, sales, and profitability.**
◆ **Significantly reduced defective PPMs.** Goal: 375 PPM; Actual: 26 PPM/YTD; Parts Produced: 978,514.

127

Combination. *Ann Klint, Tyler, Texas*

Two sizes of diamond bullets are used. The larger ones appear in the Professional Qualifications section, suggesting that the items there deserve extra attention. This writer, too, boldfaces key

ROBERT L. THORNTON

SOUND INDUSTRIES, INC. – Fort Worth, Texas   1989 – 1995

Customer Service / Technical Representative (1994–1995)

- Supervised contract labor force; extensively interacted with technicians via phone to troubleshoot problems and provide technical support for OEM industrial water heaters and boilers.
- Responsible for warranty service performed on defective equipment.
- Solicited and negotiated estimates for jobs; ensured work was completed promptly and accurately.
- Specified parts; placed orders; shipped parts, as needed.

Quality Control Inspector (1993–1994)

- Performed final inspection for finished goods.
- Ensured manufacturing personnel complied with regulations (U.L. Laboratories, ULC, A.S.M.E.).
- Promoted to Customer Service / Technical Representative.

Engineering Technician (1990–1993)

- Designed and determined instrument specifications; performed bill of material maintenance.
- Coordinated and ensured compliance with various regulatory agencies.
- **Team Leader** in implementation of new computer system.
- Served as liaison between Engineering and Manufacturing.
- Performed drafting and limited AutoCAD.
- Promoted to Quality Control Inspector.

Research and Development Technician (1989–1990)

- Conducted R&D for new product lines.
- Promoted to Engineering Technician.

◆ ◆ **Professional References Furnished On Request** ◆ ◆

words to increase their chances of being read. In boldface also are the various job positions so that you can see all of these in a quick sweep across the resume. Adequate white space is achieved mainly through blank lines.

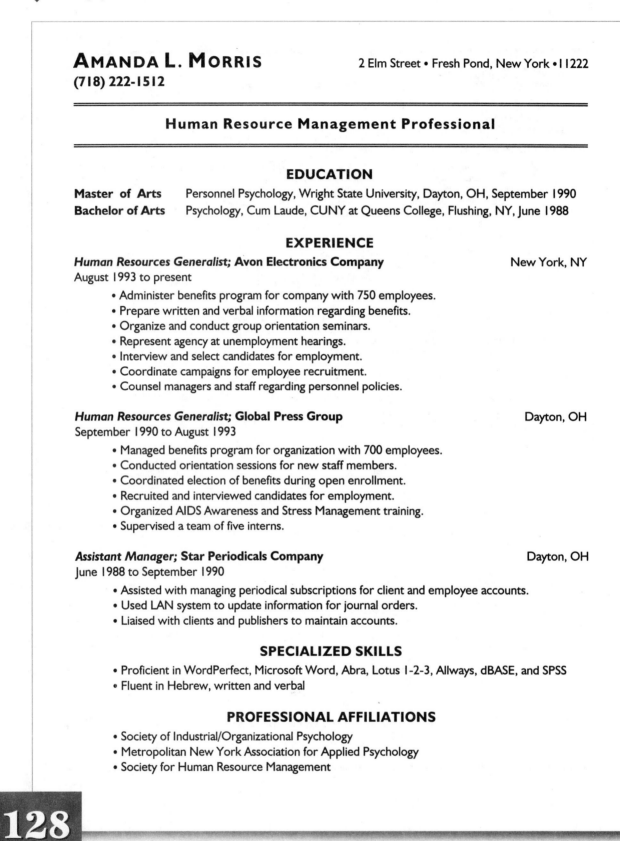

AMANDA L. MORRIS
(718) 222-1512

2 Elm Street • Fresh Pond, New York • 11222

Human Resource Management Professional

EDUCATION

Master of Arts Personnel Psychology, Wright State University, Dayton, OH, September 1990
Bachelor of Arts Psychology, Cum Laude, CUNY at Queens College, Flushing, NY, June 1988

EXPERIENCE

Human Resources Generalist; **Avon Electronics Company**   New York, NY
August 1993 to present

- Administer benefits program for company with 750 employees.
- Prepare written and verbal information regarding benefits.
- Organize and conduct group orientation seminars.
- Represent agency at unemployment hearings.
- Interview and select candidates for employment.
- Coordinate campaigns for employee recruitment.
- Counsel managers and staff regarding personnel policies.

Human Resources Generalist; **Global Press Group**   Dayton, OH
September 1990 to August 1993

- Managed benefits program for organization with 700 employees.
- Conducted orientation sessions for new staff members.
- Coordinated election of benefits during open enrollment.
- Recruited and interviewed candidates for employment.
- Organized AIDS Awareness and Stress Management training.
- Supervised a team of five interns.

Assistant Manager; **Star Periodicals Company**   Dayton, OH
June 1988 to September 1990

- Assisted with managing periodical subscriptions for client and employee accounts.
- Used LAN system to update information for journal orders.
- Liaised with clients and publishers to maintain accounts.

SPECIALIZED SKILLS

- Proficient in WordPerfect, Microsoft Word, Abra, Lotus 1-2-3, Allways, dBASE, and SPSS
- Fluent in Hebrew, written and verbal

PROFESSIONAL AFFILIATIONS

- Society of Industrial/Organizational Psychology
- Metropolitan New York Association for Applied Psychology
- Society for Human Resource Management

128

Combination. *Kim Isaacs, Jackson Heights, New York*

Enclosed within parallel lines is a headline that indicates the individual's career goal. The writer calls attention to the master's degree by making Education the first section.

Johanna Breitmorgan

2110 Sneckner Court
Morro Bay, California 90044
Telephone (213) 327-6111

Experience and education have provided detailed working knowledge of these key areas:

Financial Services	**Business Strategies**
Organization Development	**Customer Service**
Program Development	**Staffing & Training**
New Product Introductions	**Employee-Community Relations**

Highly motivated, results-oriented business professional with sixteen years of progressive accomplishments. Highly effective leadership skills, with an established track record of achievements. Fluent in French, German and English.

CRÉDITE INTERNATIONALE Morro Bay, California 1977 - Present
Have played key roles in managing change, building organizations, and working with senior management throughout this financial services organization that has 300 million cardholders in 240 countries and sales of $500 billion.

Director - Management Communications 1989 - Present
Partnering with the president and senior management of this 2,500-employee organization, created and launched programs for an executive speaker's bureau, employee communications, and community relations.

- Aggressively capitalized on opportunities and doubled the first year's number of speeches given by executive management; grew the total four-fold within three years.
- Developed and introduced a successful speech-merchandising program that, through press releases, op-ed articles, and reprints, delivered a strengthened image of Crédite as an industry leader.
- Developed a community relations program that made grant money available to non-profit organizations in which Crédite employees were working as volunteers.
- Recruited and worked closely with some 10 external speech writers.
- Planned and directed a complete re-design of the employee newsletter from improved graphics to an editorial planning calendar to meet the needs of multiple levels of management and staff.

Executive Assistant to the COO 1988 - 89
Pro-actively identified several significant corporate issues and, working with senior managers, developed plans to effect improvement.

- Resolved a growing problem of compliance between merchants and banks issuing the Crédite card.
- Revamped an out-moded mailing system to assure prompt delivery of important communications to banks.
- Prepared new policy and guidelines for employees to communicate with customers.

Director - Member Services 1985 - 88
Called in to manage a troubled, 35-employee unit that had an operating budget of $2 million and supported 80 major data centers, representing 1,500 banks, in the Western U.S. and Asia-Pacific.

- Restored high level of morale to the unit and reduced turnover to near zero.
- Managed and oversaw two complete changeovers in system software that enhanced productivity.

Earlier in member services (1981-85), presented trainings and seminars in the U.S. and Asia to enhance effectiveness and profitability of Crédite's computer systems.

Operations Coordinator 1979 - 81
Championed the development of an Fast-Pay Refund System when Crédite introduced travelers checks in 1982 and played a vital part in the worldwide implementation as liaison between the business unit and operations center.

Joined the company in Strasbourg, France, in 1977.

BA Degree - Psychology
STANFORD UNIVERSITY California

129

Combination. *Ted Bache, location unknown*

A resume that displays the progressive 16-year rise of a person within the same company. Activities move from revamping company systems to improving corporate communications.

NORMA L. KENNEDY, PHR

120 Windmill Dr., Southfield, MI 48000
(810) 555-0000

CAREER SUMMARY

- Human resources manager with six years generalist experience.
- Results-oriented, with highly developed problem-solving, decision-making, and leadership abilities.
- Trained in effective communication and conflict resolution.

ACCOMPLISHMENTS

Personnel Management

- Managed human resources and payroll for 250 employees at four Data Trust locations.
- Recruited, interviewed, hired, counselled, and separated employees.
- Managed $4.5 million annual payroll budget and $160,000 employee relations budget.
- Supervised major update of job descriptions.
- Developed, implemented and administered Personnel Policies and Procedures Manual. Results were a significant reduction in absenteeism, and more equitable disciplinary procedures.
- Reduced turnover from 22% to 10% over a two-year period.

Training

- Minimized EEO complaints by training supervisors and managers to effectively handle employee relations.
- Organized Human Resources team to develop a presentation of managed health care plan to 1,650 employees.
- Make recommendations about employee training and cross training.
- Train and supervise support staff.

Administration

- Manage corporate benefits programs for major financial institution. Administer health and welfare benefits for 4,500 employees, including health, dental, life, disability, Workers' Compensation, and pensions.
- Supervised the consolidation of more than 12,000 employee records during merger of the bank's two largest regions.
- Successfully met four-week project deadline - which had been reduced from 12 weeks - during conversion to an automated pension database.

130

Combination. *Deborah L. Schuster, Newport, Michigan*

This individual was an HR Benefits specialist, but she wanted to emphasize her earlier Generalist experience. The do this, the writer used a combination of functional and chronological formats.

Norma L. Kennedy, PHR   Page 2

EMPLOYMENT

Michigan National Bank   Canton, Michigan
Benefits Administrator   1993 to Present

Data Trust Corporation   Livonia, Michigan
Personnel Manager ('86-93), Personnel Representative ('81 - '86)   1981 to 1993

State Farm Insurance Company   Dearborn, Michigan
Office Manager   1976 to 1980

EDUCATION

Oakland Community College   Auburn Hills, Michigan
Pursuing Degree in Human Resources

Society for Human Resource Management   Dearborn Chapter
Certified - Human Resource Professional (PHR)

Plymouth High School   Plymouth, Michigan
Diploma   1975

PROFESSIONAL ORGANIZATIONS

Human Resources Association of Greater Detroit
Society for Human Resource Management
American Business Women's Association
National Association for Female Executives

The first page is functional; the second, chronological. The Education section was put near the end to downplay the person's lack of a degree. She had just enrolled in an HR degree program, so no dates were given for it.

DENNIS M. SEYMOUR
983 Rosewood Avenue
Romulus, MI 48174
(313) 946-5555

PROFILE

Purchasing Management

- Diverse background with experience in all management, purchasing, and manufacturing entities.
- Proven record of supplier cost reduction through negotiation, and through coordination of team efforts such as Kaizen programs and Value Analysis/Value Engineering (VA/VE).
- Extensive knowledge of and experience in Japanese lean manufacturing and management/team oriented techniques.
- Strong leadership and decision-making abilities. Excellent troubleshooter; solve problems on a daily basis.
- Extensive experience in developing employee training programs for the division.
- Computer literate in Excel, Word, Access, and purchasing and engineering databases.
- Adaptable – have consistently met challenges of reorganizing and restructuring departments in times of growth or downsizing.

ACHIEVEMENTS

At Ford Motor Company:

- Department led the division with an annual cost reduction averaging 2.5% per year.
- Negotiated a $3 million annual cost reduction on automotive transmission purchases.
- Helped build and establish purchasing department from the ground floor level, and set up policies and procedures for its growth.
- Completed in-depth training for ISO 9000 Quality System implementation assessment and auditing. Also serve as divisional coordinator.
- As internal Kaizen coordinator for the Purchasing Division, lead team in reducing costs of supplies, and in streamlining/automating procedures to work efficiently with reduced staff.
- Traveled to Europe to assure quality of tooling built in Germany, and to Japan for business and training.

EXPERIENCE

11/87-Present

Ford Motor Company-Dearborn Stamping Plant, Dearborn, Michigan

Leader - Administration/New Model Purchasing (2/95-Present)

Manage New Model Purchasing and Administration Department. Supervise all new model and launch activities within the purchasing division, and coordinate with all outside divisions, parent companies, and suppliers. Oversee all administrative functions within the division, including system improvement and automation. Develop overall purchasing division policies, procedures, and budgets. Coordinate the implementation of all ISO 9000 procedures and systems. Develop and implement all divisional training programs for approximately 65 employees.

Leader - Purchasing Product Procurement (3/93-2/95)

Supervised a $750 million annual buy electrical and functional part production procurement department. Approved all sourcing, pricing, and purchase orders. Conducted all high level negotiations and established long-term contracts with suppliers. Developed and implemented short and long-term business plans for the department.

131

Combination. *Deborah L. Schuster, Newport, Michigan*

The challenge was to show off the individual's excellent work history to best advantage. Because purchasing managers need to appear fiscally conservative, the writer chose a no-nonsense

Dennis M. Seymour   Resume/2

EXPERIENCE   **Ford Motor Company** (Continued)
(Continued)
                        Leader - Purchasing Product Procurement (Promotion) (4/91-3/93)
                        Supervised a $300 million annual buy interior trim production procurement department.

                        Professional / Buyer - Purchasing Product Procurement (Promotion) (11/89-4/91)
                        Specialist / Buyer - Purchasing Product Procurement (5/89-11/89)
                        Responsible for sourcing and procurement of interior and exterior trim components for all
                        vehicles from a worldwide supply base. Using detailed cost analysis, negotiated all part
                        and tool pricing from prototype through final production stages. Audited and analyzed all
                        potential suppliers and production readiness through launch phase.

                        Specialist - Purchasing Administration (11/87-5/89)
                        Developed a system for coordinating, tracking, implementing, and expediting engineering
                        changes for the Purchasing Division. Developed and implemented systems for cost
                        recovery from all local source suppliers for material rejections. Coordinated and
                        implemented supplier training of company purchasing and delivery procedures. Worked
                        directly with procurement departments in investigating, solving, and expediting resolution
                        of local source supplier issues. Developed departmental procedures.

11/83-11/87   **Chrysler Corporation-Trenton Engine Plant**, Trenton, Michigan
                        Analyst - Pre Production Purchasing (Promotion) (9/86-11/87)
                        Supervisor - Materials Handling (7/85-8/86)
                        Supervisor - Production (2/85-7/85)
                        Supervisor - Quality Control (Receiving Inspection) (12/84-1/85)
                        Supervisor - Quality Control (11/83-12/84)

EDUCATION   **University of Michigan,** Ann Arbor, Michigan
                        Bachelor of Science in Administrative Management (1983)
                        Studies toward Master of Science in Administration (Ongoing)
                             Projected Completion: Spring, 1998

format. The person had a record of steady career progress, so the writer put the dates of
overall employment with a company on the left, but placed the dates of the *individual*
positions after each job title. Note how the incomplete master's degree is handled.

IRMA M. WELSH
5206 Hampton Court
Sarasota, Florida 34692
813-242-3398

OBJECTIVE

To obtain an enhanced **Real Estate Property Management** position providing a challenging opportunity for the utilization of my expertise within this industry.

SUMMARY OF QUALIFICATIONS

Extensive experience at the Property Management level maintaining commercial real estate portfolios totaling from 500,000 S.F. to 1 million S.F. of space. Qualifications include a background of progressively responsible positions with a demonstrated performance record, and cost-effective monitoring of budgets over $1 million. Excellent communication, leadership, and motivation skills that effectively interact with staff, clients and executive management. Bilingual - fluent English and Spanish.

PROFESSIONAL EXPERIENCE

HENDERSON PARTNERS, Sarasota, FL   2/92 - Present
Property Manager
- Maintain portfolio consisting of 500,000 S.F. in office buildings and industrial service centers; **Increased commercial lease occupancy to 100%.**
- Directly responsible for overseeing annual budget, property accounting, preparation of 5-year forecasts and monthly operating reports; tenant relation programs; and contracted services.
- Coordinate tenant improvements and lease negotiations.
- Instrumental in complying with ADA (American Disabilities Act) renovation requirements.
- Supervise on-site personnel.

CDM COMMERCIAL REAL ESTATE, INC., Sarasota, FL   1/91 - 2/92
Real Estate Manager / Special Services
- Performed all management services for 3 shopping centers and 2 industrial parks totaling 500,000 S.F.
- Created annual budgets and quarterly reforecasts.
- Provided consulting services; assisted in special projects.
- Automated property management accounting for 13 properties.

USA GROUP LIMITED, Tampa, FL   4/86 - 1/91
Property Manager
- Commercial portfolio included management of an office park, service center and high-rise office building; liaison between brokers and prospective tenants; structured renegotiation of leases.
- Hired and supervised support staff; coordinated operations and maintenance plans for a building containing asbestos.

ACORN DEVELOPMENT CORPORATION, Tampa, FL   8/81 - 4/86
Property Management Administrator / Data Control
- Instrumental in the establishment of a Property Management Division responsible for overseeing a real estate portfolio consisting of 8 commercial properties totaling 1 million S.F.
- Selected and implemented a Data Base Management System (hardware and software) facilitating accounting cost controls for Corporate and 13 Regional Offices. Conducted in-house training program.

EDUCATION / SPECIALIZED TRAINING

BUILDING OWNERS & MANAGERS ASSOCIATION (BOMA)   1988
Real Property Administrator (RPA)

FLORIDA REAL ESTATE SALESPERSON'S LICENSE   1988

NEW YORK UNIVERSITY, New York, NY   1980
Bookkeeping Certificate

BRONX COMMUNITY COLLEGE, New York, NY   1972 - 1974
Associate Degree - Liberal Arts

132

Combination. *Diane McGoldrick, Tampa, Florida*

Another one-page resume accomplished by narrow margins and small type. Wider margins for the Objective statement help it stand out. Centered headings offset the wide lines.

555•123•4567

JON Q. PUBLIC
123 Main Street
Anytown, USA 12345

OBJECTIVE
*To work for a well-established construction firm in the South Bay
to Monterey area as Construction Foreman/Project Manager.*

SUMMARY OF QUALIFICATIONS
- Self-employed nine years in construction industry
- Fifteen years experience in construction related fields
- Demonstrated record of customer commitment
- Continually reading to stay on cutting edge of industry
- Responsible for the training and supervision of personnel for two years

RELEVANT SKILLS
- Plan take-off and cost estimating
- Extensive knowledge in reading blueprints
- Experience dealing with permits and inspections
- Construct and remodel residential wood structures
- Foundation and form work
- Spec home completion
- Tile-setting, glass block and custom cabinetry

EMPLOYMENT HISTORY

Self-Employed, 1983-present
Tile Setter/General Contractor

Many of the bids I secure require multiple skills to accomplish. I've dealt with
sub-contractors, coordinating schedules for the completion of a task. I am highly
organized and have worked extensively with estimating and ordering various
materials to the jobsite for an efficient operation.

- Willing to relocate, temporary or permanent, for job of company requirements
- Willing to work weekends and overtime as needed
- Wages negotiable
- References available upon request

133

Combination. *Elaine Jackson, Boulder Creek, California*

An unusual border arrangement makes this resume unique. Notice the placement of the phone
number and the slanted left alignment of contact information.

JANE WEBSTER
455 Westchester Avenue
Old Bridge, New Jersey 08857
(908) 727-5683

OBJECTIVE

To continue my career in Real Estate specializing in Property and Sales Management.

SUMMARY OF QUALIFICATIONS

Over 10 years of experience working with the public in various capacities:

Corporate Positions:

- Vice President, New Homes Division Huntington Realty, Regional Site Manager, U.S. Builders New Homes Division, Sales Associate.

Political Positions:

- Councilwoman, Old Bridge Township, Council Planning Board Representative, Council Welfare Board Representative, and Spokesperson, Burnt Fly Bog Citizens Committee and the New Jersey Environmental Federation.

- Experienced in all facets of real estate and real estate documentation relating to project development, project management, and set-up of sales forces and marketing plans.

- Familiar with mortgage documentation, public offering statements, master deeds, and bi-laws.

- Hold Real Estate Broker's License and a member of M.I.R.M. (the elite Institute of Residential Marketing.)

EXPERIENCE

11/93-Present
EGAN PROPERTY MANAGEMENT, Neptune, New Jersey
<u>Senior Accounts Manager</u>

Work with bank representatives, attorneys, and individuals handling REO and OREO. Purchase bank-owned properties; provide property management and maintenance services for residential, commercial and industrial properties. The properties are revitalized and renovated into affordable housing units.

5/91-9/93
TALL OAKS AT LAKEWOOD, INC., Lakewood, New Jersey
WARREN REALTY, Sole Proprietor
<u>Director of Sales and Rentals</u>

Implemented advertising plans and marketing strategies for project development of new homes and rental properties. Responsible for all sales and rentals. Helped clients to obtain affordable financing including FHA, VA, and FANNIE MAE mortgages for new home sales. Served as a liaison between clients and mortgage companies.

134

Combination. *Beverly Baskin, Marlboro, New Jersey*

The Summary of Qualifications indicates the dual concerns of the person, who wanted to combine corporate and political interests in a job with a U.S. Government or state housing

JANE WEBSTER   Page 2

5/88-4/90
SUPERIOR REALTY, INC., Freehold, New Jersey
Vice President, New Homes Division

Responsible for setting up real estate projects statewide. Procured listings from new developers. Hired on-site sales personnel. Set up marketing plans and sales office strategies, provided continuing education for on-site sales people. Trained employees to work with customers from the time that they enter into a contract until closing and follow-up procedures. Handled all administrative and legal forms relating to procurement of on-site sales.

6/85-5/88
U.S. HOMES NEW HOME AND LANDS DIVISION, Morristown, New Jersey
Regional Site Manager of New Home Sites

On-site sales person. Promoted in 1986 to Regional Site Manager of New Homes Division. Managed the sales of single family homes, town homes, condominiums,conversions, and revitalizations from $70,000 to $500,000. Achieved U.S. Homes Million Dollar Club.

1983-1987
COUNCILWOMAN, Old Bridge Township, Old Bridge, New Jersey

Adopted and approved all budgets; involved in the daily activities of adopting and approving legislation for the betterment of Old Bridge Township and its citizens. Worked with other council members in writing legislation for Mt. Laurel Affordable Housing to approve zoning for Affordable Housing Legislation in Old Bridge Township.

1984-1986
OLD BRIDGE TOWNSHIP PLANNING BOARD, Old Bridge Township, Old Bridge, New Jersey
Council Representative to Planning Board

Adopted and approved new master plan for Old Bridge Township to allow proper zoning for commercial and residential projects and zoning for Mt. Laurel Affordable Housing.

1985-1986
OLD BRIDGE TOWNSHIP WELFARE BOARD
Council Representative

1987-1989
NEW JERSEY ENVIRONMENTAL FEDERATION, New Brunswick, New Jersey
Spokesperson for Clean Water Action

Spearheaded campaigns for toxic waste clean-up statewide and nationally. Testified before U.S. Senate and U.S. Congress Committees in Washington D.C., New York City, and New Jersey. Also testified before New Jersey DEP Committees. Articles about my environmental projects appeared in the New York Times, Time Magazine, Business Week, and all the local and state newspapers. Appeared on Senator Bill Bradley's weekly television show. CBS produced a 15 minute spot on their Sunday Morning Show on my environmental clean up work. Guest speaker at numerous environmental and political functions. Woman of the Year Award presented by Senator Bill Bradley for the New Jersey Women's Network.

EDUCATION

N.J. Real Estate School - Broker's Course.....N.J. Real Estate School - Sales Person's Course. Attended Brookdale Community College....Member of Institute of Residential Marketing.

References and copies of Trade Publications available upon request.

agency. Dual tracks—one in real estate property and sales management and the other as a Council Representative and Councilwoman—are treated in turn with positions underlined. The business positions are in reverse chronological order; note the order of the political roles.

DONALD A. JONES

5505 Baywatch Boulevard
Treasure Island, FL 34638
(813) 569-9812

SENIOR FACILITIES/PROPERTY MANAGEMENT PROFESSIONAL

SUMMARY OF QUALIFICATIONS

- Innovative, results-oriented **Senior Management Professional** with over 11 years of solid experience in progressively responsible positions, and proven achievements in all aspects of Facilities and Property Management.

- Assimilation of company goals/objectives involving the analysis and administration of operational procedures, annual budgets, and future projections.

- Extremely focused on identifying potential problem areas, minimizing issues, formulating and executing competent solutions.

- Demonstrated expertise in strategic planning, organizational development, team building, and staff enhancement.

- Excellent communication, leadership, negotiation, trouble-shooting and motivation skills that effectively interact with staff, internal clients, community leaders, and executive management.

- Team Player with the ability to consistently provide high-level, systematic standards of performance.

PROFESSIONAL EXPERIENCE

DATA SERVICES, Tampa, FL   4/85 - Present
Facilities Manager
Responsibilities:

■ Directly accountable for the administration of an annual capital budget ($3M to $15M) and annual expense budget ($15.5M) for all Corporate Headquarters and South Area properties, combined with overseeing physical assets of buildings ($100M+) and the environmental protection of computer hardware ($200M+).

■ Efficiently and economically maintain all owned and leased buildings and ensure compliance with all applicable local, state, and federal regulations, including OSHA requirements. Analyze expansion, renovation and move plans, together with proposed changes in city or county ordinances that impact operational costs.

■ Manage and direct an in-house staff of 28 personnel, 25 full-time outside contractors, and more than 100 outside contracted service vendors.

■ Coordinate and establish the development of policies, procedures and standards consistent with providing optimum service to a customer group of 3,500+ employees. Routinely monitor all safety policies, and research and evaluate effectiveness of any required changes.

■ Oversee preventive maintenance activities for all support facilities, review established schedules, and reinforce presence of competent supervision for each activity.

Achievements:

■ Coordinated opening of new data center/office complex totalling over 1 million sq. ft. Data Center consists of 100,000+ sq. ft. of raised floor computer space.

■ Gained extensive benchmarking experience with companies in similar industries. Travelled to multiple sites conducting interviews and establishing a network of industry peers to create on-going exchange of information. Authored summary report distributed to Executive Management.

■ Initiated training procedures for upgrading customer service standards. Devised "pro-active" approach enforced by frequent customer visits to verify quality assurance. Originated survey forms to obtain customers' comments and monitor efficiency levels.

135

Combination. *Diane McGoldrick, Tampa, Florida*

The writer gives extra attention to the current position by distinguishing between Responsibilities and Achievements and providing paragraphs for each category. Square bullets have extra

DONALD A. JONES   **Page Two**

- Defined need for automated work order system. Conducted screening selection of vendors for software development to institute a tailored work order/request system for the entire department.

- Developed 24-hour emergency response service for all facilities and related service activities.

- Instrumental in structuring implementation of several programs in support of OSHA standards (i.e. Lock-Out/Tag-Out, Hazardous Communications, etc.) and overseeing compliance with the ADA (Americans with Disabilities Act).

PARADOX CORPORATION, Largo, Florida   **1/83 - 3/85**
Facilities Engineering Project Manager

As Facilities Planning Engineer, responsibilities included design and layout of office space for on-site and field office. Promoted to Project Manager - accountable for all phases of office construction and moves including preliminary research and design, cost estimating, project approval, scheduling, bidding, and supervision of all contractors from conception to completion. Structured the implementation of a Computer Aided Design and Drafting System (CADD) including instructional training on use of system.

BOAT CRAFT CORP., Sarasota, Florida   **3/82 - 11/82**
Industrial Engineer

Managed all industrial engineering functions, together with four production facilities in Florida. Reported directly to Vice President of Manufacturing Services. Conducted: Cost Studies, Cost Reduction Projects, Plant/Office Layout, Process Analyses, Determination of Standard Hour Assignments per Department. Directly supervised and coordinated $3.5 million expansion of Sarasota facilities.

PEARSON COMPANY, Cincinnati, Ohio   **6/79 - 3/82**
Industrial Engineer Coordinator

Began as co-op student engineer. Upon completion of co-op program, hired as full time Industrial Engineer. Promoted to Industrial Engineer Coordinator. Interacted with Product Development, Manufacturing Engineering, Quality Assurance and Marketing Communications Departments. Functions included: Time Studies, Cost Studies, Methods Analyses, Plant/Office Layout, Package Design, Supervision of three Shop Technicians.

<u>**EDUCATION**</u>

UNIVERSITY OF TAMPA, Tampa, Florida
Master's Degree Courses - Business Administration

UNIVERSITY OF CINCINNATI, Cincinnati, Ohio
College of Design, Architecture and Art - Graduated June, 1981
Bachelor of Science Degree - Industrial Design
(Five Year Professional Practice Program)

<u>**PROFESSIONAL EDUCATION/SEMINARS**</u>

- Achieving Results in a Changing Environment
- Managing Innovation and Change
- Advanced Management Education
- Computer Aided Design Operation
- Indoor Air Quality for Facility Managers
- Data Center Management
- Organizational Leadership I & II

<u>**AFFILIATIONS/MEMBERSHIPS**</u>

BOMA - Building Owners & Managers Association
IFMA - International Facilities Managers Association
AIPE - American Institute of Plant Engineers

weight. Uppercase is used consistently for company names, and positions and degrees are in boldface. Center-justification in the Education and Affiliations/Memberships sections provides visual relief from the paragraphs.

Joseph Executive
1178 Advantageous Road
Success, NJ 00000
555-555-1212

PRODUCTION / MARKETING / SALES EXECUTIVE

Results-driven Operating Executive with 15+ years management experience. Combines highly analytical, long range strategic planning capabilities with consistent achievement in productivity/quality improvement, personnel management and team building. Excellent communications skills demonstrated with customers and employees. Represents firms with integrity and intelligence and is diligent in growing companies from a loyalty base. Superior skills in organization effectiveness. Adept in both start-up or established environments.

Who's Who in Finance and Industry: 1994 - 1995
Who's Who in the East: 1993 - 1994

VICE PRESIDENT - PRODUCTION   8/93 - present
Davis Contractors, Inc.
Smart, NJ
Responsible for $12M in annual installations of vinyl siding, windows and cabinet refacing from production through collection: all phases of customer contact, fabricating, installing, producing jobs, vendor negotiations and purchases, scheduling, close out, P & L, payroll and litigation support as a subject matter expert. Additional responsibilities include the recruiting, staffing, training and management of 80 field employees, three production managers, one warranty service manager and five staff employees.

- Grew the business 35-40 percent per year for three years.
- Excelled in Quality Every Day (QED) - Customer Satisfaction and Quality. Received medals for national achievement in eight of ten quarters: goal was to *surprise* and *delight* the customer.
- Increased the department's productivity from $350K to $1.5M per month through a redefinition of how to do business by developing and implementing process improvements.
- Developed and implemented three Standard Operating Procedures (SOPs) to improve process flows.
- Implemented the cabinet refacing start-up business: demonstrated superior project management abilities in the design and implementation of flow charts, process plans, layout, equipment, and procedures with an adherence to OSHA regulations.
- Increased crew base 200 percent to maximize production.
- Designed and implemented a three tier pay plan for contract piece workers to incent for quality improvements. This also reduced turnover and improved morale.
- Developed workplace activities to promote loyalty, e.g., Barbecue Friday.

136

Combination. *Fran Kelley, Waldwick, New Jersey*

The contact information and the first section are center-justified. That section includes a headline indicating career fields, profile and skills information, some work-trait information,

Joseph Executive

555-555-1212   *page two*

RESIDENTIAL FIELD SALES DEVELOPMENT MANAGER   1991 - 1993
Building Products, Summit, NJ
Responsible for Outside Sales and Sales Training - Mid Atlantic States with a focus on the NJ
market with full accountability for personal sales and development of sales staff.

- Developed personal sales to a $1.6M client base.
- Implemented sales to get customer loyalty and spur business growth.
- Developed a lead generation program for contractors.
- Initiated the firm's first marketing attempts with product promotions tie - ins.
- Conducted market analysis of inventory requirements through anticipation
  of market trends.
- Developed in-home presentation and marketing sales aids.

Steel Products   1981 - 1991
Ramsey, NJ
*Played key leadership roles which contributed consistent value-added expertise with increasing
responsibilities and continuous professional development during this ten year period.*

SALES MANAGER / DIVISION SALES MANAGER / SALES PERSON / SALES TRAINEE
Responsible for all aspects of residential siding, windows and roofing at this manufacturing and
distribution company. This included recruiting, training and developing all employees. Directed
activities of six union drivers, four inside and three outside sales employees. P & L
responsibility for total operations. Also responsible for design and implementation of all
marketing and promotional programs.

- Grew personal annual sales from $1.5M to $3.5M.
- Grew branch sales from $5M to $8M.

EDUCATION

State University of New York at Albany
Master of Science in Industrial Arts and Technology Education
Advance Study in Human Resource Management
Bachelor of Science in Industrial Arts and Technology Education
Concentration: Manufacturing/Production

PROFESSIONAL AFFILIATIONS

National Association of the Remodeling Industry
Treasurer and Board of Directors   1991 - 1993
Member of the Year - NJ Chapter   1992
Waldwick Village Homeowners' Association
Treasurer   1990 - 1991
Board of Directors   1989 - 1991

and *Who's Who* references. Another center-justified statement appears at the end of the first
position mentioned on page 2. For each job held, responsibilities are indicated in a
paragraph, and bullets point to achievements.

ALYSSA M. KOCHANSKY

2815 Cypress Road, Brandon, FL 33511
813/555-5212
E-Mail Address: amk@aol.com

PROFESSIONAL PROFILE

- Proven thirteen-year background in financial services and securities
- Solid track record of promotions for outstanding performance and ability to manage projects to completion with superior results
- Strategic planning and organization development
- Instrumental in company turnaround by implementing aggressive and innovative programs
- Effectively use an empowering, participatory management style that encourages accountability, teamwork, continuous improvement and desired results
- Establish efficient quality-control standards; internal and external controls
- Results-oriented with strong analytical, networking and team-building skills
- Develop new ways to reduce costs and increase efficiency

PROFESSIONAL EXPERIENCE

MERRILL LYNCH, Philadelphia, PA   1993 to Present
Senior Vice President

Charged with meeting company objectives to ensure optimum performance of all trust department operations activities to achieve safe, high-quality, productive results including reporting accountability; coordination of intradepartmental operations; identification and development of strategic plans for company growth and innovative products; and sales of institutional products.

Selected Achievements:
- Initiated and orchestrated a strategic plan that took a $30 million company to $350 million and resulted in excellent audit reviews
- Engineered the acquisition of two additional companies and coordinated the conversion of account assets
- Manage institutional accounts in excess of $75 million
- Most senior officer in staff of 21; effectively supervise multi-state staff
- Designed and implemented new software to handle management tracking
- Expertise includes local area network, wide area network and back office processing
- Successfully integrated trust and brokerage systems

WORLDWIDE COMPUTERS, Columbia, SC   1988 - 1993
Consultant (1991 - 1993)
Product Service Representative (1990 - 1991)
Product Support Specialist (1988 - 1990)

Provided training and consulting services to trust organizations nationwide; comprehensive trust training and consulting; system and application support; processing and installation of software and hardware.

Selected Achievements:
- Identified, developed and implemented strategic plans of action resulting in operational savings averaging 30%
- Provided support services to clients utilizing NCS Series 7 Trust Processing System
- Designed, developed and instructed comprehensive trust application courses for institutions operating on VAX, T.I. or PC hardware
- Provided Quality Assurance Testing of NCS Series 7 Software

137

Combination. *Cynthia Kraft, Valrico, Florida*

A resume for an individual without a four-year degree but whose alternative education, on-the-job achievements, and record of numerous promotions enabled her to progress in the

ALYSSA M. KOCHANSKY

PROFESSIONAL EXPERIENCE (continued)

FIRST AMERICAN BANK, Philadelphia, PA   1980 - 1988
Trust Operations Officer (1986 - 1988)
Trust Management Trainee (1985 - 1986)
Various Operations Positions (1980 - 1985)
Supervised Trust Department data processing, accounting and compliance functions and directed the operations staff utilizing management policies and procedures.

Selected Achievements:
- Effective management of operations during a period of radical policy and procedure disruption
- Directed staff downsizing as a result of instituting more efficient working procedures and utilizing ADP functions
- Coordinated conversion of First American Bank Systems data processing to Premier Systems, Inc.
- Managed the conversion of all physically held securities to a DTC piggyback relationship with Mellon Custody Services
- Developed and executed a comprehensive reporting system to monitor and control income and expense items

EDUCATION

- Numerous professional seminars
- Creative Training Courses including *Train the Trainer*
- Ohio State University Continuing Education
    Increasing Your Management Skills - August 1988
    Developing Management Skills - November 1987
- Pennsylvania Trust School, Bucknell University - June 1988
    Completed three-year curriculum
- American Institute of Banking - June 1987
    Foundations of Banking
- Elizabethtown College, Elizabethtown, PA
    Coursework: *Personnel Management 101*
                              Accounting I

COMPUTERS AND SYSTEMS PROFICIENCY

Systems: Novell Netware; Wide Area and Local Area Networks; SIS/CSS Brokerage; Trust Management; Alpha 400; Windows 95

Applications: Microsoft Word Suite; SunGard Series 7; Intra- and Internet; GOLDMINE

financial services and securities industry. Positions are centered and in italic along with date ranges. By clustering jobs, the writer avoided repetition in the description of responsibilities for the various positions. A list of selected achievements is provided for each employer.

SHELDON R. MAURERTON
1005 BORDEAUX DRIVE
NORTH HAMPTON, ILLINOIS 60000
000 000.0000

PROFILE

Member of senior management team for a major corporation. Successfully contributed knowledge, solid judgement, and expertise, resulting in revenue and profit growth.

Solid record of achievement - career of increasing responsibilities - effective management executive.

Recent Significant Accomplishments:
- Surpassed income budget expectations for three consecutive years.
- Developed numerous self-insured association programs.
- Successfully managed business through two major reorganizations.
- Advised and consulted on major self-insured projects.

PROFESSIONAL EXPERIENCE

HOWARD CORPORATION
(National Third Party Administrator providing claims administration, loss control, and consulting services to self-insured clients)

REGIONAL DIRECTOR/SENIOR VICE PRESIDENT, 1993 to Present   City, State

- Conduct business of the Midwest Region which includes an eight-state area, $20+ million in revenue, and 220 employees.

- Member of Management Executive Committee – involving policy making on company-wide issues including evaluation of financial performance, monitoring new sales results, evaluation of lost or in-jeopardy accounts, roll-out of new risk information computer system, human resource issues, and development of in-house managed care program.

REGIONAL CLIENT SERVICE MANAGER/VICE PRESIDENT, 1991 to 1993   City, State

- Responsible for Midwest Region client relations; managed team of account executives; met regularly with clients to assure customer satisfaction

- Developed innovative pricing and servicing options for major accounts.

MARKETING MANAGER/ASSISTANT VICE PRESIDENT, 1989 to 1991   City, State

- Managed insurance placements for both insured and self-insured clients.

- Generated new business through creative marketing methods.

DIVISION MARKETING EXECUTIVE, 1985 to 1989   City, State

- Established numerous self-insured programs for associations and individual entities.

- Responsible for the development of self-insured workers compensation programs for public entities, schools, restaurants, and contractors in several states – programs have generated income to .   in excess of $3 million annually.

138

Combination. *Lorie Lebert, Novi, Michigan*

Lines enclosing the Profile and Recent Significant Accomplishments help this part of the resume to be seen. Because it is in the "sweet spot" from 2 to 5 inches down from the top of the page,

PROFESSIONAL EXPERIENCE (continued):

MOUNTAINSIDE PRODUCTS CORPORATION
ASSISTANT RISK MANAGER, 1983 to 1984

- Assisted manager in administration of Risk Management Department.

- Effectively negotiated settlement of several complex business interruption claims.

GINN-CITY GUARDSMAN, INCORPORATED
ACCOUNT EXECUTIVE/SALES AND SERVICE, 1981 to 1982

- Produced new business and successfully renewed assigned book of business.

MANLEY, TOUCAN, HARTIN & JONES, INC.
ACCOUNT EXECUTIVE/ASSISTANT VICE PRESIDENT, 1979 to 1981

- Successfully renewed all assigned accounts.

DANIELS CORPORATION
MARKETING REPRESENTATIVE, 1976 to 1979

- Resourcefully placed insurance coverages for major accounts using innovative marketing techniques.

MAJORFORD INSURANCE COMPANY
CLAIMS REPRESENTATIVE, 1971 to 1976

- Negotiated numerous insurance claim settlements, while serving as a multi-line adjuster.

EDUCATION

NORTHERN STATE UNIVERSITY
B.B.A. DEGREE, 1970

- *Majors:* Marketing and Business Administration

Numerous seminars and courses on insurance-related topics

OTHER INFORMATION

Board Member – Homeowners Association

Professional and personal references will be furnished on request

the chances are high that the Profile will be read. The individual's name, section headings, job positions, and academic degree are in bold small caps. Square bullets point to responsibilities and achievements. The thin-thick line at the top of page 2 echoes page 1.

Thomas J. Clifton
799 Broadway, Revere, Massachusetts 02151
(617) 555-5555 Home • (617) 555-5551 Business

SUMMARY

- Experienced business manager with specific expertise in the travel industry and strong skills in sales, marketing, and staff development.
- Entrepreneur who grew business from start-up to $3 million in annual sales through effective business planning, creative sales techniques, innovative marketing, and development of strong niche markets.
- Fluent in Spanish, French, and German.

PROFESSIONAL EXPERIENCE
1987-Present

President, ADVENTURE TRAVEL, INC., Boston, Massachusetts
Partner/owner and lead agent of highly profitable travel agency.

Business Management

- Analyzed market and re-focused business in response to market changes. Initially concentrated primarily on student travel; adapted to become corporate travel specialists and then to current area of specialization, South American travel, with emphasis on low cost and fast service. Established nationwide South American client base.
- Negotiated agreements with suppliers and vendors that resulted in significant benefits to the business, specifically: incentive income agreements with major carriers ($30,000 annual bonus income) and free automation and signing bonus upon selection of computer system vendor.
- Initiated use of and trained agency outside sales agents.
- Supervised accounting, tax return, and record-keeping activities.
- Selected and hired self-motivated sales staff and allowed them autonomy to resolve customer problems. Resulted in hard-working, customer-focused staff who required minimal day-to-day supervision.

Travel

- Lead agent personally generating over $1 million in sales annually as well as assisting with sales of outside sales agents. Focused on providing quality customer service which generated substantial referral business.
- Sabre proficient, Worldspan trained, and familiar with Apollo.
- Extensive personal travel knowledge both international and domestic.

Sales/Marketing

- Developed strong niche markets. Conceived and implemented marketing plans to acquire market share within chosen segments.
- Established name recognition and generated sales through a combination of sales and marketing techniques including cold calling, corporate account development, and judicious placement of advertising in Yellow Pages and niche market journals.
- Created and implemented promotions to spur sales including a bonus travel program for ministers of South American churches.

EDUCATION

BSBA / Finance, 1987, BABSON COLLEGE, Wellesley, Massachusetts
- Started travel business part-time by making commission sales to fellow students for an established travel agency.

PROFESSIONAL AFFILIATIONS

American Society of Travel Agents
Airline Reporting Corporation

139

Combination. *Louise M. Kursmark, Cincinnati, Ohio*

With strengths in business management, sales and marketing, and travel, this individual was "positioned for a variety of management opportunities." Lines highlight Experience categories.

Medical and Health Care

Resumes at a Glance

JOHN MARK
10 Manor Road
New City, New York 10900
914-666-4444

SUMMARY

Clinical Laboratory Scientist with eighteen years clinical and administrative experience in hospital laboratory management including Hematology, Coagulation, and Bacteriology. Detail-oriented, with strong background in quality control/assurance, cost control, and regulatory compliance. High energy, dedicated professional, committed to practical and theoretical teaching, increasing productivity, and maintaining quality and efficiency.

RELEVANT EXPERIENCE

Bronx Medical Center, Bronx, NY   1970 - present
Laboratory Manager (1994 - present)
Assistant Laboratory Manager (1977-1994)
Clinical Laboratory Technologist (1970-1977)
As **functional manager of hospital laboratory since 1990**, responsible for:
   • Directing, developing, planning, and coordinating all laboratory activities
   • Designing and implementing all quality control/quality assurance policies and procedures
   • Formulating laboratory goals and objectives
   • Preparing, analyzing, and interpreting monthly and annual reports and test results
   • Presenting laboratory in-service programs
   • Supervising and training staff of three, and interns
   • Evaluating and validating analytical data
   • Interpreting clinical diagnostic findings for medical staff
   • Performing sample determinations, preventive maintenance, and instrument repair
   • Directing medical technologists and phlebotomy team.

Significant Accomplishments include:
• Increased productivity and expanded test capability of laboratory through acquisition of sophisticated, cost-effective, analytical equipment in managed care environment.
• Successfully implemented CLIA '88 regulations, and maintained standard of excellence and exemplary standing with New York State Department of Health regarding laboratory inspection and proficiency testing.
• Authored and revised Laboratory Manual, Orientation Manual, Safety/Technical Manual, and specific discipline manuals.
• Reduced 1996 laboratory supplies budget by 15% over 1995, without changing product lines.
• Evaluated technical equipment for specialty companies.
• Coordinated internship program with Bronx Community College, and prepared interns for National Registry Examinations.

CERTIFICATIONS: New York State Department of Health - Laboratory Supervisor
                              National Certification Agency - Laboratory Supervisor; Clinical Laboratory Scientist
                                              Chemistry, Microbiology, Hematology

EDUCATION: **SUNY** - Empire State College, NY   **Bachelor of Science, 1977**
                              The New School, NY   Graduate Courses

FACULTY: **CUNY** - Bronx Community College, NY
                              Medical Laboratory Advisory Committee
                              Clinical Laboratory Associate

References available on request.

140

Combination. *Linsey Levine, Chappaqua, New York*

All of this person's experience was at one company. To avoid repetitive job descriptions, the writer clustered the jobs and gave one list of responsibilities and one list of achievements.

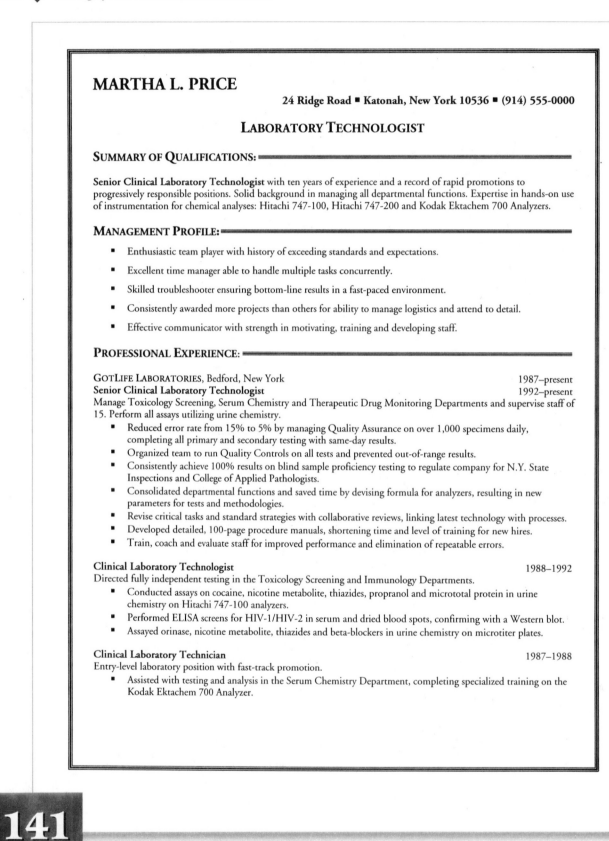

MARTHA L. PRICE

24 Ridge Road ▪ Katonah, New York 10536 ▪ (914) 555-0000

LABORATORY TECHNOLOGIST

SUMMARY OF QUALIFICATIONS:

Senior Clinical Laboratory Technologist with ten years of experience and a record of rapid promotions to progressively responsible positions. Solid background in managing all departmental functions. Expertise in hands-on use of instrumentation for chemical analyses: Hitachi 747-100, Hitachi 747-200 and Kodak Ektachem 700 Analyzers.

MANAGEMENT PROFILE:

- Enthusiastic team player with history of exceeding standards and expectations.
- Excellent time manager able to handle multiple tasks concurrently.
- Skilled troubleshooter ensuring bottom-line results in a fast-paced environment.
- Consistently awarded more projects than others for ability to manage logistics and attend to detail.
- Effective communicator with strength in motivating, training and developing staff.

PROFESSIONAL EXPERIENCE:

GOTLIFE LABORATORIES, Bedford, New York — 1987–present
Senior Clinical Laboratory Technologist — 1992–present
Manage Toxicology Screening, Serum Chemistry and Therapeutic Drug Monitoring Departments and supervise staff of 15. Perform all assays utilizing urine chemistry.
- Reduced error rate from 15% to 5% by managing Quality Assurance on over 1,000 specimens daily, completing all primary and secondary testing with same-day results.
- Organized team to run Quality Controls on all tests and prevented out-of-range results.
- Consistently achieve 100% results on blind sample proficiency testing to regulate company for N.Y. State Inspections and College of Applied Pathologists.
- Consolidated departmental functions and saved time by devising formula for analyzers, resulting in new parameters for tests and methodologies.
- Revise critical tasks and standard strategies with collaborative reviews, linking latest technology with processes.
- Developed detailed, 100-page procedure manuals, shortening time and level of training for new hires.
- Train, coach and evaluate staff for improved performance and elimination of repeatable errors.

Clinical Laboratory Technologist — 1988–1992
Directed fully independent testing in the Toxicology Screening and Immunology Departments.
- Conducted assays on cocaine, nicotine metabolite, thiazides, propranol and micrototal protein in urine chemistry on Hitachi 747-100 analyzers.
- Performed ELISA screens for HIV-1/HIV-2 in serum and dried blood spots, confirming with a Western blot.
- Assayed orinase, nicotine metabolite, thiazides and beta-blockers in urine chemistry on microtiter plates.

Clinical Laboratory Technician — 1987–1988
Entry-level laboratory position with fast-track promotion.
- Assisted with testing and analysis in the Serum Chemistry Department, completing specialized training on the Kodak Ektachem 700 Analyzer.

141

Combination. *Phyllis B. Shabad, Ossining, New York*

The writer emphasized this individual's managerial skills and her professional development (notice the Professional Development section on page 2). The person had a B.S. degree in

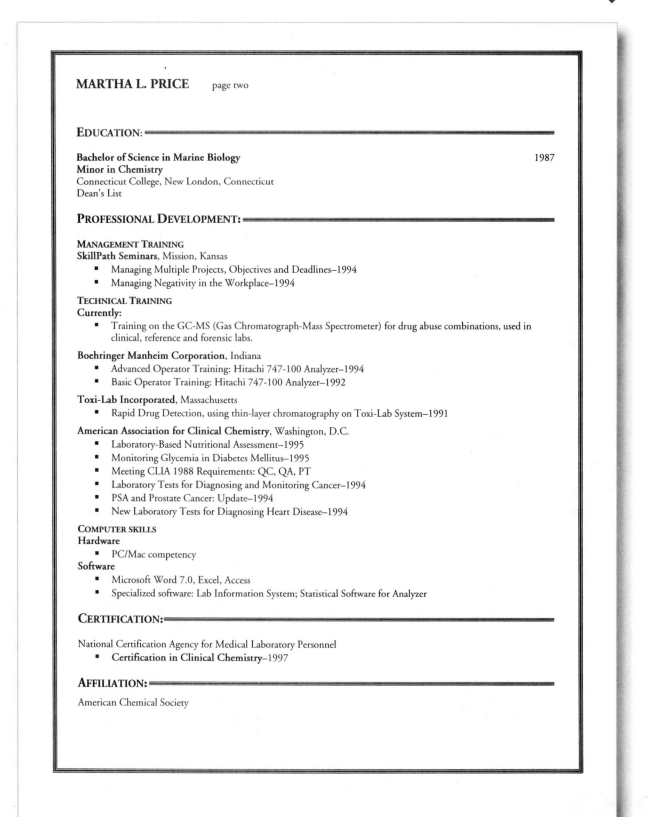

MARTHA L. PRICE   page two

EDUCATION:

Bachelor of Science in Marine Biology   1987
Minor in Chemistry
Connecticut College, New London, Connecticut
Dean's List

PROFESSIONAL DEVELOPMENT:

MANAGEMENT TRAINING
SkillPath Seminars, Mission, Kansas
- Managing Multiple Projects, Objectives and Deadlines–1994
- Managing Negativity in the Workplace–1994

TECHNICAL TRAINING
Currently:
- Training on the GC-MS (Gas Chromatograph-Mass Spectrometer) for drug abuse combinations, used in clinical, reference and forensic labs.

Boehringer Manheim Corporation, Indiana
- Advanced Operator Training: Hitachi 747-100 Analyzer–1994
- Basic Operator Training: Hitachi 747-100 Analyzer–1992

Toxi-Lab Incorporated, Massachusetts
- Rapid Drug Detection, using thin-layer chromatography on Toxi-Lab System–1991

American Association for Clinical Chemistry, Washington, D.C.
- Laboratory-Based Nutritional Assessment–1995
- Monitoring Glycemia in Diabetes Mellitus–1995
- Meeting CLIA 1988 Requirements: QC, QA, PT
- Laboratory Tests for Diagnosing and Monitoring Cancer–1994
- PSA and Prostate Cancer: Update–1994
- New Laboratory Tests for Diagnosing Heart Disease–1994

COMPUTER SKILLS
Hardware
- PC/Mac competency
Software
- Microsoft Word 7.0, Excel, Access
- Specialized software: Lab Information System; Statistical Software for Analyzer

CERTIFICATION:

National Certification Agency for Medical Laboratory Personnel
- **Certification in Clinical Chemistry**–1997

AFFILIATION:

American Chemical Society

Marine Biology but only a minor in Chemistry. Because chemical labs became her sites of employment, the writer devoted a lot of space to post-college training in management and for competency, certification, and affiliation with the chemical industry.

DONNA WARREN, M.T., ASCP

555 West Zenith Avenue
Conejo, California 55555

Home: (555) 555-5555
Work: (555) 555-5555

PROFESSION

Experienced Clinical Laboratory Technologist with 20+ year career in hospital, reference laboratory, and blood center settings. Generalist skills include:

‣ Blood Banking	‣ Microbiology	‣ Hematology
‣ Coagulation	‣ RIA Special Chemistry	‣ Urinalysis
‣ Serology	‣ Chemistry	‣ Immunology

EDUCATION, LICENSURE

STANFORD UNIVERSITY

B.A., Biology (1974)

LICENSURE

California Clinical Laboratory Technologist (1980)

PROFESSIONAL EXPERIENCE

METROPOLITAN MEDICAL CENTER, Long Beach, California
(formerly HEALTH LABORATORIES)

9/92-Present
6/76-9/92

Licensed Clinical Laboratory Technologist (9/92-Present)
(Department of Newborn Screen and Prenatal Tests Laboratory)

▣ Perform newborn screen laboratory tests required by the State of California Department of Health Services to detect genetic diseases of newborns, including phenylketonuria, galactosemia, hypothyroidism and hemoglobinopathies. Perform prenatal laboratory testing for alpha-fetoprotein in maternal serum. Maintain equipment and resolve instrumentation problems. Direct the activities of laboratory assistants as needed.

Licensed Clinical Laboratory Technologist (6/89-8/92)

▣ Performed generalist functions, with experience in all areas of the clinical laboratory (immunohematology, serology, chemistry, special chemistry, coagulation, urinalysis, hematology, microbiology, radioimmunoassay, toxicology). Monitored laboratory equipment (daily maintenance, quality control, calibration, correction of malfunctions). Assisted with rotation and inventory control of supplies. Solved technical problems using moderate degree of independent judgment with minimal supervision.

Department Head of Radioimmunoassay (1984-1989)

▣ Performed all radioimmunoassay (RIA) tests. Maintained quality control records for all assays. Documented assay and radioimmunoassay procedures and maintained safety manual for College of American Pathologist inspection. Evaluated and set-up new RIA assays. Scheduled monthly workload. Instructed student trainees in laboratory procedures. Analyzed and evaluated capital expenditures for new instrumentation and negotiated purchases. Maintained and controlled operating supplies.

142

Combination. *Susan Britton Whitcomb, Fresno, California*

The person's employer (Health Laboratories) was acquired by Metropolitan Medical Center and had already gone through two name changes. The individual originally listed each position as

Donna Warren, M.T., ASCP

Page Two

PROFESSIONAL EXPERIENCE

HEALTH LABORATORIES, continued

Prior Assignments

▶ Radioimmunoassay Specialist Technologist (1981-1984)
  Clinical Laboratory Technologist (1980-1981)
  Clinical Laboratory Temporary Technologist (1979)
  Clinical Laboratory Technologist Trainee (1978)
  Laboratory Assistant, Madera Community Hospital (1976-1977)

SO-CAL BLOOD CENTER, Long Beach, California   4/90-2/93

Per Diem Clinical Laboratory Technologist

▶ Performed laboratory work in the following technical areas: bacteriology, chemistry, hematology, and
  serology.

ADDITIONAL PROFESSIONAL ACTIVITIES

HEALTH LABORATORIES

- Secretary of Quality Assurance Committee
- Safety Committee Member
- Radiation Safety Officer
- Organized and planned activities for National Medical Laboratory Week, holiday festivities, and
  annual corporate barbecue.

PROFESSIONAL AFFILIATIONS

CALIFORNIA ASSOCIATION FOR MEDICAL LABORATORY TECHNOLOGY (CAMLT)

- Fresno Chapter, CAMLT
- Executive Committee Member
- Past Newsletter Editor, *Erythro-Sights*
- Delegate to CAMLT Annual Convention
- Sergeant at Arms, CAMLT Annual Convention
- Nominations Committee, CAMLT Annual Convention
- Secretary and Membership Chairperson
- Volunteer, Community Awareness Program

References Upon Request

with a separate employer, giving the impression of job-hopping. Identifying an employer
within parentheses eliminates this possible misperception. The writer put the resume on two
pages because of the person's experience, committee work, and affiliations.

MARTIN YRACEBORO, ARRT(N)(R), CNMT, CRT

5555 North Portsmouth Avenue
Longview, California 55555
(555) 555-5555

QUALIFICATIONS

Experienced **NUCLEAR MEDICINE TECHNOLOGIST** with 15 years in hospital and freestanding imaging facilities . . . additional experience as Radiological Technologist. Prior background in health care marketing, education, and clinical research. Credentials include:

- ◉ American Registry of Radiologic Technologists, #055555, (R) 1969, (N) 1987

- ◉ Certified Technologist, Nuclear Medicine, State of California, #RHN 555, 1989

- ◉ Certified Radiological Technologist, State of California, #55555-5555, 1985

PROFESSIONAL EXPERIENCE

IMAGING CENTER, Longview, California   3/91-Present

Nuclear Medicine Technologist II/Lead Technologist

Established start-up operating procedures for Nuclear Medicine Department, including protocol, scheduling, record keeping, computer systems, ordering, and procedures for handling, storage, and decay of radiopharmaceuticals. Performed full scope of planar, flow studies, and SPECT imaging procedures. Interviewed and made hiring recommendations for Nuclear Medicine Technologist.

Contributions:

- Researched and advised physicians regarding selection of upgraded equipment.

- Customized computer applications to automate protocol writing process.

- Received excellent bi-annual audit reviews for record keeping compliance.

- Awarded Employee of the Year. Received outstanding performance evaluations annually.

- Assumed additional responsibility for ordering of supplies for entire facility.

Staff Radiological Technologist   3/90-3/91

- Initially employed with Imaging Center's parent company, Saint Luke's Medical Center, as Staff Radiological Technologist. Performed routine radiological procedures.

- Contracted with Veteran's Administration Hospital to manage Nuclear Medicine Department on pre-arranged temporary assignment.

143

Combination. *Susan Britton Whitcomb, Fresno, California*

The individual's work history had three phases (nuclear medicine initially, then research/teaching, and then back to nuclear medicine). The person's original resume was five pages long with

MARTIN YRACEBORO, ARRT(N)(R), CNMT, CRT
Page Two

PROFESSIONAL EXPERIENCE (cont.)

1984-1990   Seven years' experience in the field of blood cell separation. Involvement extended to: supervision of **clinical trials,** including report writing and collaboration on publication of research; **technical functions** (blood cell collection and plasma exchange procedures); and **marketing** and **educational presentations** on use of blood cell separators to hospital nursing staff on a national scale.

- **Clinical Research Coordinator** (1988-1990)
  Boster Labs, Inc., Manheim, Michigan

- **Apheresis Technician, Satellite Operations** (1986-1988)
  American Red Cross, Denver, Colorado

- **Marketing Product Specialist** (1984-1986)
  Blood Bank Products Corporation, Boston, Massachusetts

1974-1984   Initial professional experience as Nuclear Medicine Technologist and Radiologic Technologist. Performed full range of procedures. Advanced to hold departmental administrative responsibilities: management of Nuclear Medicine Department; scheduling and supervision of technologists and support staff; inventory control; and budget tracking.

- **Chief Nuclear Medicine Technologist** (1980-1984)
  Radiology and Nuclear Medicine Technologist (1979-1984)
  Valley Community Hospital, Valley View, California

- **Radiology and Nuclear Medicine Technologist** (1974-1979)
  Denver Metropolitan Hospital, Denver, Colorado

EDUCATION

Graduate, Valley View Community Hospital School of Radiological Technology, 1967-1969
Certified CPR and First Aid Instructor, American Red Cross
Continuing Education requirements met through attendance at local, regional, and national meetings conferences, and seminars.

AFFILIATIONS

Society of Nuclear Medicine, Technologist Section, since 1987
Sierra Valley Society of Nuclear Medicine, since 1989

ADDITIONAL DATA

Abstracts, publications, oral presentations, and references provided upon request.

extensive descriptions of responsibilities at every employer. The writer reorganized the resume, writing first a summary paragraph for the first and second career phases, and then a more traditional listing for the most recent work with the Imaging Center.

Résumé

JOEL DAVIS McPHERSON ▪ 124 MILO ROAD ▪ MARTIN MI 49070 ▪ 222-000-2255

▪*INITIATIVE*　　▪*DEDICATION*　　▪*DEPENDABILITY*　　▪*COMMITMENT*　　▪*ACHIEVEMENT*

Career Focus and Background

- Position as a Clinical Perfusionist utilizing 18+ years of responsibility within a medical setting.
▸ **Highlights of accomplishments include**:
  - Certification and over 11 years experience as a *Clinical Perfusionist* in charge of the set-up and operation of a heart-lung machine for cardiopulmonary procedures.
  - 4 years as *Bio-Tech* involved in the evaluation and reporting of experimentation utilizing anatomical and microbiological techniques.
  - 2 years direct experience with operating room surgeons and medical support staff.

Profile

▸ Career committed with an effective combination of analytical, organizational and communications skills.
  - Ability to learn new material and procedures quickly; enthusiastic, resourceful, and trainable.
  - Capable of adapting easily to new environments; can successfully handle a wide range of responsibilities, changing workloads and special projects.

Strengths

▸ Proven effectiveness as a dedicated team player; fully sensitive and responsive to the needs of people.
  - Recognized for self-motivation and contributing to the successful management of a department.

Summary of Experience

1986-Pres:	Clinical Perfusionist.	Perfusion Associates, Inc., Kalamazoo, MI
1982-1986:	Biochemistry Technician.	Upjohn Company, Kalamazoo, MI.
1979-1981:	Clinical Perfusionist.	Borgess Hospital, Kalamazoo, MI.
1978-1979:	Operating Room Technician.	Borgess Hospital, Kalamazoo, MI.

Education

Degree in Perfusion Technology.
1993-1994:　Mississippi School of Perfusion Technology, Pelahatchie, MS.　GPA: 3.8.
1973-1977:　Western Michigan University (WMU), Kalamazoo, MI. Major: *Biology*; Minor: *Sociology*. *Working toward Bachelor of Science Degree.*

Certification

1996:　American Board of Cardiovascular Perfusion.

Associations/Community Involvements

1979-Pres:　Member: (AMSECT), *AMERICAN SOCIETY OF EXTRA-CORPOREAL TECHNOLOGY, INC.*
1985-Pres:　Vice-President: *PARENT TEACHER STUDENT ASSOCIATION, Northeastern Elementary, Kalamazoo, MI.*
1994:　Member: *IMPROVEMENT TEAM, Kalamazoo Central High School.*
1993-1994:　Vice-President: *PARENT TEACHER STUDENT ASSOCIATION, Kalamazoo Central High School.*

References

Excellent professional references will be furnished on request.

144

Combination. *Randy Clair, location unknown*

Thicker horizontal lines enclose a headline of worker traits. The remaining, thinner lines above section headings distinguish the sections visually. Note the use of bold and italic.

SALINA PIEDRA, P.A.

555 North Wickendale Drive
Selma, Alabama 55555
(555) 555-5555

PROFESSIONAL GOAL

Physician Assistant in a healthcare setting where my comprehensive clinical training and 20+ years of broad-based nursing experience will be of value.

QUALIFICATIONS

♦ **P.A. Clinical Training:** Over 1,600 hours of advanced clinical training in the role of Physician Assistant with emphasis on caring for patients of all ages from infant to geriatric, eliciting complete patient history and physical, and effectively managing and treating common acute illness and stable chronic illness.

♦ **Professional Skills:** Excellent professional judgment and documentation skills. Noted by supervisors for making well thought out decisions and utilizing consultants appropriately. Convey a sincere concern for patient's physical and emotional well-being. Excellent performance history in highly-structured managed care environments.

♦ **Prior Clinical Experience:** Well-rounded nursing experience, primarily with Foundation Medical Center, in capacities as Emergency Room Nurse, Wellness Center Nurse, Employee Health Nurse, Pre-Op/Post-Op/Recovery Nurse, Telemetry Nurse, Medical/Surgical Staff Nurse, and Oncology Staff Nurse.

♦ **Related Experiences:** Performed annual employee physicals. Assessed and treated work-related injuries. Made referrals. Provided preventative health education. Counseled individuals regarding health assessment results and lifestyle changes. Served on Emergency Department QA and Peer Review committees.

♦ **Teaching Experience:** Precepted nurse interns on medical-surgical floors (cited for my unusual patience and helpfulness). Taught nurses instructional methods for conducting pre-op classes and advising diabetic patients. Assisted in teaching EMT classes for Yellowstone National Park medics.

PROFESSIONAL EXPERIENCE

Emergency Nurse/Employee Health Nurse/Wellness Center Nurse -- Foundation Medical Center	1984-Present
Clinical and Emergency Nurse -- Yellowstone National Park	1983-1984
Telemetry Nurse/Staff Nurse -- Foundation Medical Center	1975-1982

EDUCATION, CERTIFICATION

Physician Assistant Certification -- University of California, School of Medicine	9/96
Bachelor of Science Degree, Nursing -- California State University, Long Beach	1975
Associate of Arts Degree, Liberal Arts / Minor in Child Development -- Long Beach City College	1971
Registered Nurse License (#RN 55555)	1975-Present
Advanced Cardiac Life Support	1981-Present
Certified Emergency Nurse	1985-Present
Mobile Intensive Care Nurse	1989-Present

AFFILIATIONS

California Coalition of Nurse Practitioners (CCNP); National Nurses Association (NNA)

References Upon Request

145

Combination. *Susan Britton Whitcomb, Fresno, California*

This person had just received her P.A. certification but had no paid experience as a P.A. The resume shows her strong background in acute care settings and health programs.

MEREDITH E. TYLER

1015 Wilson Avenue
Norfolk, VA 23500
804 • 496 •1569

CAREER SUMMARY

Registered Nurse with abilities and special skills in Critical Care.

PROFESSIONAL EXPERIENCE

Completing professional studies in a variety of clinical settings. These include Anna Lee Center (**Nursing Home**), BoPeep Children's Hospital (**Pediatrics**), City Central General Hospital (**Maternal Newborn**), Leyte Memorial Hospital (**Medical, Surgical, CCU/ICU**) King Arthur Nursing Home (**Long-term Care**), Waterville Psychiatric Institute (**Psychiatric**), City Central Health Department (**Community Health**).

WORK EXPERIENCE

Nurse Extern, Leyte Memorial Hospital

Organize and administer complete care for 1-2 ICU patients under Registered Nurse supervision. Duties include patient shift reports, continuous patient assessments, administering and documenting patient treatments, entering orders into the computerized hospital information processing system. November 1989 - Present

Nurse Extern, Mary Margaret Memorial Hospital

Organized and administered complete care for 1-2 ICU patients under Registered Nurse supervision. Duties included conducting patient shift reports, continuous patient assessments, administered treatments and documented actions of care, educational component to program included weekly lectures on a variety of critical care subject matters and ethics committee meetings. May - August 1989

EDUCATION

Old Dominion University, Norfolk, VA., **B.S. in Nursing**, May 1990

ACTIVITIES/AWARDS

CPR Certification - American Red Cross

146

Combination. *Anne G. Kramer, Virginia Beach, Virginia*

The candidate was a mature and highly motivated individual, as is evident in the two Experience sections. Boldfacing directs the reader's attention to key information. This Career Goals

CAREER GOALS IN CRITICAL CARE NURSING PRACTICE

The desire to pursue a career in **Critical Care Nursing** was an outgrowth of experiences after my father had numerous hospitalizations. As a teen-ager it appeared to me that being a nurse in the intensive care unit would be an exciting and challenging career. Nurses knew the disease processes, pharmacology and how to use them for the benefit of the sick. Nurses were also able to deal with the psychosocial aspects of patients and their families.

It was through these observations that I decided to become a Critical Care Nurse. I wanted to provide the best quality care possible for the sick. However, I was sidetracked along the way. When it came time for me to go to college, my family was very influential in determining exactly what should be my major. Nursing was definitely not on the list. I was told that nurses only changed bedpans and it was no way to earn a living. This career was something my family was not going to subsidize.

Being young, easily persuaded, and dependant on my family for financial support to get me through school, I pursued another field of study. In trying to meet my father's ambitions for me to become an engineer and computer wiz, I became very frustrated with the courses and ended up taking a break from school.

It was then that I made the decision I was going to do what I wanted. I would study Nursing even if it meant I had to finance my own education. Determined to pursue this goal I made my plans accordingly.

I entered nursing school in 1985. Clinical rotation experience included geriatrics, pediatrics, maternal-newborn, medical-surgical, psychiatric, critical care, long-term, and community health. Critical Care Nursing soon became my main interest and favorite clinical rotation.

This past summer I worked as an Extern at Mary Margaret Memorial Hospital in a critical care setting. The learning experience was incredible and rewarding. I could function as a registered nurse with the exception that I was not able to administer medications. Nursing was my decision, I found the work rewarding, and knew I had made the right career choice.

I will be graduating in May 1990 with a Bachelor of Science in Nursing. My immediate goal is to find an internship in the field of critical care nursing. I feel there is still much a new graduate like myself can learn. Working this past summer and currently in ICU settings, I became aware how stimulating the work can be. An internship would be the ideal way to expand my knowledge.

Eventually, I would like to return to school on a part-time basis to earn my CCRN, followed by a Masters Degree in Critical Care Nursing. I feel an individual can never have enough education.

The goals I have set for myself are more than enough to keep me busy for the next five years. With my motivation and determination each of them is attainable. My studies may have taken me a bit longer than most individuals, but my goal to become a Nurse is about to be achieved. It is something that I have always wanted and the satisfaction of knowing I did it all by myself is very exciting. With great anticipation, I now look forward to a career in Critical Care Nursing.

statement as an addendum was a change from a routine cover letter. Because of the statement's length, the resume could be shorter. This allowed the writer to focus the individual's goals in the personal statement.

93 Lyle Avenue, Ramapo, NJ 00000
(555) 555-5555

Imelda Salazar, RN, MSN, CNOR

SUMMARY

Seven years of comprehensive experience in both the clinical and business management aspects of perioperative nursing. Cognizant of the many interdependent factors that affect an institution's competitive position in the rapidly changing health care environment. Proactive liaison with staff, physicians, administration and suppliers in meeting the goal of providing the highest quality of patient care while containing costs, maximizing efficiency, and maintaining compliance with regulatory requirements. Trilingual fluency in English, Filipino and Spanish. Seeking the opportunity to direct the operating room unit of a large institution.

EDUCATION and CREDENTIALS

FAIRLEIGH DICKINSON UNIVERSITY, TEANECK, NJ
- Master of Science in Nursing Management, 1994

FELICIAN COLLEGE, LODI, NJ
- Baccalaureate of Science in Nursing, 1990

- Registered Nurse, State of New Jersey
- Certified Nurse Operating Room (CNOR)

STELLA MARIS COLLEGE, MANILA, PHILLIPINES
- Nursing Certificate, 1987

AREAS of EFFECTIVENESS

- As an OR nurse in a community hospital, assisted in every stage, pre- through post-operative, of a variety of surgeries that included: general abdominal, spinal, vascular, orthopedic, and organ transplantation procedures as well as endoscopies.

- At completion of master's program, assumed additional administrative responsibilities. Implemented policies for the organization, direction and delivery of specialized services that effectively contributed to meeting patients' health needs during surgical intervention while eliminating unnecessary paperwork.

- Established workflow processes for optimal utilization of facilities to accommodate the shift in the mix of surgical patients to less invasive procedures and same day stays.

- Increased long term value of staff by cross-training them and rotating their assignments to enable them to utilize and develop skills necessary for their professional advancement.

- Integrated the preadmission testing department into the perioperative services unit to strengthen control in this area.

- Redesigned the supply department to provide nursing staff with easy access to most commonly used materials, which simplified inventory tracking, usage charging and replenishment. Reduced supply costs through centralized purchasing and consolidation of material orders with an affiliate hospital to take advantage of quantity price breaks.

- In conjunction with other charge nurses and hospital administrators, evaluated capital equipment to be purchased for use in the operating room. Took into account such considerations as its beneficial features and ease of use, product support services, and cost of accessories. Negotiated with three vendors to obtain best prices and package deals in line with budgetary limitations.

- Participated in a technical project team, providing input on the selection and design of an OR computer system to overcome deficiencies in case scheduling, inventory control and patient charging.

- Addressed quality management issues through design of inservice seminars and multidisciplinary team participation.

147

Combination. *Melanie A. Noonan, West Paterson, New Jersey*

The person had been a nurse before emigrating to the United States from the Philippine Islands. In the United States she advanced in her career and eventually ran the operating room at a

Imelda Salazar, RN, MSN, CNOR ━━━━━━━━━━━━━━━━━━━

WORK EXPERIENCE ━━━━━━━━━━━━━━━━━━━

1993–Present   OAKMOUNT GENERAL HOSPITAL, SOUTH BERGEN, NJ
Assistant Director of Nursing/Coordinator for Surgical Services at 150-bed private hospital with 2 main operating rooms doing 1500+ surgeries per year, and a suite for minor procedures (400+ per year). Interact daily with chiefs of surgery and medical staff. Direct the activities of 5 departments: OR, PACU, Endoscopy, Same Day Stay, and Preadmission Testing, with staff consisting of 2 charge nurses, 20 RNs, 4 aides and a secretary. Contributor to upholding the hospital's highest standards, leading to its qualifying for Accreditation with Commendation by the JCAHO.

1991–1993   ST. ANTHONY'S HOSPITAL, CARTERET, NJ
Operating Room Clinical Coordinator, with 24 hour accountability. Scheduled 3 operating rooms daily for hospital performing 2,500+ surgeries per year. Supervised and evaluated a 9 member staff. Acted as both educator and manager, conducting frequent inservice training in new technologies, medications and delivery systems in conjuction with supplier contacts.

1988–1991   PROFESSIONAL HEALTHCARE AGENCY, LYNDHURST, NJ
Staff Nurse/Perioperative Nurse
Employed at Beth Israel Hospital, Passaic, NJ; Meadowlands Hospital, Secaucus, NJ; and Clara Maas Hospital, Belleville, NJ. Earlier nursing experience acquired at medical facilities in the Phillipines.

PROFESSIONAL ASSOCIATIONS ━━━━━━━━━━━━━━━━━━━

Member, National Association of Operating Room Nurses

Chairman, Education Committee for the New Jersey Chapter of PLAN: a grassroots organization of operating room, recovery room and ambulatory care managers and nurses, providing a forum for sharing ideas and networking.

small community hospital. The resume demonstrates her management skills in real situations, giving her an edge over other nurse managers whose resumes show merely a chronological listing of positions and job descriptions. The thick partial lines grab attention.

Anna Maria Delario

5555 East Middlesex Way
Fontana, California 55555
(555) 555-5555

❖ ❖ ❖

PROFILE, OBJECTIVE

Experienced Respiratory Therapist -- Qualified for licensed respiratory therapist positions with an organization that will benefit from my 16+ years' experience in home health care and acute care environments.

EDUCATION, CERTIFICATION

Registered Respiratory Therapist -- National Board of Respiratory Care
Respiratory Care Practitioner -- State of California
Exemptee Certificate -- State Board of Pharmacy for Medical Device Retailer
Bachelor of Science Degree, Respiratory Therapy -- California State University, Long Beach (1980)

PROFESSIONAL EXPERIENCE

SOUTHERN CALIFORNIA MEDICAL CENTER, Los Angeles, California   3/89-Present

Staff Lead Respiratory Therapist: Administer respiratory therapy care and life support to cardiopulmonary patients including management of home oxygen, nasal CPAP, apnea monitors, pulmonary aides, and home ventilators. Provide technical support and troubleshooting of ventilator devices and other apparatus. Conduct follow-up patient visits. *Contributions / Accomplishments:*

- ❖ Established clinical protocols in preparation for successful JCAHO survey.

- ❖ Initiated and conducted education series for patients, families, medical support staff, and other nursing agencies.

- ❖ Assumed additional administrative responsibilities (order intake, insurance verifications, purchasing, inventory).

VISTA MEDICAL CENTER, Fontana, California   11/84-2/89

Staff Therapist: Performed respiratory therapist functions similar to those listed above.

- ❖ Gained extensive ER and surgery intensive care experience, as well as ICU, CCU, NICU, PICU, and burn center experience in a regional trauma center.

TRAVELING THERAPIST CORPS (medical traveling organization)   1/83-11/84

Tuscany Medical Center, Neonatal and Pediatric ICU's, Tuscany, Mississippi:

- ❖ Held broad decision-making responsibility under progressive protocol system. Drew and ran CBGs and ABGs via arterial stick and through UAC and arterial lines. Administered aerosol therapy, IPPB, and CPT.

Saint Luke's Hospital and Medical Center, Chicago, Illinois:

- ❖ As Staff Therapist, duties included IPPB, aerosol therapy, CPT, incentive spirometry, and critical care work in units.

ADDITIONAL EXPERIENCE

Served as volunteer Respiratory Therapist on multi-disciplinary medical teams which conducted outreaches to under-served populations in Mexico, Venezuela, and Cambodia.

❖ ❖ ❖

148

Chronological. *Susan Britton Whitcomb, Fresno, California*

Chronological format is used because the person had a consistent, strong work history. Note how the Objective statement is used to express the individual's qualifications.

SHARON POLLACK

2405 Orange Grove Drive
Tampa, Florida 33618
(813) 000-0000

Career Focus	**Wellness Leadership/Health and Fitness Trainer**
Profile	High-level commitment and dedication combined with practical experience led to efficiently directing operations of exercise and fitness center. Presided over administering improvement programs, developing community outreach agendas, marketing/promotional activities, and budgeting. Outgoing and personable, exhibiting demonstrated strengths in communications, time management, and organizational skills.
Education	UNIVERSITY OF SOUTH FLORIDA - Tampa, FL **Bachelor of Science Degree** - **Wellness Leadership, May 1995** Major GPA: 3.85/4.00 Dean's List of Scholars Recipient of Faculty Scholarship Award
Certifications	-- Cardiopulmonary Resuscitation Certification (CPR) -- Standard First Aid -- ACE Personal Training Certification
Experience	PHYSICAL FITNESS WORKS - Tampa, FL **5/95 - Present** **Director** (2/96-Present) Manage daily fitness operations, structure and implement program plans, formulate annual budgets, develop membership recruitment, and supervising five instructors. Spearhead marketing/advertising of promotions and incentive programs, conduct staff evaluations, build strong membership rapport, and prepare schedules. Charged with planning Annual Health Fair focused on expanding community health awareness programs. **Exercise Instructor** (5/95-1/96) *Exhibited ability to assume leadership and managerial responsibilities that led the rapid promotion.* Performed lifestyle education/goal-setting program planning and implementation; exercise testing and prescription, exercise leadership; equipment orientation; and personal training. WELLNESS, INC. - Tampa, FL **12/95 - Present** **Co-Owner/Manager** Initiated start-up operation; participate part-time as a personal health and fitness trainer. THE CROSS WELLNESS CENTER - Winter Park, FL **1/95 - 4/95** **Internship** Completed comprehensive internship while obtaining experience in all aspects of wellness center operations. Participated in marketing activities, tracking statistics, and facilitating plans for special events. SAINT JOSEPH'S HEART INSTITUTE - Tampa, FL **5/94 - 7/94** **Internship** Measured patients' resting and exercise values and monitored electrocardiograms. Handled primary prevention, cardiac risk identification, and the National Heart Attack Risk Study.
Activities	-- Scholarship Athlete, Women's Varsity Soccer at the University of North Carolina (Greensboro) and Florida International University -- Captain, high school soccer team, junior and senior years -- All County Soccer Selection, sophomore, junior and senior years

149

Combination. *Diane McGoldrick, Tampa, Florida*

The Experience section displays development in one year from Intern to Director. The person moved to Michigan and was being considered for a fitness trainer job at General Motors.

KADINA SMITHERS

234 S.E. Main Street • Milwaukie, Oregon 97027 • (503) 657-5433

OBJECTIVE   Position as DENTAL ASSISTANT.

STRENGTHS
- Positive and enthusiastic with excellent "people" skills.
- Able to build rapport with patients.
- Punctual, dependable employee with strong work ethic.
- CDA, EFDA and X-ray certified.

EXPERIENCE   HERMAN ZORSCHY, DMD - Portland, Oregon
Dental Assistant (4/95-Present)
Assist with routine dental work, including composite and amalgam fillings, extractions, root canals and crown preparation. Take and pour impressions. Order supplies, answer phones and help maintain patient files. Take X-rays and assist with emergency exams.

JOHN JONES, DMD - Oregon City, Oregon
Dental Assistant (6/90-4/95)
Assisted dentist with various procedures, including fillings, root canals, crown preparations, composites, teeth cleaning, emergency exams and X-rays. Additionally maintained patient files, answered phones and cleaned office.

MARCUS DEMERA, DMD - Oregon City, Oregon
Intern (4/90-6/90)

EDUCATION   PORTLAND COMMUNITY COLLEGE - Portland, Oregon
Dental Assisting Program (Graduated June 1990)
Certifications: CDA, EFDA and X-ray certified

Attended school full-time while working part-time to help finance academic expenses. Maintained a 3.7 GPA.

REFERENCES   Provided upon request.

150

Combination. *Pat Kendall, Aloha, Oregon*

Relatively large type, less-than-average information, lines (page border, banner lines, and underlining), and white space (blank lines between sections) make this resume easy to read.

DEANNA SMITHERS, RDH

2345 Northwood Lane   Sherwood, Oregon 97113   (503) 642-9076

PROFILE	Highly qualified DENTAL HYGIENIST with extensive experience and up-to-date training in dental technology and periodontal therapy.

- Able to communicate effectively with all kinds of patients, including those with phobias.
- Skilled in providing comprehensive patient education and positive encouragement.
- Well-developed assessment skills.
- Good teamworker with professional attitude and appearance.

EDUCATION	University of Oregon Health Sciences Center, Portland, Oregon **B.S. Dental Hygiene**, 1982

LICENSURE	Dental Hygiene - #3423 Oregon Expanded Function Certificates:

- Pit and Fissure Sealants
- Temporary Soft Denture Relines

EXPERIENCE

1989 - Present	Martin Deberno, DMD, Portland, Oregon *Private Periodontal Practice* **Dental Hygienist**
1982 - 1989	Robert D. Peterson, DMD, Portland, Oregon *General Dentistry Practice* **Dental Assistant**

ADDITIONAL TRAINING

The Hygienist's Role in Implant Maintenance
Sean Allwood, DMD and Cathy Anderson, RDH

Infectious Disease Update: Issues in Dental Hygiene Protocol
Gary Chatsworth, DMD

Female Considerations: Periodontal Needs
Joan Derting-Howe, DMD

BDP Periodontal Study Club
Seven two-hour lectures on topics related to Dentistry and Dental Hygiene

AFFILIATIONS	American Dental Hygienists' Association

151

Combination. *Pat Kendall, Aloha, Oregon*

A resume that is easy to read down the page because of the short lines. When you read this resume, note the change in reading progress as the lines become shorter in the middle sections.

PATTY PATHOLOGIST
1521 Market Street
Wilmington, North Carolina 28405
Home: (000) 111-2222
Work: (000) 333-4444

PROFILE	Highly competent and energetic professional with demonstrated experience in developing and leading a TBI program. Experienced inservice provider. Experienced and well-qualified Speech-Language Pathologist adept in dealing with sensitive populations as part of an interdisciplinary team. Possess exceptional organization and time-management skills. Outstanding oral and written communication skills.

EDUCATION

Master of Arts in Speech-Language Pathology	1984
Bachelor of Science in Speech-Language Pathology	1983

Florida State University, Tallahassee, FL

PROFESSIONAL EXPERIENCE

Atlantic Hospital, University Medical Center, Wilmington, NC

Clinical Coordinator, Traumatic Brain Injury Program 1994 to Present

Accomplishments:

Integral part of team that designed all policies and procedures for this new facility prior to accepting the first patient. Participated in screening, interviewing, and hiring to develop staff. Instrumental in preparing for accreditation and special needs certification. Under my leadership, TBI program was under budget and over revenue with a higher than anticipated patient census.

Responsibilities:

Direct brain injury program for inpatient, day treatment, and outpatient services. Directly supervise 10 member interdisciplinary clinical staff, develop and implement program-related policies and procedures, and develop and manage annual program budget. Member of Quality Improvement Team. Clinical duties include evaluation and treatment of patients within the brain injury program, as well as assessment of swallowing disorders via modified barium swallow x-ray studies for all rehabilitation patients as needed.

Washington Memorial Rehabilitation Hospital, Washington, DC

Level III Speech-Language Pathologist, Head Injury Unit 1992 to 1994

Provided inpatient and outpatient services to neurologically-impaired adults and children including diagnostic and therapeutic treatment for speech and language, cognitive, and swallowing disorders. Supervised students, assisted with program development, and coordinated the unit's quality improvement activities.

Jellystone Hospital, Yogi, VA

Speech Pathology Supervisor 1990 to 1992

Supervisory and clinical duties associated with treatment of rehabilitation patients in an inpatient rehabilitation unit. Supervised department staff, budget planning, as well as diagnosis and treatment of patients. Caseload consisted primarily of adolescents and adults recovering from strokes and head injuries, with strong emphasis on swallowing disorders.

New Hanover County Schools, Wilmington, NC

Speech-Language Pathologist 1986 to 1990

Computer-assisted diagnostic and speech therapy services to children from pre-kindergarten through sixth grade.

152

Combination. *Sandy Adcox Saburn, Wilmington, North Carolina*

This competent professional had extensive accomplishments in her field. The resume was condensed from a five-page curriculum vitae and was well received by hiring readers. Section

Patty Pathologist **Page 2**

EXPERIENCE	*Rehabilitation Hospital of North Carolina*, Raleigh, NC
(continued)	**Speech-Language Pathologist** 1986 to 1990

Contract speech pathology services to nursing homes and home health patients, ranging from pediatrics to the geriatric population. Assisted with filing and follow-up appeals for Medicare and insurance claims.

Center for Communication Disorders, Palo Alto, NM
Speech-Language Pathologist 1985
United Way Agency providing speech-language services to children and adults with emphasis on language delay, aphasia, and articulation.

Center for Rehabilitation and Special Education, Charlotte, NC
Speech-Language Pathologist 1984 to 1985
Diagnostic and speech-language therapy services to mentally, emotionally, physically, and multi-handicapped students, ages 5 to 21, in a county-wide school program.

CERTIFICATIONS

Certificate of Clinical Competence in Speech-Language Pathology
American Speech-Language-Hearing Association, July 1985

North Carolina Licensure in Speech-Language Pathology, August 1994

RECENT CONTINUING EDUCATION

Interaction Management Series (15 month program)

The Art and Science of Rehabilitation Management Today: Surviving The Challenges

FIM Certification Workshop

1995 Carolinas Brain Injury Symposium

CARF 101: How to Prepare for a CARF Survey in Comprehensive Inpatient-Acute and Subacute Settings, Spinal Cord Injury and Traumatic Brain Injury

Dysphagia and Long Term Care

Communication Disorders after Brain Injury - Second Annual Conference

INSERVICE TOPICS

Multiple presentations of these topics to students, peers, patients and family members, rehab therapists, physicians, and nurses:
- Working with Dysphagic Patients
- Communication with the Traumatic Brain Injury Patient
- Using Videoflouroscopy to Assess Swallowing Disorders
- Augmentative Communication with the Aphasic Patient
- The Quality Improvement Process in the Rehab Setting
- Developing a Patient/Family Education Process
- Support Needs for Families of the TBI Patient

PROFESSIONAL ORGANIZATIONS

- Coastal Brain Injury Support Group, Group Facilitator
- Community Advisory Committee
- American Speech-Language-Hearing Association
- National Brain Injury Association
- Brain Injury Association of North Carolina - Member of Annual Symposium Planning Committee

headings in a separate column make it easy to see the different sections. Boldface guides the eye to academic degrees and job positions. A search for italic brings into view institutions, employers, achievements, responsibilities, and certifications.

EMMELINE WHITCOMB, P.A., J.D.
1234 North Washoe
Denver, Colorado 80283
(303) 222-0000

QUALIFICATIONS SUMMARY

SENIOR MANAGEMENT TEAM MEMBER combining 12+ years in the medical and legal professions, with career highlights including:

- As VP Medical Affairs, impressive record of addressing risk management/quality assurance, contracting, legal, physician relations, and managed care issues, positively impacting administration and medical affairs in anticipation of industry trends.

- As Risk Management Specialist for Children's Hospital, Denver, reviewed and managed contracts and implemented safety and risk management programs which considerably reduced legal fees, insurance premiums, and medical malpractice claims.

- Successful litigation experience as Associate Attorney with plaintiff medical malpractice litigation firm.

- Prior background as Board-Certified Physician Assistant in acute care hospital.

- Assistant Professor of Medicine with University of Virginia College of Medicine.

- Credentials include Juris Doctor, B.H.S. in Public Health, and Board Certification as Physician Assistant.

PROFESSIONAL EXPERIENCE

VICE PRESIDENT, MEDICAL AFFAIRS   1991-Present
Children's Hospital, Denver, Colorado

Medical Affairs: Manage administrative, financial, and technical activities of the Medical Affairs Division for 346-bed regional children's hospital, reporting to CEO and COO. Manage medical staff relations with 625 physicians and 275 active medical staff. Represent administration at all Medical Staff Committee meetings. Coordinate physician recruitment. Executive Council member, representing Medical Affairs at Board of Trustees meetings.

Management/Administration: Establish new medical programs with subspecialists and coordinate operations with hospital administration through matrix management techniques. Manage Infection Control, Quality Assurance/Risk Management, Medical Staff Office, Residency Program, Medical Library, Continuing Education, and Medical Affairs Administration with staff of 20. Manage budgeting and financial reporting functions.

Legal Affairs: Serve as liaison for all legal issues. Prepare, review, and maintain over 100 physician and medical service contracts and leases.

- Instrumental in design and development of Independent Physician Association and Physician Hospital Organization for managed care.
- Facilitated creation of Pediatric Research Division.
- Directed Medical Affairs Department in receiving JCAHO accreditation with commendation.
- Provided in-house legal services which reduced legal fees approximately 50%.
- Implemented risk management programs to reduce insurance premiums and malpractice legal fees.
- Directed successful recruiting strategies to meet physician recruitment goals.
- Controlled $8+ million operating budget, consistently finishing three consecutive years under budget.
- Promoted from Assistant Vice President, Medical Affairs in less than one year (one of two non-physicians to hold VP, Medical Affairs position among 50 children's hospitals nationwide).

153

Combination. *Susan Britton Whitcomb, Fresno, California*

The person had been a physician assistant and was now an attorney who directed legal affairs for a large children's hospital. Her original resume was three pages. The Qualifications Summary

EMMELINE WHITCOMB, P.A., J.D. Page Two

PROFESSIONAL EXPERIENCE (continued)

MEDICAL LEGAL CONSULTANT 1990-1991
Charleston, West Virginia

Consultant services included review of medical records to assess liability and damages in personal injury, workers' compensation, and medical malpractice for plaintiff and defense law firms. Additionally,

- Drafted West Virginia Academy of Physician Assistants' proposed legislation for PA section of Medical Practice Act (approximately three-quarters of legislative language was adopted).
- Lobbied state and federal legislators regarding Physician Assistant prescriptive practices and Medicare reimbursement.

PRIOR EXPERIENCE

- Litigation Associate -- Dietrich & Noble, Attorneys at Law, Charleston, West Virginia 1988-1990
- Physician Assistant -- University Hospital of Jacksonville, Florida 1985-1988

PUBLICATIONS, EDITORIAL ACTIVITIES

Editorial Board, *Journal of the American Academy of Physician Assistants* (1993-Present)
"Negotiating an Employment Contract," *Clinician's Reference Guide*, 1995.
"The Physician Assistant's Scope of Practice," *Journal of the American Academy of Physician Assistants*, 1994.
Peer reviewed chapter on Litigation for the "Liability Handbook" for health care providers.
Peer reviewed "The Physician Assistant as an Expert Witness," a position paper for the American Academy of Physician Assistants, 1992.

PUBLIC SPEAKING

Speaker for pharmaceutical company Johnson & Johnson on medical malpractice prevention:

- "The Legal Workshop or How You Too Can Think Like an Attorney"
- "Legal Relationships, in Sickness and in Health, For Richer, For Poorer"
- "Documenting for the Lawyer Looking Over Your Shoulder"

Numerous presentations to the business and medical communities on health-related topics.

EDUCATION

Juris Doctorate -- University of Colorado, School of Law (1987)
- Honors in appellate advocacy; member of Honor Court prosecutorial staff

Physician Assistant Program -- San Francisco State University, San Francisco, California (1982)
- Dean's List (6 semesters); Who's Who in American Colleges; Student Exec. Council, Medical Center

Bachelor of Health Sciences in Public Health -- University of Texas, Austin (1979)
- Graduated with Distinction; Founder, Committee on Ethics and Responsibilities

AFFILIATIONS (partial list)

Colorado Society for Health Care Attorneys; Medical Group Management Association; American Academy of Physician Assistants (active involvement, including service on Judicial Affairs committee 3 years); West Virginia Academy of Physician Assistants (active involvement, including service on Board of Directors)

References Upon Request

pulls together her medical and legal backgrounds, which make her very marketable in medical administration/management. Because the person's activities were broad in her current position, the writer categorizes these activities.

SUANN BATTLES

2904 Summerstorm Place ◆ The Woodlands, Texas 77380 ◆ (713) 367-8715

PROFILE:

HOME HEALTHCARE EXECUTIVE
Specializing in Home Health Management and Program Development
Executive Director with expertise in the strategic planning, development and leadership of freestanding and hospital-based home health agencies. Contributed to multi-million dollar revenue growth through advances in managed care concepts, contract services, market development, finance/accounting and human resources. Integrated and standardized operating and administrative systems to deliver strong and sustainable cost reductions. Expertise in areas of Quality Assurance, Clinical Auditing, Utilization Review, Reimbursement and Cost Containment.

PROFESSIONAL EXPERIENCE:

MARILAND HEALTHCARE GROUP, INC., Dallas, TX   1991 - Present
(Formerly StoneKey Home Health Management, Inc.)
<u>Area Vice President</u>   1995 - 1996
Promoted as the Senior Operating Executive challenged to position 25 hospital-based agencies, with projected visits of 900,000 (EBDITA - $9 Million), for success through the development and implementation of new programs, productivity/cost containment strategies, and administrative/operational efficiencies. Analyzed and directed the strategic integration and consolidation of agencies utilizing existing staff and facilities.
Recruited, trained and developed staff at regional and divisional levels. Served on Management Council and several Home Health Advisory Boards.
- Credited with identifying, analyzing and recommending the acquisition of several home health agencies generating 300,000+ visits. Headed up Acquisition Task Force, coordinated due diligence and directed the development of an Acquisition and Agency Consolidation Manual.
- Successfully recommended and secured home health management contracts generating over 50,000+ visits.
- Streamlined operational and administrative processes driving productivity from 3.0 to 2.0 and maintained 55 day receivables for Medicare Claims.

<u>Regional Director of Operations</u>   1991 - 1995
High profile management position monitoring total operations of Medicare-certified and private duty home care institutions in Texas, New Mexico and Florida.

Scope of responsibility was diverse and included business plan development, contract negotiations, educational training and development, program development and implementation, and cost containment.
- Led 10 agencies through State and JCAHO accreditation process.

HEALTH SOURCE ENTERPRISES , The Woodlands, TX   1990 - 1991
<u>Owner</u>
Independent Consultant providing expertise in areas of Quality Assurance, Clinical Auditing, Utilization Review, Reimbursement, Cost Containment and Licensure requirements. Trained, developed, monitored and evaluated staff personnel comprised of registered nurses, licensed vocational nurses, therapists, social workers and administrative/clerical staff. Served on several advisory committees.

- Incorporated Meals for Me, Inc., which prepared and delivered freshly cooked meals to busy professionals, homebound clients and others seeking weight reduction and healthy eating habits.

154

Combination. *Cheryl Ann Harland, The Woodlands, Texas*

A resume for an individual with an entrepreneurial background and who was seeking an executive position in another health-care group. Paragraphs after job positions contain mostly

SUANN BATTLES PAGE TWO

PROFESSIONAL   **AIM HEALTH SERVICES, INC.**, Houston, TX   1988 - 1990
EXPERIENCE:
(Cont'd.)   General Manager, Houston Operations
Directed 500-patient census with 39 full-time employees integrating Nursing, Infusion, Respiratory and Infant Monitoring Services. Guided center through State Licensing and accreditation process for NLN.

- Drove Houston contribution from 4-18% within 5 months balancing a $5 million budget.

BATTLES HEALTH CARE, INC., The Woodlands, TX   1982 - 1988
Owner
Established and directed profitable, multi-site home health agency generating over $2.5 million in annual sales revenues. P&L responsibility for total operations. Developed business plan, strategic planning, marketing and specialized programs.

Prior:

Served as Nursing Instructor and Nursing Supervisor in Massachusetts, Missouri and Rhode Island hospitals. Other nursing positions in Germany and Spain. Reimbursement Director for Anesthesiology Practice.

EDUCATION: University of Texas
College of Nursing
San Antonio, Texas 1978
Graduate Level Studies in Maternal and Child Health

Boston College School of Nursing
Chestnut Hill, Massachusetts
B.S., *Nursing*

LECTURER: South American College of Physicians and Surgeons
Bogata, Columbia
"Home Health with Outpatient Surgery"

Association of Outpatient Surgeons
Atlanta, Georgia
"Vaginal Hysterectomy in Outpatient Setting"

descriptions of responsibilities but include achievements. Square bullets point mostly to accomplishments. Experience before 1982 is summarized under the heading Prior instead of being listed as the other positions are listed.

SUSAN B. STEPHENS, M.D.

1255 West Shore Avenue
Lunenburg, MA 01246
Available for Relocation

(508) 582-0000
Facsimile: (508) 583-0000
Email: susan@snell.mit.edu.

QUALIFICATIONS

PHYSICIAN EXECUTIVE qualified for senior-level management opportunities where strengths in strategic planning, development, and visionary leadership will promote high-growth business ventures. Highlights:

♦ **Market-Driven Executive** -- Initiated business re-engineering in a 38-physician practice to address the emerging commercialization of medicine; cut operating costs through innovative cost-containment programs; brought consensus among divergent interests during transition to market-focused paradigm.

♦ **Academic Qualifications** -- MIT Executive MBA program graduate with management and financial skills backed by clinical competence of 15+ years of practice as a board-certified internist and anesthesiologist. Substantial experience in emergency services, aeromedical evacuation, and special operations.

♦ **International Orientation** -- Advanced the accessibility of health care in third world nations through commitment to international healthcare organizations (eight trips to Honduras, Mexico, and Vietnam as team chief and service as program director for an overseas teaching hospital).

♦ **White House Fellowship** -- Regional finalist among highly competitive candidate list of 800+; seeking to address global health care issues (special project: research for development of counter-strategies for medical terrorism).

PROFESSIONAL EXPERIENCE

HEALTHCARE MANAGEMENT -- Partner, Medical Consultants of Fresno, Boston, MA   1/93-Present
Partner, Medical Group, Boston, MA   1/90-12/93

Provide executive leadership as managing partner in a 38-physician group generating $18 million in annual revenue. Lead through hands-on involvement in financial affairs, professional/support staff administration, service planning, patient care, quality improvement, peer review, and credentialing. Well-versed in managed-care operations and negotiation of managed care/capitation contracts. Provide comprehensive anesthesia services and internal medicine consultations for Boston Memorial and other locations. **Accomplishments:**

- Led practice through successful transition to thrive in a managed-care environment utilizing new market-driven, community-oriented patient care model.
- Delivered significant savings through development of operational enhancements and strategic alliances.
- Researched and implemented computerized digital technology for cellular, paging, and voice mail services.
- Consultant for critical start-up of innovative home pain management therapy service.
- Resolved sensitive physician relations issues as member of Medical Staff Quality Council for 300-bed hospital.
- Mentored new physicians, helping to grow practice by 30%.

OPERATIONS MANAGEMENT -- Chief, Aerospace Medicine, Virginia Air National Guard   1989-Present

Plan and direct medical services to ensure health and combat readiness of 72 aircrew and over 1,500 ground personnel. Liaison between flying squadron and medical services. Participate regularly in flying missions including active duty deployments and mission qualification in RF4-C, a supersonic fighter aircraft. Directly supervise 25 officers and enlisted personnel. Additionally accountable for public health and safety, bio-environmental engineering, and occupational health issues.

♦ continued ♦

155

Combination. *Susan Britton Whitcomb, Fresno, California*

A Physician Executive who was pursuing an MBA to work in a management role, preferably as President/VP of a management care organization or other health-care-related company.

Susan B. Stephens, M.D.

Accomplishments:

- ▸ Selected for fast-track promotion to rank of Major and Lt. Colonel.
- ▸ Designed and implemented innovative flying safety and emergency medical training programs.
- ▸ Recipient of two Air Force Achievement Medals, Air Force Outstanding Unit Award, Armed Forces Reserve Medal, and National Defense Service Medal.
- ▸ Authored 100-pg guide to human factors and physiological stress in flying advanced tactical fighter aircraft, providing flight surgeon support for the zero mishap record during the ANG transition to F-16 aircraft.
- ▸ Formerly served as Chief, Clinical Services (1989-1992); Commander, Squadron Medical Element (1984-1989); and General Medical Officer (1982-1984).

Prior Experience:

▸ Clinical Faculty, Department of Internal Medicine, Boston Medical Center	1980-1982
▸ Attending Physician, Emergency Dept., New Bedford County Medical Center	1979-1980
▸ Medical Director, Medical Clinic	1978-1979

EDUCATION

M.B.A., Management -- Massachusetts Institute of Technology (MIT)	1994-1996
Residency in Anesthesiology -- Boston Medical Center, Theilen, MA	1983-1986
Residency in Internal Medicine -- Boston Medical Center, Theilen, MA	1979-1981
M.D. -- San Francisco State University School of Medicine, San Francisco, CA	1978
B.S., Biology (cum laude) -- Arizona State University, Tempe	1973

CERTIFICATION, LICENSURE

Diplomate -- National Board of Medical Examiners
Diplomate -- American Board of Internal Medicine
Diplomate -- American Board of Anesthesiology
Flight Surgeon -- USAF School of Aerospace Medicine
Medical Licensure -- Massachusetts, Arizona, New York

AFFILIATIONS

American College of Physician Executives
Aerospace Medical Association
American Society of Pathologists
Massachusetts Society of Pathologists
Undersea and Hyperbaric Medical Society
American Medical Association

PROFESSIONAL APPOINTMENTS

Utilization Review Committee -- Boston Medical Center
Medical Staff Quality Council -- Boston Medical Center
Chair, Department of Pathology -- Children's Hospital
District Director and Board of Directors -- Massachusetts Society of Pathologists

ADDITIONAL DATA

Commercial Pilot
Concert Violinist
Conversant in Spanish, French, and Italian

◆ ◆ ◆

Emphasis is placed on management achievements rather than clinical experience, publications, and so on. The original resume was more than nine pages of a prior curriculum vitae. The writer rewrote the resume for a total of only two pages.

JAMES BRADFORD, M.D.

Business:
1255 W. 24th, Clovis, NM 75432
Conf. Voice Mail: (201) 555-5555

Residence:
34 N. 9th, Clovis, NM 75432
Home/Fax: (201) 444-4423

QUALIFICATIONS

EXPERIENCED MANAGEMENT PROFESSIONAL with administrative competence reflected by positive impacts in the areas of operations, program planning/service development, and profit performance. Strengths include:

- ♦ Critical Start-up, Turnaround
- ♦ Regional Strategic Planning, Implementation
- ♦ Capital & Operations Budgeting

- ♦ Recruitment of Key Personnel
- ♦ Teambuilding, Training & Development
- ♦ Operations/Service Planning & Management

PROFESSIONAL EXPERIENCE

MANAGEMENT:

Directly accountable for P&L performance of a high-volume outpatient medical facility staffed with 22 physicians and support team of 57. Manage through hands-on involvement in operations, financial affairs, professional/support staff administration, service planning, patient care, and quality improvement.

- ‣ Successful in leading department though critical reorganization and turnaround.
- ‣ Improved customer perceived satisfaction by 9% through retraining of medical staff.
- ‣ Managed a culturally diverse staff using a consensus building model.
- ‣ Designed staffing plan which accommodates tremendous seasonal fluctuations in demand for services; system improved accessibility to care despite annual decreases in operating budget.

Member of executive management team challenged with critical start-up and management of new 120-bed hospital. Participated in strategic planning, policy development, minimum training requirements, etc. to obtain state accreditation. Ongoing management responsibilities as Chief of Pediatric Medical Staff includes daily operations, quality improvement process, patient care, peer review, physician discipline, and credentialing.

- ‣ Team member directly involved in budget planning, capital acquisitions, space planning, staffing mix, scope of services, physician/management recruitment, and infrastructure development.
- ‣ Instituted medical staff policies and established physician credentialing process.
- ‣ Obtained JCAHO accreditation with no significant deficiencies on first attempt.
- ‣ Realigned services to assure quality of care and staff expertise.

Serve at corporate level as member of Regional Chiefs for the Medicus Medical Group, collaborating on issues relating to regional strategic priorities impacting 26 facilities throughout a four-state area.

- ‣ Co-developed systems relating to physician relations, customer service, quality of care, accessibility to care, patient satisfaction, salary recommendations, and education.
- ‣ Provided leadership in consolidation of services to support the "Centers of Excellence" model.

FISCAL ACCOUNTABILITY:

Participate in allocation process for $43 million in operating funds. Directly administer $3 million departmental budget. Determined capital appropriations for advanced medical and information technologies. Manage and approve over $200,000 in professional fees to outside providers.

- ‣ Member of management team which met budget expectations for facility while adhering to corporate directive of no involuntary reduction of FTE's.
- ‣ Participated in negotiation of fee agreements and service parameters with outside providers.
- ‣ Managed transition from FTE-based budget to dollar-based budget.
- ‣ Intricate knowledge of fiscal issues associated with managed care.

156

Combination. *Susan Britton Whitcomb, Fresno, California*

This physician was fed up with managed care restrictions and decided that he would rather manage/administer than practice medicine. This resume drew from his Chief of Pediatrics

JAMES BRADFORD, M.D.
Page Two

PROFESSIONAL EXPERIENCE (Continued)

HUMAN RESOURCE MANAGEMENT:

Directly supervise management team consisting of 2 nurse managers and 14 physicians supported by technical and clerical staff of 20+ FTE's. Consult on hiring, discipline, dismissals, and evaluations. Manage physician recruitment, discipline, and evaluations.

- Catalyst for internal reengineering of management structure -- brought staffing in line with regional norms (from 30+ FTE's to 20 without sacrificing service quality), achieved performance improvement through cross-training and teambuilding, and turned-around department to record levels for morale, cooperation, and commitment.
- Launched a physician/staff retraining series to meet the challenge of healthcare initiatives in a fast-paced, customer-driven environment.
- Balanced resources to support new "open access" policy which enabled customers same-day access to services.
- Resolved complex service issues and customer concerns.

EDUCATION

UNIVERSITY OF COLORADO

- **M.D.** (1969)
- **B.S., Business Administration** (1966)

PROFESSIONAL DEVELOPMENT SEMINARS (partial list)

- **Leadership Development Process** -- Program includes training in TQM, CQI, DISC Personality Profiling, Teambuilding, and Managing Transition and Change.

- **Physician's Management Course** -- Program includes training in Leadership Styles, Legal Issues, Problem-Solving & Decision-Making, Cultural Diversity, Communication Styles, Recruitment, Hiring, Evaluations, and Managing Employee Performance.

- **Managing in a Union Environment** -- Program includes training in EEO, Cultural Diversity, Sexual Harassment Issues, Progressive Discipline, Seniority, and Grievance Processes.

EMPLOYMENT SUMMARY

Chief of Pediatrics, Medicus Foundation Hospital, Albuquerque, New Mexico	1994-Present
Chief of Pediatrics, Medicus Foundation Hospital, Albuquerque, New Mexico	1992-Present
Pediatrician, Medicus Hospital, Albuquerque, New Mexico	1988-Present
Private Practice, Albuquerque, New Mexico	1979-1988
Emergency Department Physician, Christian Hospitals, Denver, Colorado	1975-1978
Staff Pediatrician, US Army Hospital, Ft. Carson, Colorado	1972-1975
Intern and Resident, Walter Reed Army Medical Center	1969-1972

References Upon Request

experience, special assignments, and leadership training. M.D. was used after his name even though he wasn't looking for a clinical position. The reason was that the M.D. might make readers pay more attention to his resume.

THOMAS P. STEVENS, R.PH.
1608 Cimmarron Trail
Tyler, Texas 75703
(903) 599-8833

PHARMACEUTICAL SALES PROFESSIONAL

HIGHLIGHTS OF QUALIFICATIONS

- **Licensed Pharmacist** with broad-based knowledge of pharmaceuticals / pharmaceutical industry uniquely coupled with **proven pharmaceutical sales success**; expertise in **Influential Professional Sales / Marketing** ◆ **Strategic Planning / Development** ◆ **Client Relationship Management**.

- In-place **cultivated positive relationships** with physicians and pharmacists in the East Texas area.

- Exceptional **presentation, client service, communication,** and **interpersonal** skills; easily establish trusting rapport with healthcare professionals and people of diverse backgrounds and personalities.

- Strong computer literacy of customized pharmaceutical / pharmaceutical sales software applications using networked PCs and laptop computers.

- **Exemplary integrity** and **professional ethics**. Highly **career-** and **goal-oriented**.

EDUCATION / LICENSURE

THE UNIVERSITY OF TEXAS AT AUSTIN – Austin, Texas
Bachelor of Science Degree in Pharmacy
Graduated with **Honors** in 1985

Licensed Pharmacist, Texas State Board of Pharmacy

PROFESSIONAL EXPERIENCE

INDEPENDENT PHARMACY   Tyler, Texas
Licensed Pharmacist / Assistant Manager   August 1997 – Present
- Serve as Assistant Manager and Staff Pharmacist of community pharmacy; supervise staff of five.
- Formulate compounds; provide professional advice to physicians; maintain high level of accuracy/precision and alertness to contraindications with other medications and allergies of clients.
- Counsel clients regarding potential reactions/side effects, medication contraindications, and accurate intake.

PREMIUM PHARMACEUTICAL COMPANY   Tyler, Texas
Professional Pharmaceutical Sales Representative   December 1991 – August 1997
- Effectively managed East Texas territory with client base of approximately 400 physicians and 100 pharmacies for $5 billion Fortune 500 company.
- Marketed antihistamine, nasal steroid, bronchodilator, antibiotic, and interferon drugs.
- Organized/coordinated speaker programs for healthcare professionals; engaged speakers to present medical topics of educational interest to physicians and pharmacists.
- **Accelerated market share every month** during first three years of promoting Claritin.
- **Ranked above-average nationally**.

157

Combination. *Ann Klint, Tyler, Texas*

The person was a pharmacist who wanted to return to pharmaceutical sales. The writer used the prescription symbol to add interest. The same page border on each page ties the two pages

THOMAS P. STEVENS, R.PH. Page Two

MAJOR MEDICAL CENTER Tyler, Texas
Licensed Pharmacist August 1990 – November 1991

- Extensively interacted with healthcare professionals in hospital pharmacy of 400-bed medical center as Staff Pharmacist; supervised IV technician.
- Performed compounding and IV admixture (including chemotherapy); disbursed prescriptions primarily to nursing staff for delivery to patients.
- Conducted inservice training for medical center nurses pertaining to pharmaceuticals and drug reactions.
- Operated networked computer; ensured accuracy of data entry and maintenance of computerized records.

STEVENS-RAWLINS PHARMACY Tyler, Texas
Owner / Manager / Pharmacist-in-Charge September 1985 – August 1990

- Full P&L responsibility of community pharmacy in close proximity of two major hospitals and myriad physician clinics; staffed, trained, directed, and supervised staff of up to 15.
- In addition to filling prescriptions, managed all aspects of business which encompassed personnel recruitment/ supervision, payroll, purchasing, inventory / financial management, cost-control, and customer service.

PROFESSIONAL AFFILIATIONS

RHO CHI SOCIETY (*National Pharmaceutical Honor Society*)

TEXAS PHARMACEUTICAL ASSOCIATION

SMITH COUNTY PHARMACEUTICAL ASSOCIATION

♦ ♦ **Professional References Furnished As Addendum** ♦ ♦

together visually. Boldfacing makes it easier for the reader to spot the person's name, contact information, headline, section headings, key words, academic degree and professional license, positions, achievements, and affiliation.

DOREEN PINCHET, R.Ph.

555 E. Longfellow ♦ Denver, CO 55555 ♦ (555) 555-5555

PROFESSIONAL EXPERIENCE

PHARMACEUTICS PLUS, Denver, Colorado
(6/93-Present)

Key Contributions:

℞ Developed pharmacy technician training program which impacted quality assurance, increasing scores from 87% to 99%.

℞ Spearheaded implementation of system for computerized billing, insurance reconciliations, prescription authorizations, and patient data, significantly enhancing pharmacy productivity.

℞ Established protocol for security of controlled substances and disposal of hazardous waste.

<u>Pharmacist</u> -- Provide full range of services as community pharmacist:

▸ Compound and dispense prescribed medications, drugs, and other pharmaceuticals for patient care.

▸ Identify, evaluate, and interpret physician-issued prescriptions to assure accuracy and determine ingredients needed.

▸ Counsel pharmacy customers on possible drug interactions, side effects, dosage, and storage of pharmaceuticals; interpret clinical data in patient medication record system.

▸ Consult with physicians, nurses, and other health care professionals.

<u>Acting Pharmacy Manager</u> -- Additional responsibilities:

▸ Supervise staff of 12 Pharmacy Technicians in packaging and labeling of drugs, servicing patients, and processing insurance records and other documentation.

▸ Manage total store operations with staff of 65-75 in absence of General Manager.

EDUCATION

UNIVERSITY OF COLORADO -- SCHOOL OF PHARMACY
Denver, Colorado

Bachelor of Science Degree, Pharmacy (1992)

LICENSE, AFFILIATIONS

Licensed Pharmacist, State of Colorado (#55555)
Member, Colorado Pharmacy Association
President, Denver Metro Pharmacy Alliance
Volunteer Counselor, House of Hope Homeless Shelter

♦ ♦ ♦

158

Chronological. *Susan Britton Whitcomb, Fresno, California*

The person had only three years of experience. Readers would know what a pharmacist does, so the writer began with Key Contributions with prescription symbol bullets.

Professional Service

Resumes at a Glance

Marcus R. Coy

Objective: Master cake decorator in search of leadership position with company catering to clientele in demand of high-quality bakery products.

Specialties

Marzipan florals • characters • coverings
Poured and rolled fondant
Gum paste florals • ornaments • figurines
Royal icing flowers • Pulled and spun sugar
Portfolio available upon establishment of mutual interest

Highlights of Qualifications

- Able to handle a multitude of details at once, meeting deadlines under pressure.
- Sharp, innovative, quick learner; proven ability to adapt quickly to a challenge.
- Capable of speed and organization in a highly productive setting.
- Committed to harmonious working environment.
- Work cooperatively with a wide range of personalities.

Work History

1988-Present	*Cake Decorator*	DRAEGER'S GOURMET MARKET, Menlo Park, CA
1986-88	*Cake Decorator*	KELLY'S FRENCH PASTRY, Santa Cruz, CA
1986 (*3 mos.*)	*Apprentice Pastry Chef*	HANSEL AND GRETEL'S, Los Gatos, CA
1980-86	*Cake Decorator*	BAKER'S SUPERMARKETS, Omaha, NB
1978-80	*Cake Decorator*	EMMINGER BAKERY, Omaha, NB
1978-80	*Apprentice*	THE CAKERY, INC., Omaha, NB
1976-78	*Cleanup Crew*	ROTELLA'S ITALIAN BAKERY, Omaha, NB

Professional Experience

Design & Decorating
- Designed centerpiece cake for Mutual of Omaha benefit attended by the Ambassador to Great Britain, which included baking and extensively detailed cake decoration.
- Baked, decorated and assembled wedding cakes of all sizes and complexities.
- Fashioned variety of gum paste flowers for stunning visual effects, including cake tops and floral arrangements of violets, tulips, lilies, orchids, fresia, and roses.
- Devised gum paste figurines in designer fashions made of gum paste for cake tops or as individual gifts, including four "dolls" presented to Bill Blass "wearing" his designs.
- Operated Kopy Kake machine, emblazoning company logos, photos and other designs on cake surfaces; also used airbrush to enhance color, shadows and other artistic details.

Instruction
- Successfully trained apprentices in the art of cake decorating, teaching how to construct and ice cakes, create marzipan roses and other basic skills.
- Instructed series of gum paste flower classes at various cake supply shops in San Jose area.
- Demonstrated creation of marzipan animals at Menlo Park street fair.

Customer Relations
- Identify customer's desires concerning cake design, recommending cake flavors and decorations.
- Resolve wide range of customer problems, including dissatisfaction with taste and texture of cakes and frostings, design discrepancies, occasional misplaced orders and other miscommunication problems.

Education

Advanced and Lambeth Continental courses,
WILTEN SCHOOL OF CAKE DECORATING AND CONFECTIONARY ART
Woodridge, IL — 1985

1307 Burrows Road • Campbell, CA • 95008 • (408) 555-0913

© THE WORDSMITH, Sallie Young, 1992

159

Combination. *Sallie Young, Riverton, Utah*

The background screen was done in Freehand and imported along with text in PageMaker. The original was printed on colored Decadry Print birthday cake paper.

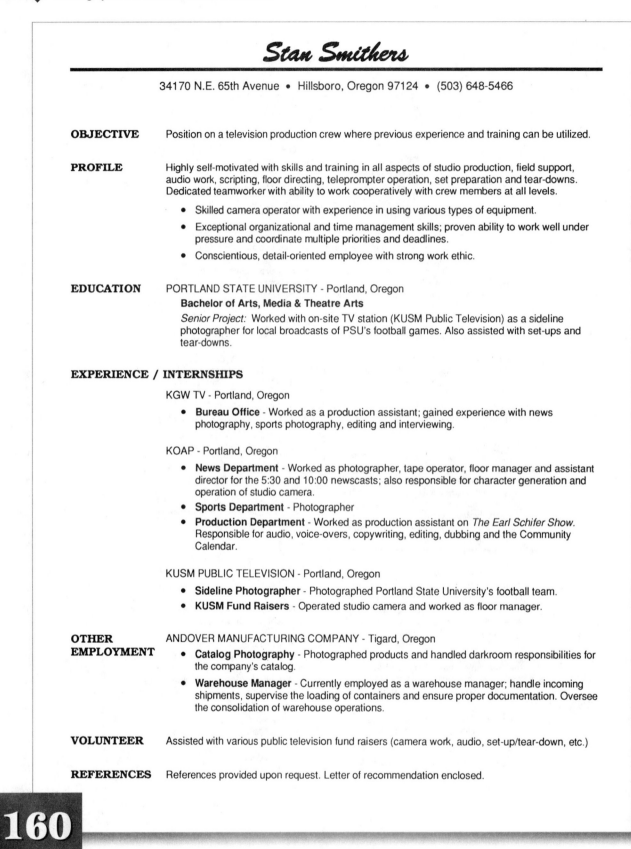

Stan Smithers

34170 N.E. 65th Avenue • Hillsboro, Oregon 97124 • (503) 648-5466

OBJECTIVE
Position on a television production crew where previous experience and training can be utilized.

PROFILE
Highly self-motivated with skills and training in all aspects of studio production, field support, audio work, scripting, floor directing, teleprompter operation, set preparation and tear-downs. Dedicated teamworker with ability to work cooperatively with crew members at all levels.

- Skilled camera operator with experience in using various types of equipment.
- Exceptional organizational and time management skills; proven ability to work well under pressure and coordinate multiple priorities and deadlines.
- Conscientious, detail-oriented employee with strong work ethic.

EDUCATION
PORTLAND STATE UNIVERSITY - Portland, Oregon
Bachelor of Arts, Media & Theatre Arts
Senior Project: Worked with on-site TV station (KUSM Public Television) as a sideline photographer for local broadcasts of PSU's football games. Also assisted with set-ups and tear-downs.

EXPERIENCE / INTERNSHIPS

KGW TV - Portland, Oregon
- **Bureau Office** - Worked as a production assistant; gained experience with news photography, sports photography, editing and interviewing.

KOAP - Portland, Oregon
- **News Department** - Worked as photographer, tape operator, floor manager and assistant director for the 5:30 and 10:00 newscasts; also responsible for character generation and operation of studio camera.
- **Sports Department** - Photographer
- **Production Department** - Worked as production assistant on *The Earl Schifer Show*. Responsible for audio, voice-overs, copywriting, editing, dubbing and the Community Calendar.

KUSM PUBLIC TELEVISION - Portland, Oregon
- **Sideline Photographer** - Photographed Portland State University's football team.
- **KUSM Fund Raisers** - Operated studio camera and worked as floor manager.

OTHER EMPLOYMENT
ANDOVER MANUFACTURING COMPANY - Tigard, Oregon
- **Catalog Photography** - Photographed products and handled darkroom responsibilities for the company's catalog.
- **Warehouse Manager** - Currently employed as a warehouse manager; handle incoming shipments, supervise the loading of containers and ensure proper documentation. Oversee the consolidation of warehouse operations.

VOLUNTEER
Assisted with various public television fund raisers (camera work, audio, set-up/tear-down, etc.)

REFERENCES
References provided upon request. Letter of recommendation enclosed.

160

Combination. *Pat Kendall, Aloha, Oregon*

Notice the different kinds of type. The person's name is in a cursive font, the section headings are in a serif font, and the text is in a sans serif font. Note, too, the use of bold.

IMA PIANIST
107 MUSICAL WAY
MELODIC, CA 00000   **(000) 000-0000**

SUMMARY OF QUALIFICATIONS

Versatile pianist with extensive repertoire including Italian, show tunes, classical, operatic and jazz. Able to create and sustain a festive atmosphere through personal entertainment and people skills. Extensive repertoire from memory. Bilingual - English and French. Excellent interpersonal and organizational skills. Able to improvise and play requests.

PROFESSIONAL EXPERIENCE

PIANIST   **1992-present**
Major Productions
Los Angeles, California
Play requests from classical to contemporary. Interface with wide range of celebrities, business professionals and people from all walks of life.

PIANIST   **1990-present**
Elite Department Store
Status, California
Play piano in atrium for clientele of upscale department store. Play requests from patrons. Loyal following. High degree of interaction with patrons.

PIANIST   **1960-present**
The Best Catering Company
Delicious, California
Entertain at all catered special events - weddings, anniversaries, birthdays, bar mitzvahs, graduations and communions for #1 catering house in California. Customize repertoire according to function for audiences from 10 to 1,000 people.

PIANIST
1995 Man of the Year Dinner honoring John Doe, Prestigious, California

PIANIST
American Cancer Society Fund-raiser, Los Angeles, California. Played for a dinner audience of 1,000.

SPECIAL APPEARANCES
-Television Specials-

	PBS	
Carnegie Hall	California Cable	Hotel One Fifth Avenue
Radio City Music Hall		San Remo West
Westbury Music Fair		Meson Madrid

OPERA COORDINATOR - DIRECTOR
Music Lovers' Restaurant, San Francisco, California
Directed Opera company - all aspects of production and music selection. Recruited and scheduled performers and substitutes. Solved problems. Acted as liaison between performers and management.

EDUCATION: Bachelor of Fine Arts
                        Julliard School of Music

LANGUAGES: English and French   **EQUIPMENT:** Smith portable keyboard

REFERENCES AND AUDIO TAPE AVAILABLE ON REQUEST

161

Combination. *Fran Kelley, Waldwick, New Jersey*

Another resume which uses thematic, decorative paper that illustrates the career of the candidate. The Special Appearances and Education sections are strong later elements.

♪ **ANTHONY ("TONY") ZIMMERMANN** ♪
Three Blue Key
Birch, New York 00000-0000
Tel: (555) 555-5555 • Email: xxxxxxxx@aol.com

TOP PRODUCING MUSIC EXECUTIVE

RESULTS ORIENTED professional with a 20-year proven track record in strategic planning, development and business expansion • Ability to foster relationships with recording corporations, labels and artists • Unique talent in discovering new label interests and business ventures • Easily identifies up and coming trends with a talent for recognizing cutting-edge styles • Creating and recognizing hit singles • Dynamic, aggressive, persistent and consistent • Extensively versed in studio production • Experienced in both European and U.S. tour management • Confident decision maker and successful risk taker • Knowledge of music spans pop, rock, metal, R&B, alternative, rap, new age and country • Totally versed in state-of-the-art computerized environments • Areas of expertise include:

♪ ARTIST/LABEL PROJECT MANAGEMENT AND DEVELOPMENT
♪ NEGOTIATING/SIGNING NEW ARTISTS
♪ GENERATING, DEVELOPING AND IMPLEMENTING NEW LABEL BUSINESS
♪ TARGET AND CREATE INNOVATIVE LABEL INVESTMENT OPPORTUNITIES
♪ PRODUCTION MANAGEMENT AND DISTRIBUTION

PROFESSIONAL EXPERIENCE:

SPHERE PRODUCTIONS   New York, New York
PRESIDENT • 1986 - Present

Challenged to lead a successful music production company from inception through full operations. Discover and develop extreme talent into cross-over markets. Forecast future trends into mainstream music marketplace.

- Currently managing **Lynn Richardson**, an up and coming female performer.
- Produced MACHINE for **Paul Simon's** production company, *"Night After Night, LTD."*
- Discovered and launched career of **Jewel through** GRP *"Rap to Rock"* CD compilation of new artists.
- Participant in 20th anniversary **KISS** project and current **KISS** conventions (interviews and personal appearances).
- Maintain high-profile engagement with R&B artists **Elexus Quinn and Ziggy True** and pop/rock artist **Oona Falcon** (major attraction throughout Europe).
- Diverse areas of expertise encompass **Harper-Josef**, a New Age project.
- Contributed to the success of numerous music videos and films.
- Accountable for daily operations, including P&L, budgeting, marketing, strategic planning, staff development and contract negotiations.

(continued...)

162

Combination. *Alesia Benedict, Rochelle Park, New Jersey*

Graphics add interest in a resume as long as they are not too many or too cute and don't distract the reader. The writer achieves a satisfying mix in this resume through a variety

ANTHONY ("TONY") ZIMMERMANN Tel: (555) 555-5555   **- Page Two -**

PROFESSIONAL EXPERIENCE: continued…

<u>TOGA PRODUCTIONS</u>   New York, New York

FOUNDER, CO-OWNER • 1982 - 1986

High-profile position in full service music and video production company. Managed projects for artists and groups. Provided live and video coverage for special events. Launched and produced video-magazine concept in association with The Industry Network System (TINS).

PROJECT/ARTIST HIGHLIGHTS:

♪   *Machine* (Paul Simon's Night After Night productions)
♪   *Rod Stewart* (1988 World Tour)
♪   *KISS* (20th anniversary project)
♪   *Oona Falcon* (European Starlight Express and tour)
♪   *Myth* (Beatles' attorney, Walter Hofer project)
♪   *Lynn Richardson* (up and coming female artist)
♪   *Jewel* (Rap to Rock GRP project)
♪   *Elexus Quinn and Ziggy True* ("Nothing is Meaningless" project)
♪   *Breakfast Special* (national tour)
♪   *Hunter* (former members with Billy Squire)
♪   *Hawkeye* ("Great Seal" film documentary, Mill Valley Productions)
♪   *Dreams* in Color (in association with Joe Serling)
♪   *Alexia* (managed by Rolling Stones partner, Pete Rudge)

PROFESSIONAL ATTRIBUTES:

◆ Founding member (drummer) of rock group KISS with Gene Simmons, Paul Stanley and Brooke Ostrander.
◆ Recipient of numerous awards and tributes in recognition of writing popular songs and lyrics.
◆ Featured in trade publications including *Modern Drummer*.
◆ Co-wrote and produced material for successful bands and major production companies.
◆ Instrumental in production of video projects and film clips.

EDUCATION:

Bachelor of Arts degree
University of Miami • Coral Gables, Florida

of bullets: eighth notes and an embedded bullet in the contact information, embedded bullets and sixteenth notes in the Profile (not so named), bullets for the current position, sixteenth notes again but in a Highlights section, and diamond bullets near the end.

Marc Aigner

14 Sundale Place ★ Scarsdale, NY 10583 ★ (914) 555-0000

Feature Films ★ Theatre ★ Television ★ Shorts ★ Video ★ Documentaries

Creative Profile

Highly creative **production manager** and **independent filmmaker** with more than 15 years of diversified industry experience. Well-regarded, warm and energetic **teacher** who readily shares technical expertise and passion for filmmaking. Outstanding management, communication and collaborative skills that help get the job done. Effective troubleshooter whose strengths include *producing, directing, writing* and *editing.* Expertise in *camerawork* and *direction of photography.*

Career Highlights

★ **Management**

Manage university Film Production Office and Facilities, including sound stage, film, video, computer-editing, mixing and transfer rooms and equipment.

" ... particular strengths are commitment, energy, knowledge of cameras and concern for students."
—Tom Gunning, Author, "D.W. Griffith and the Origins of American Narrative Film."

- Spearheaded and managed a turnaround operation for university film department. Improved viability and quality of production/post-production film equipment by determining complex repair needs and establishing controls.

- Served as catalyst for increased productivity among faculty and students for on-time project completion of independent films.

- Creatively used budget allocations for staffing needs and facilities upgrades.

★ **Independent Filmmaking**

Collaborated in the making of numerous feature, television, short and documentary films.

- Director of Photography/Producer: "European and Poetic," 90 min. Stefano Mario Baratti, Director.

- Writer/Producer/Director: "Gypsy Cab," 16mm, 30 min., in color. Original project filmed on location in The Bronx, depicting an immigrant man's struggle to adapt to a new life. Screened at area film festival.

" Mr. Aigner has many of the same admirable personal values that former Film Chair Avakian possessed" ... "he is patient and willing to help in problem-solving, and takes a personal interest in student projects."
—Richard Dawson, NYU colleague.

- Cameraman: "Vinal," 16mm, 30 min., in color. Director, Marissa Benedetto.

- Assistant Director: "The Suitors," 35mm, 90 min. Director, G. Ebrahimian.

- Cameraman: "Bone White," 16mm, 60 min., in color.

- Director of Photography: "Vanitas," 16mm, 60 min., in black and white. Stefano Mario Baratti, Director.

- Production/Camera Assistant: Ebra Films. Several documentary projects for BBC, French and Italian Television.

★ **Instruction**

Hire and supervise work/study students, offering group and one-on-one instruction. Support film faculty in organizing film festivals and outside screenings.

- Designed and taught course *Production Workshop* focusing on proper operation of cameras, lighting, sound, editing, mixing and transfer equipment.

- Simplified instructional methodology and improved student morale by completely rewiring sound-mixing studio, creating universal access to sophisticated controls.

163

Combination. *Phyllis B. Shabad, Ossining, New York*

A resume for a creative individual with a managerial role. For control, the writer used desktop publishing as well as word processing. Note the graphics, the boldfacing of key words, the

Employment History

1990–present	**Film Production Manager** and **Instructional Support**, Film Department, New York University, New York, NY.
1988–1989	**Cameraman.** WVVA-TV (NBC affiliate), Bluefield, West Virginia.
1982–1988	**Independent Filmmaker.** Ebra Films, New York, NY.

Education

New York University, New York, NY:
Bachelor of Fine Arts in Film Production, 1985.
Additional coursework in engineering.

Special Talents

Languages:
Trilingual—Fluency in written and spoken English/French; spoken Italian.

Technical:
- Adept in using all 16mm and 35mm film equipment, and applying latest technology such as DVD.
- Use specialized software such as *Movie Magic* and *Final Draft*.

Related Professional Activities

Participated in several film productions that appeared at the:
Sundance Film Festival, 1997 (Winner—First Prize).
Empire State Exhibition Film Festival, 1995.
Cannes Film Festival, 1988.

testimonials in the left column of the first page, the three categories—each preceded by a star bullet—in the Career Highlights section, the italic explanations of these activities, and the inclusion of Special Talents and Related Professional Activities.

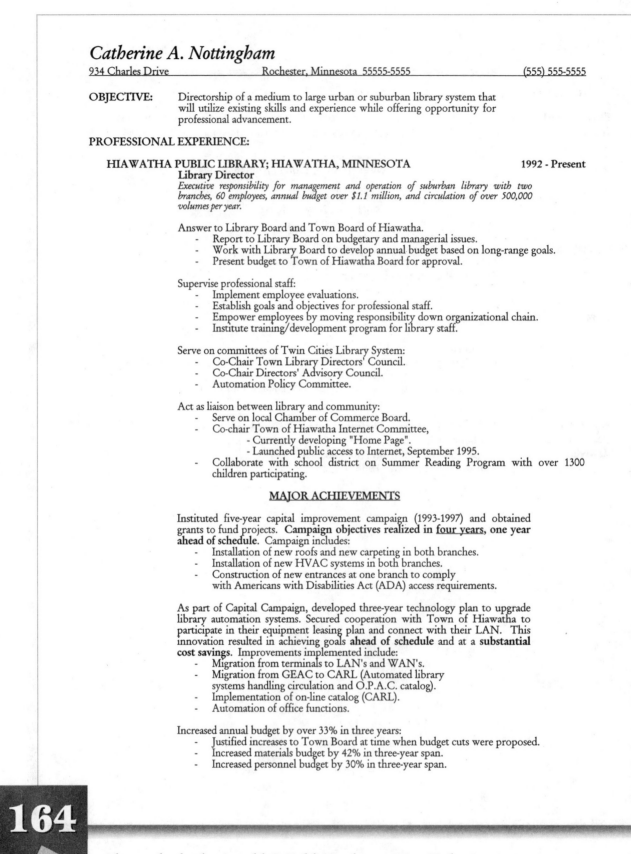

Catherine A. Nottingham

934 Charles Drive   Rochester, Minnesota 55555-5555   (555) 555-5555

OBJECTIVE: Directorship of a medium to large urban or suburban library system that
will utilize existing skills and experience while offering opportunity for
professional advancement.

PROFESSIONAL EXPERIENCE:

HIAWATHA PUBLIC LIBRARY; HIAWATHA, MINNESOTA   1992 - Present
Library Director
*Executive responsibility for management and operation of suburban library with two
branches, 60 employees, annual budget over $1.1 million, and circulation of over 500,000
volumes per year.*

Answer to Library Board and Town Board of Hiawatha.
- Report to Library Board on budgetary and managerial issues.
- Work with Library Board to develop annual budget based on long-range goals.
- Present budget to Town of Hiawatha Board for approval.

Supervise professional staff:
- Implement employee evaluations.
- Establish goals and objectives for professional staff.
- Empower employees by moving responsibility down organizational chain.
- Institute training/development program for library staff.

Serve on committees of Twin Cities Library System:
- Co-Chair Town Library Directors' Council.
- Co-Chair Directors' Advisory Council.
- Automation Policy Committee.

Act as liaison between library and community:
- Serve on local Chamber of Commerce Board.
- Co-chair Town of Hiawatha Internet Committee,
  - Currently developing "Home Page".
  - Launched public access to Internet, September 1995.
- Collaborate with school district on Summer Reading Program with over 1300
  children participating.

MAJOR ACHIEVEMENTS

Instituted five-year capital improvement campaign (1993-1997) and obtained
grants to fund projects. **Campaign objectives realized in <u>four years</u>, one year
ahead of schedule**. Campaign includes:
- Installation of new roofs and new carpeting in both branches.
- Installation of new HVAC systems in both branches.
- Construction of new entrances at one branch to comply
  with Americans with Disabilities Act (ADA) access requirements.

As part of Capital Campaign, developed three-year technology plan to upgrade
library automation systems. Secured cooperation with Town of Hiawatha to
participate in their equipment leasing plan and connect with their LAN. This
innovation resulted in achieving goals **ahead of schedule** and at a **substantial
cost savings**. Improvements implemented include:
- Migration from terminals to LAN's and WAN's.
- Migration from GEAC to CARL (Automated library
  systems handling circulation and O.P.A.C. catalog).
- Implementation of on-line catalog (CARL).
- Automation of office functions.

Increased annual budget by over 33% in three years:
- Justified increases to Town Board at time when budget cuts were proposed.
- Increased materials budget by 42% in three-year span.
- Increased personnel budget by 30% in three-year span.

164

Chronological. *Arnold G. Boldt, Rochester, New York*

Educated in Massachusetts and New York, this librarian has worked in Minnesota her entire
career. Through blank lines and some short lines, the resume exhibits considerable white

Catherine A. Nottingham   *Resume - Page 2*

ADDITIONAL PROFESSIONAL EXPERIENCE:

ST. PAUL PUBLIC LIBRARY; ST. PAUL, MINNESOTA   1981 - 1992

Department Head, Interlibrary Loan & Centralized Reserves   1986 - 1992
Planned, coordinated, and managed all interlibrary loan and centralized reserves services for the Pioneer Library System, which encompassed over 100 individual branches in a five county region of southern Minnesota. Provided ILL services to Twin Cities Regional Library Council, school library systems, and MSILL on contract basis.

- Supervised staff of 18 employees.
- Recommended and implemented policy and procedural changes.
- Prepared and monitored departmental budget.
- Represented ILL services at Central Division Heads' meetings.
- Served on regional and state-wide committees relating to interlibrary loan.
- Provided training to member libraries on ILL services.
- Assisted in planning/implementation of automated circulation system.
- Chaired Office Automation Committee for Central Library.

Special Librarian, Central Library   1986
Established and coordinated usage of automated circulation system (GEAC) for Central divisions. Trained staff on use of GEAC and responded to user problems.

Science and Technology Reference Librarian   1981 - 1985
Selected titles and developed Science and Technology collection. Assisted member libraries with reference and collection development. Supervised pages, library assistants, and interns.

HARRIETVILLE PUBLIC LIBRARY; HARRIETVILLE, MINNESOTA   1978 - 1980

Acting Director   1979
Assumed Director's duties for seven month period shortly after move into new facility with doubled circulation.

Adult Services Librarian   1978 - 1980
Developed adult, reference, and Audio/Visual collections for large suburban library. Assisted Library Director in planning and management.

PROFESSIONAL AFFILIATIONS:

Minnesota Library Association:
Continuing Education Committee
Interlibrary Loan Committee

American Library Association

EDUCATION:

Master of Library Science
School of Library and Information Science
State University College at Cuylerville
Cuylerville, New York

Bachelor of Science, Biology
Holy Cross College
Worcester, Massachusetts

space even though the document presents much information. A short italic paragraph after each job position in boldface summarizes the position. Boldfacing also highlights key achievements and academic degrees.

MAKEUP ARTISTRY
CONCEPT THROUGH DESIGN

1(800) 435-2835

Coast to Coast Coverage!
California, Florida, North Carolina

FILMS AND TELEVISION

Where the Dead Are
Twilight Zone Movie
Stars: Patrick Bergin, Jack Palance

In My Daughter's Name
Overruled Productions
Stars: Donna Mills, Lee Grant

Race day
TNN Motor Sports
5 TV Episodes

Tom Smith Interviews
Capitol Satellite & FLTV

Country Hitkickers
Halloween Special
Fox Television

Candlelight
Sound Rep Group

Callia
Steele Films, Inc.

Bikini Summer II
PM Entertainment
Stars: Jessica Hahn, Jeff Conaway

Outside
Panoptikon Films
Stars: Alex Courtney, Bill Dunlevy

Sunset Strip
PM Entertainment
Starring: Jeff Conaway

Unbecoming Age
Ringlevision
Stars: Diane Salinger, Colleen Camp

**Free Aspirin and
Tender Sympathies**
Lopes Productions
Starring: Efrain Figueroa

COMMERCIALS AND INFOMERCIALS

WESTERN AUTO
4 Commercials
Avatar Group Int.

FOOD LION
24 Commercials
Avartar Group Int.

BRENDLE'S
3 Commercials
Avatar Group Int.

VLASIC PICKLES
Commercial
MC Group

OSCAR MAYER
Commercial
MC Group

TWILIGHT ZONE
Commercial
Steele Films, Inc.

LEVIS
Commercial
Burton Pierce Co.

DALIPRINTS
Commercial
2M Productions

CHARLOTTE AD CLUB
2 PSA's
Doggett Advertising

CUB FOODS
8 Commercials
Avatar Group Int.

JOHNSON & JOHNSON
Commercial
Avatar Group Int.

LEGGETT'S
3 Commercials
Archdale Advertising

WHEELS RACING
Commercial
Avatar Group Int.

BELK
9 Commercials
Wildwood Prod.

LA Z BOY
3 Commercials
Peter Corbett & Company

ALL DATA
Commercial
2M Productions

METROLINA EXPO
3 Commercials
Avatar Group Int.

FOOD LION RESPONSE
Infomercial
FLTV

BURGER KING
6 Commercials
Even the Bigger
Picture Prod.

SOMINEX
5 Commercials
Whitewater Productions

WATSON INSURANCE CO.
Commercial
Avatar Group Int.

LEGAL BRIEFS
2 Commercials
Avatar Group Int.

COMMUNITY CASH
5 Commercials
Avatar Group Int.

NBA AUTHENTICS
Commercial
NBA Entertainment

HAVOLINE OIL
2 Commercials
Crash Films, Inc.

LEGGETT'S
4 Commercials
Tularosa Film Co.

GRAND PIANO & FURNITURE CO.
4 Commercials
Boulevard Films

SOMINEX
2 Infomercials
Whitewater Prod.

REFUND AMERICA
Commercial
Avatar Group Int.

INSTRUCTION, INDUSTRIAL and PROMOTIONAL VIDEOS

Refund America
Promotional
Avatar Group Int.

General Motors
Promotional
Parallel Productions

Wix-Dana Corporation
Corporate / Promotional
Thirty's Film & Tape

Club Armageddon
Promotional Video
Marlis Seefe
Productions

The Hampton Zone II
Industrial Video
SBL Vision Merchants

TRAINING AND REFERENCES
The Institute of Studio Makeup, Ltd.
James Brown, President (555) 555-1313

Tim Brown	Panoptikon Films	(555) 444 4444
Jim Ross	Makeup Artist	(555) 212-5553
Victor Long	Avatar Group Int.	(555) 212 -2222

Motion Picture ★ Video ★ Television ★ Prosthetics ★ Beauty ★ Horror ★ Special Effects

165

Functional. *Rose Montgomery, Charlotte, North Carolina*

A resume that looks like an ad for this makeup artist. Experience is grouped by categories and placed in boxes. In the original the name (not evident here) is white on black.

Psychology and
Social Work

Resumes at a Glance

Employee Assistance Programs
Substance Abuse Counseling
Case Management

MARY JAYNE SMYTH, C.S.W., CEAP

279 Bay Ridge Drive ⬥ Hyde Park, New York 12538 ⬥ (914) 555-5555

Licensed Clinical Social Worker with over thirteen years experience in the diagnosis and treatment of work-related and family issues. Implement treatment plans involving intervention, short-term and long-term therapy, or intermittent treatment. Conduct management/supervisory consultations. Collaborate with other professionals and community organizations.

QUALIFICATION *HIGHLIGHTS*	⬥ Conduct comprehensive client assessments encompassing crisis intervention, chemical dependency, psychiatric, family/marital, and job stress issues
	⬥ Coordinate employee wellness programs
	⬥ Develop work-site program for cancer survivors
	⬥ Serve as project director of federal government contract
	⬥ Supervise in-house and sub-contracted consultants in assessment, follow-up, referral and short term counseling
	⬥ Interdisciplinary team member providing long-term counseling to geriatric patients with a variety of physical and psychological ailments
	⬥ Provide on-going counseling and monitoring for mandated and self-referred employees to substance abuse program
	⬥ Administer twenty-four hour on-call coverage as external provider of employee assistance and managed care programs

EMPLOYMENT	**Case Manager,** <u>*Oppenheimer Associates, Inc.,*</u> *Eastchester, NY*	*1995-Present*
	Consultant, <u>*Jernberg Corp.,*</u> *Worcester, MA*	*1995-Present*
	Consultant, <u>*PepsiCo Inc.,*</u> *White Plains, NY*	*1990-Present*
	Senior Associate, <u>*Paul Sherman & Associates*</u>, *Rye, NY*	*1989-1990*
	Associate, <u>*Archeus Foundation, Ltd.,*</u> *New York, NY*	*1988-1989*
	Counselor, <u>*Central Labor Rehabilitation Council*</u>, *New York, NY*	*1985-1987*
	Intern, <u>*District Council 37*</u>, *New York, NY*	*1984-1985*
	Intern, <u>*Hebrew Home for the Aged*</u>, *Riverdale, NY*	*1983-1984*

EDUCATION	**Master of Social Work,** Columbia University	*1985*
	Bachelor of Arts in Social Work, University of Oklahoma	*1982*

TRAINING/SEMINARS	Stress Management	Sexual Harassment	Working With Resistant Clients
	Workplace Violence	Managed Care	Suicide Prevention

CERTIFICATIONS	Certified Employee Assistance Professional	*1988*
	Certified Social Worker	*1986*

PROFESSIONAL *AFFILIATIONS*	Employee Assistance Professionals Association National Association of Social Workers American Cancer Society, Oncology Social Work Committee

166

Combination. *Marian Kozlowski, Poughkeepsie, New York*

This person provided substance abuse and employee assistance to several large companies. The writer consolidated the person's experience into a Qualifications section.

═══ *Thomas J. Allen, Ph.D., M.C.C.* ═══

5849 Pine Cove
Jefferson, Michigan 46587
(526) 313-5214

● *Professional Objective:*

Seeking a challenging position as a psychological counselor / therapist utilizing my education and life experience most successfully, and where there is *"opportunity to serve others in need."*

● *Summary of Qualifications:*

- 11 years experience in counseling others on a variety of human issues and emotions
- **Areas of counseling include:** marriage, pre-marriage, depression, anxiety, grief work, co-dependency, divorce, single parenting, victimization, adultery, anger, self control, self esteem, rejection, fear, inter/intro personal conflict, jealousy, guilt, loneliness, thought life, and habits.
- Experienced utilizing a variety of psychological test / profiles
- Ability to counsel well, one-on-one or in group sessions
- Compassionate, good listener, and very supportive in client recovery
- Ability to work with individuals from a variety of backgrounds and social sectors

● *Education:*

Evers University, Dixon, MO
Ph.D. - Doctorate in Counseling (Psychology), May 1993

Christian College, Santa Mesa, New Mexico
M.C.C. - Masters in Christian Counseling, December 1991

Christian College, Santa Mesa, New Mexico
Bachelors of Theology, December 1989

● *Certifications / Licenses:*

Licensed Pastoral Counselor - Lic. No. A8760987
DSM 111-R Clinical Procedures - April 1993
Candidate For: Adolescent Therapy - June 1993
Crisis and Grief Specialists - June 1993
Clinical Counselors License - January 1994

● *Internship:*

Worked under the direction of Dr. Richard Ontorio, Ph.D., (the executive director of the Psychologist Counseling Association). Duties included counseling on a variety of human issues. Obtained a total of 3000 counseling hours. Traveled extensively including trips to Bilice, Mexico and the Philippines (1986-1988). Researched and wrote masters thesis 1989-1991.

See following page for additional counseling experience

167

Combination. *P. J. Margraf, New Braunfels, Texas*

Large bullets point to section headings throughout the resume, unifying the two pages. Small bullets in the Summary of Qualifications call attention to skills in one section.

Resume Continued

══ *Thomas J. Allen, Ph.D., M.C.C.* ══

● <u>*Work Experience:*</u>

<u>Life Center, Jefferson, Michigan</u>   1984 to Present
Counselor / Therapist
Work with individuals counseling in areas of marriage, pre-marriage, relationships, depression, anxiety, and victimization. Conduct group counseling (26 session per week) teaching self image concepts and principles to an enriched life. Provide one-on-one consultation at any hour, if needed. Additionally, offer a variety of assessment test: TAP - Temperament Analysis Profile,   Mate - Premarital and Marriage Perception Analysis, Family Relations Inventory, Slossen Intelligence Test (I.Q.), and Occupational Interest Test.

<u>Marriage Retreat, Mexico City, Mexico</u>   1984 - 1986
Counselor
Provided marriage counseling first week of each month.

● <u>*Professional Organizations / Achievements:*</u>

Member: National Counselors Associations - July 1992
<u>Achievements as a member of the National Counselors Association:</u>
License Pastoral Counselor -Sept. 1992
Professional Clinical Member - Jan. 1993
Diplomat - April 1993
Member: Michigan Christian Counselors Association - May 1993

● <u>*Personal / Hobbies:*</u>

Single, non-smoker. Enjoy fishing, camping and children.
Also enjoy flying an airplane and travel in general.

References Available Upon Request

Thin-thick lines are top and bottom borders on both pages, further unifying the resume. The recurrence of the person's name within border segments is a third unifying device. Boldface makes counseling areas, the Ph.D., positions, and achievements more visible.

Curriculum Vita

Marion E. Appleby, Ph.D.

555 Main Street
Jonesburg, IL 55555
(505) 505-5050

Education

Boston University, Ph.D., 1979 — Clinical Psychology, APA approved
Boston University, M.A., 1976 — Psychology
Wesleyan University, B.A., 1973 — Psychology

Clinical Experience

Private Practice
Director of Appleby Psychological Associates   1983–Present
Jonesburg, Illinois
    Provide psychotherapy, psychological evaluation, and consultation to a diverse patient
    population as well as manage seven full-time psychologists, four consultants, and support staff.

Post-Doctorate Intern
New York Child Guidance Clinic, Family Therapy Training   Summer 1983

Associate Director and Director of Training
Affiliated Mental Health Services   1981–83
Newton, Massachusetts
    Responsible for managing six programs in a 85-staff comprehensive community mental health
    center.

Director of Training, Consultation and Education Coordinator, Staff Psychologist
The Mental Health Clinic of Boston   1979–81
Brookline, Massachusetts
    Responsible for providing staff training, community consultation, psychotherapy to children
    and families, coordinating psychology internship program, and personnel selection for four
    municipal police departments.

Staff Clinical Psychologist
Tri-Town Mental Health Center   1978–79
Wakefield/Reading, Massachusetts

Clinical Psychology Intern
Boston Psychiatric Hospital   1977–78
Boston, Massachusetts

Teaching Experience

   Lecturer, Graduate Psychology Department, Northwestern University — 1983–Present
   Adjunct Professor, Graduate Counseling Department, Boston University — 1980–83
   Teaching Fellow, Psychology Department, Boston University — 1976–77

168

Traditional C.V. *Jan Melnik, Durham, Connecticut*

Typical for the psychology profession, pure white parchment was preferred as the stationery
of choice. Slightly atypical was the inclusion of some key identifying information regarding

Marion E. Appleby, Ph.D. *Vita Page Two*

Workshops

Have presented over 75 workshops on a range of mental health topics to various groups and agencies including hospitals, clinics, chambers of commerce, school systems, police departments, attorneys, business groups, and medical staffs.

Research Interests

Selected Papers and Presentations

Appleby, M.E. Imitation of resistance to temptation in male children. Paper presented at Northeastern Psychological Association, Boston, MA, May 1979. (Master's Thesis).

Appleby, M.E. The process of description and perception of stigmatized and non-stigmatized persons. Paper presented at National Psychological Association, New York, NY, March 1981.

Appleby, M.E. and Smith, L.S. Alcohol and Drug Services to a Rural Community. Paper presented at Annual National Alcohol and Drug Abuse Conference, Chicago, IL, September 1983.

Appleby, M.E. Psychotherapeutic Applications of the MMPI: Beyond Assessment, Feedback and Outcome Evaluation. Paper presented at the 21st Symposium on Recent Developments in the Uses of the MMPI, Washington, D.C., March 1989.

Appleby, M.E. The MMPI and its Specific Use as a Therapeutic Tool in Marital Therapy. Paper presented at the 22nd Symposium on Recent Developments in the Uses of the MMPI, Boston, MA, May 1990.

Appleby, M.E. Assessment of Marital Strength and its Use in Couples' Psychotherapy, presented to the Illinois Psychological Association, Chicago, IL, May 1993.

Professional Affiliations

American Psychological Association — Division 12

Illinois Psychological Association

National Register of Psychologists

Association for the Advancement of Psychology

Licensed Psychologist, State of Illinois

Affiliate Medical Staff, Illinois State Psychiatric Hospital, Chicago, Illinois

Affiliate Medical Staff, City Hospital, Chicago, Illinois

responsibilities within several key positions. The person operated a successful and well-known psychology practice and used this vita to secure a variety of high-level consulting arrangements with national organizations and Fortune 50 companies.

LAWRENCE BURTON, Ph.D.
Clinical Psychologist
123 White Road
Westchester, NY 10000
(914) 222-2222

Objectives: **Counselor/Teacher in College Setting**
Psychologist in Clinical Setting

HIGHLIGHTS OF QUALIFICATIONS

- Licensed clinical psychologist; 30 years professional experience as college counselor
- Strong practical and theoretical foundation in variety of therapeutic modalities
- First-hand experience with multi-cultural differences as they relate to
    counseling, therapy, and teaching environments
- Excellent planning, organizational, communication and administrative skills
- Energetic, innovative, dedicated, adaptable, intuitive problem solver
- Conversant in Spanish

PROFESSIONAL EXPERIENCE

College Counseling and Teaching
- Counseled a wide range of individual multi-cultural students regarding personal, social,
    and academic difficulties interfering with success in college
    - Assisted students in planning for meaningful realistic career choices.
    - Devised academic strategies which included referral to college and
        community resources
    - Collaborated with teaching faculty in tracking and providing intervention to
        maximize academic success.
- Created and implemented syllabus for group counseling with students on academic
    probation which enabled group members to explore and rectify roots of problems
- Developed and implemented innovative programs for counselors to use in their daily work
    including mentoring and transfer student orientation programs
- Coordinated, supervised, and administrated a unit staff of eighteen counselors
- Taught freshmen orientation and development courses, as well as introductory psychology
    and adjustment problems of aging.

Psychotherapy and Psychological Testing
- Provided individual psychotherapy for adolescents and adults for the past 25 years, using
    a psychodynamic approach
- Conducted goal-oriented couples counseling
- Provided psychodiagnostic testing for adolescents and adults, including over 100 OVR
    evaluations.

169

Combination. *Linsey Levine, Chappaqua, New York*

Center-alignment for the contact information and the Objectives at the beginning of the
resume, and for the Professional Organizations and Education sections at the end, gives

Lawrence Burton, Ph.D. Page 2

EMPLOYMENT HISTORY

Professor/Counselor Dept. of Special Programs	The City College, CUNY New York, NY	1966-present
Psychotherapist Private Practice	Westchester, NY	1970-present
Staff Psychologist	Manhattanville College Purchase, NY	1972-1977
Staff Psychologist	Westchester County Dept. of Mental Health, Yonkers, NY	1968-1972
Lecturer	Bronx Community College Bronx, NY	1967-1968
Psychotherapist	Mental Health Consultation Center West Nyack, NY	1965-1968
Staff Clinical Psychologist	V.A. Hospital Montrose, NY	1964-1966

RECENT PUBLICATIONS

Burton, L., "Success Rate of Transfer Students Enrolled in a Program for the Underprepared at a Senior College": <u>Journal of College Student Development</u>:11, 56-60,1993

Backner, B.L., and Burton, L., "A Survey of Disadvantaged Students Attitudes Toward a Special College Program": <u>Journal of Human Resources</u>: V.2, 1992.

PROFESSIONAL ORGANIZATIONS

American Psychological Association
Westchester County Psychological Association

EDUCATION

State University of NY at Buffalo, Buffalo, NY
Ph.D., Clinical Psychology, 1964
Brooklyn College, Brooklyn, NY
B.S. Psychology, 1958
NY State Certification Exam Passed, 1965

vertical symmetry to the resume—that is, the sense that it opens and closes the same way. Large bullets point to listed items on the first page. Boldface emphasizes items on the second page, such as the positions in the Employment History.

Yvette Winhauser, LCSW, LPC

172 Tilden Court
Creve Coeur, Missouri 63141
(314) 555-1224

SPECIALTIES & QUALIFICATIONS

- Licensed clinical social worker; nationally licensed counselor.
- Dedicated to establishing cooperative family relationships, building self-esteem and providing effective parenting information and support.
- Accomplished speaker, trainer and consultant for hospitals, schools, corporations, professional and community service organizations.
- Frequent featured guest in major newspapers, magazines and on nationally syndicated talk shows.
- Co-author of internationally-acclaimed books addressing fresh and positive approaches to parenting.

PROFESSIONAL EXPERIENCE

12/89 - Present
- Manage clinical counseling services for individuals, married couples and families in crisis.

1/77 - Present
- Develop and cultivate time-limited parent education groups for metropolitan community organizations.

9/87 - 11/89
- Licensed counselor for Comprehensive Clinical and Consulting Services, providing individual, marriage and family counseling.

11/81 - 12/83
- Parent Educator and Family Counselor, providing professional individual, family and marriage counseling to patients in a pediatric practice.

1981 - 1982
- Adjunct Professor at Maryville College, Webster University, and University of Missouri at St. Louis. Taught "Building Self-Esteem in Children."

EDUCATION

- **M.A., Counseling Psychology,** Alfred Adler Institute of Chicago, IL
- **M.A.T.,** Webster University, St. Louis, MO
- **B.A., Elementary Education,** Washington University, St. Louis, MO

PUBLICATIONS

- Winhauser, Y., & Friedman, K. (1991).
  <u>Stop Struggling with Your Child</u>. Harper Collins.
- Winhauser, Y., & Friedman, K. (1988).
  <u>Stop Struggling with Your Teen</u>. Viking Penguin, Inc.
- Winhauser, Y. (1978).
  <u>A practical guide to family meetings</u>.
- Collaborated with writing and production of ABC News week-long series, "The Parent Test", St. Louis, MO
- Collaborated with writing and production of six-week parenting news special on WCPO-TV, Cincinnnati, OH sponsored by St. Elizabeth Hospital.

PROFESSIONAL ORGANIZATIONS

- North America Society of Individual Psychology
- American Counseling Association
- National Speaker Association
- National Committee for Prevention of Child Abuse

170

Combination. *John Suarez, location unknown*

The shaded left column, containing headings and dates, balances visually text on the right. The bullets are useful because the text is single-spaced and some items occupy two lines.

Sales/Marketing

Resumes at a Glance

MARION I. GORDON
1717 Seabird Circle
Westport, Washington 00000
555-555-5555

OBJECTIVE

Enthusiastic, hardworking and self-motivated individual with excellent interpersonal skills seeking a sales position in the travel industry, where my successful background in the sales field will help your company improve market share.

QUALIFICATION SUMMARY

More than 10 years of experience in sales. Personable and persuasive, with excellent negotiation skills. Delivered consistent revenue growth through expertise in:

- *Client Recruiting*
- *Account Development*
- *Product Expertise*
- *Client Needs Analysis*
- *Trade Show - Presentations*
- *Import/Export Experience*
- *Client Retention*
- *Trade Show - Booth Design*
- *Multi-Cultural Experience*

PROFESSIONAL EXPERIENCE

Sales Associate, Chandlers Way, Poulsbo, WA   1995 - Present
Upscale department store in bay-side community geared to serve heavy boating/tourist population.
- Provide friendly and professional customer service in sale of large inventory of designer fashions, accessories and jewelry. Promote add-on sales.
- Serve regular customer-base of over 60 business women as "personal sales consultant." Maintain current files on sizes and preferences of style and color, notify customer when appropriate merchandise is received and special order items to meet specific requests.
- Develop window and in-store merchandise displays to increase sales.
- Operate electronic cash register, balance/close-out till, stock and price merchandise.

Wholesale Representative, Seaside Trading Company, Seattle, WA   1989 - 1994
In this import/export business started as part-time office worker, trained in all aspects of customer service, commissioned sales, shipping and product development. Promoted to Wholesale Representative.
- Developed and instituted ongoing "Net 30" account development guarantee program.
- Established new accounts such as Waterfront Landmark, Captain's Galley and the Columbia River Maritime Museum.
- Traveled extensively to promote products and service accounts.
- Initiated and instituted new ideas on product packaging and display. Designed jewelry.
- Developed and organized trade show exhibits. Supervised booth layout, setup and staffing. Greeted current and prospective customers, providing information and demonstrations.

Sales/Marketing Representative, Maritime Welding, South Beach, WA   1985 - 1989
Provided primary administrative services for this small family-owned welding business.
- Developed regional market for wood stove sales. Pursued UL listing for stoves produced.
- Marketed "Davit Arm" lift mechanism to marinas in the Pacific Northwest. Developed marketing brochure to increase product visibility and clarify function.
- Serviced regional accounts.

EDUCATION

Graduate, Marquis Modeling Academy, Seattle, Washington
Graduate, Bellevue North High School, Bellevue, Washington

REFERENCES AVAILABLE UPON REQUEST

171

Combination. *Lonnie L. Swanson, Poulsbo, Washington*

The individual wanted to work in gift shops on cruise ships. Because such work is people-oriented, the writer emphasized the person's sales and customer service skills.

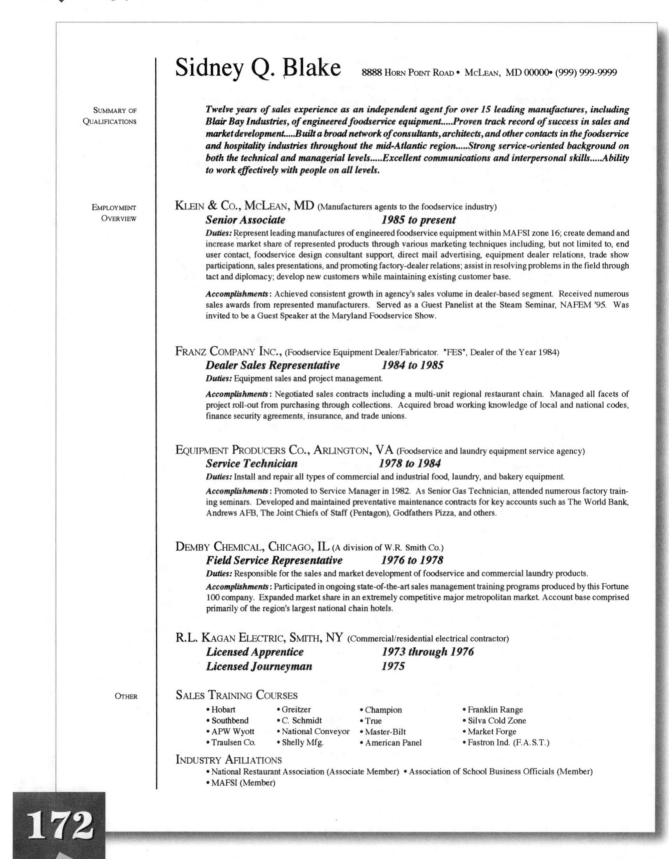

Sidney Q. Blake
8888 HORN POINT ROAD • MCLEAN, MD 00000• (999) 999-9999

SUMMARY OF QUALIFICATIONS

Twelve years of sales experience as an independent agent for over 15 leading manufactures, including Blair Bay Industries, of engineered foodservice equipment.....Proven track record of success in sales and market development.....Built a broad network of consultants, architects, and other contacts in the foodservice and hospitality industries throughout the mid-Atlantic region.....Strong service-oriented background on both the technical and managerial levels.....Excellent communications and interpersonal skills.....Ability to work effectively with people on all levels.

EMPLOYMENT OVERVIEW

KLEIN & CO., MCLEAN, MD (Manufacturers agents to the foodservice industry)
Senior Associate   1985 to present
Duties: Represent leading manufactures of engineered foodservice equipment within MAFSI zone 16; create demand and increase market share of represented products through various marketing techniques including, but not limited to, end user contact, foodservice design consultant support, direct mail advertising, equipment dealer relations, trade show participationn, sales presentations, and promoting factory-dealer relations; assist in resolving problems in the field through tact and diplomacy; develop new customers while maintaining existing customer base.

Accomplishments: Achieved consistent growth in agency's sales volume in dealer-based segment. Received numerous sales awards from represented manufacturers. Served as a Guest Panelist at the Steam Seminar, NAFEM '95. Was invited to be a Guest Speaker at the Maryland Foodservice Show.

FRANZ COMPANY INC., (Foodservice Equipment Dealer/Fabricator. "FES", Dealer of the Year 1984)
Dealer Sales Representative   1984 to 1985
Duties: Equipment sales and project management.

Accomplishments: Negotiated sales contracts including a multi-unit regional restaurant chain. Managed all facets of project roll-out from purchasing through collections. Acquired broad working knowledge of local and national codes, finance security agreements, insurance, and trade unions.

EQUIPMENT PRODUCERS CO., ARLINGTON, VA (Foodservice and laundry equipment service agency)
Service Technician   1978 to 1984
Duties: Install and repair all types of commercial and industrial food, laundry, and bakery equipment.

Accomplishments: Promoted to Service Manager in 1982. As Senior Gas Technician, attended numerous factory training seminars. Developed and maintained preventative maintenance contracts for key accounts such as The World Bank, Andrews AFB, The Joint Chiefs of Staff (Pentagon), Godfathers Pizza, and others.

DEMBY CHEMICAL, CHICAGO, IL (A division of W.R. Smith Co.)
Field Service Representative   1976 to 1978
Duties: Responsible for the sales and market development of foodservice and commercial laundry products.

Accomplishments: Participated in ongoing state-of-the-art sales management training programs produced by this Fortune 100 company. Expanded market share in an extremely competitive major metropolitan market. Account base comprised primarily of the region's largest national chain hotels.

R.L. KAGAN ELECTRIC, SMITH, NY (Commercial/residential electrical contractor)
Licensed Apprentice   1973 through 1976
Licensed Journeyman   1975

OTHER

SALES TRAINING COURSES
• Hobart	• Greitzer	• Champion	• Franklin Range
• Southbend	• C. Schmidt	• True	• Silva Cold Zone
• APW Wyott	• National Conveyor	• Master-Bilt	• Market Forge
• Traulsen Co.	• Shelly Mfg.	• American Panel	• Fastron Ind. (F.A.S.T.)

INDUSTRY AFILIATIONS
• National Restaurant Association (Associate Member) • Association of School Business Officials (Member)
• MAFSI (Member)

172

Combination. *Thomas E. Spann, Easton, Maryland*

Boldface draws the eye to the person's name, Summary of Qualifications, job titles, dates for the positions, duties, and accomplishments. Note the range of type size.

SUMMARY OF EXPERIENCE

Produced Market Development Report and Marketing Plan for environmental services group. Designed agricultural chemical programs to assist clients with environmental compliance. Managed agricultural chemical remedial investigations and correction action design projects. Managed hazardous waste and petroleum release, transportation and disposal program for an environmental services company. Four years environmental regulations experience with extremely hazardous chemical category. Nine years marketing experience with major agricultural chemical accounts. Extensive experience in establishment and maintenance of customer accounts and creation of successful Agricultural Chemical Facility Compliance Plans.

PROFESSIONAL EXPERIENCE

ENVIRONMENTAL COMPANY
xxxx - xxxx   **Independent Contractor - Market Development**
- Developed Agricultural Chemical Market Development Report
- Designed Agricultural Chemical Marketing Action Plan
- Focused program on site investigation and remediation

ENVIRONMENT CONSULTANTS
xxxx - xxxx   **Agricultural Chemical Specialist**
- Managed agricultural chemical remedial investigations and corrective action design projects
- Worked with Agricultural Chemical Response and Reimbursement Account (ACRRA)
- Prepared an agricultural chemical section of the corporate marketing plan

ENVIRONMENTAL SERVICES
xxxx - xxxx   **Transportation and Disposal Coordinator**
- Managed 85 plus Hazardous Waste Transportation and Disposal Projects
- Worked on Hazardous Waste and Petroleum LUST sites
- Negotiated contracts with major hazardous waste disposal firms and national transporters
- Interfaced with federal and state environmental regulatory agencies
- Supervised field technician transportation and disposal-related activity

LARGE COMPANY
xxxx - xxxx   **Agrichemical Sales Representative**
- Sold agricultural chemicals and programs to key customers
- Exceeded $1 million territory sales budget
- Maintained control over project budgets
- Completed IBM, Lotus 1-2-3 training

AGRICULTURAL PRODUCTS COMPANY
xxxx - xxxx   **Technical Sales Representative**
- Provided market analysis and recommendations
- Implemented Time and Territory Management Plan
- Negotiated product performance inquiries

EDUCATION

UNIVERSITY OF STATE
College of Agriculture
Bachelor of Science-Agronomy, *xxxx*

GOVERNMENT INSTITUTE, INC.
Environmental Law Course: CERCLA, EPCRA, TSCA, OSHA, SDWA, NEPA, FIFRA, RCRA, UST.

LADY ENGINEER ● 1234 Any Street ● Anytown, ST 12345 ● (000) 555-1234

173

Combination. *Linda Morton, Lawrence, Kansas*

A resume for a manager not by title but by responsibility and activity. The resume is different because of the vertical double line and information rotated 90 degrees.

LADY S. LOOKING

1234 Any Street • Anytown, State 66049 • (913) 749-4235

PROFILE

Marketing/Customer Relations professional with management experience in the tour and travel industry; demonstrated organization and planning skills.
+ Accomplished facilitator; able to coordinate multiple/complex projects
+ Skilled at problem mediation and resolution while successfully upholding company objectives
+ Highly adaptable to rapidly changing requirements and situations
+ Task-oriented and precise, with high performance standards
+ Well developed awareness and understanding of different cultures
+ Excellent mass communicator...experienced with people from East and West Coasts, Midwest and Europe

EDUCATION

B.S. Communication Studies (xxxx), *University,* Anytown
+ Emphasis: Organizational and Interpersonal Communication
+ *100%* financial responsibility for education

EXPERIENCE

Travel Company, Anytown, State (xxxx-Present)
Supervisor, Reservations Department
Market over 150 tour packages to international and domestic travel agencies. Oversee 10 reservation clerks. Interact with individuals from clerks to top management. Create and maintain professional rapport with travel industry vendors. Perform site inspections to assure customer satisfaction.
ACHIEVEMENTS
+ Instrumental in developing international markets for tour packages. **Increased bookings from 10 to 100** in first year.
+ Created and produced procedures/training manual for reservation clerks
+ Established training process; implemented manual and trained new employees
+ Visited hotels, museums, and restaurants in 30 international and domestic locations *on my own time* to evaluate quality and suitability for consumers

Bar and Grill, Anytown, State (xxxx-xxxx)
Assistant Bar Manager
Organized and controlled liquor inventories. Served a diverse clientele.

Day Care Center, Anytown, State (xxxx-xxxx)
Home Care Assistance Provider
Prepared meals; transported students from school to day care center.

University Motor Pool, Anytown, State (xxxx-xxxx)
Office Assistant
Scheduled and reserved university automobiles and lift van rides for handicapped students. Managed accounts payable and receivable.

EXCELLENT REFERENCES AVAILABLE UPON REQUEST

174

Combination. *Linda Morton, Lawrence, Kansas*

Distinctive bullets (variants of plus signs) tie together visually the three sections of this resume. Italic and boldfacing are used to call attention to names, positions, and key ideas.

JOHN ANYBODY
1111 South Anywhere Drive, #224, Tampa, Florida 335116
(813) 111-1111

OBJECTIVE
Dynamic, energetic professional seeks position where advancement potential is based on initiative and skills. Background focused on effectively developing skills to enhance company's "bottom line" and enable me to compete and excel in the sales/marketing field.

SUMMARY OF QUALIFICATIONS
- Proven track record in telecommunication sales and management
- Positive and enthusiastic, highly motivated, excellent leadership techniques, and professional attention to detail supplemented by the ability to influence and stimulate others
- Communicate well with business professionals, easily establishing rapport and gaining client confidence; extremely sociable, articulate; professional in appearance and manner

WORK EXPERIENCE
MMM ATLANTIC, New Jersey, Chicago & Tampa   1992 - Present
Account Executive
- Outside sales - selling commercial telephone systems to medium-sized businesses
- Set up office in Chicago including training of 25 sales representatives; promoted to supervisor
- Wrote and presented program on selling and closing sales
- Motivational and technical speaker at weekly meetings
- Conducted Sales Training seminars
- Transferred to Tampa July 1994

Achievements:
- **MMM Achiever's Club** (awarded to only 5% of all MMM personnel)
- **Met 100% of quota in first year**
- **Accommodation Plaque/Monetary bonus for successful Chicago operation**

ANYWHERE COMPANY, INC., Newark, NJ   1991 - 1992
Sales Representative
- Cold calling, canvassing and creating leads.
- Closed sales, maintained accounts and kept detailed records of all contacts

GOLF UNLIMITED, INC., Park Ridge, NJ   1990 - 1991
Owner/Manager
- Overall operation of custom golf store
- Repairs, sales, merchandising/marketing, purchasing and record keeping

DC ELECTRONICS, Upper Saddle River, NJ   1988 - 1990
Sales Representative
- Cold calls, direct customer contact, negotiated and closed sales for telephone peripheral equipment
- Installed equipment and followed-up to ensure customer satisfaction; maintained accounts and expedited orders

Achievements:
- **One of the top two salesman throughout the tri-state area**
- **Top salesman of branch office**

EDUCATION
Anytown College, Anywhere, NJ   1988
Major: Business Management, Computers and Marketing

175

Combination. *M. Carol Heider, Tampa, Florida*

A resume that shows how boldface, italic, all-uppercase letters, and bullets can be used in a resume for emphasis. Note the two levels of bullets—the second by indentation.

Daniel D. Schumm

805 South County Line Road
Hebron, Indiana 46341

(219) 996-6110

OBJECTIVE

Professional Sales/Management—Pharmaceuticals, medical equipment with or leading to management responsibility utilizing my communication, marketing, and public relations skills.

PROFILE

- ♦ Territorial sales in wholesale/retail/institutional medical markets including sales plans, promotions, formulary approval, ongoing account management and administration.
- ♦ Self-motivated and positive attitude to meet/exceed goals unsupervised as well as in team member/team leader role.
- ♦ Effective interpersonal skills; Creative flexibility in sales presentation based on professional's product posture; and Organized, detailed-minded problem-solver.
- ♦ Proactive to strengthen a high-growth, entrepreneurial organization that values and rewards results in an atmosphere whose primary concerns are integrity and teamwork.

PROFESSIONAL EXPERIENCE

Professional Medical Representative

05/99-Present

ABC Laboratories, Chicago, Illinois

Responsibilities:

Present and persuade designated target physicians and medical institutions to promote, prescribe and/or purchase the use of *ABC* pharmaceutical products in the Northern Indiana territory; Consult with physicians and hospital staff for direct sales and formulary approval of all *ABC* products; Update sales binder to analyze, plan and implement *ABC's* sales and marketing plan; Document every sales call; Communicate with regional office; and File weekly reports.

Accomplishments:

- ♦ Attended *A Career Ladder Program,* Chicago, IL. Successfully completed the specific courses designed by *ABC* to improve product knowledge and sales.
- ♦ Consistently, have either met or exceeded High Quality (HQ) ranking in year-end review conducted by *ABC's* management.
- ♦ **1999-99:** Recipient six (6) times of *Achiever's Club Award* for attaining top ranking in overall sales performance.
- ♦ **1999:** Finished in top quantile for *Suprax* salesman for the South Chicago district.
- ♦ **1999:** Finished fourth (4th) in the Chicago region for *The Gold Cup* which is the highest recognition award in honor of achieving the position of top sales performer.

Executive Sales Agent

05/99-05/99

XYZ Insurance Company, Merrillville, Indiana

Responsibilities:

Presented and persuaded prospective clients to promote and/or purchase the use of *XYZ Insurance* products in the Northern Indiana territory; Consulted with clients for direct sales; Worked with policies, contracts and scheduling; Implemented and updated sales plans to meet company's goals; and Personally delivered *XYZ's* products to clients.

176

Combination. *Susan K. Schumm, Carmel, Indiana*

The lines under the contact information are repeated in the header at the top of page 2. Small caps are used for the section headings. Separate subheadings for Responsibilities

Daniel D. Schumm

Accomplishments:

♦ Promoted from Sales Agent to Executive Sales Agent in first 12 months (usually occurs after first year).

Assistant Manager

05/99-05/99

ABC Drugstore, Chicago, Illinois

Responsibilities:

Managed and supervised the daily operations including: inventory control, merchandising, displays, promotions, personnel scheduling and performance, payroll, and cashier assistance.

STRENGTHS

Have professional and personal relationships with many of the key influential physicians and decision-makers in the business community in Northwest Indiana region.

EDUCATION

Bachelor in Business Administration (BBA)

1999-1999

University of North Dakota, Grand Forks, North Dakota ♦ MAJOR: Marketing

Accomplishments:

♦ Member: University of North Dakota Varsity Basketball Team, Scholarship (2 years).

Associate of Arts (AA)

1999-1999

Iowa Central Community College, Fort Dodge, Iowa ♦ MAJOR: Business

Accomplishments:

♦ Member: Iowa Central Community College Varsity Basketball Team, Scholarship (2 years).
♦ Recipient of *Mike Algoe Award* for Outstanding Student Athlete.

INTERESTS

Golf, Running, Basketball Official, and 4-H Committee Member.

REFERENCES

Furnished upon request.

and Accomplishments make the information for these two categories readily apparent in the Professional Experience and Education sections. Italic is used for company and institution names and for the names of awards.

RESUME

Robert Biscay
7000 East Feldon Way
Phoenix, AZ 00000

EDUCATION

> Attended Flagstaff City College 1980-1983, General
> Education W. Smith High School   Graduated 1980

EMPLOYMENT HISTORY

> 1986-Present
> > ROUTE SALESMAN - Colorado Waters Co., Phoenix, AZ
> > Duties include servicing existing accounts,
> > soliciting new accounts, billing and collections
> > of all accounts

> 1985-1986
> > MACHINIST - Arizona Equipment, Phoenix, AZ
> > Rebuilt old drivelines and made new drivelines

> 1984-1985
> > ROUTE DRIVER - Watersoft, Flagstaff, AZ
> > Route included exchanging the water softening
> > tanks

> 1980-1984
> > DRIVER/REPAIRMAN - Business Machines, Inc.,
> > Flagstaff, AZ
> > Made all necessary deliveries, I also made minor
> > repairs and cleaned the calculators

> 1978-1980
> > CASHIER/ASSISTANT NIGHT MANAGER - McDonald's,
> > Flagstaff, AZ
> > Worked as a cashier and balanced money drawer at
> > closing

PERSONAL STRENGTHS

> I am very strong in math skills, work well with my co-
> workers as well with clients. I am a very loyal and
> responsible employee

SALARY REQUIREMENT

> Minimum of $30,000.00 per year

REFERENCES FURNISHED UPON REQUEST

177

Chronological (Before). *Susan Britton Whitcomb, Fresno, California*

The person's original resume. It begins with an Education statement that shows graduation only
from high school send ends with a Salary Requirement, which invites rejection.

ROBERT BISCAY

2222 East Feldon Way
Fresno, California 93722
(209) 222-2222

OBJECTIVE

Outside Sales ▪ Route Sales position with a company that will benefit from my proven ability to generate new business, service and develop existing accounts, and earn bottom-line profits.

PROFESSIONAL EXPERIENCE

COLORADO WATERS COMPANY, Phoenix, Arizona   1986-Present

Route Salesman, Bottled Water Division: Over six years' commission sales experience, managing business growth, account retention, and deliveries to Phoenix area customers. Developed new business through prospecting and referrals. Serviced over 800 commercial and residential accounts. Prepared daily activity reports to track sales, inventory, collections, and cash receipts. Accustomed to heavy work load and long hours. (1986-1992)

- Increased territory volume approx. 155% despite influx of new competition.
- Continually exceeded goals, generating sales to warrant territory division into three separate routes.
- Selected for Hall of Fame two years (top 10% for sales, add-on sales, and new customers).
- Collected cash on 37% of accounts, well above the company norm.
- Trained 10 new salesmen over tenure, many of whom are now top producers.

Route Salesman, Coffee Division: Presently managing coffee route for two territories, covering some 100 miles daily. Perform sales, sales recordkeeping, and training responsibilities similar to those listed above. (1992-Present)

- Built number of accounts from 90 to 150 in just one year.
- Demonstrated company loyalty and longevity throughout seven-year tenure (average employee turnover for industry is two years).

ARIZONA EQUIPMENT, Phoenix, Arizona   1985-1986

Machinist: Built drivelines for diesel trucks and automobiles using high-technology equipment.

WATERSOFT, Flagstaff, Arizona   1984-1985

Route Driver: Scheduled and made deliveries of water softening tanks throughout the Central Valley.

BUSINESS MACHINES, INC., Flagstaff, Arizona   1980-1984

Driver/Repairman: Part-time employment concurrent with college.

EDUCATION

Accounting/General Education -- Flagstaff City College, Flagstaff, Arizona

References Upon Request

178

Chronological (After). *Susan Britton Whitcomb, Fresno, California*

The preceding resume developed into a resume that got an excellent response. Notice the expanded description of the current position. Education now appears last.

BETH BENDIX
16 Fillerman Road
Maybrook, New Jersey 00000
(555) 555-5555

SUMMARY *of* QUALIFICATIONS

A highly successful and knowledgeable sales professional with a proactive approach and a dynamic personality. Strong interpersonal skills with the ability to interface with individuals at all levels. Possesses a strong entrepreneurial spirit. Commitment to excellence is demonstrated through professional and academic achievements. Demonstrated strengths include:

SALES AND MARKETING	GOAL ORIENTED	TEAM PLAYER
INTERPERSONAL SKILLS	RESOURCEFUL	PROBLEM RESOLUTION
CLIENT RELATIONS	TECHNICAL APTITUDE	ENTREPRENEURIAL SKILLS

PROFESSIONAL AFFILIATIONS

R.S. GRAPHIC SUPPLIES   Landisville, New Jersey
Technical Sales Representative   *1996 - Present*

- Market graphic arts equipment and supplies to printers, publishers, advertising agencies, graphic designers and in-plant printing operations throughout New York/New Jersey metropolitan area.
- Comprehensive product line includes pre-press and press equipment, encompassing imagesetters, color separation scanners, file servers, desktop computers and computer-to-plate (CtP) systems.
- Instrumental in developing a corporate emphasis on system integration services.

LINOTYPE-HELL COMPANY   Hauppauge, New York
Territory Manager   *1990 - 1996*

- High profile position accountable for direct and channel sales of entire product line to high end users in the graphic arts pre-press marketplace. Linotype-Hell Company is a software developer and hardware manufacturer of imagesetters and raster image processors, color separation scanners, high-end color correction and photoretouching workstations, and computer-to-plate systems.
- Additionally, drove revenue through marketing of Linotype-Hell's system integration services.
- Targeted accounts throughout northern and central New Jersey, including color preparation trade shops, high quality printers, financial printers, publishers, ad agencies, graphic designers, service bureaus and large corporate in-plant printing operations. Territory generated over $2.5 million annually.
- Conducted plant surveys to analyze production flow and profitability levels.
- Recommended systems to reduce overhead and streamline production.
- Produced detailed proposals and secured contracts with average sales of $200,000+.

   ♦ **Generated sales in excess of $2.5 million; ranked 7 among 60 Territory Managers nationwide.**
   ♦ **Attained success and high close ratio in rapidly diminishing marketplace.**
   ♦ **Inducted into the President's Club for outstanding sales achievements.**

(continued...)

179

Combination. *Alesia Benedict, Rochelle Park, New Jersey*

The Summary of Qualifications ends with a three-column list of strengths. Column format makes it easy to alter the list for a different job target. Horizontal lines in the Professional Affiliations

BETH BENDIX   (555) 555-5555   -Page Two-

PROFESSIONAL AFFILIATIONS continued...

INFORMATION SYSTEMS CORP.   Westwood, Illinois
Media Sales Consultant, Eastern Region Sales Manager   *1985 - 1990*

- As **Media Sales Consultant for the Eastern Region**, contributed to the company's transition from a direct sales environment to sales through independent system integrators.
- Managed a $2.5 million territory.
- Pursued strategic alliances with new system integrators.
- Provided technical field support for certified system integrators.
- Conducted plant surveys to analyze production flow and current profitability levels.
- Configured detailed computer networks to meet client production requirements to ensure higher productivity and enhance profitability level.
- Responded to detailed request for proposals; negotiated and secured contracts with average sales exceeding $500,000.

  ◆ **Ranked in the top percentage in sales volume.**
  ◆ **Achieved and sustained an average sales figure of $500,000+, against company standard of $250,000.**
  ◆ **Launched a successful marketing campaign in an untapped market, without name recognition, and won sales from established industry leaders including ATEX, Triple-III, Harris Corporation, Cybergraphic Corporation, and System Integrators, Inc.**

COMPUGRAPHIC CORP.   Wilmington, Massachusetts
Senior Sales Representative   *1982 - 1985*

- Successfully marketed product line for a manufacturer of phototypsetting equipment and front-end newspaper systems.
- Targeted the newspaper and commercial publishing industries throughout the midwest and managed a $1.5 million territory.
- Recognized by upper management for generating superior sales volume and exceeding sales quotas.

MERGENTHALER LINOTYPE   Melville, New York
Sales Engineer   *1979 - 1982*

- Marketed phototypesetting equipment; prospected typography houses, printing companies, advertising agencies, newspapers, book publishers, graphic design agencies and corporate in-plant art departments throughout the highly competitive New York metropolitan territory.

EDUCATIONAL BACKGROUND

Hofstra University • Hempstead, New York • **Bachelor of Arts in Psychology**
GPA of 3.5 • Dean's List

TECHNICAL PROFICIENCY

Client/Server Technology • PC Hardware • Macintosh
Novell Networks • UNIX Operating System • Microsoft Windows • Windows NT • MS DOS
Microsoft Works • WinWord • QuarkXpress • Corel Draw • Relational Databases

section help the reader find quickly each position, employer, and dates and place of employment. Bullets indicate responsibilities. Diamond bullets are effective in pointing to quantified achievements. Page borders are a finishing touch.

CHRISTOPHER S. JADEN

369 Harborside Drive
Lakeland, Florida 33810
(941) 555-5555

SENIOR SALES REPRESENTATIVE
Expert in Sales Account Development and Servicing

Dynamic sales leader with expertise in creating customer-driven strategies designed to stimulate sales and increase presence within the industry. Exceptional account management skills with the ability to inspire confidence in customers and gain trust through attentive service and efficient problem-solving.

PROFESSIONAL EXPERIENCE

Outside Sales Representative   **FLORIDA PAPER COMPANY,** Orlando, Florida *(1983-Present)*
➤ Sell paper products, chemicals, and packaging materials from a broad line of 7,000 products representing 60-70 manufacturers.
➤ Develop and maintain accounts for **Templeton Gasoline, Johnson Department Stores, Inc., ThirstQuench Foods Division, Global Mining Corporation, Hamilton Furniture Brokers, Florida Specialties Clinic, and Adams Insurance Company.**
➤ Procure and follow up on new leads through cold calling; formulate and deliver presentations to prospective accounts.
➤ Analyze existing sales methods and develop new strategies to re-direct the sales focus and enhance product awareness.
➤ Work closely with senior management to position the company for continued growth and market expansion.

SPECIFIC ACCOMPLISHMENTS

➤ Produced the third highest total profit margin in 1995 among 16 representatives, $158,000. Successfully maintained this ranking during the first quarter of 1996 by bringing in nearly $40,000, a 16.4% growth over the first quarter of 1995.
➤ Rated third for overall total sales volume produced in 1995, which was $751,000; improved to second in 1996 with a first-quarter volume of nearly $215,000, a 9% increase over the first quarter of 1995.
➤ Built sales territory from a $10,000 to $63,000 per-month volume in thirteen-year career; increased number of base accounts from 20 to 65; retained 44% of customer base for more than five years.

OTHER EXPERIENCE

Account Manager   **ORLANDO TRUCK RENTAL,** Winter Park, Florida *(1979-1982)*
➤ Sold lease and maintenance agreements to fleet companies.
➤ Awarded *Rookie of the Year* honors for the Florida market.

District Manager   **DIVISION OF FORESTRY,** Orlando, Florida *(1972-1979)*
➤ As District Manager, oversaw all facets of the district covering a three-county area including staffing, equipment, and annual budget.
➤ As Urban Forester, worked with the Brevard County Planning Department to develop new program ideas and write sections of the County's Master Development Plan.
➤ Presented preservation proposals to the Brevard County Commission; performed public speaking duties to educate the community regarding forestry issues and environmental education.

EDUCATION

Bachelor of Science - Forestry *(1969)*   **NORTH CAROLINA STATE UNIVERSITY,** Raleigh, North Carolina

180

Combination. *E. René Hart, Lakeland, Florida*

The lines enclosing the profile information (not so named) increase the chances that this first section under the contact information will be seen and read. Special tip bullets point to

CONTINUING EDUCATION AND TRAINING

Continuous self study and improvement in sales technique and strategy.
Recent programs include:

Spin-Selling by Neil Rackham
Advanced Selling Techniques by Brian Tracey
The Zone by Barry Sears

Course work and study in business computer applications, including:

Introduction to Computers, Microsoft Windows - Brevard Technical Center *(1996)*
Business Applications on the Internet - Orlando Community Bookshop *(1996)*

MILITARY EXPERIENCE

Honorable Discharge - United States Army - SICV Intelligence, Saigon, Vietnam *(1971)*

COMMUNITY INVOLVEMENT

Assistant Scoutmaster of Troop 54, Orlando. Active in Scouting since 1986.
Awarded the Wood Badge in 1994 from the Boy Scouts of America.

responsibilities and accomplishments in the Professional Experience section, and to
responsibilities in the Other Experience section. Boldfacing is used to highlight key
information such as a degree, account names, self-study programs, and course work.

WILLIAM A. SALES
2 Dynamo Lane
Buyme, CT 33333
(333) 333-3333

OBJECTIVE
A position in sales or sales management.

PROFILE
- ★ 11 years of successful, diverse experience in sales and management.
- ★ Well-liked, customer service oriented professional: I establish and maintain long term relationships with customers by building good rapport; known for excellent follow through after the sale.
- ★ Received awards for outstanding sales achievement.
- ★ Exercise common sense and have the ability to "think on the run."
- ★ Possess entrepreneurial spirit, experience, and wisdom.

RELEVANT EXPERIENCE AND ACCOMPLISHMENTS

Sales and Customer Service
- Received awards for achieving high sales volumes in a wide range of brewed and non-alcoholic beverages; service accounts on a weekly basis, including restaurants, grocery/convenience stores and liquor stores, *Town Refreshments.*
- Managed sales and customer relations which resulted in contracting more business during my first quarter than was attained in the previous three quarters combined, *Honeycomb Producers.*
- Attained steady sales growth in a depressed industry through detailed product knowledge and commitment to customer service. Over a 3-year period, doubled sales income for a 100% commission sales route, *Morgan & Conway, Ltd.*
- Obtained positive sales growth and established excellent customer relations for franchise, *Muffins for You, Inc.*
- Distributed and sold videotapes, *New England Viewing.*

Sales Awards
- "Summer Sun-Up" award, Beer Brewing Company: for increasing sales of two new products by 18% and 21% within 3 months, 1995.
- "Top Ten" award, Ale Brewing Company: for surpassing sales by 10% during first ten weeks, 1995.
- "Champion" award, Beer Brewing Company: for achieving 9% sales growth in 3-month time period, 1994.

Management and Administration / Entrepreneurial Ventures
- Performed business administration duties including contract research, bidding, scheduling subcontractors, purchase and delivery of materials, procuring necessary permits and coordinating inspections by town officials, *Honeycomb Producers.*
- Successfully leased restaurant from a family that owned and operated it for 20 years; managed entire operation, including hiring, purchasing and menu selection, *Country Restaurant.*
- Purchased franchise and established excellent relationship with parent firm; received offer to participate in Supervisor Training program, *Muffins for You, Inc.*
- Purchased exclusive distribution rights for selling videotapes in Connecticut - films produced by Ocean Entertainment at Universal Studios in Florida, *New England Viewing.*
- Substantial earlier experience in grocery store management, including personnel supervision and training, vendor and sales relations, cash management, and inventory control.

WORK HISTORY
1993-present	**Route Sales/Merchandising**	*Town Refreshments,* City, CT
1992-1993	**Owner/Operator**	*New England Viewing,* Rural, CT
1989-1991	**General Manager**	*Honeycomb Producers,* Rural, CT
1988-1989	**Manager/Operator**	*Country Restaurant,* Rural, CT
1986-1988	**Wine and Liquor Route Sales**	*Morgan & Conway, Ltd.,* City, CT
1984-1986	**Franchise Owner/Route Sales**	*Muffins for You, Inc.,* City, OH

EDUCATION
Completed coursework in personnel management for small business, **Community College.**
Completed SBA small business start-up courses, **State University.**

181

Combination. *Annamarie Pawlina, location unknown*

This resume has the look of a resume for a manager: narrow margins, small type, and much information on a page. Star bullets point to Profile statements that sell the person.

JOHN KLINGER

600 10th Street
Virginia Beach, Virginia 23456
804 • 391 • 1295

OBJECTIVE: A career in *Sales* and *Marketing* with a stable company where comprehensive experience will benefit the employer and offer promotional opportunities.

QUALIFICATIONS:
- Extensive experience in sales and marketing. Exceptional sales performance as account representative for yellow pages company.
- Self-motivated and able to work independently. Have a high degree of creativity and initiative culminating with exemplary results.
- Responsible for positively motivating and influencing the thinking and behavior of others.
- Have the ability to achieve and increase sales performance to exceed quotas and goals.
- Able to prospect new clients and design advertising for accounts. Proficient in sales strategies, preparing oral and written proposals resulting in significant revenues.
- Maintain continuous client contact and follow-up. Achieve goals set forth by managers.
- Convey strong professional image, ability, initiative, and judgment. Work well with people on all levels.
- Fundamental knowledge of computers including MIS systems and the ability to grasp new concepts.

EXPERIENCE: Detail Data, Virginia Beach, VA. 1992-Present.
Yellow pages sales consultant.

ABC Vending Company, Virginia Beach, VA. 1991-1992.
Founded vending machine company to subsidize college education.

XYZ Chemical Company, Virginia Beach, VA. 1988-1989.
Territorial Manager. First runner-up as Zone Rookie of the Year-1988

Moon Building Company, Portsmouth, VA. 1986-1987.
Marketing representative of building related products.

Rough Utilities, RahRah, NY. 1979-1985.
Responsible for all inside, outside sales, advertising and marketing. Supervised five employees.

EDUCATION: St. Jupiter College, Norfolk, VA. B.A. Business Management, Cum Laude. 1992.
Monroe Community College, RahRah, NY. A.A.S. Marketing. 1984.

MISCELLANEOUS: Virginia Beach Oceanfront Jaycees (V.P. Management Development).

182

Combination. *Anne G. Kramer, Virginia Beach, Virginia*

The three-line line stands out as uncommon. Section headings down a blank column ensure white space. Bold Experience comments are to the point and therefore effective.

Amy Lou Smithers

1234 Main Street, Aloha, Oregon 97007
Telephone: (503) 543-5555

Professional Profile

Over 14 years of experience in developing, maintaining and maximizing sales production in the highly competitive home furnishings market. Proficient in all aspects of merchandising, training and customer service.

- Experienced in planning and conducting training seminars; able to develop effective presentations and tailor training programs to meet individual needs.
- Proven ability to develop a high level of referral and repeat business.
- Excellent follow-up and time management skills.

Experience

Design Consultant – 1992 to Present

Innovation Interiors, Tigard, Oregon

Call on local contractors and develop positive relationships to encourage referrals. Meet with customers, define needs, prepare estimates, make presentations and close sales. Plan and coordinate the installation process.

Accomplishments: Rated as #1 producer; consistently exceeded all sales goals.

Account Representative – 1984 to 1992

Advent Fabrics, New York, New York

Represented the fabric division to retail establishments and manufacturers in Washington, Oregon and Idaho. Managed over 550 existing accounts. Provided training at sales meetings and conducted customer training seminars.

Accomplishments: Successfully expanded the company's least productive territory; increased sales from $400,000 to $2,432,000 by demonstrating a thorough understanding of customer needs and providing relevant product education.

Sales Representative – 1978 to 1984

Design Group & Associates, Bellevue, Washington

Coordinated sales and customer service functions for accounts in Washington and Oregon. Also managed a 3,000 square foot designer showroom.

Accomplishments: Named "Rookie of the Year" in 1979.

Education

Bachelor of Arts – Interior Design, Portland State University, 1980
Sales Training – Dale Carnegie Sales Course, 1991

References

Provided upon request.

183

Combination. *Pat Kendall, Aloha, Oregon*

"Dot leaders" instead of horizontal lines are a pleasing alternative for separating the resume sections visually. Bullets are no longer just bullets but echoes of the dot leaders.

William Troise, Jr.

323 West High St.   Elviratown, New York 55555   (000) 000-0000

EDUCATION

State University of New York, College of Technology, Canton, New York
Associate in Applied Science Degree: *Retail Business Management,* May 1995

Related Courses
Accounting, Marketing, Advertising, Retailing, Business Law, Sales Management,
Business Organization & Management, Human Resource Management.

RELATED EXPERIENCE

Retail Management
- Assisted Store Manager in maintaining/operating a retail drug store
- Functioned as manager in the Store Manager's absence
- Assisted in monitoring and controlling store expenses within budget guidelines
- Progressed to Night Manager of a convenience store
- Closed out register; reconciled accounts; carried out nightly inventory of selected items
- Supervised up to three other workers
- Wal-Mart Department Manager - Department of Paper and Chemicals

Sales
- Maintained department; kept shelves well stocked; assigned customers; operated cash register during rush times.
- Took telephone orders for product from established food service customers
- Maintained excellent customer relations
- Loaded truck and made deliveries
- Made contact with potential customers attempting to establish new accounts

EMPLOYMENT HISTORY

Assistant Manager, November 1995 - Present
Fays, Anywhere, New York

Department Manager, August 1995 - November 1995
Wal-Mart, Anywhere, New York

Carpenter/Mason and Heavy Construction Mechanic, 1993 - Present
New York National Guard, Somehwere, New York

Heavy Equipment Mechanic, May 1989 - May 1993
United States Army, Fort Happy Drum, New York

Sales Associate, January - May 1989
K-Mart Department Store, Elviratown, New York

Laborer, June - September 1988
House Doctor Construction, Elviratown, New York

Guard, February - June 1988
Burns International Security, Elviratown, New York

Sales/Delivery, May 1987 - February 1988
Eddy Dale Farms, Elviratown, New York

Night Manager, April 1985 - May 1987
Buckey's Convenience Store, Elviratown, New York

Infantryman/Heavy Equipment Mechanic, December 1984 - April 1985
United States Army Reserve/Training, Fort Leonard Wood, Missouri

184

Combination. *Betty Geller, Elmira, New York*

An unusual format. The Related Experience section summarizes work in various jobs. A typical chronological format would have meant much repetition of similar responsibilities.

PETER S. MANAGER
1122 Waterford Court • Somewhere, NJ 11223
(555) 555-5555

MANAGEMENT / SALES REP / MANUFACTURING REP
Expertise in...Servicing Existing Accounts...New Account Development...Team Building

SUMMARY OF QUALIFICATIONS
- Strong presentation, negotiation, and sales closing skills. Utilize verbal communication and listening abilities to identify client needs and/or problems; superior grasp of product knowledge.
- Solid work ethic; ability to set short- and long-term goals; computer literate.
- Extremely focused on identifying potential problem areas, minimizing issues, formulating and executing competent solutions.
- Assimilation of company goals/objectives involving the analysis and administration of operational procedures, annual budgets, and future projections.

PROFESSIONAL EXPERIENCE
BEST DEPARTMENT STORE, Anywhere, NJ, FL   1995 - Present
Department Manager
Responsible for inventory control of hard lines including ordering merchandise, stocking shelves, and setting displays.
- *Largest turnover of merchandise in store.*
- *Instituted methods to increase productivity and reduced work force.*

ANASCH'S INC, Anywhere, NJ   1994 - 1995
Regional Sales Manager
Wholesale dry cleaning establishment headquartered in Small Town, NJ. Territory encompassed the state of New Jersey, from Anywhere to Somewhere.
- *Established route; started with 10 accounts and generated approximately 40 new accounts per month.*

WHOLESALE CLEANERS, INC., Anywhere, NJ   1986 - 1994
President
Mid-sized cleaning established with on-premises cleaning facilities generating approximately $700,00 in annual revenues. Hired, trained, supervised, and evaluated 13+ employees. Complete P&L and budget responsibility.
- *Founder and majority stockholder; turned profit in first year.*
- *First wholesale dry cleaner to cater exclusively to the hotel industry.*
- *Major clients included Best Known hotel, Better Known hotel, and Grand hotels.*
- *Successfully negotiated profitable sale.*

Early relevant career experience includes: *General Manager* of large local cleaner with $1 million+ in revenues. Directly responsible for P&L, budget, hiring, training, supervising of 48+ employees. Redesigned physical facilities thus improving productivity. Increased sales; initiated computerized sales system; initiated development of new outlets in downtown locations. **Office Manager** of large wholesale printing supply company. Clients included printers throughout the state of New Jersey. Responsible for inventory, sales, and customer service.

EDUCATION
University of New Jersey, Anywhere, NJ   1983
  Major: Management
Community College, Anywhere, NJ
  Associate of Science, Business Management   1982

MILITARY/AFFILIATIONS
United States Navy Reserve
- Honorable Discharge   1982
- Citation, The Commander Submarine Force, U.S. Atlantic Fleet
Rotary Club   1985 - 1987

185

Combination. *M. Carol Heider, Tampa, Florida*

Lines enclosing a career banner with areas of expertise help to make this opening part of the resume visible to the reader. Elsewhere in this resume, notice the use of italic.

JACK YONG
40 View Avenue • Oakland, Maryland 00000 • (555) 555-5555

CAREER OBJECTIVE:

DEDICATED individual seeks a position with advancement opportunities that will utilize acquired skills and experience to contribute to organizational success. Areas of interest include:

MANAGEMENT • MARKETING • SALES

PROFILE SUMMARY:

A highly energetic, dynamic professional with a track record in situations where exceptional achievement and quality performance are the keys to success • Dedicated and achievement-oriented with a proven base of knowledge upon which to draw that will assist organizations in meeting their objectives. Fluent in Chinese (Cantonese). Computer skills include MS Word, Excel, Lotus 1-2-3 and Windows 95.

PROFESSIONAL EXPERIENCE:

COLLECTOR'S SQUARE   Piedmont, Maryland
Manager   *1993 - Present*
- Oversee sales, customer relations and all daily operations of a distributor and purveyor of diversified collectibles.
- Recruit, train and develop staff to peak levels of performance.
- Communicate and negotiate with vendors and suppliers.
- Collaborate with owner on budgeting, purchasing, marketing and merchandising strategies.
- Market products to clientele and conduct comprehensive research to track/locate rare collectibles.
- Maintain inventory and perform bookkeeping functions.

 ◆ *Drove sales by 300% within 3 years.*
 ◆ *Increased sell-through of merchandising through innovative marketing strategies including direct mail campaigns, catalogs and on-line web sites.*
 ◆ *Increased net profit through introduction of new inventory and cyclic sheet system.*
 ◆ *Slashed wholesale costs by expanding vendor base.*

MEIN CORPORATION   Jaywerd, California
Plant Manager   *1995 - 1996*
- Scheduled daily production, delivery routes and sales force routes for a company specializing in non-perishable food products.
- Directed a staff of production personnel and sales staff.
- Solicited and secured new customers.
- Accountable for procurement, ordering and daily operations.

 ◆ *Significantly increased sales through promotional pricing structure.*
 ◆ *Empowered staff and improved management/employee relations and employee morale.*

W.S. PLUMBING AND FIRE PROTECTION, INC.   San Francisco, California
Assistant Manager   *1994 - 1995*
- Provided leadership to a crew of 10 employees for a construction company concentrating in plumbing and fire protection systems.
- Drafted and submitted private contract bids and proposals.
- Scheduled assignments and projects.
- Versed in building permits and inspections.

EDUCATION:

Bachelor of Science in Managerial Economics (1994)
University of California • Davis, California

186

Combination. *Alesia Benedict, Rochelle Park, New Jersey*

Eye-catching diamond bullets indicate achievements in italic for this manager. Italic is used also for the Profile Summary and for the job titles and their dates. Education is last.

RICARDO M. SMITHERS

Sales & Marketing

5677 S.W. Avalon Drive • Lake Oswego, Oregon 97034 • 503-636-7089

BACKGROUND SUMMARY

Aggressive marketing professional with solid experience in territory development, major account management and public relations.

- Excellent communication skills; able to establish productive, long-term relationships with corporate decision-makers.
- Highly self-disciplined with ability to prioritize tasks and work independently with minimum supervision.
- Resourceful and trainable with readily transferable skills.

EXPERIENCE

CABLE SYSTEMS, INC. - Portland, Oregon   1995-Present
Account Manager
Hired to rebuild business that was lost during company's downsizing and re-organization in 1989. Responsible for price negotiations and continuous maintenance of account files. Set up territory call schedules and entertain account decision-makers.
- Despite decline in market conditions, successfully rebuilt account base to previous levels.

ADVO EQUIPMENT CORPORATION - Portland, Oregon   1989-1995
Sales Representative
Sold construction equipment to contractors, construction companies, municipalities and rental yards. Priced new equipment and appraised trade-ins. Sold financing and developed comprehensive sales presentations.
- Consistently met or exceeded sales quotas.

CABLE SYSTEMS, INC. - Portland, Oregon   1985-1989
Territory Manager
Managed territory that showed significant growth and sales increases each period.
- Two-time winner of the "Gold Circle" sales excellence award.

CANADIAN VIP SERVICES - Alberta, Canada   1982-1985
Sales Representative
Managed large sales territory and successfully developed new accounts.
- Built yearly sales from -0- to $2,000,000 in two years.
- Member, Achievers' Club.

EDUCATION

PORTLAND STATE UNIVERSITY - Portland, Oregon
B.S. Business Administration (1982)

TOM HOPKINS SALES TRAINING SEMINAR - Portland, Oregon (1990)

REFERENCES

Provided upon request.

187

Combination. *Pat Kendall, Aloha, Oregon*

Enclosed contact information, headings in a separate column, caps for employer names, bold for job titles, bullets for key points, and blank lines make this a readable resume.

EMMA COHEN

15 Avenue I • Brooklyn, New York • 12121
(718) 222-3333

SUMMARY

Experienced Retail Manager with proven strength in Customer Service, Sales, and Negotiations. Skilled at marketing, advertising, strategic planning, and promoting products. Highly analytical and logical with excellent research and writing skills. Successful in developing strategies to attract new customers and maintain their loyalty.

EXPERIENCE

NORTHERN HOME STORES, Brooklyn, NY
General Manager, 1993 to present
Oversee fifteen 5,000 square foot stores/warehouses throughout the U.S. Supervise twenty employees. Foster an atmosphere of teamwork and empower staff to make decisions. Design store layouts to maximize attractiveness and sales. Represent company and promote products to retail operations.

- Increased sales by 15% in 1996 and helped company achieve its highest sales level in 15 years.
- Coordinate monthly store exhibits that draw 10,000 customers.
- Overhauled pricing structure that increased profits by 10%.
- Implemented employee retention plan that reduced staff turnover rate by 50%.

Assistant Manager, 1991 to 1993
Assisted with staff supervision and product marketing. Designed layout and wrote copy for quarterly product catalogues. Promoted to General Manager.

AMERICAN STORES, Forest Hills, NY
National Inventory Director, 1988 to 1991
Inspected operations throughout the U.S. and solved inventory problems.

- Developed comprehensive system for handling damaged furniture.
- Decreased defective furniture by 75% in California and 85% in New York.
- Successfully negotiated with factories to receive credits for furniture.
- Improved appearance of warehouses and stores.

APEX INVESTMENT CORPORATION, New York, NY
Account Executive, 1985 to 1988
Researched and visited companies to determine growth potential. Advised investors on strategies and helped them make informed decisions.

- Managed up to 75 accounts worth a total of $300,000.
- Earned Series 7 and Series 63 Licenses.

COMPUTERS

- Proficient in Microsoft Office (Word, Excel, Access, PowerPoint)
- Knowledge of WordPerfect, Lotus 1-2-3, Quotron, and PageMaker

EDUCATION

B.A. in Economics, 1985
St. John's University, Jamaica, NY
Financed education 100%

188

Combination. *Kim Isaacs, Jackson Heights, New York*

Like the preceding resume, an easy-to-read document with some similar features. The chief difference is the filled (shaded) Summary box that is also shadowed.

Helen K. Lewis

44311 Blue Field Road
East St. Louis, Illinois 62269
(618) 555-3512

"...energetic, willing, and enthusiastic worker."
—E. Pepperidge, Customer

"...makes customers feel warm and appreciated..."
—Capt. Paul Jamison
Department of the Air Force
Lackland AFB, TX

"...genuinely dedicated and professional individual..."
—Jerry M. Wallace
Branch Brigade Exchange
Fort Sam Houston, TX

"...an exceptional employee with outstanding job knowledge, desire to excel, and willingness to satisfy customers."
—Robert Matthews, General Manager
Scott Main Exchange, SAFB, IL

"...sales driven and an excellent merchandiser..."
—Cherry Kamen, Retail Manager
Scott Main Exchange, SAFB, IL

"...unbridled energy and passion for her duties..."
—Georgia McLeod, Retail Manager
Fort Leavenworth Exchange
Fort Leavenworth, KS

"...a joy to customers and very knowledgeable in all product areas...personally insures that all patrons receive the best possible service."
—Kevin Roberts, Exchange Manager
Four Seasons/Toyland
Lackland AFB, San Antonio, TX

Profile

Experienced **Sales Manager** with retail sales and management career spanning 20+ years in increasingly responsible positions with military exchange service. Bottom-line oriented with consistent record of exceeding standards and expectations. Aggressive and organized, with exceptional ability to motivate and train team workers and subordinates. Demonstrated drive and skills needed for successful progression in field.

Professional Experience

Sales & Merchandise Manager   1992-1993
ARMY & AIR FORCE EXCHANGE SVC, Scott Air Force Base, IL

Planned, coordinated, and directed selling, reordering, and merchandising activities for all store selling departments for on-base military retail store with average monthly sales of $2.3 million. Trained and supervised four department managers.

Accomplishments:
- Employed aggressive sales management techniques to increase sales by over 10% over previous year.
- Motivated department managers and workers resulting in 13% increase in productivity over 1-year period.

Sales & Merchandise Manager   1991-1992
ARMY & AIR FORCE EXCHANGE SVC, Ft. Leavenworth, KS

Supervised store operations for $1.9 million/month retail sales operation. Managed 3 department supervisors.

Accomplishments:
- Maintained planned turn rates and established sales goals—despite decreased activity—during and after major renovation of store.
- Supervised in-store merchandising programs and maintained inventory variance well above tolerance.

Operations Manager   1990-1991
ARMY & AIR FORCE EXCHANGE SVC, Scott Air Force Base, IL

Managed administrative, customer support, and sales and expenditures activities in 4 major areas: stock room, accounting office, customer support, and central checkout/cashier's cage. Also supervised RPOS computer operations and related support activities.

Accomplishments:
- Instituted expense controls resulting in net decrease in overall expenditures of 1.2% over prior year.
- Mastered schedules and MSO program for drop in personnel costs and measurable increase in productivity.
- Contributed to increase in sales of over 10% above previous year.

189

Combination. *Carla Culp Coury, Glen Carbon, Illinois*

A stellar resume for a person whose work experiences were all from the military and relatively similar. Several letters of recommendation were the source of the testimonials.

Helen K. Lewis 2

Store Manager 1989-1990
FOUR SEASONS/TOYLAND STORE, Ft. Sam Houston, TX

Managed outdoor recreation, lawn and garden, furniture, live plant, and toy merchandise with monthly sales averaging over $260,000.

Accomplishments:
- Increased monthly sales activity 62% during one-year period.
- Closely supervised accountability controls resulting in improved variance figures for year.
- Developed extensive product knowledge of outdoor merchandise.

Store Manager 1986-1989
FOUR SEASONS/TOYLAND STORE, Lackland AFB, TX

Managed outdoor recreation, lawn and garden, furniture, live plant, and toy merchandise with monthly sales averaging over $215,000.

Accomplishments:
- Decreased bloated inventory levels and excess damaged merchandise resulting in financial improvement in all areas.
- Aggressive leadership style resulted in new products, new services, and customers brought into facility.

Retail Manager 1984-1986
BRANCH EXCHANGE, Ft. Sam Houston, TX

Managed all areas of small retail operation on base.

Accomplishments:
- Contributed to high growth rate in sales and productivity of installation's retail activities with personal leadership ability, management skills, and experience.

Special Training

Numerous specialized supervisory, management, and retail sales training courses:

"Professional Retail Management Seminar" (1 week, 1992)
    University of Arkansas, Fayetteville
"Challenge of Retailing"
"Retailing for Manager"
"Retail Accounting Procedures"
"Retail Management Review"
Toy, Jewelry and Outdoor Living Seminars
Retail Branch Store Operations
Shoppette Seminars and Workshops
Audio, Photographic, Camera & Electronics Products Seminars

Personal and professional references provided upon request

More testimonials on this page would have been overkill. Those on the first page offset fears employers might have of functional information or gaps in employment and education. Accomplishments after each work experience are a strong marketing tool.

GARY S. MCKAY

6789 Antelope Lane ■ Hometown, Arizona 5555 ■ 5555.555.5555

Manages $3 million sales territory, generating new business
and maximizing existing account sales for *NASDAQ* listed heavy equipment distributor.
Thirteen years with company, offering a broad spectrum of administrative experience
in the areas of management, training, customer service and program development.

SELECTED ACHIEVEMENTS

- Demonstrated ability to **increase** gross sales volume by up to 200%.
- **Expanded** market penetration 30% in past two years, continually exceeded **sales** targets.
- #1 sales representative with **highest** sales volume of $3.5 million+, recognized with numerous awards for excellent salesmanship.
- **Tripled** attachment sales resulting in increased gross profit margins of $100,000.

QUALIFICATIONS SUMMARY

- Expertise in servicing existing accounts, new account development and closing the deal.
- Skilled in management, sales and marketing of heavy equipment and attachments.
- Proficient in interpersonal relations, load and resource management; strong communication skills with customers, staff and management.
- Ability to facilitate, organize and direct staff, implement systems and procedures.
- Self motivated individual but also an effective member of a decision making team.
- Consistently exceeds company profit projections based upon performance.
- Trains, develops, supervises, schedules and motivates staff.
- Analyze needs, submit recommendations, and implement cost-effective programs encompassing market research, public relations, target relationship marketing, strategic alliances, sales support materials and customer assistance.

PROFESSIONAL EXPERIENCE

ACE EQUIPMENT COMPANY 1984 to present Hometown, Arizona
Largest heavy equipment dealer in North America
Promotions based on performance led to present position. Skilled manager and **effective** motivator who "learned by doing" and leads by example.

MANAGER/SALES 1995 to present Hometown, Arizona
- ▹ Generated volume increase from $1.5 to $3 million, doubled territory.
- ▹ Responsible for profits of both new heavy equipment and attachments, consumer relations management, safety and systems management.

SALES COORDINATOR 1992 to 1995 Big City, Arizona
- ▹ Coordinated sales, vendors, purchasing, billing and invoicing.
- ▹ Managed inventory control for State of Arizona.

PARTS MANAGER 1990 to 1992 Big City, Arizona
- ▹ Supervise parts, service and warranty departments, schedule deliveries.
- ▹ Developed strong customer service alliances through follow up.

PARTS SALES/WAREHOUSE 1984 to 1990 Big City, Arizona

PROFESSIONAL DEVELOPMENT - *SEMINARS, WORKSHOPS*

- Dale Carnegie How to . . .Influence People
- Brian Tracy's Psychology of Sales
- Customer Oriented Marketing and Service Strategies
- *ACE EQUIPMENT COMPANY'S* Extensive Training Courses in Sales, Marketing and Customer Service

190

Combination. *Patricia S. Cash, Prescott, Arizona*

This person was very motivated and accomplished. The task was to de-emphasize his lack of higher education and to highlight his professional development through other training.

DAVID M. MERCHANDISER

12587 New York Avenue, Winterpark, NC 69317   (555) 898-9898

MANAGEMENT • BUYER

Experienced professional with a proven track record in merchandising and closing sales. Solid management, communication, situation assessment, problem solving, and organizational skills. Expertise in:

- Floor Management
- Product Ordering/Distribution
- Quality Control/Improvement

- Merchandising/Inventory Control
- Personnel Training/Supervision
- Retail Sales Management/Customer Service

PROFESSIONAL EXPERIENCE

Buyer/Sales Manager   1987 - Present
GOOD FURNITURE, Ft. Myers/Jacksonville, FL

Primary responsibility for the coordination of merchandise inventory for four high volume furniture stores. Maintain $3M inventory; plan and prepare budget. Work independently with little or no supervision. Familiar with custom software maintenance programs. Take charge in manager's absence. Key responsibilities include:
- Train, schedule, supervise, and evaluate the work performance of a staff of 10+.
- Maintain/update inventory, documents, and control procedures.
- Recommend procedural changes to expedite product movement, control, and accountability.
- Set advertising and coordinate product movement through four Metro stores.
- Meet with manufacturer's reps to resolve problems regarding defective products.
- Instrumental in closing of floor sales.
- Voted "Employee of the Month."

Audio/Video Manager   1984 - 1987
BEST APPLIANCE, Anywhere, OH

Supervised entire audio/visual department. Scope of responsibilities included merchandising/displaying of established and new product offerings. In charge of inventory control functions.

Appliance Sales/Cashier Supervision   1982 - 1984
DISCOUNT LAND, Anywhere, OH

Responsibilities included audio/visual sales, inventory control, and customer service.

Assistant Manager   1980 - 1982
DISCOUNT WORLD, Anywhere, OH

Supervision of 30+ personnel. Reported directly to President. Diverse responsibilities included personnel training, employee scheduling, sales, merchandising, product management, pricing, advertising, customer service, and opening and closing store.

Manager   1979 - 1980
HIP FASHIONS, Anywhere, OH

Responsibilities included supervision and scheduling of 5+ personnel, merchandising, displays, and overseeing store operations.

191

Combination. *M. Carol Heider, Tampa, Florida*

Two pairs of lines enclose key information: a career headline and the heading for the Professional Experience section. Between the two pairs is a profile with areas of expertise.

Susan Steinfeld

12 Browertown Road
Little Falls, NJ 07424
(201) 785-3011

Objective

Senior administrative management position with an innovative company, where the professional execution of their special events and various marketing programs will be valued.

Personal Profile

Entrepreneurial, creative manager with strong leadership and motivational skills; extremely service oriented; unique combination of intuitive and analytical abilities; astute at recognizing areas in need of improvement, with the vision to develop action steps and see them through to a prompt and successful completion, well within budgetary framework; knowledge of conversational French.

Areas of Expertise

Special Event/Meeting Planning

- Eleven years of experience in the start to finish management of high budgeted, multi-faceted projects for the hospitality, franchise and other industries.

- Demonstrated exceptional ability to plan and organize a broad range of considerations from site negotiations to finishing details and amenities, with the style and panache befitting events such as grand openings, major conferences, fundraisers and employee/corporate functions.

- Screen and select agency personnel, freelancers and in-house staff, promoting harmonious working relationships throughout entire event staging process. Scope of involvement includes: coordination of attendees and presentors, travel/accommodations planning, theme-oriented decor, room set-up, food and beverage services, entertainment, audio-visual productions, and more.

Marketing Communications

- Heavy exposure to the entire creative execution of corporate marketing plans, guided only by minimal directives from management.

- Contract for and direct the activities of implementation teams which include: communications consultants, print and audio-visual production houses, photographers, artists, designers and public relations agencies, in addition to internal support staff, to produce creative promotional materials reflective of the corporate image.

- Awarded recognition for multiple print and other corporate communications pieces such as annual reports, franchise brochures, videos, consumer information bulletins, and company newsletters.

... Continued

192

Combination. *Melanie A. Noonan, West Paterson, New Jersey*

Filled square bullets are used with paragraphs throughout this resume. The Areas of Expertise section contains two groups of three paragraphs for a balanced look. The Professional

Susan Steinfeld

Professional Experience

HOST SERVICES INTERNATIONAL, New York, NY   1991-Present

Director of Event Marketing for hotel property franchisor controlling 2500+ Howard Johnson's, Days Inn and Ramada facilities. Report to Executive Vice President of Marketing. Responsible for planning and executing major special events including annual conferences, cause related marketing, corporate meetings, and creative contributions to marketing plans.

- Within six months, orchestrated two successful major meetings normally requiring two years from inception of plans.
- Utilized economics of scale to produce two corporate functions with similar themes, back to back at the same location, saving the company at least $500,000 had they taken place at different times of the year.

BILLY BOB'S CHUCKWAGON, INC., Houston, TX   1981-1991

Director of Marketing Communications Services (1988-91) at Corporate Headquarters of $1.4 billion, 2400+ unit international restaurant chain.

- Reported to the Vice President of Corporate Communications and managed a staff of four in the areas of corporate communications/public relations, special events, publications, audio-visuals, and large scale meetings. Controlled a $1.2MM meeting budget.
- Promoted through the ranks of the marketing organization to director post by proving ability to take charge of problem areas and effect beneficial solutions.
  - ... Initiated marketing information center to answer various inquiries from individual franchise operators; published a quarterly directory listing contacts for available services.
  - ... Facilitated distribution of newly introduced but difficult to obtain marketing items. Traced cause of problem to short term lack of inventory and developed monitoring system to prevent recurrences.
  - ... Took over meeting planner responsibility upon former incumbent's resignation three months before annual convention. With brand new management, developed and executed plans quickly, smoothly and to their satisfaction.
- Assumed permanent charge of event planning for the next seven years, each year progressively improving it with regard to increased attendance, quality of service and graphic design.
- Received Billy Bob's Outstanding Performance Award (four years) for quality and prompt execution of projects and recognition for award-winning annual reports.

Education

McGill University, Montreal, Canada (1975-77). Major in Marketing and Advertising. Management and Creative Writing seminars while at Billy Bob's.

Memberships

Meeting Planners, Inc.
Women in Communications

References and portfolio available upon request.

Experience section indicates two places of work. The bullets call attention to achievements, and more information is given about the longer of the two jobs held. Ellipses (. . .) are used as second-level bullets.

Dana S. Forest

7549 Farmhouse Lane ■ Loveland, Ohio 45140 ■ (513) 555-7549

Profile

Business management professional with strengths in strategic planning, finance, marketing, and the assessment and development of human resources.

History of successful business leadership and resulting growth in diverse corporate and entrepreneurial environments.

Proven ability to lead and motivate both teams and individuals and to create consensus for goal achievement.

Consistent accomplishments in:

- Department leadership and management
- Long- and short-range marketing and sales planning
- Development of business operation systems
- Organization planning

- Strategic planning
- Planned growth
- Financial planning
- Team building

Professional Experience

AKERBLOM & FOREST ASSOCIATES, Cincinnati, Ohio   1992-Present
Organizational development consulting firm
Partner / Sales and Administrative Manager

Business Management
Developed corporate strategic plan and marketing strategy; responsible for revenue/expense and balance sheet management; presented and sold consulting services to organizations of all sizes.

Key Consulting Accomplishments
Conducted employee assessments for organizations of 10 to 100-plus employees to establish root causes of identified problems; developed and delivered organizational change programs that led to:
- Improved productivity;
- Employee buy-in of corporate goals;
- Increased profitability;
- Improved employee retention and satisfaction.

WELBY MANAGEMENT ASSOCIATES, INC., Cincinnati, Ohio   1987-1992
Management consulting firm
Operations Manager

Business Management
Led start-up company to profitable, planned growth. Managed revenue, expenses, and balance sheet operations. Developed and implemented all control systems, office operations and policies.

Marketing/Sales
- Created corporate marketing plan and established client base.
- Implemented innovative and effective database for sales staff that contributed to significant sales growth in six-figure range in first twelve months.

Key Consulting Accomplishments
- Led turnaround of troubled third-party insurance administrator with 50 employees — introduced organizational structure and controls and reestablished company's ability to achieve profitable and planned growth.
- Developed public relations program and succeeded in restoring client company's tarnished image with clients and customers, resulting in improved efficiency and profitability.

193

Combination. *Louise M. Kursmark, Cincinnati, Ohio*

This person was a "generalist" with small business and consulting experience. She had a diverse background and needed to focus her experience in several specific areas. The writer used

Dana S. Forest Page 2

Professional Experience (continued)

FINANCIAL PLANNERS, INC., Cincinnati, Ohio   1982-1987
Consulting and brokerage firm
Chief Operating Officer/Treasurer

Business Management
> P&L and overall management responsibility; specific operations assignments in the areas of financial management, strategic planning, staff management, and oversight of information systems.
> - Developed customized software program to enhance high-growth marketing and customer services. Selected programmer and provided detailed specifications for time-efficient programming process.

Marketing/Sales
> - Created structure and marketing programs that led to 400% growth in 5-year time frame. Recipient of Crescendo Award as one of Cincinnati's 50 fastest-growing firms.
> - Created highly profitable and high-growth niche marketing services; established focus on customer service and support.

PREMIER SPECIALTY STORES, Cincinnati, Ohio   1980-1982
Merchandising Manager

Business Management
> Accountable for new product development, purchasing, inventory control and marketing services.
> - Structured, formalized and streamlined the buying function, leading to 20% increase in cash flow, elimination of distressed inventories, and establishment of businesslike operations.

Marketing/Sales
> - Contributed to 20% sales growth through redefined marketing strategies and effective vendor negotiations.

MERCANTILE DEPARTMENT STORES, Cincinnati, Ohio   1975-1980
Buyer

> Fast-track promotion through management training program.

Education

BS, Business/Marketing, UNIVERSITY OF OHIO, Columbus, Ohio   1975

Computer Skills
Proficient in DOS- and Windows-based word processing, spreadsheets, financial software. Experience includes specifying functions and working closely with programmers to create customized business management software.

Professional and Community Activities

Board Member, Social Health Alliance
Fund-raising Team Leader: American Red Cross/Northeast
Chairman, Community Outreach: Grace Episcopal Church
Chairman, Advisory Board: Loveland Elementary School

subheadings like Business Management and Marketing/Sales to make achievements more readable. Because the person was going to target nonprofit agencies for management opportunities, the writer included volunteer and community experience.

SELL M. MOORE

1515 Gogetem Crescent
Any City, USA   22222

Home: (808) 666-6666
Business: (808) 444-4444

RETAIL SALES / MANAGEMENT

Seeking position in retail sales where extensive experience can be utilized. Capabilities include:

- Operations Management
- Leasing Negotiations
- Budget Control
- Customer Relations

- Store Design/Set Up
- Cash Management
- Personnel Management
- Personnel Training

- Inventory Control
- Advertising / Media Buying
- Forecasting
- Merchandising

RETAIL EXPERIENCE

Owner / Manager, The Great Store, Any City, VA   1986 - present

Developed and built business from ground floor level.   Generated annual sales to a high of $2,100,000. Actively involved in all operations.

- Negotiated contracts for leasing of space and pricing from suppliers.
- Designed store lay-out and merchandise display.
- Supervised staff of 9 full-time employees and 8 - 12 part-time/seasonal employees.
- Handled all aspects of advertising including media buying, writing ad copy, and co-op advertising with suppliers.
- Full responsibility for sales projections, budgeting, and inventory control.

Vice President, The Best Possible Company, Any City, VA   1979 - 1985

Began as manager of one store with annual sales of $1.5 million. Within 3 years, advanced to supervisor of six stores. In 1983, promoted to Vice President with responsibility for twelve stores.

- Developed leases to open new stores.
- Coordinated store design with architects and contractors.
- Actively involved in set up and opening of all new stores.
- Monitored expense budgets/sales projections for each store.
- Supervised store managers. Wrote training manuals for use by managers.
- Handled all advertising including media buying, writing ad copy, generating co-op advertising dollars from suppliers.

Manager Trainee, World's Best Company, This City, VA   1977 - 1978

Completed 1 year management training program.

EDUCATION

Bachelor's Degree, The Greatest University, Any Town, USA

194

Combination. *Susie Brady, location unknown*

A symmetrical resume that opens with a scan list of abilities enclosed within a pair of horizontal lines. In the Retail Experience section, paragraphs indicate achievements.

SUSAN E. BRITTON

1234 N. West ● Fresno, CA 93704
(209) 222-7474

QUALIFICATIONS

TOP-PRODUCING SALES MANAGER with nine years' experience building and managing high-growth sales organization for Fortune 50 industry leader. Led district **from mid-range performance to #1** in western United States, with overall sales increase of $12 million. Strengths include:

- ◆ Sales Team Recruitment, Development & Coaching
- ◆ Market Analysis, Sales Forecasting & Fiscal Management
- ◆ Strategic Planning & Positioning in Anticipation of Industry/Market Trends

PROFESSIONAL EXPERIENCE

THE BEST FORTUNE 50 COMPANY, Anywhere, USA   1979-Present

Promoted through positions as Sales Representative (1979-82); Sales Specialist (1982-86); District Manager (1986-94); (requested lateral move) Sales Consultant (1994-95); and Senior Sales Consultant (1995-Present).

AS DISTRICT MANAGER, directed sales/marketing functions in eight eastern states generating $16 million in annual sales. Primary responsibilities included management of sales team of nine (plus telemarketing and sales support staff), sales planning/forecasts, corporate reporting, and marketing including direct accountability for $250,000 marketing budget.

- ‣ Increased overall sales from $4 to $16 million -- $7.9 million of which was achieved in past 3 years during challenging economic period for industry.

- ‣ Launched two new products in 1992 and 1993, generating $430,000 versus goal of $300,000 and $522,000 versus goal of $272,000.

- ‣ Exceeded annual goals by 21.2%, 19.2%, 20.4%, and 9.9% for years ending 1990-1993.

- ‣ Consistently earned recognition as #1 or #2 district among 12-15 in the eastern United States.

- ‣ Established new district which ranked #1 in sales growth in its first year.

- ‣ Initiated effective marketing and business planning policies, subsequently adopted region-wide.

- ‣ Developed inexperienced sales representatives to receive numerous honors as Academy winners (top 10% nationwide), two of whom promoted to District Manager.

AS SENIOR SALES CONSULTANT, accountable for marketing and sales development among producers and suppliers in $17 million territory.

- ‣ As Senior Sales Consultant (1995-Present), achieved an 18% rate of sales growth in a static market.
- ‣ As Sales Consultant (1994-1995), achieved 20% gain during first quarter in territory, building sales volume from $3 to $4 million in a one-year period.

EDUCATION

State Polytechnic University

- ‣ Bachelor of Science Degree (1979)
- ‣ Major: Agricultural Business Management
- ‣ Outstanding Senior, School of Agriculture

Professional Development & Continuing Education

- ‣ IBM Leadership Institute
- ‣ Wharton Strategic Marketing
- ‣ Company-sponsored Seminars and Training

◆ ◆ ◆

195

Combination. *Susan Britton Whitcomb, Fresno, California*

This individual was seeking a management position after she had stepped down into a direct sales role with her Fortune 50 company. The writer emphasized sales increases.

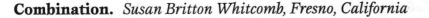

6000 Belleton Way	**William C. Burton**	(000) 000-0000

San Jose, CA 00000

OBJECTIVE: Position utilizing my skills in sales and management of high-end products and graduate degree with emphasis in telecommunications in a major telecommunications company in the Bay area.

EDUCATION: UNIVERSITY OF CALIFORNIA, Los Angeles (UCLA)
M.B.A. Telecommunications, May '91; Courses in Telecommunications Applications & Management, Systems Planning and International Telecommunications.
UNIVERSITY OF CALIFORNIA, Santa Barbara
B.S. Business Administration, 1980

EMPLOYMENT HISTORY:

'91-Present   Territory Manager   MIS-ADVANCEMENT, INC., San Jose, CA
Sold hardware, software and factory communication solutions to auto dealerships throughout Central San Joaquin Valley.   Achieved 126% of gross sales in first year and President's Club in second year. Recognized at the 1992 Western Division Strategy Convention as having "increased territory by 100%."

1989   General Sales Manager   PACIFIC LINCOLN-MERCURY/MAZDA, Sacramento, CA
Responsible for profits of both new and used car divisions.   Trained and supervised sales staff of 12. Succeeded in closing deals on sales and leases which were previously considered lost sales, increasing sales beyond established goals.

'87-'89   General Sales Manager   HARLY LINCOLN-MERCURY, Oakland, CA
Coordinated the finance and insurance department of Harly Motor Sales.   Achieved over $100,000 in finance income with less than 100 cars delivered.   Promoted to G.S.M. one month after hire.   Recruited, trained and motivated sales staff of 12, emphasizing professional sales approaches.   Doubled per car gross income within sixty days.   Maintained consistently high closing ratio and achieved store record sales volume in September '88.   At the same time, supervised extensive customer follow-up, advancing from 17th to top 3 in customer satisfaction of all northern California Lincoln-Mercury dealers.

'86-'87   Finance & Insurance Coordinator/Sales Manager   BELLEVIEW TOYOTA, Chatsworth, CA
Recruited, trained and supervised eight business managers at flagship store.   Introduced a new computer system organization-wide (eight dealerships) and a step sell and package sell concept approaches to Finance and Insurance Department.   Consistently top sales producer from my sales crew.   Improved faltering sales at new Toyota franchise.   Increased sales from 7 to 47 units in the first month, making it the top retail Toyota dealership in the Southwestern United States for October '86.

'82-'85   Branch Manager   AMERICAN FINANCE, A Bank of New York Co., Aristo, CA
Joined growing division of a leading financial services corporation to enhance management skills. Responsible for the 1983 Eastern Region Office of the Year Award with a quarter of a million dollar budget and a staff of five.   Conducted sales presentations to clients, bankers and brokers and enlarged dealer portfolio tenfold.   Introduced new financial service products to spur future investments.

EDUCATIONAL RECOGNITION:
National Communications Association (NCA) Telecommunications Scholarship Recipient '92-'93.
Dean's List '79; Edward Bennett Award for Outstanding Athletic and Scholastic Ability '79.

ADDITIONAL TRAINING:
IBM Strategic Sales Training, Chicago, Illinois
Tom Hopkins International Advanced Sales Training, Los Angeles, California
Total Quality Management Training, Phase I and II, San Francisco, California
Bank of New York, Effective Leadership Program, San Francisco, California
Dale Carnegie Sales Course, Anaheim, California

Additional work experience at various auto dealerships in sales, sales management and business operations.

196

Chronological (Before). *Susan Britton Whitcomb, Fresno, California*

Narrow margins make room for a wealth of material, but it worked against this person because most of it drew attention to his "car salesman" experience.

WILLIAM C. BURTON

1111 Belleton Way
San Jose, California 94444
Voice Mail: (800) 222-2222, ext. 2222

EXPERTISE

Sales ▪ Sales Management ▪ Business Development ▪ Account Retention

PROFESSIONAL EXPERIENCE

MIS-Advancement, Inc., San Jose, California   6/90 - Present

TERRITORY MANAGER

Manage $1.6 million sales territory, generating new business and maximizing existing account sales for largest international supplier of data processing technology. Make sales presentations for capital expenditures which exceed $100,000 per sale; present ROI analysis and schematic configurations; obtain buy-in from multiple departments. As technical specialist, consult management on applications for Xenix-based operating system with new technology for multi-user groups of up to 90 including system configuration and interface for 20 software applications.

- Doubled territory volume, generating increase from $800,000 to $1,600,000.
- Produced 126% of quota in just nine months of FY 1991/92.
- Earned membership in President's Club, exceeding corporate directives in FY 1992/93.
- Achieved 100% of quota to date for FY 1993/94.
- Selected among nine Territory Managers as representative to attend customer trade show in New York.

EDUCATION

M.B.A., Telecommunications, University of California, Los Angeles (UCLA)
- Partial list of coursework includes Telecommunications Applications and Management, Systems Planning, and International Telecommunications.
- International Communications Association Telecommunications Scholarship Recipient.

B.S., Business Administration, University of California, Santa Barbara

SPECIALIZING TRAINING

IBM Strategic Sales Training, Chicago, Illinois
Tom Hopkins International Advanced Sales Training, Los Angeles, California
Total Quality Management Training, Phase I and II, San Francisco, California
Bank of America, Effective Leadership Program, San Francisco, California
Dale Carnegie Sales Course, Anaheim, California

PRIOR EXPERIENCE

Financed M.B.A. coursework through concurrent full-time employment in Sales/Management. Prior career highlights include:

- Three years in branch management for American Finance, a Bank of New York Company, earning Eastern Region Office of the Year Award for profits and growth;
- Achieved record sales volume, won regional customer satisfaction award, and ranked as top producing unit in various retail sales management responsibilities.

197

Combination (After). *Susan Britton Whitcomb, Fresno, California*

An example in which "less is more." The writer cut much of the material, focused on the person's current experience and MBA, and delivered a far more marketable resume.

Confidential
Professional Resume

ADAM MYLES

Objective: Director of Sales / Marketing / Key Account Management

Qualifications

- 8 years of sales in financial accounting, tax preparation, distribution, and payroll / human resources software
- skilled in facilitation, generation of new leads, canvassing, and referral networks
- formation of strategic alliances with outside consultants nationwide and management of key account relationships
- development of individualized presentations for each new account relying on strong negotiation, closing, and troubleshooting skills
- high achiever, with numerous awards as Top Sales Producer
- preparation of monthly new business forecasts and annual business plans
- willing to travel or relocate

Education and Personal Development

- University of Wisconsin at Madison
  - BS in Economics, with minor in Finance and Mathematics — 1987
  - MBA — 8 credit hours
- Specialized software training programs
  - HR, payroll, accounting, tax preparation and MRP II manufacturing
- H&R Block Tax Prep (ranked #2 in class) ▸ SPIN Selling Workshop
- Series 7 Certification earned via self-study program

198

Combination. *Beverley Drake, Rochester, Minnesota*

"A resume chock full of statistics, awards, and accomplishments." It looks different because it *is* different. It has a title, which is placed above the name of the person. Other contact

Adam Myles, 411 Dringler Road, Milwaukee, Wisconsin 50000

(414) 555-0000

Sales & Marketing Professional

- very strong communication, presentation, and leadership skills
- completed 5 semesters college-level Spanish
- advocate of team building, cross training, and employee empowerment
- knowledgeable regarding needs of the changing workplace of the '90s: flexibility, work ethics, cost reduction, quality, project teams, MRP II
- aggressive sales rep / manager inspired by challenge

Technology Skills

- AS/400 software systems ▶ Programming in FORTRAN and BASIC
- PC Windows and DOS environments, including Lotus, PC Tools, Executive Information Systems

Sales and Marketing Experience

REGIONAL SALES ACCOUNT MANAGER   1993 to present

FAMOUS DATA, INC. (Anytown, WI) — a $14 million company listed in "The Hidden Job Market" as one of the fastest growing companies in Wisconsin; well-known for application software for AS/400 computers (MRP II systems; purchasing; order entry; inventory management; financial accounting; payroll; human resources; and PC executive information systems).

Achievements and Oversight
- numerous awards include: 2 Eagle awards for 1994 and 1995 monthly sales in excess of $100K; "Salesperson of the Month" 3 times; 2nd highest company sales in 1995 with revenue increase of 27%; "Rookie of the Year" in 1994 for $263K sales revenue (a record in the company for non-manufacturing software)
- licensed sales representative for payroll, financial, HR, and distribution software
- direct the activities of sales and support personnel
- assisted in development of training coursework for new hires in company

ACCOUNT REPRESENTATIVE   1990 to 1993

COMPUTER SOFTWARE GROUP (Largetown, WI) — known worldwide for top-level PC-LAN tax prep software for accounting and law firms.

Achievements and Oversight
- 1991-92, ranked #1 as Division Sales Representative (out of 12 sales reps in 3 states) and #4 out of 130 nationwide sales reps
- scored 2nd highest on tax preparation course
- managed $900K territory in Wisconsin and Michigan's Upper Peninsula

SALES REPRESENTATIVE   1987 to 1990

BIG FINANCIAL GROUP (Captown, WI) — a brokerage subsidiary of Otherstate Life Insurance with sales of mutual funds, group life, and disability insurance.

Achievements and Oversight
- opened 2nd office in Noted Bank as a result of developing successful financial planning / marketing strategies for executive clientele
- honored in 1988 among approximately 300 1st yr. rookies for top 5% new sales nationwide
- earned status as "resident expert" with company's financial planning software

Personal Interests

golf ▶ guitar ▶ skiing ▶ tennis ▶ softball and volleyball leagues

---

information is put at the top of page 2. The four-line "bar" looks gray rather than black, giving the resume some "color." The Objective is above the bar rather than below it. Small, light, sans serif type contrasts with the large bold headings, and so on, and so on.

confidential

N. Jonathan Coster

1715 Normand Drive
Memphis, Tennessee 37100

✆ [615] 555-5555
njcoster@msn.com

WHAT I BRING TO EDUTECH AS A **DIRECTOR OF SALES AND TRAINING:**

✦ **Skill** that penetrates and holds tough new markets.

✦ **Experience** that guides people to higher goals.

✦ **Knowledge** that keeps production costs low.

RECENT WORK HISTORY WITH EXAMPLES OF SUCCESS:

✦ June 96 – Present: **National Sales Manager**, Education Technology, Plano, Texas
Education Technology is the national leader in bringing the newest technologies into the educational market. Annual sales projection: $2M.

  ✦ Report directly to CEO. Supervise 20 sales professionals.

  ✦ Hired away by president to build national sales force from scratch. Single-handedly created our marketing plan, budgets, territories, quotas, cost of sales, pricing, sales manual, and presentations. *Payoffs:* Twenty sales professionals **covering 33 states in just 90 days.**

  ✦ Penetrated market dominated by single competitor who enjoyed 18-month lead. We were unknowns. Our products cost four times his. *Payoffs:* **Beating sales projections by 20%.** Now at 70% of quota despite late start in very short buying season.

  ✦ Expanded our market vertically through strong presentations to senior executives and administrators. *Payoffs:* **Customers'** central decision makers now **"pre-selling"** our products and services.

✦ November 89 – June 96: **District Manager,** Reference Division *promoted to* **Midwest Sales Manager,** Electronic Learning Division *promoted to* **Southeastern Regional Manager,** Instructional Materials Division, Encyclopaedia Britannica Educational Corporation, Chicago, Illinois
Britannica is the former global industry leader in reference materials for libraries and media centers. Annual sales: $35M.

  ✦ Sold new curriculum products at 10 times the unit cost of "tried and true" traditional materials offered by competitors. Proved cost-per-student attractive. Positioned our lines as key to the Federal and state funding on which our customers lived. Increased student achievement and boosted teacher efficiency. *Payoffs:* **Beat** as many as **15 competitors to win large sales** in three of four state adoption presentations.

  ✦ Turned around sales in economically depressed territory after seven other professionals failed to make their goals for five years. Targeted the right market segments. *Payoffs:* Topped six other publishers. Made sales targets and **sold entire catalog** product line. My first job in educational sales.

✦ February 86 – November 89: **Director of Admissions**, Southeastern Paralegal Institute, Nashville, Tennessee
Southeastern Paralegal is the only school in the Southeast sanctioned by the American Bar Association.

  ✦ Built admissions department from the ground up. Coordinated placement of our students as interns with prospective employers. *Payoffs:* **Increased enrollment 333%.**

confidential

199

Combination. *Provided by Don Orlando, Montgomery, Alabama*

Another resume in which you can learn much by studying it. The word *confidential* in the top- and bottom-left corners and the phone symbol are early signs that this resume is special. The

confidential

| N. Jonathan Coster | Director of Sales and Training | [615] 555-5555 |

ADDITIONAL WORK EXPERIENCE:

◆ January 84 – February 86: **Director of Admissions, Corporate Programs Administrator** and Faculty Member, Davidson Educational Center, Nashville Tennessee

◆ May 83 – Feb 84: **Field Representative**, United States Chamber of Commerce, Washington, D.C.

◆ May 81 – May 83: **Institutional Sales Manager** and **Operations Manager,** Page and Taylor's Sporting Goods, Clarksville, Tennessee

◆ Aug 76 – May 81: **Academic Department Head** and Assistant Athletic Director, Houston County School System, Erin, Tennessee

AWARDS:

◆ Seven consecutive memberships in President's Club (120% of sales goals) or Honors Club (110% of goals), Encyclopaedia Britannica Educational Corporation.

◆ "Rookie of the Year" for highest grossing new salesperson, Encyclopaedia Britannica Educational Corporation.

◆ Five time winner as "Instructor of the Quarter," Davidson Educational Center.

PROFESSIONAL DEVELOPMENT AND EDUCATION:

◆ Management Internship, Encyclopaedia Britannica, 91 – 92 *Chosen by VP for Corporate Planning as one of five from 300 eligibles to be groomed for more managerial responsibility.*

◆ **Practica for College Recruiting Professionals**, College Administrators' Institute, Harvard University, Boston, Massachusetts, 86 – 87 *Passed competitive examination and interviews to attend this program fully paid by my employer.*

◆ Pursued M.S., **Educational Administration**, Appalachian State University, Boone, North Carolina, **GPA 3.8**, 78 – 79

◆ Pursued M.S., **Educational Administration**, Austin Peay State University, Clarksville, Tennessee, 76 – 78

◆ B.S., **History** and **English** (double major), Middle Tennessee State University, Murfreesboro, Tennessee, **cum laude**, 76

COMPUTER LITERACY:

◆ Expert: Internet search techniques, Decide Right (decision analysis software), MAC OS, Write Now, Inspiration, Publish It Now, MultiMedia Level III

◆ Proficient: HTML, Java, Winsock, Excel, Windows 3.x, Windows 95, ACT!, Word for Windows, WordPerfect 6.1, Quicken, MS Money, PowerPoint

SPECIAL SKILLS

◆ Strong background in technical writing and the drafting of educational proposals and grant applications

confidential

Page two

headings are special. The bullets are special. The italic comments about each firm are special: they don't just say something about the firm but indicate how it is *significant*. The use of *payoffs* for achievements is special. . . . The resume is fresh in every way.

Charles Kane

165 Pleasant Avenue
Bayonne, NJ 00000
(201) 555-5555

✦✦✦ CAREER FOCUS ✦✦✦

International marketing or **traffic management** position for a manufacturer, wholesale distributor or high volume retailer. Willing to travel and/or relocate.

✦✦✦ QUALIFICATIONS ✦✦✦

Import/Export Operations

- ✦ Knowledge of worldwide origination points for all types of goods and the movement process through multiple trade lanes, including the Far East, Europe, Middle East, South America and Canada.
- ✦ Experience with the operational documentation procedures and regulatory compliance required to clear shipments through United States Customs.

Pricing and Contract Negotiations

- ✦ Instrumental in negotiating mutually beneficial contracts for any type of material being shipped to the United States from foreign ports.
- ✦ Skilled in marketing cost effective, timely and hassle-free cargo movement services to and from distributors abroad, including the pricing of oversized shipments.
- ✦ Proven capability as intermediary to facilitate the opening of overseas markets for domestic manufacturers.

Customer Service Management

- ✦ Strongly committed to quality in every aspect of internal and external customer service.
- ✦ Expertise in managing both people and projects, with the vision to strategize the action steps needed to attain long and short term goals.
- ✦ Confident team leader, successful in developing and motivating a culturally diverse administrative staff to work cooperatively by promoting open lines of communication.
- ✦ Recognized for maintaining working relationships built on trust and respect with numerous industry contacts, thereby contributing to profitability in a highly competitive market.

Technical Liaison

- ✦ Interface with systems staff to provide information from a management standpoint for the development of advanced capabilities, most notably: customer activity tracking; follow-through on complaints and inquiries; and acceleration of response to sales leads.
- ✦ Familiarity with the various features of the Microsoft Office suite for Windows to create text and graphic materials for management presentations.

200

Combination. *Melanie A. Noonan, West Paterson, New Jersey*

The individual wanted a career change. He had worked eight years for a major overseas shipping line, had learned all about imports and how exports find their way to foreign markets, and

Charles Kane

Page 2

✦✦✦ EMPLOYMENT ✦✦✦

AQUATERRA CONTAINER LINES, INC., Port Newark, NJ   1988 to Date
U.S. headquarters of one of world's largest transoceanic shipping companies.

Career Progression

SENIOR MANAGER, CLIENT RELATIONS	1994 to Date
MANAGER, PAN AMERICAN MARKETS	1992 to 1993
MARKET ANALYST, EUROPEAN GROUP	1991 to 1992
MARKET ANALYST, HONG KONG/TAIWAN	1989 to 1991
PRICING AND DOCUMENTATION REPRESENTATIVE	1988 to 1989

Accountabilities and Accomplishments

✦ Monitored daily activity of high volume accounts that generated at least $1 million in revenue per year. Opened and personally oversaw import activities for leading manufacturers of toys, consumer electronics and athletic footwear.
  ▷ Marketed target accounts to be pursued by sales representatives.
  ▷ Developed all pricing from U.S. East Coast to Far East destinations.
  ▷ Prepared weekly management reports of sales activities in targeted areas, which also included recommendations to overcome operational weaknesses.
  ▷ Submitted proposals considered feasible to management for consideration and allocation of funds.
✦ Supervised the service center with staff of 17 engaged in receiving and shipping cargo, documentation, waybilling, assessing charges, and collecting fees for shipments. Set their goals, motivated them to exceed performance standards, and supported their career development.
  ▷ Received departmental recognition by the company as its benchmark work group for maintaining a high morale and low turnover rate.
  ▷ Established improvements in communications between corporate staff, service center and outside sales force, which corrected serious inconsistencies with information flow.
  ▷ Developed new procedures for tariff rate filings to circumvent the obstacles caused by non filed rates.
✦ Effected staffing changes brought about by company's reorganization from regional to centralized functions early in 1994.
  ▷ Headed the work group to facilitate the adoption of the AquaTerra Quality System, based on the Philip Crosby Quality Awareness Program.
  ▷ Trained over 50 employees in the various modules of the process.
  ▷ Organized a committee to recognize individual employee contributions.

✦✦✦ EDUCATION ✦✦✦

Fairleigh Dickinson University, Teaneck, NJ
B.S. in Business Management, May 1988

believed that he could help manufacturers participate in the global economy. The writer used a double-line page border, stylized diamond bullets, and open triangle sub-bullets for interest. She used bullets in the headings to suggest ocean waves.

FLORENCE ADAMS
REGISTERED PHARMACIST

999 N. Overlook Street
Camden, MD 21601
(999) 999-9999

OBJECTIVE

Pharmaceutical sales position with Bayview Medicals in the Camden, MD district.

SUMMARY OF QUALIFICATIONS

- Over 40 years experience as a Registered Pharmacist.
- Ten years business management experience.
- In-depth knowledge of Bayview products.
- In-depth knowledge of competing pharmaceutical products.
- Thorough understanding of product differences in pharmaceuticals.
- Thorough understanding of the flow of pharmaceutical products from manufacturer to consumer.
- Excellent interpersonal and communications skills.
- Establishes excellent rapport with physicians and other health care professionals.
- Highly motivated, goal directed individual.

PROFESSIONAL BACKGROUND

JOHNSON'S DRUG STORE, CAMDEN, MD   5/92 to present
Pharmacist/Manager Governor's Lane Pharmacy

WINTER'S PHARMACY, CAMDEN, MD   7/82 to 5/92
Owner/Manager/Pharmacist

UNIVERSITY OF NEW YORK, TROY, NY   1972 to 1975
Guest Lecturer, Senior Nursing--Medical Surgical Course

GOODFELLOWS HOSPITAL, TROY, NY   1959 to 1964
Registered Pharmacist

NEW YORK PHYSICIANS APOTHECARY, HAMPTON, NY   1958 to 1959
Resistered Pharmacist

DENTON APOTHECARY, DENTON, FL   1956 to 1958
Registered Pharmacist

WELLS-FARGO DRUG CO., WELLS FARGO, IL   1953 to 1956
Registered Pharmacist

EDUCATION

UNIVERSITY OF NORTH CARLONIA, WINCHESTER,NC   1953
Bachelor of Science, Pharmacy

OTHER

- Currently holds Registered Pharmacist licenses in Maryland and New York.
- Previously served on the Drug Utilization Committee of New York.

201

Combination. *Thomas E. Spann, Easton, Maryland*

The vertical line looks gray, making the page seem two-color. Compared to the tiny section headings, the text looks more important. The Summary avoids repetitive job descriptions.

Technology/
Engineering/Science

Resumes at a Glance

WALTER ROBERTS
P.O. Box 1234
Hawthorne, Nevada 00000

555-555-5555

QUALIFICATION
SUMMARY

More than five years experience in most phases of domestic and foreign automobile maintenance and repair.

TOOLS/
EQUIPMENT

Hand Tools	Gauges	Test Meters
Vacuum Tester	Pressure Tester	Voltmeter
Hydraulic Jack	Drill Press	Lathe
Chassis Aligner	Acetylene Torch	Misc. Power Tools

EXPERIENCE

- ❏ Perform tune-ups: remove and replace or adjust spark plugs, points, coil/alternator.
- ❏ Replace defective chassis parts: shock absorbers, ball joint suspension, brake shoes, and wheel bearings.
- ❏ Inspect, test and repair cooling systems.
- ❏ Repair and overhaul brake systems, replacing brake shoe units or attaching new brake linings. Repair and replace leaky brake cylinders.
- ❏ Repair and adjust carburetors: test needle valves, repair or replace defective parts, reassemble carburetor and gas filter and install.
- ❏ Align wheels, axles, frames, torsion bars, and steering mechanisms. Straighten axles and steering rods. Adjust shims, tie rods, and joining pins to align wheels.
- ❏ Remove, repair, and replace transmission and clutch assemblies.
- ❏ Rebuild domestic and imported engines.

WORK
HISTORY

1991 - Present	Mike's Auto Service	Hawthorn, Nevada
1994 - 1996	Auto Experts	Hawthorn, Nevada

EDUCATION

1991 - 1993	Desert Sands Vocational Skills Center
	Automotive Technology
	CAD Training
	Computer Programming
1993	Sierra High School (Graduate), Hawthorn, Nevada

202

Combination. *Lonnie L. Swanson, Poulsbo, Washington*

This person—having technical experience but lacking confidence—did not want to look "too good" and just wanted something basic. Without being fancy, the resume shows his worth.

Charlie A. Brown
9999 Channel Loop Road
Wilmington, North Carolina 28409
910-123-4567

OBJECTIVE A position as a **Machinist** with proven ability to generate products that meet or exceed specifications within very tight tolerances. Nearly three years experience machining both metal and plastic.

SKILLS CNC and manual milling machines and lathes
Blueprint Reading
Micrometers
Dial Calipers
Intra Micrometers
Height Gauge
Go No Go Gauges
Optical Comparator
Maintain safe working environment

EXPERIENCE *Quality Machines*, Wilmington, NC
Machinist - August 1994 to Present
Set up and operate manual and CNC milling machines and lathes. Lead person for cross-drill department.

Acme Machine Shop, Leland, NC
Machinist (Temporary/Part-Time) - August 1993 to December 1993
Contract machining of replacement and custom parts for manufacturing companies.

Machines Inc., Wilmington, NC
Machinist - September 1992 to July 1993
Set up and operated manual and CNC milling machines and lathes to manufacture plastic parts for fitness center equipment. Ensured parts were to specifications by using precision measuring instruments.

Construction & Machines Corporation, Leland, NC
Fork Lift Operator - June 1990 to June 1991
Transported raw materials to storage areas using fork lift.

EDUCATION *Cape Fear Community College*, Wilmington, NC
Diploma in Machining Technology - August 1992

Courses included:
Machine Shop Math   Algebra
Trigonometry   Blueprint Reading

REFERENCES Provided upon request

203

Combination. *Sandy Adcox Saburn, Wilmington, North Carolina*

A strong Objective and Skills section are supported by the strong Experience section. A manager of a well-known international firm liked the resume and gave "Charlie" the job.

JAMES D. JOYNER

22222 SPICER ROAD • CHEVY CHASE, MD • 11111• (000) 999-9999

Occupational Objective	*A position as a maintenance mechanic/industrial mechanic.*

Career Highlights

In the U.S. Navy, repeatedly commended for superior performance of duties during normal operating conditions, and during Operational Propulsion Plant Examinations. At Easton Memorial Hospital, received letter of appreciation for Outstanding Performance from Director of Plant Operations. Consistently cited for outstanding troubleshooting and problem solving skills in the repair and maintenance of high capacity boilers. Recognized in evaluations for ability to effectively supervise and train personnel

Experience

SMITH'S CONTROLS, CHEVY CHASE, MD   5/96 TO PRESENT
Maintenance Mechanic
> Responsible for all building maintenance and repair. Perform preventative maintenance and corrective maintenance on HVAC and electrical systems. Responsible for the upkeep of all outside grounds areas.

BLADES TESTING AND BALANCING, HARDY, MD   6/95 TO 10/95
Air Balance Apprentice
> Duties included setting up new and existing HVAC equipment. Adjusting the air handlers for proper CFMs and static pressures.

GOOD CARE HOSPITAL, EASTON, MD   4/90 TO 2/95
HVAC Mechanic, Stationery Engineer 1st Grade
> Responsible for the operation, preventative maintenance and repair of all air handling units, pumps, boilers, steam traps and cooling towers. Recorded temperatures, humidity, and operating pressures. Made adjustments on environment controls. Tested condenser water and boiler/feedwater. Inspected mechanical and electrical equipment.

UNITED STATES NAVY, USS MERRIMACK (AO-179), FPO, NEW YORK   9/86 TO 3/90
Boiler Technician/Fireroom Supervisor BT-3
> Responsible for the safe operation of two 600 lb. top-fired, watertube boilers. Additional duties included supervision of the Division's Valve Maintenance Program and analysis/testing of power plant fuel and boiler feedwater. Performed preventative maintenance on boilers, pumps, forced draft blowers, de-aerating feed tanks, condensers, ejectors and heat exchangers. Supervised crew of four technicians. (Honorably discharged 1/94).

Education/ Special Training

MARYLAND STATE BOARD OF EXAMINING ENGINEERS	1994
Successfully completed requirements for 1st Grade Engineer license	
SMITH'S CONTROLS, INC., ORLANDO, FL	1994
DSC-8500 Operations/Troubleshooting Course	
SMITH'S CONTROLS, INC., SALISBURY, MD	1991
Automatic Temperature Control, Basic Course	
U.S. NAVY FLEET TRAINING CENTER, NEWPORT, RI	1989
Engineering Training School	
U.S. NAVY FLEET TRAINING CENTER, NORFOLK, VA	1989
Basic Boilerwater/Feedwater Testing School	
U.S. NAVY ATLANTIC FLEET SCHOOLSHIP	1989
Engineering Training Team	
U.S. NAVAL PROPULSION ENGINEERING SCHOOL, GREAT LAKES, IL	1986
Boiler Technician "A" Course, Service School Command	
CAROLINE COUNTY VOCATIONAL SCHOOL, RIDGLEY, MD	1985
Graduated, Auto Mechanic	

204

Combination. *Thomas E. Spann, Easton, Maryland*

The thick-thin page border lends authority to the resume even before you read it. The Career Highlights section presents achievements. Indented paragraphs show duties.

MARY C. ADAMS   3333 MILLS VALLEY RD. • HAYES, MD 00000 • (000) 000-0000

SUMMARY OF KEY
QUALIFICATIONS

- Twelve years experience in industrial electrolysis.
- Received "Perfect Attendance Awards", 1991-1995.
- Distinguished service record in the U.S. Army Reserves.
- Consistently cited by superiors for outstanding job performance.
- Excellent supervisory and interpersonal skills.
- Reliable and dependable team player.

EXPERIENCE

RANKIN TECHNOLOGIES, HAYES, MD   4/84 TO PRESENT
Electrolysis Plater - Group Leader

Performs electrolysis plating functions, in addition to supervising crew of six factory workers responsible for cooper, gold, nickel and silver plating of micro circuits, relays, switches, breakers and other electronic components. Operates ultrasonic circuit machine. Promoted to position of group leader after nine years of plating experience. Group Leader duties include:

- Preparing daily and weekly work assignments.
- Conducting monthly crew meetings.
- Attending Group Leader meetings.
- Conducting feedback sessions with crew members.
- Providing coaching and counseling for crew members.
- Conducting annual performance evaluations.
- Writing employee reprimands as needed.
- Processing time sheets and time cards.
- Preparing weekly summary reports for management.

PRICE'S FAMILY RESTAURANT, INC., RUSTON, MD   1/84 TO 4/84
Cashier/Waitress

EDUCATION/
SPECIAL
TRAINING

LOMA COLLEGE, ROLLE, CA
Coursework in English, Math, History, 1993

PINEHURST HIGH SCHOOL, PINEHURST, CA
Graduated, general diploma, 1982

RANKINTECHNOLOGIES, HAYES, MD
Training Courses:
   "Design of Experiments: The Taguchi Method", 1994
   "Basic Statistical Process Control", 1992
   "Precision Measurements", 1989
   "Reading Electronic Blueprints", 1987

NATIONAL SEMINARS GROUP, BALTIMORE, MD
Training Course:
   "How to Deal with Difficult People", 1996

UNIVERSITY OF PENNSYLVANIA, COLLEGE PARK, PA
Training Course:
   "Hazardous Materials Awareness" (1992) administered by the Pennsylvania Fire and
   Rescue Institute.

MILITARY

UNITED STATES ARMY RESERVES   10/87 TO 11/95
Served in the 109th Service and Supply Battalion, Essex, DE. Successfully completed training course in "Tactical Telecommunications Center Operations". Awarded U.S. Army Commendation Medals in 1987and 1988. Honorably discharged, 1995.

205

Combination. *Thomas E. Spann, Easton, Maryland*

The vertical bar points to the individual's name in small caps. Small caps are used also in the rest of the contact information, the section headings, and the firms and institutions.

HAROLD C. HOPPES, JR.
160 South Main Street
Milltown, New Jersey 08850
(908) 846-5487

OBJECTIVE: To obtain a position as an Electronic Technician/Troubleshooter utilizing my extensive experience in repair and maintenance of production equipment.

SUMMARY:
- Quality Control
- PLC Design
- Circuit and Software Testing
- Corrective Actions and Redesign
- Training and Supervision of Assemblers
- Field Service and Repair

EXPERIENCE:

1981-Present **RELIANCE ELECTRIC COMPANY**, Edison, NJ

1988-Present **Electronic Technician**

- Involved with implementation of custom specifications for AC and DC variable speed motor drives.
- Work directly with application and control engineers to work up schematics and specifications.
- Test functionality to precisely meet customer requirements.
- Extensive involvement with quality control and assurance.
- Final testing and inspection of all completed drives.
- Document all changes using CAD system.
- Update all new test procedures to take advantage of greater precision and speed of testing equipment.
- Make field modifications to existing customer equipment.

1981-1988 **Electro-Mechanical Assembler**

- Built complete control systems for AC and DC motor controls.
- Performed diverse and complex operations for a full range of products.
- Promoted to Electronic Technician because of recognized capabilities.

1980-1981 **CONTINENTAL CONTAINER CORP.**, Piscataway, NJ
Line Maintenance Mechanic

- Responsible for maintenance and repair of plastic blow molding and extrusion machinery.
- Supervised machine operators and directed their production.
- Managed material handlers to ensure continuous production.

EDUCATION: Received ongoing training and attended seminars given by Reliance Electric.

Middlesex County College, Edison, NJ
Completed 2 courses in Electrical Engineering, 1988

Middlesex County Vocational-Technical High School, East Brunswick, NJ
Successfully completed classes in basic electrical fundamentals, residential and commercial wiring, and blueprint reading, 1985-1986.

206

Combination. *Beverly Baskin, Marlboro, New Jersey*

If you read a resume from the bottom up, as in this resume, you gain a sense of the development of an individual in a field and why he is ready for the goal in the Objective.

LANCE A. MATHIAS

Post Office Box 55555
Fremont, California 55555

(555) 555-5555

SUMMARY OF QUALIFICATIONS

HIGHLY SKILLED HVAC TECHNICIAN offering 20 years' diverse experience including:

❏ Installation, troubleshooting, overhaul, and repair of computer-regulated environmental control systems for residential, commercial, and industrial establishments (A/C units ranging from ½-ton to 250-ton chillers).

❏ Supervised apprentice level air conditioning and refrigeration maintenance workers and electricians.

❏ Experienced and certified to instruct community college classes in air conditioning, refrigeration, and heating.

❏ Successful business experience owning and managing an air conditioning and heating repair business.

PROFESSIONAL EXPERIENCE

MATHIAS MAINTENANCE, Pasadena, CA   1986-Present

HVAC Technician / Principal

Built new business from start-up to sales in excess of $300,000. Provide design, installation, repair, and maintenance services for air conditioning, refrigeration, and heating systems. Sourced and secured service contracts with major educational institutions, government agencies, regional shopping malls, and manufacturing companies.

CAL WEST TECHNICAL COLLEGE, Pasadena, CA   1982-Present

Instructor - Air Conditioning, Refrigeration & Heating

Teach course providing basic theory and hands-on experience in installing, troubleshooting, and repairing environmental control systems.

ENVIRONMENTAL-AIR, Cambria, CA   1974-1986

Air Conditioning / Refrigeration Maintenance Technician

Installed, repaired, and performed preventative maintenance on commercial and large, complex industrial systems. Also held position as Electrician.

EDUCATION

CAL WEST TECHNICAL COLLEGE, Pasadena, California

- **Certificate in Air Conditioning Technology**
- **Graduated with 4.0 GPA**

❏ ❏ ❏

207

Combination. *Susan Britton Whitcomb, Fresno, California*

The tool graphic is distinctive and provides marketing appeal. The person was using this resume as part of an application for a bank loan. The writer therefore puts $300,000 first.

Thomas R. Breedveld

8666 Marsh Drive, Zeeland, MI 49464 • Day Phone: 555-000-0022, Evening Phone: 555-222-5522

Professional Profile

▪ 9 years successful sales experience with major sound and audio equipment retailers; excellent working knowledge of a wide range of consumer electronic products; 10 years experience as Sound Technician and Technical Director over 25-30 technicians:

   ▸ currently in charge of *state-of-the-art* audio/visual operations for 5,000 seat and 1,800 seat auditoriums; supervise operation of 56 channel sound mixer to include, CD players; tape players; graphic equalizers; amplifiers; VCRs; and systems for reverberation, special effects, mixing, and time aligning and delay; hands-on experience in troubleshooting, maintenance, and setup of technical equipment and accessories; demonstrated ability to pinpoint problems and initiate creative and workable solutions.

Technical Service

▪ Experienced in the installation of technical equipment for special projects and presentations; integrate the use of lighting, sound, and visuals for maximum front-of-the-house effectiveness.

   ▸ perform board- and component level repairs and maintenance; strong diagnostic abilities; can take items from initial testing and analysis through complete restoration to manufacturers' specifications; *accomplishments include*: technical installation and troubleshooting of off-site auditorium production involving 110 voice choir and 45 piece orchestra; presently oversee annual holiday productions and approximately 3 musical dramas per year; serve as "intro" announcer for Church services recordings.

Organizational Skills

▪ Supervise work crews and coordinate work schedules for Church Technical Volunteers; answer technical questions related to equipment installation and use.

   ▸ have trained service and volunteer personnel in equipment handling, maintenance, operation, and systems interface; coordinated efforts for planning, selection, purchase, and installation of audio and video components for First Assembly of God 5,000 seat auditorium; coordinated efforts with consultants, technical experts, and support crews; functioned as Video Engineer to ensure proper integration and arrangement of sound and camera networks.

Communications & Interpersonal Abilities

   ▸ Experienced and organized with demonstrated ability to successfully supervise large crews performing numerous responsibilities.
   ▸ Ability to coordinate assignments within a technical environment; exceptional follow-through from concept to finished project.
   ▸ Excellent human relations skills with the ability to develop and maintain sound working relationships with all contacts.
   ▸ Strong belief in quality workmanship and the desire to "do things right the first time."

Work History

1990-Pres.	**Technical Director.**	First Assembly of God, Wyoming, MI.
1985-1990.	**Production Coordinator.**	First Assembly of God, Wyoming, MI.
1984-1985.	**Volunteer, Sound Technician.**	First Assembly of God, Wyoming, MI.
1982-1984.	**Production Supervisor.**	Kessler, Inc., Grand Rapids, MI.
1979-1982.	**Sales/Technical Service Writer.**	Sound Room, Grand Rapids, MI.
1976-1979.	**Sales Manager.**	Electronic Sound, Grand Rapids, MI.
1973-1976.	**Sales Assistant.**	Steketees Audio, Grand Rapids, MI.

Education/Training

   ▸ San Diego County College, San Diego, CA. Liberal Arts studies, 2 years.
   Numerous technical seminars with NAM: National Association of Music Manufacturers.

Computer Experience

   ▸ MAC/IBM computers and graphics/word processing software: Adobe PhotoShop, Macromedia 4.0, MS Word, Teach-Text.

Military Background

   ▸ United States Air Force. Airman First Class; Radio Operator/Non-Morse Intercept Operator. Honorable Discharge.

Memberships

   ▸ Church Technical Directors Association.

208

Combination. *Randy Clair, location unknown*

Small san serif type makes it possible to fit much information into paragraphs and bulleted items. That way, you can get a lot of text on a page and still have white space.

WILLIAM WELDER
P.O. Box 11517
Wilmington, North Carolina 28412
(910) 123-4567

SUMMARY

- 20 years welding/fitting, hands-on and supervisory experience in nuclear, chemical and pulp and paper industries.
- Qualified to the following welding processes and codes: SMAW, GTAW, GMAW, FCAQ, ASME III, VIII, XI, B31.1, AWS D1.1, D1.2 and D1.3. Certified welder for nuclear power and pressure vessels.
- Supervisory skills include supervision of crews from 30 to 120 technicians.
- Trained in welding overlays - recirc piping.

EXPERIENCE

- Coordinate design changes between engineering and construction management.
- Supervise operations of outages - both major shutdowns and weekend outages.
- Install and repair seismic supports as directed by engineering packages.
- Experienced with pre-fabbing jacketed pipe and steam trace lines for products, also with pickle pipe.
- Perform liquid penetrate tests on steam drums.
- Extensive experience with boilers including ripout and replacement of damaged tubes, piping and supports.
- Rebuild catalyst system including relining catalyst tank with carbon cladding and aluminum liner and associated piping modifications.
- Modify drywell and CRD supports.
- Reline hoppers that have been corroded by flash, water from leaking ducts, and expansion joints.

EMPLOYMENT HISTORY

BLUE & GREEN CONSTRUCTION GROUP
POWER PLANT MAINTENANCE
Foreman - Wilmington Plant   1988 - Present
General Foreman - Charlotte Plant   2/93 - 7/93

DECOY CONSTRUCTION COMPANY
Fitter/Leadman - Nuclear Plant - CP&L   7/93 - Present
Foreman/Coordinator - Wilmington Plant   4/92 - 2/93
Welder/Fitter - Raleigh Plant   7/90 - 12/91 & 8/88 - 2/89
Welder/Fitter/Equipment Operator - CP&L   1/85 - 4/86

209

Combination. *Sandy Adcox Saburn, Wilmington, North Carolina*

When in an Employment History many job titles are the same because an individual's specialized skills are needed by many different companies, you can avoid much repetition in job descriptions

WILLIAM WELDER   **PAGE 2**

EMPLOYMENT HISTORY (CONTINUED)

MILNER CONSTRUCTION
Pipe Welder/Fitter - Cobert Industries   2/92 - 4/92

ATLANTIC PAPER
Welder/Fitter   2/90 - 7/90

IRON WORKS
Foreman/Welder   6/89 - 2/90

CAPITAL MAINTENANCE, INC.
Foreman/Welder   3/89 - 6/89 & 2/88 - 6/88

POWER PLANT COMPANY
Foreman/Welder - Pella Power   10/88 - 2/88 & 4/86 - 9/86

MINING AND MILL COMPANY
Foreman/Welder - Atlantic Chemical   6/87 - 9/88

NEW YEAR CONSTRUCTION
Equipment Operator/Fitter   4/83 - 1/85

REFERENCES

Available upon request

if you summarize activities and experience common to the various jobs. Boldfacing helps you to see the different job positions held by this person. Many of them were short-term projects that were finished, instead of signs of job-hopping.

ROBERT L. POPICK
4 Two Bridge Place
Paramus, New Jersey 00000
(201) 555-5555

CAREER OBJECTIVE:

EXPERIENCED ENGINEERING professional seeks a position with advancement opportunities that will utilize acquired skills and experience to contribute to organizational growth. Areas of expertise include:

PROJECT MANAGEMENT • DESIGN DOCUMENTATION • STAFF DEVELOPMENT

PROFILE SUMMARY:

A dedicated and highly energetic professional with a strong background that encompasses various aspects of engineering, design and drafting • Proficient in CAD software, consisting of Futurenet and Orcad (Schematic and Net List Generation) and Generic CAD (Mechanical Drawing) • Adept at providing technical support and developing new processes through successful evaluation and improvement of process performance and profitability • Functions effectively in a team approach to ensure goals are achieved.

PROFESSIONAL EXPERIENCE:

<u>ATERON CORP.</u>   Parsippany, New Jersey
Manager, Engineering Services   *1984 - Present*
- Directs daily design documentation operations for an engineering firm providing automatic test equipment design and consulting services.
- Recruits, trains and develops a staff of drafters, mechanical engineers and computer operators to peak levels of performance.
- Develops and implements drafting standards to ensure adherence with Good Commercial Practices.
- Develops tracking systems for drafting electronic media.
- Maintains purchased software and upgrades all PC's.

Highlights:

- ◆ *Established and implemented a Computer Aided Design capability.*
- ◆ *Instrumental in the conversion of military armored vehicle and tank maintenance manuals to highly sophisticated, computerized, electronic manuals, consisting of over 20,000 scanned drawings.*
- ◆ *Developed a database to track over 30,000 presentation viewgraphs used in marketing campaigns and client instruction courses requiring visual aides.*
- ◆ *Managed the design and packaging of custom electronic test equipment, retailing at up to $2 million.*

210

Combination. *Alesia Benedict, Rochelle Park, New Jersey*

The Profile Summary acquaints the reader with the background and experience of this person. Double-underlining calls attention to company names. Diamond bullets and italic help to make

ROBERT L. POPICK
(555) 555-5555
- Page Two -

PROFESSIONAL EXPERIENCE: continued...

<u>DATASCOPE CORP.</u>   Paramus, New Jersey
Manager, Engineering Services   *1982 - 1984*
- Directed a staff of 12+ professionals in all drafting activities.
- Attended weekly design review meetings.
- Established and instituted drafting priorities and schedules.

Highlights:

- *Chaired Change Review Board; member of Special Products Committee, Product Data Management Committee and Product Safety Committee.*
- *Established and instituted a microfilm file for all drawings.*
- *Developed a CAD/CAM system for printed circuit board design.*

<u>INSTRUMENTATION ENGINEERING</u>   Franklin Lakes, New Jersey
Chief Draftsman   *1968 - 1982*
- Developed and implemented drafting priorities, managing a staff of up to 21 drafters.
- Accountable for reviewing change requests.
- Interfaced extensively with manufacturing and engineering staff.

EDUCATIONAL BACKGROUND:

Newark College of Engineering • Newark, New Jersey
Mechanical Engineering

Regularly attends advanced training in:
drafting electronics, product data management and organizational management

visible achievements in the Highlights sections. The individual did not have a degree, so the writer mentions merely the field of study and then tells of additional training. The impression is that the person continually pursues education.

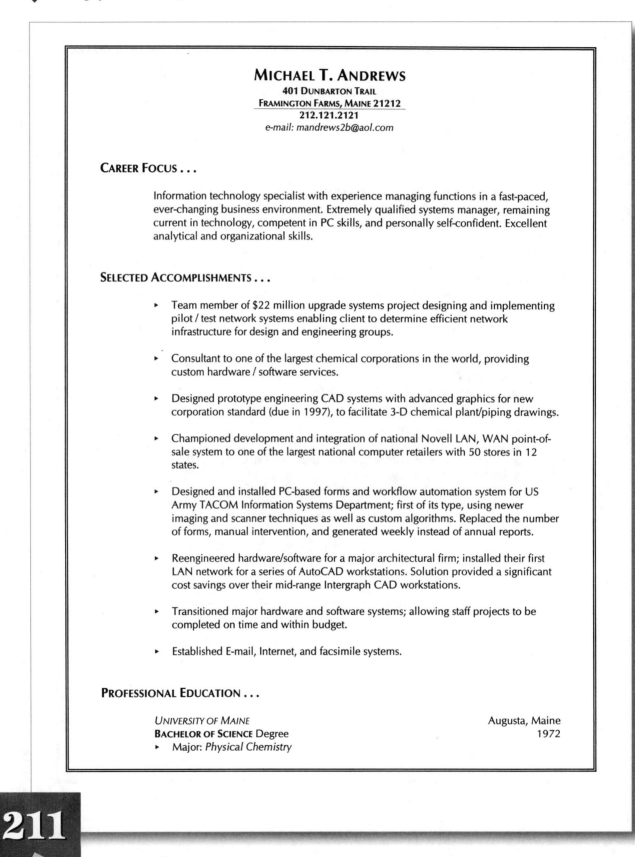

MICHAEL T. ANDREWS
401 DUNBARTON TRAIL
FRAMINGTON FARMS, MAINE 21212
212.121.2121
e-mail: mandrews2b@aol.com

CAREER FOCUS . . .

Information technology specialist with experience managing functions in a fast-paced, ever-changing business environment. Extremely qualified systems manager, remaining current in technology, competent in PC skills, and personally self-confident. Excellent analytical and organizational skills.

SELECTED ACCOMPLISHMENTS . . .

▸ Team member of $22 million upgrade systems project designing and implementing pilot / test network systems enabling client to determine efficient network infrastructure for design and engineering groups.

▸ Consultant to one of the largest chemical corporations in the world, providing custom hardware / software services.

▸ Designed prototype engineering CAD systems with advanced graphics for new corporation standard (due in 1997), to facilitate 3-D chemical plant/piping drawings.

▸ Championed development and integration of national Novell LAN, WAN point-of-sale system to one of the largest national computer retailers with 50 stores in 12 states.

▸ Designed and installed PC-based forms and workflow automation system for US Army TACOM Information Systems Department; first of its type, using newer imaging and scanner techniques as well as custom algorithms. Replaced the number of forms, manual intervention, and generated weekly instead of annual reports.

▸ Reengineered hardware/software for a major architectural firm; installed their first LAN network for a series of AutoCAD workstations. Solution provided a significant cost savings over their mid-range Intergraph CAD workstations.

▸ Transitioned major hardware and software systems; allowing staff projects to be completed on time and within budget.

▸ Established E-mail, Internet, and facsimile systems.

PROFESSIONAL EDUCATION . . .

UNIVERSITY OF MAINE   Augusta, Maine
BACHELOR OF SCIENCE Degree   1972
▸ Major: *Physical Chemistry*

211

Combination. *Lorie Lebert, Novi, Michigan*

A resume for an individual who entered the workforce as a chemistry major but who became savvy with computers in a big way—as an applications user, programmer, systems manager,

EXPERIENCE . . .

TECHNOLOGY ARTS, INC.
CONTRACT PROFESSIONAL, 1996-current
- ▸ Currently assigned to Bell Graham at the Internal Motors Technical Center.
- ▸ Providing systems reengineering and project management skills.

BASF CORPORATION
SENIOR SYSTEMS ENGINEER CONSULTANT, 1992-96
- ▸ Provided LAN, software, and overall systems integration, including design and implementation of several site-wide operational and engineering systems.

INACOMP COMPUTER CENTERS, INC.
MICRO SYSTEMS MANAGER, 1989-92
- ▸ Managed a staff of ten programmers and technicians.
- ▸ Responsible for all design, implementation, and support of headquarters and company-owned stores.

Previous Employment:
CONSULTANT
- ▸ Various contract assignments for programming, sales, support, and technical training for industries / companies including: ABCarr; Phearson, Hegman, and Bolton; O/E Learning Systems; Telbec Corporation; Jones, Gryllisman & Smythe.

TECHNICAL SUMMARY . . .

HARDWARE
- ▸ IBM PC-XT, AT, PS-2; PC clones: Acer, Dell, Gateway, Compaq Systems pro file servers; Apple Macintosh and Apple Talk hubs to server; Intel; WAN gateways; Novell wiring types-Ethernet, ARCnet, Token Ring, Fiber Optic; Network hubs-Synoptics, Thomas Conrad, 3Comm; Mainframe interconnects-VAX Cluster with VMS, HP9000, IBM 36/38/AS400; communication gateways, muxes, and modems.

OPERATING SYSTEMS
- ▸ Windows NT, 95, 3.11; MS DOS 3.1-6.22; Novell 2.15, 3.15, 4.0, 4.1.

LANGUAGES
- ▸ Microsoft Basic, Quick Basic, Visual Basic.

OFFICE AUTOMATION SOFTWARE
- ▸ Microsoft Word, Excel, Access, PowerPoint, Mail; Q&A, WordPerfect; Lotus 1-2-3; Paradox; Harvard Graphics; Aldus PageMaker; Phone Line; Perform Form and Filler; Corrective Action; Math CAD; Engineering Aid.

CAD SYSTEMS
- ▸ Microstation; Autosketch; AutoCAD.

INTERNET AND INTRANET
- ▸ Netscape; Web page creation using HTML script and Hot Dog.

UTILITIES
- ▸ Norton Utilities; Cross Talk; Irwin, Emerald, and Mountain tape back-up systems; X.25 gateway and routers; Hewlett Packard printer/scanner configurations; CD ROM catalog systems; Rumba; PC Emulation.

systems engineer, network installer, and so on. The Selected Accomplishments section is an indication that this individual is a high achiever. The reference to an IBM PC-XT in the Technical Summary shows early acquaintance with PCs.

Steven P. Weston

8425 North Division Street ▪ Appleton, Wisconsin 54911
414/784–7548

Qualifications Overview

- Instrumental in reversing a manufacturing company to a profit position in a one-year period.
- Successfully marketed quality/productivity improvement software to Fortune 1000 companies.
- Domestic and international manufacturing and industrial engineering management experience.
- Demonstrated skills in motivation, team-building, problem solving, and management.

Professional Experience

XYZ Products, Inc. — May 1986 to Present
Manufacturer of industrial machinery and components

Vice President; Green Bay, Wisconsin

Full P&L responsibility including strategic planning, capital and operating budgets; implementing major cost reduction programs, and renegotiating union contract.

- Accomplished successful turnaround by reducing inventory, manufacturing costs, and distribution/administrative expenses. Restructured all outstanding debt.
- Increased sales by 62% over two-year period.
- Orchestrated facility expansion and installation of state-of-the-art computer-controlled equipment.
- Brought previously subcontracted accounting procedures in-house through the purchase and installation of a computer network and related software packages.

Advanced Technologies, Inc. — September 1977 to May 1986
Supplier of educational textbooks, computer hardware and software

Vice President – National Sales Manager, Boston, Massachusetts (1/86 to 5/86)

Full responsibility for managing a national sales staff of nine. Position required strong interpersonal and communication skills in dealing with all corporate levels from union workers to board of directors.

Vice President – Eastern Division, Boston, Massachusetts (1/82 to 1/86)

Designed and implemented sales/marketing plans for the Eastern Division comprised of 21 states.
- Division exceeded sales goals by 28% in 1985, including personal achievement of $1.1M.

Regional Sales Director, Charleston, West Virginia (10/77 to 1/82)

Conducted seminars, in-house management and union presentations, productivity/feasibility audits, proposal writing, and presentations to executive management of primarily Fortune 1000 companies.
- Achieved largest sales year in history of the company.
- Recognized by the International Computer Programming Society for sales in excess of $1M.

212

Combination. *Kathy Keshemberg, Appleton, Wisconsin*

This candidate was vice president of a manufacturing company and secure in his position. He was interested in testing the waters to see what other jobs might be available in another part

Steven P. Weston

ABC Company — 1968 to March 1977
International manufacturer of construction equipment.

Manager Industrial Engineering, Cincinnati, Ohio (11/73 to 3/77)

Responsible for the administration and supervision of the tool crib, tool design, maintenance, and industrial engineering departments. Supervised 109 people. Developed and controlled multi-million dollar operating and capital budgets.

- Visited Japan to review their high technology equipment and procedures.

Foreman – Machine Department, Cincinnati, Ohio (1/73 to 11/73)

Directly supervised 27 union employees; met schedules, cost reduction, and quality control goals. Requested assignment to acquire hands-on experience in this first-line management position.

Project Engineer, Paris, France (6/72 to 1/73)

Special overseas assignment to establish an Industrial Engineering Department for this new facility.

Corporate Staff Industrial Engineer, Seattle, Washington (11/70 to 6/72)

Audited all manufacturing plants in performance and cost reduction areas, capital equipment selection/utilization, capital budget review and justification.

From 1968 to 1970, positions included Manager Industrial Engineering – Assembly Plant, Methods and Standards Supervisor, and Unit Industrial Engineer; all in St. Louis, Missouri

Education

Washington State University; Seattle, Washington
Fully admitted M.B.A. student; 50% completion towards degree prior to relocation in 1977

University of Wisconsin-Madison – 1969
Bachelor of Science – Industrial Engineering (Cooperative education work-study program)

of the country. The resume was designed to show his progressive career advancement and diverse industry experience. The Qualifications Overview quickly points out choice accomplishments and key areas of expertise.

JOHN A. DOE

Any Street
Any Town, USA 00000
(000) 000-0000

QUALIFICATION SUMMARY

Acquired 23 years experience in the technology, planning, and monitoring of U.S. South Communications' network facilities in Florida and Mississippi. Overall achievements include development of detailed network configurations for local loop access architecture involving multiple alternatives, end user customer needs, and overall economics of implementation; provisioning high capacity digital service; and maximizing current utilization and investment of the embedded base. Specific responsibilities include developing strategic network plans to deploy fiber/digital electronics in local loop, calculating capital funds required for construction of infrastructure, participating in market unit sales strategy sessions to position the network to be available for sales, and interfacing with numerous network segments to implement recommendations.

PROFESSIONAL EXPERIENCE

SOUTHEASTERN BELL TELEPHONE/U.S. SOUTH COMMUNICATIONS   1980 - Present

Planning Engineer, Network Facilities
Responsible for western half of Florida (11/92 - Present)
Responsible for western half of Mississippi (1980 - 11/92)

SOUTHWESTERN BELL TELEPHONE COMPANY

Design Engineer, Network Facilities	1978 - 1980
Communications Technician	1974 - 1978

AMERICAN TELEPHONE and TELEGRAPH COMPANY   1970 - 1974

Microwave Radio Technician

UNITED STATES GOVERNMENT   1966 - 1970

Electronics and Radar Technology Technician
Civilian employee with the Department of the Navy (1969 - 1970)
United States Army (1966 - 1969)

213

Combination. *Claudia Stephenson, location unknown*

Dates show a continual stream of professional experience from 1966 to the present. The Qualification Summary focuses on 23 years of experience with telephone companies.

RELATED TRAINING   **U. S. SOUTH COMMUNICATIONS**

* Loop Electronics Inventory Module (LEIM) (40 hrs.)   1992
* Loop Planning Economic Computer Module (PLAN) (40 hrs.)   1988
* Economic Selection Module/Loop Engineering Assignment Data (ESM/LEAD) (40 hrs.) 1988
* Integrated Services Digital Networks (40 hrs.)   1987
* Lightwave Design Technology (24 hrs.)   1984
* Digital Communications Technology (32 hrs.)   1983
* Subscriber Carrier Planning (40 hrs.)   1983
* Loop Feeder Administration (40 hrs.)   1982
* Long Range Outside Plant Planning (60 hrs.)   1980
* Engineering Economics (16 hrs.)   1979
* Network Facilities Basic Engineering (40 hrs.)   1978

EDUCATION

Technical Level Education:

Mississippi Institute of Electronics - Tupelo, MS   1970
• Electronics Technology course

Redstone Arsenal - Huntsville, AL   1968
• Electronics Technology course

College Level Education:

Georgia State University - Atlanta, GA   1972
• Completed 16 quarter hour credits in accounting and psychology

University of Florida - West Palm Beach, FL   1969
• Completed 27 semester hour credits in basic college courses

AWARDS/CERTIFICATES

* Received Engineering Merit Awards for Individual Performance (1992, 1987, 1985, 1984, 1982)
* Certified Radio Technician through National Association of Business and Educational Radio
   (1989 - Present)
* Hold Federal Communications Commission First Class License (1970 - Present)

This second page is devoted to related training, education, certification, and licensing.
The extensive amount of related training is put first and arranged chronologically.
Right-alignment of the dates makes it easy to compare them.

John H. Maddox
300 Green Road • Delmar, MD 00000 • (000) 000-0000

Senior level Health Care Engineer with extensive background in managing all phases of hospital plant operations. Five years experience as Director of Plant Operations at a major, 300,000 sq. ft., regional hospital complex.

Professional Experience	Aug 1996 to Present	WORCESTER HEALTH SYSTEMS, INC., DELMAR, MD (Formerly Franklin Memorial Hospital and Fairlawn General Hospital) ***Manager of Plant Operations/Franklin Memorial Hospital at Delmar, MD***

1992 to Aug 1996   FRANKLIN MEMORIAL HOSPITAL AT DELMAR, MD
Director of Plant Operations/Hospital Safety Officer
Responsible for overall administration of all hospital plant operations including building systems (HVAC, electric, plumbing, boiler plant, etc), new construction, renovations, building and grounds maintenance, equipment maintenance and repair, security and safety.

- Planned and implemented budget reduction measures which resulted in savings of $243,000 in annual plant operating expense. Among other measures this included reductions in department personnel, implementing steps to reduce energy costs, and restructuring rates of rental properties.
- Drafted construction plans for Washington Pediatric Clinic. Reviewed and approved change orders for construction of Hambry Diagnostic Center.
- Designed and implemented staff cross training program between maintenance and environmental services personnel. Results were an improved level of patient care, greater operating efficiency and higher staff morale.
- Designed and implemented a mandatory in-service Safety Training Program for 1,400 hospital employees.
- Led team of workers to win first prize in a hospital wide competition designed to identify cost savings measures based on employee suggestions.

1991 to 1992   ***Director of Plant Operations***
1986 to 1991   ***Assistant Director of Plant Operations***
1984 to 1986   ***Chief of Power Plant and Security***
1982 to 1984   ***Chief Stationary Engineer***

1976 to 1982   FAIRLAWN GENERAL HOSPITAL, CAMBRIDGE, MD
Stationary Engineer

1975 to 1976   THE TOWN OF BISHOP, BISHOP, MD
Town Engineer

1974 to 1975   TECH-COM, BISHOP, MD
Chief Engineer

1973 to 1974   FIBERTECH, INC., CAMBRIDGE, MD
Quality Control Engineer

1971 to 1973   GRAYSON AUTOMOTIVE CO., JAMESTOWN, MD
Division Manager, Parts

1967 to 1970   UNITED STATES NAVY
Marine Propulsion

1965 to 1967   GRAYSON AUTOMOTIVE CO., JAMESTOWN, MD
Division Manager, Parts

214

Chronological. *Thomas E. Spann, Easton, Maryland*

The profile-like statement at the top of the first page and below the contact information can serve also as objective statement if what the person is, is what he still wants to be. Reading

John H. Maddox

300 Green Road • Delmar, MD 00000• (000) 000-0000

Education		
	1993	AMERICAN SOCIETY OF HOSPITAL ENGINEERS
		Training for certification as Safety Officer
	1991	MARYLAND HEALTH CARE EDUCATION INSTITUTE
		Coursework in Management Leadership, and Public Speaking
	1991	LINCOLN COLLEGE, WATER MILLS, MD
		Coursework in Management, Criminal Justice and Computer Aided Drafting
	1980	INTERNATIONAL CORRESPONDENCE SCHOOL
		Coursework in Leadership, and Mechanical Engineering
	1976	ESSEXSTATE UNIVERSITY, ESSEX, MD
		Training for certification in Wastewater Treatment, and Water Treatment
	1969	UNIVERSITY OF MEXICO,
		Earned 30 credit hours towards Bachelor of Science in Mechanical Engineering (CLEP)
	1968	UNITED STATES NAVY
		Basic Propulsion and Engineering - Nuclear Power School
	1965	GREEN ACRESSENIOR HIGH SCHOOL, GREEN ACRES, MD
		Academic Diploma

Professional Affiliations

AMERICAN SOCIETY OF HEALTH CARE ENGINEERS

NATIONAL FIRE PROTECTION ASSOCIATION

AIRCRAFT OWNERS AND PILOTS ASSOCIATION

Licenses

FIRST GRADE STATIONARY ENGINEER

PRIVATE PILOT'S LICENSE

SAFETY OFFICER (ASHE)

Special Skills

LIFE SAFETY CODE 101 (NFPA STANDARDS)

ENVIRONMENT OF CARE STANDARDS (JCAHO)

COMPUTER AIDED DRAWING AND DRAFTING

WORD PERFECT 6.0/MICROSOFT WORKS

this resume from the bottom up—that is, from 1965 forward—gives a clear idea of the progression of his career. The information about his preceding work experience (1992–1996) gives you an idea of the depth of his experience.

GERALD G. FEINSTEIN
2020 MAPLE STREET – SOME CITY, MONTANA 12345
321 123.3210

PROFESSIONAL PROFILE

Enthusiastic, responsible, and results-oriented engineer. Able to manage multiple responsibilities and assignments with efficiency. Quality directed, team player with a vision of company and customer.

QUALIFICATIONS SUMMARY

- ➤ Manages quality issues and related tasks effectively.
- ➤ Excellent verbal and written communication; documenting results and informing others of conclusions and outcomes.
- ➤ Works well with customers and principals; maintains professionalism, sensitivity, and confidentiality.
- ➤ Team-member perspective; builds strong supportive relationships.
- ➤ Moderate understanding of the German language.
- ➤ **Computer** knowledge includes: Windows, Lotus 1-2-3, Ami Pro, MS Works, Peachtree Accounting, CADD 2-D.

EMPLOYMENT HISTORY

SMITH & BROOKSIDE AMERICA, INC.   City, State
International designing, developing, and manufacturing of electromechanical components for automotive, communication, computer, and other industries.

APPLICATIONS ENGINEER   1992 to Present
- ➤ Engineering liaison between customers, sales staff, technical personnel.
- ➤ Manage computer programming and maintenance; purchasing, implementing, maintaining, and training of software and hardware.

QUALITY CONTROL MANAGER
- ➤ Responsible for all aspects of quality, PPAP submissions, material rejections, 8-D reports, and parts inspection.

OTHER RESPONSIBILITIES
- ➤ Design and develop according to customer specifications.
- ➤ Assume sales and support responsibilities with major accounts.

EDUCATION AND TRAINING

ORCHARD UNIVERSITY   City, State
B.S.E.E. DEGREE, 1992
- ➤ 4-year varsity baseball, senior year as captain; all-academic first team

QS9000 Seminars

215

Combination. *Lorie Lebert, Novi, Michigan*

Lines enclose the Professional Profile, ensuring that it will be seen. The striking arrow-tip bullets do their job of calling attention to key skills and responsibilities.

3
P · A · R · T

Best Cover Letter Tips

Best Cover Letter Tips at a Glance

Best Cover Letter Writing Tips

In an active job search, your cover letter and resume should complement one another. Both are tailored to a particular reader you have contacted or to a specific job target. To help you create the "best" cover letters for your resumes, this part of the book mentions some common myths about cover letters and presents tips for polishing the letters you write.

Myths about Cover Letters

1. **Resumes and cover letters are two separate documents that have little relation to each other.** The resume and cover letter work together in presenting you effectively to a prospective employer. The cover letter should mention the resume and call attention to some important aspect of it.

2. **The main purpose of the cover letter is to establish friendly rapport with the reader.** Resumes show that you *can* do the work required. Cover letters express that you *want* to do the work required. But it doesn't hurt to display enthusiasm in your resumes and refer to your abilities in your cover letters.

3. **You can use the same cover letter for each reader of your resume.** Modify your cover letter for each reader so that it sounds fresh rather than canned. Chances are that in an active job search, you have already talked with the person who will interview you. Your cover letter should reflect that conversation and build on it.

4. **In a cover letter, you should mention any negative things about your education, work experience, life experience, or health to prepare the reader in advance of an interview.** This is not the purpose of the cover letter. You might bring up these topics in the first or second interview, but only after the interviewer has shown interest in you or offered you a job. Even then, if you feel that you must mention something negative about your past, present it in a positive way, perhaps by saying how that experience has strengthened your will to work hard at any new job.

5. **It is more important to remove errors from a resume than from a cover letter, because the resume is more important than the cover letter.** Both your resume and your cover letter should be free of errors. The cover letter is usually the first document a prospective employer sees. The first impression is often the most important one. If your cover letter has an embarrassing error in it, the chances are good that the reader may not bother to read your resume or may read it with less interest.

6. **To make certain that your cover letter has no errors, all you need to do is proofread it or ask a friend to "proof" it.** Trying to proofread your own cover letter is risky, even if you are good at grammar and writing. Once a

document is typewritten or printed, it has an aura about it that may make it seem better written than it is. For this reason, you are likely to miss typos or other kinds of errors.

Relying on someone else is risky too. If your friend is not good at grammar and writing, that person may not see any mistakes either. Try to find a proofreader, a professional editor, an English teacher, a professional writer, or an experienced secretary who can point out any errors you may have missed.

7. **After someone has proofread your letter, you can make a few changes to it and not have it looked at again.** More errors creep into a document this way than you would think possible. The reason is that such changes are often done hastily, and haste can waste an error-free document. If you make *any* change to a document, ask someone to proofread it a final time just to make sure that you haven't introduced an error during the last stage of composition. If you can't find someone to help you, the next section gives you advice on how to eliminate common mistakes in cover letters.

Tips for Polishing Cover Letters

You might spend several days working on your resume, getting it "just right" and free of errors. But if you send it with a cover letter that is written quickly and contains even one conspicuous error, all of your good effort may be wasted. That error could be just the kind of mistake the reader is looking for to screen you out.

You can prevent this kind of tragedy by polishing your cover letter so that it is free of all errors. The following tips can help you avoid or eliminate common errors in cover letters. If you become aware of these kinds of errors and know how to fix them, you can be more confident about the cover letters you send with your resumes.

Using Good Strategies for Letters

1. **Use the postal abbreviation for the state in your mailing address.** See resume writing strategy 1 in Part 1.

2. **Make certain that the letter is addressed to a specific person and that you use this person's name in the salutation.** Avoid using such general salutations as Dear Sir or Madam, To Whom It May Concern, Dear Administrator, Dear Prospective Employer, and Dear Committee. In an active job search, you should do everything possible to send your cover letter and resume to a particular individual, preferably someone you've already talked with in person or by phone, and with whom you have arranged an interview. If you have not been able to make a personal contact, at least do everything possible to find out the name of the person who will read your letter and resume. Then address the letter to that person.

3. **Adjust the margins for a short letter.** If your cover letter is 300 words or longer, use left, right, top, and bottom margins of one inch. If the letter is shorter, the width of the margins should increase. How much they increase is a matter of personal taste. One way to take care of the width of the top and bottom margins is to center a shorter letter vertically on the page. A maximum width for a short cover letter of 100 words or fewer might be two-inch left and right margins. As the number of words increases by 50 words, you might decrease the width of the left and right margins by two-tenths of an inch.

4. **If you write your letter with word processing or desktop publishing software, use left-justification to ensure that the lines of text are readable with fixed spacing between words.** The letter will have a "ragged right" look along the right margin, but the words will be evenly spaced horizontally. Don't use justification in an attempt to give a letter a printed look. Unless you do other typesetting procedures, like kerning and hyphenating words at the end of some lines, full justification can make your letter look worse with some extra-wide spaces between words.

Using Pronouns Correctly

5. **Use *I* and *My* sparingly.** When most of the sentences in a cover letter begin with *I* or *My,* the writer may appear self-absorbed, self-centered, or egotistical. If the reader of the letter is turned off by this kind of impression (even if it is a false one for you), you could be screened out without ever having an interview. Of course, you will need to use these first-person pronouns because most of the information you put in your cover letter will be personal. But try to avoid using *I* and *My* at the beginnings of sentences and paragraphs.

6. **Refer to a business, company, corporation, or organization as "it" rather than "they."** Members of the Board may be referred to as "they," but a company is a singular subject requiring a singular verb. Note this example:

    > New Products, Inc., was established in 1980. It grossed over a million dollars in sales during its first year.

7. **If you start a sentence with *This,* be sure that what *This* refers to is clear.** If the reference is not clear, insert some word or phrase to clarify what *This* means. Compare the following lines:

    > My revised application for the new position will be faxed to you by noon on Friday. *This* should be acceptable to you.

    > My revised application for the new position will be faxed to you by noon on Friday. This *method of sending the application* should be acceptable to you.

    A reader of the first sentence wouldn't know what *This* refers to. Friday? By noon on Friday? The revised application for the new position? The insertion after *This* in the second sentence, however, tells the reader that *This* refers to the use of faxing.

8. **Use *as follows* after a singular subject.** Literally, *as follows* means *as it follows,* so the phrase is illogical after a plural subject. Compare the following lines:

Incorrect:	My plans for the day of the interview are as follows:
Fixed:	My plans for the day of the interview are these:
Correct:	My plan for the day of the interview is as follows:
Better:	Here is my plan for the day of the interview:

    In the second set, the improved version avoids a hidden reference problem—the possible association of the silent "it" with *interview.* Whenever you want to use *as follows,* check to see whether the subject that precedes *as follows* is plural. If it is, don't use this phrase.

Using Verb Forms Correctly

9. **Make certain that subjects and verbs agree in number.** Plural subjects require plural forms of verbs. Singular subjects require singular verb forms. Most writers know these things, but problems arise when subject and verb agreement gets tricky. Compare the following lines:

Incorrect:	My education and experience has prepared me. . . .
Correct:	My education and experience have prepared me. . . .

Incorrect:	Making plans plus scheduling conferences were. . . .
Correct:	Making plans plus scheduling conferences was. . . .

   In the first set, *education* and *experience* are two things (you can have one without the other) and require a plural verb. A hasty writer might lump them together and use a singular verb. When you reread what you have written, look out for this kind of improper agreement between a plural subject and a singular verb.

   In the second set, *making plans* is the subject. It is singular, so the verb must be singular. The misleading part of this sentence is the phrase *plus scheduling conferences.* It may seem to make the subject plural, but it doesn't. In English, phrases that begin with such words as *plus, together with, in addition to, along with,* and *as well as* usually don't make a singular subject plural.

10. **Whenever possible, use active forms of verbs rather than passive forms.** Compare these lines:

Passive:	My report will be sent by my assistant tomorrow.
Active:	My assistant will send my report tomorrow.

Passive:	Your interest is appreciated.
Active:	I appreciate your interest.

Passive:	Your letter was received yesterday.
Active:	I received your letter yesterday.

    Sentences with passive verbs are usually longer and clumsier than sentences with active verbs. Spot passive verbs by looking for some form of the verb *to be* (such as *be, will be, have been, is, was,* and *were*) used with another verb.

    A trade-off in using active verbs is the frequent introduction of the pronouns *I* and *My.* To solve one problem, you might create another (see Tip 5 in this list). The task then becomes one of finding some other way to start a sentence.

11. **Be sure that present and past participles are grammatically parallel in a list.** See Tip 48 in Part 1. What is true about parallel forms in resumes is true also in cover letters. Present participles are action words ending in *-ing,* such as *creating, testing,* and *implementing.* Past participles are action words usually ending in *-ed,* such as *created, tested,* and *implemented.* These are called *verbals* because they are derived from verbs but are not strong enough to function as verbs in a sentence. When you use a string of verbals, control them by keeping them parallel.

12. **Use split infinitives only when *not* splitting them is misleading or awkward.** An *infinitive* is a verb preceded by the preposition *to,* as in *to create,*

to test, and *to implement.* You split an infinitive when you insert an adverb between the preposition and the verb, as in *to quickly create, to repeatedly test,* and *to slowly implement.* About 50 years ago, split infinitives were considered grammatical errors, but opinion about them has changed. Many grammar handbooks now recommend that you split your infinitives to avoid awkward or misleading sentences. Compare the following lines:

Split infinitive:	I plan to periodically send updated reports on my progress in school.
Misleading:	I plan periodically to send updated reports on my progress in school.
Misleading:	I plan to send periodically updated reports on my progress in school.

The first example is clear enough, but the second and third examples may be misleading. If you are uncomfortable with split infinitives, one solution is to move *periodically* further into the sentence: "I plan to send updated reports periodically on my progress in school."

Most handbooks that allow split infinitives also recommend that they not be split by more than one word, as in *to quickly and easily write.* A gold medal for splitting an infinitive should go to Lowell Schmalz, an Archie Bunker prototype in "The Man Who Knew Coolidge" by Sinclair Lewis. Schmalz, who thought that Coolidge was one of America's greatest presidents, split an infinitive this way: "*to instantly and without the least loss of time or effort find. . . .*"[1]

Using Punctuation Correctly

13. **Punctuate a compound sentence with a comma.** A compound sentence is one that contains two main clauses joined by one of seven conjunctions (*and, but, or, nor, for, yet,* and *so*). In English, a comma is customarily put before the conjunction if the sentence isn't unusually short. Here is an example of a compound sentence punctuated correctly:

    I plan to arrive at O'Hare at 9:35 a.m. on Thursday, and my trip by cab to your office should take no longer than 40 minutes.

    The comma is important because it signals that a new grammatical subject (*trip,* the subject of the second main clause) is about to be expressed. If you use this kind of comma consistently, the reader will rely on your punctuation and be on the lookout for the next subject in a compound sentence.

14. **Be certain not to put a comma between compound verbs.** When a sentence has two verbs joined by the conjunction *and,* these verbs are called *compound verbs.* Usually, they should not be separated by a comma before the conjunction. Note the following examples:

    I *started* the letter last night *and finished* it this morning.

    I *am sending* my resume separately *and would like* you to keep the information confidential.

---

[1] Sinclair Lewis, "The Man Who Knew Coolidge," *The Man Who Knew Coolidge* (New York: Books for Libraries Press, 1956), p. 29.

Both examples are simple sentences containing compound verbs. Therefore, no comma appears before *and*. In either case, a comma would send a wrong signal that a new subject in another main clause is coming, but no such subject exists.

Note: In a sentence with a series of three or more verbs, use commas between the verbs. The comma before the last verb is called the *serial comma*. For more information on using the serial comma, see resume writing style Tip 63 in Part 1.

15. **Avoid using *as well as* for *and* in a series.** Compare the following lines:

Incorrect:	Your company is impressive because it has offices in Canada, Mexico, as well as the United States.
Correct:	Your company is impressive because it has offices in Canada and Mexico, as well as in the United States.

    Usually, what is considered exceptional precedes *as well as,* and what is considered customary follows it. Note this example:

    > Your company is impressive because its managerial openings are filled by women as well as men.

16. **Put a comma after the year when it appears after the month.** Similarly, put a comma after the state when it appears after the city. Compare the following pairs of lines:

Incorrect:	In January, 1994 I was promoted to senior analyst.
Correct:	In January, 1994, I was promoted to senior analyst.
Incorrect:	I worked in Chicago, Illinois before moving to Dallas.
Correct:	I worked in Chicago, Illinois, before moving to Dallas.

17. **Put a comma after an opening dependent clause.** Compare the following lines:

Incorrect:	If you have any questions you may contact me by phone or fax.
Correct:	If you have any questions, you may contact me by phone or fax.

    Actually, many writers of fiction and nonfiction don't use this kind of comma. The comma is useful, though, because it signals where the main clause begins. If you glance at the example with the comma, you can tell where the main clause is without even reading the opening clause. For a step up in clarity and readability, use this comma. It can give you a "feel" for a sentence even before you begin to read the words.

18. **Use semicolons when they are needed.** See resume writing style Tip 64 in Part 1 for the use of semicolons between items in a series. Semicolons are used also to separate main clauses when the second clause starts with a *conjunctive adverb* like *however, moreover,* and *therefore.* Compare the following lines:

Incorrect:	Your position in sales looks interesting, however, I would like more information about it.
Correct:	Your position in sales looks interesting; however, I would like more information about it.

The first example is incorrect because the comma before *however* is a *comma splice,* which is a comma that joins two sentences. It's like putting a comma instead of a period at the end of the first sentence and then starting the second sentence. A comma may be a small punctuation mark, but a comma splice is a huge grammatical mistake. What are your chances for getting hired if your cover letter tells your reader that you don't recognize where a sentence ends, especially if a requirement for the job is good communication skills? Yes, you could be screened out because of one little comma!

19. **Avoid putting a colon after a verb or a preposition to introduce information.** The reason is that the colon interrupts a continuing clause. Compare the following lines:

> Incorrect: My interests in your company *are:* its reputation, the review of salary after six months, and your personal desire to hire handicapped persons.
>
> Correct: My interests in your company *are these:* its reputation, the review of salary after six months, and your personal desire to hire handicapped persons.
>
> Incorrect: In my interview with you, I would like *to:* learn how your company was started, get your reaction to my updated portfolio, and discuss your department's plans to move to a new building.
>
> Correct: In my interview with you, I would like to discuss *these issues:* how your company was started, what you think of my updated portfolio, and when your department may move to a new building.

Although some people may say that it is OK to put a colon after a verb like *include* if the list of information is long, it is better to be consistent and avoid colons after verbs altogether.

20. **Understand colons clearly.** People often associate colons with semicolons because they sound alike, but colons and semicolons have nothing to do with each other. Colons are the opposite of dashes. Dashes look backward, and colons usually look forward to information about to be delivered. One common use of the colon does look backward, however. Here are two examples:

> My experience with computers is limited: I have had only one course on programming, and I don't own a computer.
>
> I must make a decision by Monday: that is the deadline for renewing the lease for my apartment.

In each example, what follows the colon explains what was said before the colon. Using a colon this way in a cover letter can impress a knowledgeable reader who is looking for evidence of writing skills.

21. **Use slashes correctly.** Information about slashes is sometimes hard to find because *slash* often is listed under a different name, such as *virgule* or *solidus*. If you are not familiar with these terms, your hunt for advice on slashes may lead to nothing.

At least know that one important meaning of a slash is *or*. For this reason, you often see a slash in an expression like ON/OFF. This means that a condition or state, like that of electricity activated by a switch, is either ON or OFF but never ON and OFF at the same time. This condition may be one in which a change means going from the current state to the opposite (or alternate) state. If the current state is ON and there is a change, the next state will be OFF, and vice versa. With this understanding, you can recognize the logic behind the following examples:

Incorrect:	ON-OFF switch (on and off at the same time!)
Correct:	ON/OFF switch (on or off at any time)

Correct:	his-her clothes (unisex clothes, worn by both sexes)
Correct:	his/her clothes (each sex had different clothes)

Note: Although the slash is correct in *his/her* and is one way to avoid sexism, many people consider this expression clumsy. Consider some other wording, such as "clothes that both men and women wear" or "unisex clothes."

22. **Think twice about using *and/or*.** This stilted expression is commonly misunderstood to mean *two* alternatives, but it literally means *three.* Look at the following example:

> If you don't hear from me by Friday, please phone and/or fax me the information on Monday.

What is the person at the other end to do? The sentence really states three alternatives: just phone, just fax, or phone *and* fax the information by Monday. For better clarity, use the connectives *and* or *or* whenever possible.

23. **Use punctuation correctly with quotation marks.** A common misconception is that commas and periods should be placed outside closing quotation marks, but the opposite is true. Compare the following lines:

Incorrect:	Your company certainly has the "leading edge", which means that its razor blades are the best on the market.
Correct:	Your company certainly has the "leading edge," which means that its razor blades are the best on the market.

Incorrect:	In the engineering department, my classmates referred to me as "the guru in pigtails". I was the youngest expert in programming languages on campus.
Correct:	In the engineering department, my classmates referred to me as "the guru in pigtails." I was the youngest expert in programming languages on campus.

Unlike commas and periods, colons and semicolons go *outside* double quotation marks.

Using Words Correctly

24. **Avoid using lofty language in your cover letter.** A real turn-off in a cover letter is the use of elevated diction (high-sounding words and phrases) as a bid to seem important. Note the following examples, along with their straight-talk translations:

Elevated:	My background has afforded me experience in. . . .
Better:	In my previous jobs, I. . . .

Elevated:	Prior to that term of employment. . . .
Better:	Before I worked at. . . .

Elevated:	I am someone with a results-driven profit orientation.
Better:	I want to make your company more profitable.

Elevated:	I hope to utilize my qualifications. . . .
Better:	I want to use my skills. . . .

In letter writing, the shortest distance between the writer and the reader is the most direct idea.

25. Check your sentences for an excessive use of compounds joined by *and*. A cheap way to make your letters longer is to join words with *and* and do this repeatedly. Note the following wordy sentence:

> Because of my background and preparation for work and advancement with your company and new enterprise, I have a concern and commitment to implement and put into effect my skills and abilities for new solutions and achievements above and beyond your dreams and expectations. [44 words]

Just one inflated sentence like that would drive a reader to say, "No way!" The writer of the inflated sentence has said only this:

> Because of my background and skills, I want to contribute to your new venture. [14 words]

If, during rereading, you eliminate the wordiness caused by this common writing weakness, your letter will have a better chance of being read completely.

26. Avoid using abstract nouns excessively. Look again at the inflated sentence of the preceding tip, but this time with the abstract nouns in italic:

> Because of my *background* and *preparation* for *work* and *advancement* with your *company* and new *enterprise*, I have a *concern* and *commitment* to implement and put into *effect* my skills and *abilities* for new *solutions* and *achievements* above and beyond your *dreams* and *expectations*.

Try picturing in your mind any of the words in italic. You can't because they are *abstract nouns,* which means that they are ideas and not images of things you can see, taste, hear, smell, or touch. One certain way to turn off the reader of your cover letter is to load it with abstract nouns. The following sentence, containing some images, has a better chance of capturing the reader's attention:

> Having created seven multimedia tutorials with my videocamera and Gateway Pentium computer, I now want to create some breakthrough adult-learning packages so that your company, New Century Instructional Technologies, Inc., will exceed $50,000,000 in contracts by 2001.

Compare this sentence with the one loaded with abstract nouns. The one with images is obviously the better attention grabber.

27. Avoid wordy expressions in your cover letters. Note the following examples:

at the location of (at)
for the reason that (because)
in a short time (soon)
in a timely manner (on time)
in spite of everything to the contrary (nevertheless)
in the event of (if)

in the proximity of (near)
now and then (occasionally)
on a daily basis (daily)
on a regular basis (regularly)
on account of (because)
one day from now (tomorrow)
would you be so kind as to (please)

After each of these phrases is a suitable substitute in parentheses. Trim the fat wherever you can, and your reader will appreciate the leanness of your cover letter.

28. **At the end of your cover letter, don't make a statement that the reader can use to reject you.** For example, suppose that you close your letter with this statement:

> If you wish to discuss this matter further, please call me at (555) 555-5555.

This statement gives the reader a chance to think, "I don't wish it, so I don't have to call." Here is another example:

> If you know of the right opportunity for me, please call me at (555) 555-5555.

The reader may think, "I don't know of any such opportunity. How would I know what is right for you?" Avoid questions that prompt yes or no answers, such as "Do you want to discuss this matter further?" If you ask this kind of question, you give the reader a chance to say no. Instead, make a closing statement that indicates your optimism about a positive response from the reader. Such a statement might begin with one of the following:

> I am confident that . . . .
> I look forward to . . . .

In this way, you invite the reader to say yes to further consideration.

Exhibit of Cover Letters

The following Exhibit contains sample cover letters that were prepared by professional resume writers. In most cases, the names, addresses, and facts have been changed to ensure the confidentiality of the original sender and receiver of the letter. For each letter, however, the essential substance of the original remains intact.

Use the Exhibit of cover letters as a reference whenever you need to write a cover letter for your resume. If you have trouble starting and ending letters, look at the beginnings and ends of the letters. If you need help on writing about your work experience, describing your abilities and skills, or mentioning some of your best achievements, look at the middle paragraph(s). Search for features that will give you ideas for making your own cover letters more effective. As you examine the Exhibit, consider the following questions:

1. **Does the person show a genuine interest in the reader?** One way to tell is to count the number of times the pronouns *you* or *your* appear in the letter. Then count next the number of times the pronouns *I, me,* and *my* occur in the letter. Although this method is simplistic, it nevertheless helps you see where the writer's interests lie. When you write a cover letter, make your first paragraph *you*-centered rather than *I*-centered. *See also* Tip 5 earlier in Part 3.

2. **Where does the cover letter mention the resume specifically?** The purpose of a cover letter is to call attention to the resume. If the letter fails to mention

the resume, the letter has not fulfilled its purpose. Besides mentioning the resume, the cover letter might direct the reader's attention to one or more parts of the resume, increasing the chances that the most important part(s) will be seen by the reader. It is not a good idea, however, to put a lot of resume facts in the cover letter. Let each document do its own job. The job of the cover letter is to point to the resume.

3. **Where and how does the letter express interest in an interview?** The immediate purpose of a cover letter is to call attention to the resume, but the *ultimate* purpose of both the cover letter and the resume is to help you get an interview with the person who can hire you. If the letter doesn't display your interest in getting an interview, the letter has not fulfilled its ultimate purpose.

4. **How decisive is the person's language?** This question is closely related to the preceding question. Is interest in an interview expressed directly or indirectly? Does the person specifically request an interview on a date when the writer will be in the reader's vicinity, or does the person only hint at a desire to "meet" the reader some day? When you write your own cover letters, be sure to be direct and convincing in expressing your interest for an interview. Avoid being timid or wishy-washy.

5. **How does the person display self-confidence?** As you look through the Exhibit, notice the cover letters in which the phrase "I am confident that . . ." (or a similar expression) appears. Self-confidence is a sign of management ability but also of essential job-worthiness. Many of the letters display self-confidence or self-assertiveness in various ways.

6. **How does the letter indicate that the person is a team player?** From an employer's point of view, an employee who is self-assertive but not a team player can spell T-R-O-U-B-L-E. As you look at the cover letters in the Exhibit, notice the many letters in which the word *team* appears.

7. **How does the letter make the person stand out?** As you read the letters in the Exhibit, do some letters present the person more vividly than other letters? If so, what does the trick? The middle paragraphs or the opening and closing paragraphs? Use what you learn here to help you write distinctive cover letters.

8. **How familiar is the person with the reader?** In a passive job search, the reader will most likely be a total stranger. In an active job search, the chances are good that the writer will have had at least one conversation with the reader by phone or in person. As you look through the cover letters in the Exhibit, see whether you can spot any letter which indicates that the writer has already talked with the reader.

After you have examined the cover letters in the Exhibit, you will be better able to write an attention-getting letter—one that leads the reader to your resume and to scheduling an interview with you.

Edward G. Masterson

456 River Lane, Trenton, MI 48183
(313) 555-0000

June 15, 1996

Mr. Ralph Hotshot
Vice President
ABIG Corporation
987 Industrial Blvd.
Detroit, MI 48226

Dear Mr. Hotshot:

I am writing to express my interest in working for your company as a Design Engineer. Highlights of some of my qualifications are:

➢ **Design:** 3-D designer with extensive experience in PDGS. I have experience designing both products and tooling.

➢ **Management:** Experience managing both people and projects. I can motivate and train employees to excel in their work performance and efficiency. My #1 goal is to increase efficiency and cut costs on a <u>daily</u> basis.

➢ **Personal Traits:** I'm highly motivated and have a strong commitment to continuing my education and expanding my skills. Since I enjoy learning new systems, I tend to learn them very quickly. Fueled by past successes, I strongly believe that the achievement of all of my goals is within my reach.

I am seeking a position that would offer additional challenges and continued growth opportunity. I'm confident that I can use my skills and experience to make a positive contribution to your company. I will be calling you soon to answer any questions you may have about my background. Thank you for your attention, and I look forward to our conversation.

Sincerely,

Edward G. Masterson

Deborah L. Schuster, Newport, Michigan

A two-paragraph letter in which the first paragraph introduces three bulleted items, each beginning with a category in boldface. In the last paragraph the person plans to do the follow-up.

Dale M. Hightower

753 Main Street
Andover, Massachusetts 01810
(508) 475-0000

Dear :

During my professional career I have acquired broad experience and honed diverse skills that I believe will be of interest to your organization.

- **Sales and Management** — My experience includes the successful turnaround of an entrepreneurial venture through business analysis, the implementation of innovative merchandising and strict quality control.

- **Leadership and Supervision** — With proven success in widely divergent environments, I have the skill and experience to recruit and hire, train, lead and motivate both individuals and teams.

- **Program Implementation** — My professional experiences have been enhanced by valuable volunteer leadership positions requiring the ability to plan, organize, and follow through to ensure that programs meet their objectives.

At this point in my career I seek a position in which I can use my creative thinking, innovative problem-solving, and strong persuasive skills to achieve successful outcomes. I would be interested in discussing with you how these skills, complemented by strong business experience and abilities, can make a difference to your organization. When can we schedule an appointment?

Sincerely,

Dale M. Hightower

enclosure: resume

2

Louise M. Kursmark, Cincinnati, Ohio

Another two-paragraph letter. Three bulleted items illustrate the first paragraph by indicating experience and skills. The second paragraph ends with a question.

CYNTHIA NURSE, R.N., A.D.N.
123 Healthcare Lane
Medville, MA 12345
(222) 222-2222

Dear Human Resources Director:

I am an **experienced registered nurse** who is interested in exploring employment opportunities with your health care facility/department. I have enclosed my resume for your consideration.

As my resume illustrates, I have enjoyed a well-rounded progressive career in nursing. My record is one of increased responsibility and accomplishments. I am especially known for my professional and caring attitude toward patients and staff, being a good resource person for other nurses, efficiency and organization, and loyalty. In addition to these personal attributes, I feel my experience in the following areas would be most beneficial to you:

- Case management for quality assurance and cost effective care.
- Third party payer requirements and processing insurance paperwork.
- Direct patient care including geriatrics, adult health, and maternal/infant health.
- Received recognition from current employer for developing SIDS consultation standards to be followed by state visiting nurses.

I would appreciate the opportunity to meet with you to discuss your employment needs and my qualifications in greater detail. I may be reached at (222) 222-2222. Thank you for your time and consideration. I look forward to hearing from you.

Sincerely,

Cynthia Nurse, R.N., A.D.N.

Enclosure: resume

Annamarie Pawlina, location unknown

A three-paragraph letter in which the second paragraph introduces a series of bulleted items indicating areas of experience. The third shows interest in a response for an interview.

HARRY ALBRIGHTON
9926 California Court
Wilmington, North Carolina 28412
(000) 111-2222

August 2, 19xx

Joe Schmoe
Human Resources Director
Heavenly Apparel
1121 North Front Street
Wilmington, NC 28401

Dear Mr. Schmoe:

Thank you for taking the time to talk with me regarding the Department Supervisor position available with Heavenly Apparel. My resume highlights my skills and qualifications and follows this letter.

My career is highlighted by significant improvements to quality, production, and profitability of leading manufacturing plants. I am a hands-on manager with emphasis on safety and efficiency. With my varied experience in garment manufacturing I am confident that I have the qualifications to fill this position.

The opportunity to meet with you to discuss this matter further would be appreciated. I am available Tuesday through Thursday mornings and would be happy to meet you at your convenience. I look forward to hearing from you in the near future.

Sincerely,

Harry Albrighton

Enclosure: Resume

Sandy Adcox Saburn, Wilmington, North Carolina

A three-paragraph letter that is basic and straightforward, which is the individual's style. The person leaves the initiative with the reader for a response.

Charles W. Broadway
2000 Victoria Boulevard
Sandhurst, Alabama 36100
℘[555] 555-5555

November 15, 1995

Ms. Carla Harlow
Chief Financial Officer
DataStar Corporation
1000 Argent Circle
Suite 100
Marston, Alabama 36100

Dear Ms. Harlow:

It has taken me four years to write this letter. That's how much time it requires to build a track record you probably demand from any computer systems manager who wants to joint the DataStar team.

In my résumé you will see specific results in a series of increasingly responsible positions. In each case, I earned the trust of every key player from senior management to user to customer. Nowhere was this more important than in my work in a major study on quality control for pharmacies. Because planners could readily understand my methods, they approved the plan with only minor changes. My work allowed users to see – through computer graphics they could quickly generate – the impact of 32 types of errors quickly.

Now I'd like to expand my career by contributing my skills to a growing company. May I meet you to discuss how I might serve your organization as a computer systems manager? I will call in a few days to arrange a date that fits your schedule.

Sincerely,

Charles W. Broadway

One enclosure: Résumé

Don Orlando, Montgomery, Alabama

The letter begins with a lead that compels further reading. The letter not only refers to the resume but also comments about it. The sender keeps control at the end for follow-up.

WINNFRED H. SUCCESS

0000 East Heather
Anywhere, USA
(000) 000-0000

April 26, 2000

Joseph Smith, President
Idaho Growers, Inc.
P.O. Box 0000
Anywhere, USA

Dear Joe:

While working in the Idaho state potato industry, I became acquainted with John Smith of your organization. My business dealings with both Idaho Growers and all of its representatives were very positive, which has prompted me to contact you. At this time, I am actively exploring a return to the Boise area and opportunities in the potato industry.

As a 20-year veteran of the produce industry, I offer comprehensive experience in marketing, management, and grower relations. Briefly, my strengths include:

- **Operations:** Performed hands-on management functions for grower/packer/shipper with over $50 million in sales. Operational accountability extended to packing plant operations (receiving, packing, storage, shipping), plant upgrades and maintenance, computerized accounting/recordkeeping systems, quality control, contract negotiations, staffing and supervision, and grower relations. **Results:** tripled production and increased net profits by over 200%.

- **Sales/Marketing:** Well-versed in all phases of sales and marketing including development of new market opportunities/distribution channels, formation of business partnerships/alliances to capitalize on market opportunities, domestic marketing, expansion into international markets, and consumer packaging/value-added products. **Results:** achieved a 100% or better increase in sales and distribution.

I have enclosed a résumé which more specifically details my accomplishments as a proactive manager and entrepreneur. Should there be needs within your organization which might benefit from my background, I would enjoy visiting with you. I will follow-up with a telephone call in the upcoming week and look forward to speaking with you at that time.

Sincerely,

Winnfred H. Success

Enclosure

6

Susan Britton Whitcomb, Fresno, California

The second paragraph introduces two bulleted paragraphs for two different areas of strengths. Each bulleted paragraph ends with a Results statement.

JOHN ANYBODY
1111 South Anywhere Drive, #224, Tampa, Florida 335116
(813) 111-1111

November 7, 1995

Mr. Bigwig
President/CEO
Anycompany
Anystreet
Anytown, USA

Dear Mr. Bigwig:

I would like to explore the possibility of career employment opportunities within your organization. The enclosed resume highlights my extensive career experience and abilities.

I am particularly interested in a position with your company because of my background in sales and telecommunications. My success in the past has stemmed from my strong commitment and sense of professionalism. Evidence of my ability to be a solid contributor to your company includes:

- Ability to create and present an excellent image of the company and its services to customers, and to coordinate and communicate well with clientele and management at all levels; special skills in sales closings.

- Successfully started up and staffed a 25-employee office in the Chicago area.

- Selected for membership in MMM Achiever's Club.

If your need is for someone with my qualifications, drive and enthusiasm, you may reach me by phone at (813) 111-1111. This is a confidential inquiry. I would appreciate an opportunity to meet with you personally to discuss how my knowledge and proven track record can make an immediate impact in your organization.

Sincerely,

Enc.

M. Carol Heider, Tampa, Florida

The second paragraph introduces three bulleted items as evidence of the person's ability to contribute to the target company. Initiative for a follow-up is left with the reader.

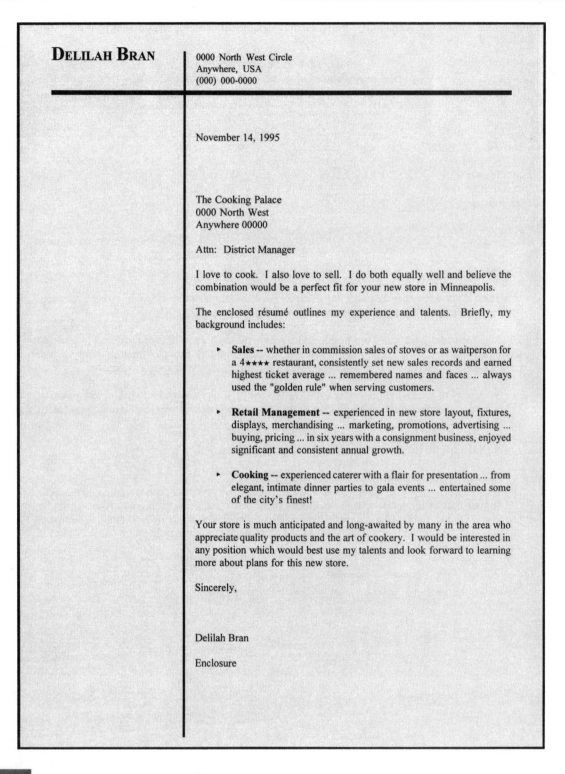

DELILAH BRAN

0000 North West Circle
Anywhere, USA
(000) 000-0000

November 14, 1995

The Cooking Palace
0000 North West
Anywhere 00000

Attn: District Manager

I love to cook. I also love to sell. I do both equally well and believe the combination would be a perfect fit for your new store in Minneapolis.

The enclosed résumé outlines my experience and talents. Briefly, my background includes:

- ▸ **Sales** -- whether in commission sales of stoves or as waitperson for a 4★★★★ restaurant, consistently set new sales records and earned highest ticket average ... remembered names and faces ... always used the "golden rule" when serving customers.

- ▸ **Retail Management** -- experienced in new store layout, fixtures, displays, merchandising ... marketing, promotions, advertising ... buying, pricing ... in six years with a consignment business, enjoyed significant and consistent annual growth.

- ▸ **Cooking** -- experienced caterer with a flair for presentation ... from elegant, intimate dinner parties to gala events ... entertained some of the city's finest!

Your store is much anticipated and long-awaited by many in the area who appreciate quality products and the art of cookery. I would be interested in any position which would best use my talents and look forward to learning more about plans for this new store.

Sincerely,

Delilah Bran

Enclosure

8

Susan Britton Whitcomb, Fresno, California

The second of three paragraphs introduces bulleted background categories. The last paragraph expresses interest in a position and anticipation of more information.

ALAN A. ALADIN

0000 N. West Avenue
Anywhere, USA

Residence (000) 000-0000
Cellular (000) 000-0000

As an experienced **Economic Development Specialist,** I am writing to inquire of opportunities which might be available on a full-time or contract basis with your firm. The enclosed résumé outlines my 20-year history with the City of Bilton and the County of Attowa.

Strengths and experiences which may be of particular interest to you include:

- Sourced, negotiated, and secured over $255 million in new commercial/industrial development for the City of Bilton, an achievement which created $57 million in new single-family and multi-family construction and more than doubled population growth during my tenure.

- A creative problem-solving approach to financing, including experience with public/private sector partnerships, creation of assessment districts, and bond financing (as well as traditional financing methods) which enabled the city to underwrite over $28 million in new public works projects.

- Numerous contacts within, and ability to service, a broad client base including state, county and city agencies, lending institutions, and varied business interests representing utility, retail, and manufacturing concerns.

- Proactive leader with the ability to inspire cooperation, communication, and consensus among varied interests (public agencies, private sector, support staff, media, and the community-at-large).

Should you have need for an individual with my skills and experience, I would appreciate an opportunity to meet with you to explore our mutual interests. I will be in touch.

Sincerely,

Alan A. Aladin

Enclosure

Susan Britton Whitcomb, Fresno, California

The second paragraph introduces four bulleted statements, which include achievements. The last paragraph shows interest in a meeting. The person keeps control for a follow-up.

Charles M. Downer

2114 Pitt Street
Alexandria, Virginia, 23100

☎ [703] 555-5555 (Home)
[703] 555-6666 (Office)

October 9, 1995

Mr. Charles W. Morgan
Chairman
Coleman County Board of Education
2315 Wesley Street
Coleman, Georgia 30243

Dear Mr. Morgan:

Whenever I speak with colleagues in educational leadership, the conversation often focuses on measuring the value of what we do. But now, after some 26 years of administering educational programs, I am persuaded that *who* does the measuring is as important as the measures themselves. Simply put, I am happiest – and therefore most successful – helping teachers and principals and, most important, students succeed. If that approach appeals to the Coleman County Board of Education, I would like to explore joining your team as your Chief Executive Officer.

My curriculum vitæ should help you learn about my background. I have even included a very small sampling of the successes I helped obtain. However, such documents cannot explain *how* I made progress for my organizations. In everything I do I hold to these principles:

- ꙩ I must show that I care about the mission through deeds, not words,
- ꙩ I reward the extra time it takes for staff members to make themselves visible and accessible,
- ꙩ My organization's mission is ultimately measured in the success of the community from which my students come,
- ꙩ I reward taking prudent risks if the goal is to further the mission, and
- ꙩ I do not care who gets the credit as long as objective measures show we are doing our mission very well.

I am employed by an organization that values my services. However, I want to return to the field I love most. And so I am "testing the waters" with this confidential application. May I call in a few days to explore the possibility of an interview?

Sincerely,

Charles M. Downer

One enclosure: Résumé

10

Don Orlando, Montgomery, Alabama

This writer makes every attempt to avoid clichés and succeeds, as is evident here. Have you ever read another cover letter like this one? Even the bullets are different.

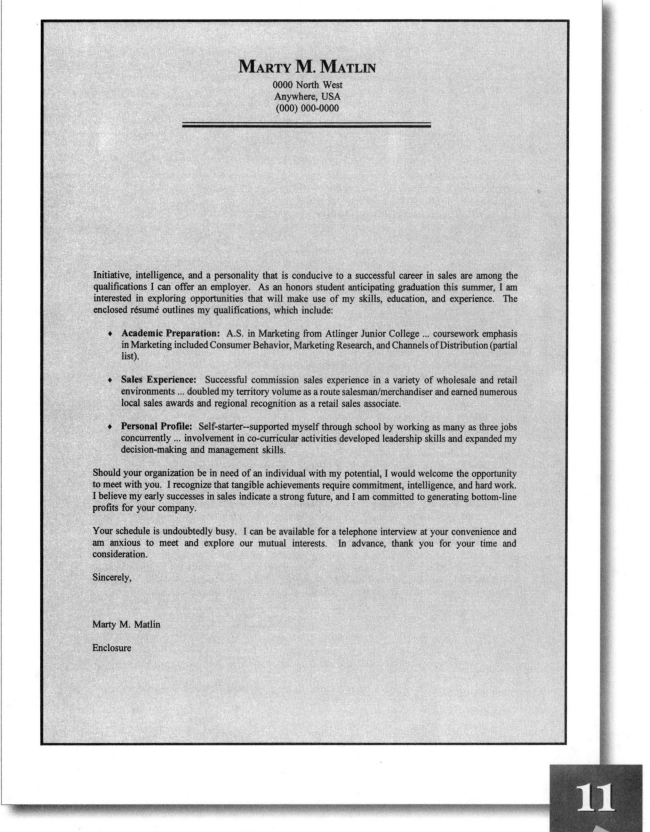

MARTY M. MATLIN
0000 North West
Anywhere, USA
(000) 000-0000

Initiative, intelligence, and a personality that is conducive to a successful career in sales are among the qualifications I can offer an employer. As an honors student anticipating graduation this summer, I am interested in exploring opportunities that will make use of my skills, education, and experience. The enclosed résumé outlines my qualifications, which include:

♦ **Academic Preparation:** A.S. in Marketing from Atlinger Junior College ... coursework emphasis in Marketing included Consumer Behavior, Marketing Research, and Channels of Distribution (partial list).

♦ **Sales Experience:** Successful commission sales experience in a variety of wholesale and retail environments ... doubled my territory volume as a route salesman/merchandiser and earned numerous local sales awards and regional recognition as a retail sales associate.

♦ **Personal Profile:** Self-starter--supported myself through school by working as many as three jobs concurrently ... involvement in co-curricular activities developed leadership skills and expanded my decision-making and management skills.

Should your organization be in need of an individual with my potential, I would welcome the opportunity to meet with you. I recognize that tangible achievements require commitment, intelligence, and hard work. I believe my early successes in sales indicate a strong future, and I am committed to generating bottom-line profits for your company.

Your schedule is undoubtedly busy. I can be available for a telephone interview at your convenience and am anxious to meet and explore our mutual interests. In advance, thank you for your time and consideration.

Sincerely,

Marty M. Matlin

Enclosure

11

Susan Britton Whitcomb, Fresno, California

The first of three paragraphs introduces three bulleted items, which show qualifications. Initiative for a follow-up is passed to the reader but not without expressing thanks.

ROBIN BRIMM, MHSL
0000 North West Avenue
Anywhere, USA
(000) 000-0000

December 15, 2000

John Shirley, Ph.D.
Associate Vice President for Academic Administration
THE UNIVERSITY OF FLORIDA MEDICAL BRANCH
000 Miami Boulevard
Miami, Florida 00000-0000

Dear Dr. Shirley:

John Daggel, Administrator--Pediatrics with Children's Hospital, suggested I contact you regarding the position of Program Development Manager, Department of Radiology with The University of Florida Medical Branch. The enclosed résumé outlines my management experience in health care, as well as pertinent industry involvement and graduate preparation in health systems leadership. With respect to your requirements, my qualifications include:

Administration: Presently hold full administrative authority for the nation's largest freestanding radiology center ... accountable for strategic planning, management of operating and capital equipment budgets, contract negotiations, business development, marketing ... positioned center to control major market share despite nationwide decline in imaging center services.

Development of Service Lines: Identified and developed comprehensive service line, augmenting facility with women's services, 3D imaging, and MRI mammography. Successfully introduced new lines through strategic marketing and communications campaign.

Human Relations: Strength in establishing and fostering cohesive relationships, particularly with physicians ... equally effective with administrators, employees, the medical community, and the community at large ... extensive experience in addressing sensitive physician-related matters.

Dr. Shirley, based on my brief conversation with John, I am very interested in this position. Given my background, I believe I have much to contribute toward your center's evolution and expansion, as well as the administrative expertise to support new business growth.

I will be in touch and look forward to learning more about this opportunity.

Sincerely,

Robin Brimm, MHSL
Enclosure

Susan Britton Whitcomb, Fresno, California

The lead for this letter is mention of a referral. The first paragraph introduces without bullets three qualifications areas. In the last paragraph the person controls the follow-up.

Robert F. Bailes

793 Broadway, Revere, Massachusetts 02151 • (617) 251-0000

Dear :

I am interested in exploring career opportunities with your organization and have enclosed my resume for your review.

In more than fifteen years of management experience I have held responsibility for operations both large and small. In addition, as a business owner I have overseen all business functions and been accountable for bottom-line profitability. Strong skills in financial management, employee supervision and concept development have been enhanced and utilized to bring success to the businesses with which I was associated.

Having just finalized the sale of my business, I am currently seeking an opportunity where my skills will be an asset to the organization and where I may continue to grow and increase my capabilities. I would be interested in meeting with you to discuss management opportunities at any level within your organization; may we schedule an appointment?

Thank you.

Sincerely,

Robert F. Bailes

enclosure

13

Louise M. Kursmark, Cincinnati, Ohio

A four-paragraph letter in which the fourth paragraph is merely Thank you. The letter is direct and clear, saying, in effect, "I'm interested. I can do it. I want to meet. Thanks."

OTTO MEKANIC

555 Any Street
Anytown, USA 00000
(000) 000-0000

LETTER OF INTRODUCTION

I am writing regarding my interest in an entry-level management position within your dealership. Therefore, I am enclosing my résumé which will provide you with my educational and professional achievements in the automotive repair industry. In advance, thank you very much for taking the time to review my qualifications.

As the résumé indicates, I have recently earned my degree in Automotive Technology from Any Junior College, graduating #1 in my class. While earning my degree, I have been working as a Line Technician at Happytown Motors. I started out as an apprentice and quickly promoted to Line Technician, due to my outstanding performance.

I feel confident that my extensive knowledge of automotive repair, plus my exceptional people skills and organizational abilities, would make me an excellent candidate for a management position with your dealership. I will contact you next week to see if we might schedule an exploratory meeting at a mutually convenient time.

Thank you for your consideration and I look forward to meeting you.

Sincerely,

Otto Mekanic

Résumé enclosed.

Joellyn Wittenstein, Arlington Heights, Illinois

A cover letter as a letter of introduction. The first paragraph displays tact and gratitude; the second, qualifications by degree and experience; the third, confidence and initiative.

JoanClaire May, R.D.H.

555 West Right Street
Elmira, NY 00000
(555) 000-0000

Dear Doctor:

I would like to offer the enclosed résumé as an application for a possible position with your practice as a full-time dental hygienist.

I have an excellent background in all facets of dental hygiene care, as well as experience with a wide range of patients including those with mental and physical disabilities. I am particularly meticulous concerning charting and documentation, and I am fully able to handle general office duties as well. I maintain excellent rapport with patients, and I particularly enjoy the challenge of helping to ease the anxiety many patients bring to the chair, turning their visits into a positive experience "at the dentist's."

Please consider my credentials and experience in your search for a qualified, enthusiastic addition to your professional staff. I can be reached at the above address and phone to arrange for a personal interview at your convenience. I will be happy to furnish references; however, until a mutual interest is established, I would request that you do not contact my present employer.

Thank you for your time and consideration of my qualifications. I hope to hear from you soon.

Sincerely,

JoanClaire May, R.D.H.

Enclosure

15

Betty Geller, Elmira, New York

The four paragraphs express in turn the letter's purpose; a profile of the applicant; a request for consideration, an interview, and confidentiality; and thanks and hope.

ROBERT E. FORD

72727 Gateside, Suite #305
Royal Oak, Michigan 48009
800 555.1234

Fourteen years of experience has equipped me in troubleshooting, communicating with customers and their concerns, and being involved in electrical, electronic and mechanical functions.

My responsibilities have steadily increased, due to a consistently good work performance, an assured employment ethic, and excellent knowledge of the industry. Therefore, I am enclosing my résumé to better show my qualifications and accomplishments.

I believe that we would both benefit from a personal interview. I would be interested in knowing the requirements and responsibilities of your company, and I could answer any questions that you may have.

Thank you for your time in review of my résumé and for consideration of permanent, full-time employment. I look forward to your response.

Sincerely,

Robert E. Ford

Enclosure: Résumé

16

Lorie Lebert, Novi, Michigan

Experience, qualifications, mutual benefits from an interview, and thanks and anticipation are the themes of this letter's four paragraphs. The drop cap is "different."

$\mathscr{S}$*arah* $\mathscr{V}$*ilempa*

555.987.6543   *19842 Wildwind*
                                                                 Framington, IL 60006

With degree in hand, I am pursuing full-time employment. I graduated from Loyola University a few months ago, and am trying to break into the "Professional Business World."

Besides the experience listed on my enclosed résumé, please know that I am a responsible person and employee. I offer a company diligence, an uncompromising work ethic and an ambitious outlook.

I would be more than happy to answer any questions that you might have or discuss how I could be a benefit to your company. Since my calendar is quite open at the present time, I would be available to meet with you personally to further discuss opportunities. Please call me at the telephone number at the top of this letter.

Thank you very much for your time in review of my résumé, and I look forward to hearing from you in the near future.

Sincerely,

Sarah Vilempa

Enclosure: Résumé

17

Lorie Lebert, Novi, Michigan

The person announces her new degree and interest in finding work. She sketches her worker traits and requests a phone call. Thanks and anticipation end the letter.

Thomas A. Miller

1712 E. Capital Drive   *Work* — 414 / 784-8514
Appleton, Wisconsin 54911   *Home* — 414 / 788-1847

■ ■

November 16, 1995

Timothy Downers
Director, Human Resources
XYZ Company
123 Main Street
Appleton, WI 54915

Dear Mr. Downers:

Please accept the enclosed resume in application for potential opportunities within your Sales Department.

Throughout my career with Food Corporation of America, I have realized top level sales performance and achievements. While satisfying, all challenges have been attained, and therefore, I am interested in employment which will provide advancement opportunities as well as fresh goals and objectives.

You will find me to be highly effective in the sales arena, with an inept ability to secure appointments, counter customer objectives, and close difficult sales. In addition to proven performance in these areas, I have a demonstrated ability to recruit and train others to do the same. My communication, leadership, and organizational skills, combined with my drive to succeed and achieve goals, would enable me to become a positive team player for XYZ Company.

A brief meeting to discuss my qualifications further would be appreciated. Thank you for your consideration.

Sincerely,

Thomas A. Miller

Enclosure

18

Kathy Keshemberg, Appleton, Wisconsin

Purpose, performance, and profile are the dominant themes in turn of the first three paragraphs. The fourth shows interest in an interview and expresses thanks for interest.

Edward V. McConnell
75 Main Street, Reading, Massachusetts 01867
(617) 942-0000

Dear :

I am responding with interest and enthusiasm to your recent advertisement for a Computer Service Technician. My skills appear to be a good match for the position requirements.

Having just completed an accelerated, intensive program in PC/network support, I am expertly qualified to provide PC service and support to your employees. My recent internship with the Boston Computer Society, a full-time position, has provided opportunities to gain experience in "real world" computer repair and reconfiguration. The systems that are donated to the Recycling Committee come in a wide variety of configurations, and I enjoy the challenge of repairing and assembling these systems to provide a valuable resource to non-profit organizations. This PC experience is complemented by a thorough understanding of electronic assembly gained through extensive experience as an Electronics Technician.

One of my real strengths is the ability to communicate with individuals at all levels. I am able to explain technical issues in layman's terms and have a genuine commitment to providing outstanding customer service.

I would appreciate a personal interview to learn about this opportunity and to provide you with additional details of my background and qualifications. Thank you for your consideration.

Sincerely,

Edward V. McConnell

enclosure

19

Louise M. Kursmark, Cincinnati, Ohio

Here the sequence of key themes per paragraph is purpose, qualifications, strengths and skills, and interest in an interview. An indication of thanks closes the letter.

Kimberly Lisherness

RFD 3, Box 467   Houlton, ME 04730   (555) 324-9506

May 24, 1995

Jane Rancourt
Human Resources Specialist
Insurance Associates
P.O. Box 25
Lewiston, ME 04240

Dear Ms. Rancourt,

Please consider my qualifications, as summarized on the enclosed résumé, for an office support position with your company. The organizational and communication skills I have displayed over the years have resulted in efficient completion of duties ranging from data entry to customer service.

Throughout my varied office experiences for legal, lodging, architectural, and data processing establishments, I have been:

- successful at managing time and prioritizing projects;

- gracious in meeting the needs of numerous and sometimes demanding guests;

- mature and professional when assisting clients/customers by phone or in person.

DEDICATION—to work, scholastic and personal matters—has always been my trademark. I could very well be your most committed candidate. Taking on assignments without being asked, "going the extra mile" for a valued client, or re-checking the details on an important project are all things I do because it's my nature!

If your office could benefit from someone with secretarial training, clerical/customer service experience, and a proven work record, please give me a call. I look forward to meeting you and your staff in a personal interview.

Sincerely,

Kimberly Lisherness

Enclosure

20

Elizabeth (Lisa) M. Carey, Waterville, Maine

A four-paragraph letter with three bulleted statements about worker traits. All four paragraphs, however, are about qualifications, qualifications, qualifications—a strength.

AMY D. MOSSE

444 Old Copper Drive	*Home: 555 444-3333*
South Port, Maine 12345	*Office: 555 666-7777*

"Human Resources"

If the *Human Resource Department* is looking for a *Human Resource Person* to join their team, please look over my enclosed résumé to see if my qualifications conform to your requirements.

I have almost ten years of experience directly involved in Human Resources. Please know that I have a high energy level and enjoy personal involvement and creativity. I like working with people and possess a particular talent for informing and helping.

My employment has included involvement on committees such as the Diversified Services Group Task Force, a Quality Improvement Program and the Human Resource Information System User Group.

I would appreciate a personal interview to further review employment possibilities. Or, if you have any questions that I could answer or expand on, please don't hesitate to call.

Thank you very much for your time in review of my résumé and I look forward to meeting with you in the near future.

Sincerely,

Amy D. Mosse

Enclosure: Personal Résumé

21

Lorie Lebert, Novi, Michigan

A five-paragraph letter that expresses in turn a request for a review, experience and worker traits, committee work, interest in an interview, and thanks with anticipation.

ART STORMAN JR.

120 N. Jefferson
Trenton, IL 62293
(618) 555-3300

June 25, 1995

Charlie Jones
Inside Sales Manager
Better Music
100 Fazoli Ave.
St. Louis, MO 63133

Dear Mr. Jones:

Dave Bonham, a new employee of yours, suggested I write and express my interest in working for your company. I realize you are not hiring right now, but hope you will consider my qualifications should the need for additional staff arise in the near future.

As the enclosed resume indicates, I have been generating sales for one of your competitors, MIDCO, since August of 1992 to the tune of nearly $750,000. I enjoy my current position but would like to try my luck in a more competitive, aggressive and challenging environment.

My accumulated sales figures for 1992-1995 include:

- Guitars, $190,000
- Drums and Hardware, $56,000
- Accessories, $425,000
- Miscellaneous Equipment, $67,000

I welcome the opportunity to further discuss how my background can help increase bottom-line profits for Better Music as well. Feel free to call me at the number above or confidentially at MIDCO (800) 555-4556, ext. 425.

I look forward to talking with you soon.

Sincerely,

Art Storman Jr.
Enc.

22

John A. Suarez, location unknown

This letter says, in effect, "Hire me, and one of your competitors will suffer. Its sales will decrease, but your sales will increase." It's a ploy that appeals to the reader's greed.

John DeFlyer

5005 Beechcraft Court, Apartment 5 ✈ Jennersville, Iowa 55555   (555) 555-0000

April 3, 1995

Mr. Peter Janes, Director of Aviation Services
PDS Aviation Services
3737 East Bonanza Way
Phoenix, Arizona 85034

RE: Aircraft/Sheetmetal Mechanic or Assistant Position

Dear Mr. Janes:

I would like the opportunity of being considered for an **Aircraft/Sheetmetal Mechanic** or **Assistant** position with your company, where I can further my experience in the field of aviation maintenance. My enthusiasm and dedication in this field has earned me a GPA of 3.8 in the Aviation Maintenance Technology program at Vincennes University. And, during four years as an Aviation Structural Mechanic in the U. S. Marine Corps., I have consistently demonstrated my ability to perform any tasks assigned with little or no supervision.

My qualifications include:

    ✈   Background and training commensurate with career objectives.
    ✈   Practical hands-on experience as an aircraft/helicopter mechanic/metal-smith.
    ✈   Solid training in leadership, supervision, and management.
    ✈   Own personal tools.

After finishing this year I will have acquired my Airframe and Power Plant certificates.
I have had extensive training and experience in sheet metal repair and the fabrication of structural parts during my enlistment in the Marine Corp. I have also attended technical schools concerning composite aircraft repair, reinforcing my positive commitment to this field.

I have enjoyed a reputation for being a hard-working, industrious individual. My motivation is to completely utilize my accumulated experience and to exercise my technical abilities to the fullest extent possible, becoming a valuable asset for the right company.

I would appreciate the opportunity to demonstrate my capabilities.

Sincerely,

John DaVania

23

Colleen S. Jaracz, Vincennes, Indiana

The topic (RE:) line is distinctive in this five-paragraph letter. The second paragraph introduces four bulleted statements preceded by airplane bullets.

Robert L. Norwood
3220 Mountain Ridge Road
Montgomery, Alabama 36100
[334] 555 -1575 Residence   [334] 555 -1066 Cellular

October 3, 1998

Mr. John Carmody
President
Four Hills Country Club
1520 Tramway Boulevard, NE
Albuquerque, New Mexico 87112

Dear Mr. Carmody:

My club sought me out to guide them through a $2,000,000 renovation and expansion. Now that the project is nearly finished, I want to make the same kind of contribution to another club. That is why I am exploring — very confidentially — opportunities in Albuquerque.

My specialty is constantly finding what club members want, then giving them more than they expect. Of course, members must have more than extraordinary service in gracious settings. They want confidence that their club will *always* be the best. I deliver that reassurance. If adding a General Manager with that personal standard appeals to Four Hills, we should talk.

I will seek out *anyone* whose ideas will help make my club shine. Sometimes that person is on the board, very often it is a member. But I go beyond the obvious sources to talk with employees and suppliers. I am as comfortable walking with the president as I am in talking with the janitor.

Not infrequently there are tangible payoffs: cutting supply costs by $35,000 in a single year while *improving* the service we offered. At times the results are intangible: the pride in our members' eyes after a garden party for the Secretary of Defense.

As a first step in putting my drive and energy to work for you, I have enclosed my résumé. It can only hint at my track record. Because words on paper cannot replace personal conversations, I encourage you to test me for yourself in a telephone interview soon.

Sincerely,

Robert L. Norwood

One enclosure: Résumé

Don Orlando, Montgomery, Alabama

The lead is a $2 million project. The rest of this original letter is a refined, subtler appeal to the reader's economic self-interest. The last paragraph is exceptional.

Jane L. Benderson

77111 Spring Street   Anaconda, MT 59711   (406) 555-5555

May 31, 1995

U.S. Forest Service
c/o Anaconda Job Service
Anaconda, MT 59711

Dear Recruiter:

As referred to me by the Anaconda Job Service, I am submitting this letter and the enclosed resume as my formal application for the **Survey Aide** vacancy you listed.

I graduated from the Division of Technology of Montana Tech in May 1995 with an Associates of Applied Science Degree in Civil Engineering Technology, at the top of my class. The course work has been stimulating, and I especially enjoyed the special projects conducted in the field. The project at the Grant Kohrs Ranch in Deer Lodge, Montana allowed us to use so many of the concepts we learned in the classroom. My traverses with the EDM were usually right on target.

As a non-traditional student, I brought to my course work a unique blend of experience. My focused work ethic was established young in my life. Many of the positions I held involved working with heavy machinery, where I learned first hand the need for safety practices. These lessons, coupled with my experience working as a First Responder on the Anaconda Ambulance crews, were of great help when I studied for and received my HAZMAT certification in April of 1995.

Challenging projects have always attracted my interest. Both inside and outside the classroom, I have assumed leadership roles and have been able to creatively solve problems. Serving as the President of the Civil Engineering Technician Student Society, I was able to use both my communication and people skills.

After reviewing my qualifications, should you have any questions, I would be happy to personally answer them at a time convenient to your schedule. I look forward to discovering what opportunities await me within your organization, and I know that I will give my usual 110% to any project to which I would be assigned.

Sincerely,

Jane L. Benderson   Enclosure

25

Kathlene Y. McNamee, Butte, Montana

The tone of this letter is conversational and autobiographical. Much of the letter reads like a personal narrative. When we get to the last paragraph, we know the person is sincere.

CARYN C. ESSAR

6602 Marcus Lane, Newman, NJ 00000   **(555) 555-5555**

October 5, 1995

Darlene Kensington
Customer Service Manager
Janson Industries
504 Dalton Lane
Cameron, NJ 00000

Dear Ms Kensington:

If your organization is in need of an experienced, bright, and extremely professional customer service representative, please contact me for an interview.

As noted on my enclosed resume, I am presently employed as a customer service representative with Chilton-Elms Insurance Corporation, handling dental insurance enrollments and changes for corporate accounts. Answering and responding to over 100 calls daily on a busy "employer hotline" comprises a large part of my job. I've demonstrated the ability to remain calm, poised, and extremely productive in a demanding, fast-paced environment.

I have established excellent relationships with corporate clients by listening closely to their concerns and providing prompt follow-up. I've received numerous requests from representatives of client companies to personally handle their accounts.

When I don't have all the information needed to assist my clients, I research through computer files and consult with appropriate company employees until I find the information. Thorough and accurate documentation is also very important in my position. My quality review scores, which assess productivity and accuracy, have been in the 90-100% range.

I am confident that my skills and experience can help your organization in maintaining a solid customer base. I look forward to hearing from you soon.

Sincerely,

Caryn C. Essar

Enclosure

26

Rhoda Kopy, Toms River, New Jersey

Interest in an interview is expressed up-front in the first paragraph. The person can do this because she exudes confidence, ability, and successfulness throughout the letter.

BEVERLY A. ROBERTS, R.N.

(904) 775-0916 • 815 Volusia Ave. • Orange City, FL 32763

Dear Prospective Employer:

I am forwarding my résumé in response to your recent advertisement in *The Orlando Sentinel* for a Medical Sales Representative. Comparison of my qualifications with your requirements, as specified in the advertisement, suggests that I would be an excellent candidate for this position. I am a top-producing representative with a comprehensive background in home health and hospital care.

In my most recent position as an Account Executive at Coram Healthcare, I marketed infusion, and perinatal services to various primary and specialty physicians. I have developed and presented contracts to managed care companies, nursing home facilities and nursing associations in the Volusia, Orange, Seminole, Osceola, and Lake county areas and have cultivated and earned their trust and confidence.

As an experienced medical liaison, I possess strong interpersonal, communication, and leadership skills. My medical background includes over seven years as a Registered Nurse in both Florida Hospital and Central Florida Regional Hospital.

Educationally, I have an Associates of Science Degree in Nursing. My computer skills include familiarity with Word Perfect, Microsoft Word and DOS as well as a custom medical tracking/evaluation program on a notebook computer complete with a fax and modem.

Would you please consider my request for a personal interview so that you may evaluate my qualifications, abilities and creativity for yourself? I am confident that I can make a significant contribution to your company. I can be reached at 904-775-0916.

Thank you for your consideration. I look forward to meeting and talking with you.

Sincerely,

Beverly A. Roberts, R.N.

Enc.

27

Beverly Harvey, Pierson, Florida

In this six-paragraph letter the person displays in turn experience, competency, a diversified background, computer literacy, and confidence in her request for an interview.

Maria Eléna Navarro, CRTT
127 Pine Street, Unit D
Morris Plains, NJ 55555

(000) 000-0000

October 9, 1995

Karen Sargent
Human Resources Department
Willow Grove Hospital
Route 10 at Delaney Street
Hanover, NJ 07936

Dear Ms. Sargent:

I am interested in applying for a Respiratory Therapist position at Willow Grove Hospital, as advertised in the October 2nd edition of the ADVANCE publication. My resume is enclosed, which details my credentials and background.

I am a graduate of an AMA approved program in respiratory care and have some experience in a long term care facility with both adult and pediatric patients. As your requirement states, I am also certified in basic life support systems.

My background includes competency in intubation, as well as pediatric and neonatal ventilation and critical care experience. Currently, I am employed at a home care agency, but have kept up my clinical skills with per diem assignments in a hospital setting.

I have developed the ability to organize my schedule, set priorities and use my time efficiently to get more done. Using my communicative skills in English and Spanish, I have maintained effective working relationships with clients and medical professionals.

Among my responsibilities, I have instituted home care for infants with apnea episodes following their release from the hospital. I instructed parents on how to troubleshoot the ventilators and monitors for continuous accurate readings. In addition, I recommended filters and tubing replacements, balancing infection control with cost cutting.

I am sure I could make a worthwhile contribution to your respiratory care staff and would we glad to met with you to discuss the possibility of joining your organization. Thank your for your consideration.

Sincerely,

Maria Eléna Navarro

28

Melanie A. Noonan, West Paterson, New Jersey

A developed, six-paragraph letter covering interest in a position, credentials, background, skills, responsibilities, and interest in an interview. Thanks ends the letter.

RONALD GRIFFITH, RN
650 Wellmont Place, Prospect Park, NJ 55555
(000) 000-0000

July 25, 1995

Maryanne Rossiter, RN
Nurse Recruiter
St. Martin's Hospital Center
112 Ridgeview Avenue
Ridgeview, NJ 07450

Dear Ms. Rossiter:

I have been advised by Barbara Fredericks, a nurse manager at St. Martin's Hospital Center, that you may be seeking recently certified RNs. If so, I would appreciate your consideration of me. I graduated this May from the Bergen Community College Associates program in Nursing, and also received my State Board Certification on July 14, 1995. My studies involved a comprehensive curriculum and a variety of clinical rotations, including medical-surgical, pediatrics, maternity, and orthopedics. These assignments have given me some exposure to working with a professional staff and participating in the delivery of high quality nursing care.

Coming from a family background in the profession, nursing has always been my ideal career choice, even though it has taken me several years before I could enroll in an academic study program. My mother was a nurse for 40 years, serving as a role model of caring and dedication. Her inspiration strongly influenced me and my two sisters to also became nurses. My experience in the U.S. Army, with emphasis on performing at one's best, further reinforced my commitment.

My greatest satisfaction comes from helping people, whether or not there are monetary rewards for my services. A lot of my free time is spent in volunteer activities through my church to better the lives of disadvantaged youth and adults. As a nurse, I would want nothing more than to contribute to the efficiency of a professional care team, and to be regarded by my coworkers and patients as someone who is always there for them whenever needed. It would give me great pride to earn the respect of those I serve and work with. To me, being a nurse is not just a job; it's what I am.

I realize that in order to fulfill my ambition takes ongoing training. From what I have been told, the training program at St. Martin's provides the type of supportive atmosphere conducive to attaining the level of proficiency I aspire to.

As you read my resume, I hope you will find my qualifications desirable and consider me for any of the staff positions open for new recruits. I am particularly interested in the area of critical care which is a specialization at St. Martin's Hospital Center, and I can be available to work any hours or shifts, part time or full time.

I will be glad to discuss in a personal interview how I may be able to benefit your institution, and eagerly await hearing from you.

Yours truly,

Ronald Griffith

29

Melanie A. Noonan, West Paterson, New Jersey

A six-paragraph letter in which the first three paragraphs are more developed than the last three. In its length the letter is more self-revealing than a typical cover letter.

Catherine A. Nottingham

934 Charles Drive   Rochester, Minnesota 55555-5555   (555) 555-5555

September 12, 1996

Mr. Edward Broderick
Woodstream Public Library
George Washington Plaza
Woodstream, Nebraska 77777

Dear Mr. Broderick:

As a professional librarian with a sixteen year career in positions of increasing responsibility, leading to management, I read with great interest your recent advertisement in *Library Journal* for a Library Director.

Currently, I serve as Library Director of the Hiawatha Public Library in a major suburb of Rochester, Minnesota, with a budget of **$1.1 million** and over 60 employees. During my four years in this position, I have instituted a capital improvement campaign and a plan for **upgrading the library's automation systems**. I have been **successful in raising funds from public sources** for repairs and improvements to buildings and grounds. Working with the Library Board, I have been able to **establish long-range goals** for the library and **plan annual budgets** based on those long-range goals. The five-year capital improvement campaign has been successfully completed in four years, a year ahead of schedule.

Through community involvement, I have **improved the library's image** in the eyes of town residents. I have successfully justified **increased funding from town government** in an environment of spending cuts, growing the annual budget by 33% in three years. We are currently cooperating with a local school district on a **Summer Reading Program** that involves over **1300 children** and offers incentives for books read.

While serving as Department Head of Interlibrary Loan for the St. Paul Public Library, I managed all interlibrary loan and centralized services for the **Pioneer Library System**, which covered a **five county area** in southern Minnesota. Services were provided to over **100 individual branches** that included large **urban** libraries, **suburban** libraries with a high level of activity, and very small **rural** libraries. My department also provided services to school libraries on a contract basis. In addition to supervising a staff of 18, I served on regional and state-wide committees and provided training to member libraries on ILL services.

I believe that I have the experience, desire, and vision to effectively meet the challenges that will face the new Library Director for the Woodstream Public Library. I would enjoy speaking with you, or any members of the Library Board, about how I can help your library achieve its objectives. Please call me at **(555) 555-4444** (office) or **(555) 555-5555** (home) to arrange a meeting. I look forward to speaking with you soon.

Thank you.

Sincerely yours,

Catherine A. Nottingham

Enclosure

30

Arnold G. Boldt, Rochester, New York

This substantial letter includes boldfacing of key information so that the reader can see quickly information that otherwise would be hard to find in developed paragraphs.

List of Contributors

List of Contributors

The following persons are the contributors of the resumes and cover letters in this book. All of the contributors are professional resume writers. To include in this appendix the names of these writers and information about their business is to acknowledge with appreciation their voluntary submissions and the insights expressed in the letters that accompanied the submissions. Resume and cover letter numbers after a writer's contact information are the *numbers of the writer's resumes and cover letters* included in the Gallery, not page numbers.

Alabama

Montgomery

Donald Orlando
The McLean Group
640 South McDonough
Montgomery, AL 36104
Phone: (334) 264-2020
Fax: (334) 264-9227
E-mail: orlandores@aol.com
Member: PARW
Certification: MBA, CPRW
Resumes: 79, 80, 199
Cover letters: 5, 10, 24

Arizona

Prescott

Patricia S. Cash
Resumes For Results
P.O. Box 2806
Prescott, AZ 86302
Phone: (520) 778-1578
E-mail: geow@goodnet.com
Member: PARW
Certification: CPRW
Resume: 190

California

Boulder Creek

Elaine Jackson
Sincerely Yours, Business Services
10130 Highway 9 (Central Avenue)
Boulder Creek, CA 95006
Phone: (831) 338-3000
Fax: (831) 338-3666
E-mail: ejackson@hwy9.com
Resume: 133

Fresno

Susan Britton Whitcomb
Alpha Omega Services
757 E Hampton Way
Fresno, CA 93704
Phone: (559) 222-7474
Fax: (559) 222-9538
E-mail: topresume@aol.com
Web site: www.careerwriter.com
Member: NRWA, PARW
Certification: NCRW, CPRW
Resumes: 1, 7, 8, 9, 11, 13, 14, 65, 66,
    142, 143, 145, 148, 153, 155, 156, 158,
    177, 178, 195, 196, 197, 207
Cover letters: 6, 8, 9, 11, 12

Galt

Nancy Karvonen
A Better Word and Resume
771 Adare Way
Galt, CA 95632
Phone: (209) 744-8203
E-mail:
   careers@aresumecoach.com
Web site: aresumecoach.com
Member: PARW
Certification: CPRW, IJCTC
Resumes: 3, 45, 116

Orange

Nita Busby
Resumes, Etc.
438 E. Katella, Ste. F
Orange, CA 92867
Phone: (714) 633-2783
Fax: (714) 633-2745
E-mail: resumes100@aol.com
Web site: www.resumesetc.net
Member: NRWA, CA Assn. of
  Personnel Consultants,
  contributing writer to
  www.smallbusinessresources.com
Certification: CPRW, ValueStar
Resume: 47

Connecticut

Bristol

Debra O'Reilly
A First Impression Resume Service
16 Terryville Avenue
Bristol, CT 06010
Phone: (860) 583-7500
E-mail:
  debra@resumewriter.com
Web site:
  www.resumewriter.com
Member: PARW
Certification: CPRW, JCTC
Resume: 95

Durham

Jan Melnik
Absolute Advantage
P.O. Box 718
Durham, CT 06422
Phone: (860) 349-0256
E-mail: CompSPJan@aol.com
Web site:
  www.yourabsoluteadvantage.com
Member: NRWA
Certification: CPRW
Resumes: 28, 59, 168

Florida

Mary Roberts
Phone: (727) 942-7002
Fax: (727) 944-4117
E-mail: Rezwizard@aol.com
Certification: CPRW, JCTC
Resume: 5

Lakeland

E. René Hart
First Impressions Resume &
  Career Dev. Svcs.
7100 Pebble Pas Loop
Lakeland, FL 33810
Phone: (941) 859-2439
E-mail: ReneHart@aol.com
Web site:
  www.ResumesForSuccess.com
Member: PARW
Certification: CPRW
Resume: 180

Melbourne

Laura A. DeCarlo
Competitive Edge Career Service
1665 Clover Circle
Melbourne, FL 32935
Phone: (407) 752-0880
(800) 715-3442
Fax: (407) 752-7513
E-mail: getanedge@aol.com
Web site:
  www.acompetitiveedge.com
Member: NRWA, PARW
Certification: CPRW, ICCC
Resumes: 41, 44, 70

Pierson

Beverly Harvey
Beverly Harvey Resume & Career
  Services
P.O. Box 750
Pierson, FL 32180
Phone: (904) 749-3111
E-mail:
  beverly@harveycareers.com
Web site: harveycareers.com
Member: PARW, NRWA
Certifications: CPRW, JCTC
Cover letter: 27

Tampa

M. Carol Heider
Heider's Resume Center
10014 North Dale Mabry,
  Suite 101
Tampa, FL 33618
Phone: (813) 282-0011
Fax: (813) 926-0170
E-mail: HSSHEIDER@aol.com
Web site: http://browser.to/
  heidersresumecenter
Member: PARW, NRWA
Certification: CPRW
Resumes: 40, 175, 185, 191
Cover letter: 7

Tampa

Diane McGoldrick
Business Services of Tampa Bay
2803 W. Busch Ave., #103
Tampa, FL 33618
Phone: (813) 935-2700
Fax: (813) 935-4777
E-mail:
  mcgoldrk@ix.netcom.com
Member: PAEW, NAJST, *Who's*
  Who Among Professionals, CMI
Certification: CPRW
Resumes: 52, 89, 103, 132, 135

Valrico

Cynthia Kraft
Executive Essentials
P.O. Box 336
Valrico, FL 33595
Phone: (813) 655-0658
Fax: (813) 685-4287
E-mail: CPRWck@aol.com
Web site: www.exec-
  essentials.com
Member: PARW, NRWA, CMI
Certification: CPRW
Resume: 137

Georgia

Savannah

Carol Lawrence
P.O. Box 9826
Savannah, GA 31412
Phone: (912) 832-4438
Certification: CPRW
Resume: 88

Illinois

Arlington Heights

Joellyn Wittenstein
A-1 Quality Résumés
2786 N. Buffalo Grove Rd., Unit
  206
Arlington Heights, IL 60004
Phone: (847) 255-1686
Fax: (847) 255-7224
E-mail: Joellyn@interaccess.com
Member: NRWA
Certification: CPRW
Cover letter: 14

Glen Carbon

Carla Culp Coury
10 Downing Place
Glen Carbon, IL 62034
Phone: (618) 288-1625
E-mail:
  ccoury@empowering.com
Certification: CPRW
Resume: 189

Indiana

Carmel

Susan K. Schumm
The Printed Page
327 Parkview Place
Carmel, IN 46032
Phone: (317) 581-1057
Fax: (208) 248-6088
E-mail:
  theprintedpage@email.com
Web site: http://
  theprintedpage.cjb.net/
Resumes: 24, 176

Vincennes

Colleen S. Jaracz
Innovative Computer Concepts
2581 S. Harvest Acres Drive
Vincennes, IN 47591
Phone: (812) 882-2009
Fax: (812) 882-2192
E-mail: kokolar1@hotmail.com
Cover letter: 23

Iowa

Iowa City

Elizabeth J. Axnix
Quality Word Processing
329 East Court Street
Iowa City, IA 52240
Phone: (319) 354-7822
E-mail: axnix@earthlink.net
Member: PARW
Certification: CPRW, JCTC
Resumes: 69, 115, 118

Kansas

Lawrence

Linda Morton
Transcriptions
1012 Massachusetts, Suite 201
Lawrence, KS 66044
Phone: (785) 842-4619
Fax: (785) 842-2846
E-mail:
  morton_sscm@compuserve.com
Member: PARW
Certification: CPRW
Resumes: 21, 46, 47, 48, 81, 173,
  174

Louisiana

West Monroe

Melanie Douthit
305 Arlington Drive
West Monroe, LA 71291
Phone: (318) 396-7513
Resume: 124

Maine

Waterville

Elizabeth (Lisa) M. Carey
Connections Secretarial Services
6 Boutelle Ave.
Waterville, ME 04901
Phone: (207) 872-5999
Fax: (207) 872-5999
E-mail: RezWriter@aol.com
Certification: CPRW
Cover letter: 20

Maryland

Easton

Thomas E. Spann
Lee Edwards Associates
7605 Dover Woods Rd.
Easton, MD 21601
Phone: (410) 822-2876
E-mail: resumes@skipjack-
  bluecrab.org
Web site: http://
  www.bluecrab.org/members/
  resumes
Resumes: 12, 97, 108, 172, 201,
  204, 205, 214

Massachusetts

Needham

Wendy Gelberg
Advantage Résumés
21 Hawthorn Ave.
Needham, MA 02192
Phone: (781) 444-0778
Fax: (781) 444-2778
E-mail: wgelberg@aol.com
Member: NRWA
Certification: CPRW, JCTC
Resume: 19

Northboro

Steven P. Green
Career Path
242 Brewer St.
Northboro, MA 01532
Phone: (508) 393-5548
Fax: (508) 393-6120
E-mail:
  Steven@WorkingSmart.com
Certification: MA, MPA
Resumes: 64, 68

Michigan

Flint

Janet L. Beckstrom
Word Crafter
1717 Montclair Ave.
Flint, MI 48503
Phone: (800) 351-9818
Fax: (810) 232-9257
E-mail: wordcrafter@voyager.net
Member: PARW
Resumes: 83, 98, 99, 100, 102

Fremont

Patricia L. Nieboer
401 Miller Street
Fremont, MI 49412
Phone: (231) 924-0594
E-mail: zemo@ncats.net
Certification: CPS, CPRW
Resume: 109

Newport

Deborah L. Schuster
The Lettersmith Résumé Service
P.O. Box 202
Newport, MI 48166
Phone: (734) 586-3335
Fax: (734) 586-2766
E-mail: lettersmith@foxberry.net
Web site:
  www.thelettersmith.com
Member: PARW, CareerMasters
Certification: CPRW
Resumes: 105, 107, 111, 117, 130,
  131
Cover letter: 1

Novi

Lorie Lebert
Résumés for Results
P.O. Box 267
Novi, MI 48376
Phone: (248) 380-6101
Fax: (248) 380-0169
E-mail: DoMyResume@aol.com
Web site:
  www.DoMyResume.com
Member: PARW, CareerMasters
Certification: CPRW, JCTC
Resumes: 5, 138, 211, 215
Cover letters: 16, 17, 21

Minnesota

Rochester

Beverley Drake
CareerVision Resume & Job Search
  Systems
1816 Baihly Hills Drive SW
Rochester, MN 55902
Phone: (507) 252-9825
Fax: (507) 252-1559
E-mail: bdcprw@aol.com
Member: PARW, AJST
Certification: CPRW, IJCTC
Resume: 198

Montana

Butte

Kathlene Y. McNamee
The Word Wizard
523 East Front Street
Butte, MT 59701
Phone: (406) 782-1063
Fax: (406) 782-1063
Web site:
  www.lifepathcreations.com
Member: PARW
Certifications: CPRW, JCTC
Resumes: 82, 85, 91
Cover letter: 25

New Jersey

Marlboro

Beverly Baskin
Baskin Business & Career Services
6 Alberta Drive
Marlboro, NJ 07746
Other offices: 120 Wood Ave. S,
  Iselin, NJ 08830; 116 Forrestal
  Blvd., Princeton, NJ 08540
Phone: (800) 300-4079
Fax: (732) 972-8846
E-mail: bbcs@att.net
Member: NRWA, PARW, NCDA,
  NECA, ACA
Certification: MA, NCC, CPRW,
  LPC, NAJST
Resumes: 22, 26, 86, 114, 134,
  206

Rochelle Park

Alesia Benedict
Career Objectives
151 W. Passaic St.
Rochelle Park, NJ 07662
Phone: (800) 206-5353
Fax: (800) 206-5454
E-mail: careerobj@aol.com
Web site:
  www.getinterviews.com
Member: PARW, CMI (Board),
  AJST
Certification: CPRW, JCTC
Resumes: 73, 162, 179, 186, 210

Toms River

Rhoda Kopy
A HIRE IMAGE™
26 Main Street, Suite E
Toms River, NJ 08753
Phone: (732) 505-9515
Fax: (732) 505-3125
E-mail: ahi@injersey.com
Web site:
  jobwinningresumes.com
Member: PARW, NRWA,
  CareerMasters
Certification: CPRW
Resumes: 104, 119
Cover letter: 26

Waldwick

Fran Kelley
The Résumé Works
71 Highwood Ave.
Waldwick, NJ 07463
Phone/Fax: (201) 670-9643
E-mail:
  twofreespirits@worldnet.att.net
Web site: http://home.att.net/
  ~ twofreespirits/index.html
Member: PARW, NRWA,
  CPADN, SHRM, IACMP
Certification: MA, CPRW, SPHR,
  JCTC
Resumes: 37, 57, 90, 136, 161

West Paterson

Melanie A. Noonan
Peripheral Pro
560 Lackawanna Ave.
West Paterson, NJ 07424
Phone: (973) 785-3011
Fax: (973) 785-3071
E-mail: PeriPro1@aol.com
Member: PARW, NRWA
Certification: CPS
Resumes: 147, 192, 200
Cover letters: 28, 29

New York

Chappaqua

Linsey Levine
Career Counsel
11 Hillside Place
Chappaqua, NY 10514
Phone: (914) 238-1065
Fax: (914) 238-5822
E-mail: LinZlev@aol.com
Member: PARW, NRWA, NCDA,
  IACMP, NAJST
Certification: MS, JCTC
Resumes: 25, 54, 75, 140, 169

Elmira

Betty Geller
Apple Résumé & Career Services
456 West Water Street
Elmira, NY 14905
Phone: (607) 734-2090
Fax: (607) 734-2090
E-mail: appleresumes@aol.com
Web site:
  www.accessresumes.com
Member: NRWA
Certification: CPRW, NCRW
Resumes: 184
Cover letter: 15

Jackson Heights

Kim Isaacs
Advanced Career Systems
34-41 85th St., Ste. 6-G
Jackson Heights, NY 11372
Phone: (888) 565-9290
Fax: (718) 565-1611
E-mail:
  support@resumesystems.com
Web site: http://
  www.resumesystems.com
Member: NRWA, PARW
Certification: CPRW, NCRW
Resumes: 10, 23, 123, 128, 188

Medford

Deborah Wile Dib
Advantage Résumés of New York
77 Buffalo Ave.
Medford, NY 11763
Phone: (631) 475-8513
Fax: (631) 475-8513
E-mail:
  gethired@advantageresumes.com
Web site: http://
  www.advantageresumes.com
Member: NRWA, PARW, AJST,
  CMI, CPADN
Certification: CCM, NCRW,
  CPRW, JCTC
Resumes: 42, 56

New York

Etta R. Barmann
Compu-Craft Business Services,
  Inc.
124 East 40th St., Suite 403
New York, NY 10016
Phone: (212) 697-4005
Fax: (212) 697-6475
E-mail: erbarmann@aol.com
Member: PARW
Certification: MSW, CSW, CPRW
Resume: 110

Ossining

Phyllis B. Shabad
CareerMasters
95 Woods Brooke Circle
Ossining, NY 10562
Phone/Fax: (914) 944-9577
E-mail: target@CareerIQ.com
Member: NRWA, PARW
Certification: NCRW, JCTC
Resumes: 120, 141, 163

Poughkeepsie

Marian K. Kozlowski
MKK Resume Consulting Service
47 S. Gate Dr.
Poughkeepsie, NY 12601
Phone/Fax: (914) 462-0654
E-mail: MKozlo4371@aol.com
Member: SHRM
Resumes: 49, 63, 166

Rochester

Arnold G. Boldt
Arnold-Smith Associates
625 Panorama Trail Bldg. 2, Ste.
  200
Rochester, NY 14625
Phone: (716) 383-0350
Fax: (716) 387-0516
E-mail: Arnoldsmth@aol.com
Web site: www.resumesos.com
Member: PARW
Certification: CPRW
Resume: 164
Cover letter: 30

Yorktown Heights

Mark D. Berkowitz
Career Development Resources
1312 Walter Rd.
Yorktown Heights, NY 10598
Phone: (888) 277-9778
   (914) 962-1548
Fax: (914) 962-0325
E-mail: cardevres@aol.com
Web site:
   CareerDevResources.com
Member: CMI, PARW, NCDA,
   ACA
Certification: NCC, NCCC,
   CPRW, JCTC
Resumes: 20, 125

North Carolina

Asheville

Dayna J. Feist
Gatehouse Business Services
265 Charlotte St.
Asheville, NC 28801
Phone: (828) 254-7893
Fax: (828) 254-7894
E-mail: Gatehous@aol.com
Member: PARW
Certification: CPRW, JCTC
Resume: 30
Cover letter: 24

Charlotte

Rose Montgomery, Owner
Mail Order Resume Service
P.O. Box 25155
Charlotte, NC 28229
Phone: (704) 366-9749
Fax: (704) 364-2737
E-mail: deskpub@aol.com
Resume: 165

Wilmington

Sandy Adcox Saburn
Innovative Coaching Group
3608B Oleander Drive, Suite 103
Wilmington, NC 28403
Phone: (910) 251-9598
Fax: (910) 251-9564
E-mail: icoach@bellsouth.net
Web site:
   www.innovativecoaching.net
Certification: CPRW
Resumes: 43, 62, 74, 152, 203,
   209
Cover letter: 4

Ohio

Athens

Melissa L. Kasler
Résumé Impressions
One N. Lancaster St.
Athens, OH 45701
Phone: (740) 592-3993
Fax: (740) 592-1352
E-mail:
   mkasler2@eurekanet.com
Member: PARW, NRWA
Certification: CPRW
Resumes: 61, 94

Cincinnati

Louise M. Kursmark
Best Impression Career Services,
Inc.
9847 Catalpa Woods Court
Cincinnati, OH 45242
Phone: (888) 792-0030
Fax: (513) 792-0961
E-mail:
   LK@yourbestimpression.com
Web site: http://
   yourbestimpression.com
Member: PARW, NRWA, AJST
Certification: CPRW, JCTC, CCM
Resumes: 16, 53
Cover letters: 2, 13, 19, 139, 193

Oklahoma

Bartlesville

Laura C. Karlak
936 Sandstone Drive
Bartlesville, OK 74006
Phone: (918) 333-5925
Fax: (918) 333-5925
E-mail: lkarlak@aol.com
Certification: CPRW
Resume: 27

Oregon

Aloha

Pat Kendall
Advanced Résumé Concepts
18580 S.W. Rosa Rd.
Aloha, OR 97007
Phone (503) 591-9143
Fax: (503) 642-2535
E-mail: reslady@aol.com
Web site: www.reslady.com
Member: NRWA
Certification: JCTC, NCRW
Resumes: 4, 67, 150, 151, 160,
   183, 187

Pennsylvania

Edinboro

Wendy A. Lowry
5624 Obed Heights Drive
Edinboro, PA 16412
Phone: (814) 734-7552
Resume: 32

Huntingdon

Margaret M. Hilling, Owner
Huntingdon County Resume
   Service
RR 2, Box 385
Huntingdon, PA 16652
Phone: (814) 643-1663
Resume: 92

Tennessee
Hendersonville

Carolyn S. Braden
Braden Résumé Solutions
108 La Plaza Dr.
Hendersonville, TN 37075
Phone: (615) 822-3317
Fax: (615) 826-9611
E-mail:
    bradenresume@home.com
Member: PARW
Certification: CPRW
Resumes: 34, 58, 106

Texas
New Braunfels

P.J. Margraf
The Career Consulting Corner
1492 Cloud Lane
New Braunfels, TX 78130
Phone: (830) 625-9515
E-mail: career30@careercc.com
Web site: www.careercc.com
    or
    www.careerconsultingcorner.com
Resume: 167

Tyler

Ann Klint
Ann's Professional Résumé Service
1608 Cimmarron Trail
Tyler, TX 75703
Phone: (903) 509-8333
Fax: (734) 448-1962
E-mail: Resumes-Ann@tyler.net
Member: PARW, NRWA
Certification: CPRW, NCRW
Resumes: 2, 15, 96, 127, 157

The Woodlands

Cheryl Ann Harland
Résumés By Design
25227 Grogan's Mill Rd., Suite
    125
The Woodlands, TX 77380
Phone: (281) 296-1659
Fax: (281) 296-1601
E-mail:
    cah@resumesbydesign.com
Web site:
    www.resumesbydesign.com
Member: PARW
Certification: CPRW
Resumes: 35, 36, 51, 78, 154

Utah
Riverton

Sallie Young
12421 Harvest Avenue
Riverton, UT 84065
Phone: (801) 253-9339
one_writer_2000@yahoo.com
Resumes: 93, 126, 159

Virginia
Virginia Beach

Anne G. Kramer
Alpha Bits
4411 Trinity Ct.
Virginia Beach, VA 23455
Phone: (757) 464-1914
E-mail: akramer@livenet.net
Member: PARW
Certification: CPRW
Resumes: 38, 39, 146, 182

Washington
Poulsbo

Lonnie L. Swanson
A Career Advantage
21590 Clear Creek Road
    Northwest
Poulsbo, WA 98370
Phone: (360) 779-2877
E-mail:
    resumewriter@amouse.net
Member: PARW
Certification: CPRW
Resumes: 29, 101, 112, 171, 202

West Virginia
Charleston

Barbie Dallmann
Happy Fingers Word Processing &
    Résumé Service
1205 Wilkie Dr.
Charleston, WV 25314
Phone: (304) 345-4495
Fax: (304) 343-2017
E-mail:
    BarbieDall@mindspring.com
Web site: www.ibssn.com/
    happyfingers
Member: NRWA
Certification: CPRW
Resumes: 71, 113

Wisconsin
Appleton

Kathy Keshemberg
A Career Advantage
1615 E. Roeland, #3
Appleton, WI 54915
Phone: (920) 731-5167
Fax: (920) 739-6471
E-mail: kathyKC@aol.com
Web site:
    www.acareeradvantage.com
Member: NRWA
Certification: NCRW
Resumes: 50, 87, 122, 212
Cover letter: 18

Location Unknown
Ted Bache, Resumes 6, 128
Susie Brady, Resumes 17, 194
Steven M. Burt, Resume 121
Randy Clair, Resumes 60, 77, 84,
    144, 208
David Newbold, Resumes 55, 72
Annamarie Pawlina, Resumes 18,
    181; cover letter 3
Claudia Stephenson, Resume 213
John Suarez, Resumes 33, 76,
    170; cover letter 22

For those who would like to contact the Professional Association of Résumé Writers, its address is as follows:

Professional Association of Résumé Writers
1388 Brightwaters Blvd., N.E.
St. Petersburg, FL 33704
Phone: (727) 821-2274
Toll-free: (800) 822-7279
Fax: (813) 894-1277
E-mail: parwhq@aol.com
Web site: www.parw.com

For those who would like to contact the National Résumé Writers' Association, write to Ms. Pat Kendall (NRWA President) at reslady@aol.com or call 1-888-NRWA-444. For membership information, contact Tisha Silvers (tmsilvers@yahoo.com).

Occupation Index

Current or Last Position

Note: Numbers are resume numbers in the Gallery, not page numbers.

Features Index

Note: Numbers are resume numbers in the Gallery, not page numbers.

The following commonly appearing sections are not included in this Features Index: Work Experience, Work History, Professional Experience, Related Experience, Other Experience, Education (by itself), and References. Variations of these sections, however, *are* included if they are distinctive in some way or have combined headings. As you look for features that interest you, be sure to browse through *all* the resumes. Some important information, such as Accomplishments, may not be listed if it is presented as a subsection of an Experience section.